Jane Austen: Two Centuries of Criticism

Studies in English and American Literature and Culture:
Literary Criticism in Perspective

About *Literary Criticism in Perspective*

Books in the series *Literary Criticism in Perspective* trace literary scholarship and criticism on major and neglected writers alike, or on a single major work, a group of writers, a literary school or movement. In so doing the authors — authorities on the topic in question who are also well-versed in the principles and history of literary criticism — address a readership consisting of scholars, students of literature at the graduate and undergraduate level, and the general reader. One of the primary purposes of the series is to illuminate the nature of literary criticism itself, to gauge the influence of social and historic currents on aesthetic judgments once thought objective and normative.

JANE AUSTEN

Two Centuries of Criticism

Laurence W. Mazzeno

CAMDEN HOUSE
Rochester, New York

First published 2011
by Camden House

Camden House is an imprint of Boydell & Brewer Inc.
668 Mt. Hope Avenue, Rochester, NY 14620, USA
www.camden-house.com
and of Boydell & Brewer Limited
PO Box 9, Woodbridge, Suffolk IP12 3DF, UK
www.boydellandbrewer.com

ISBN-13: 978-1-57113-394-6
ISBN-10: 1-57113-394-1

Library of Congress Cataloging-in-Publication Data

Mazzeno, Laurence W.
    Jane Austen: two centuries of criticism / Laurence W. Mazzeno.
        p. cm. — (Studies in English and American literature and culture.
Literary criticism in perspective)
    Includes bibliographical references and index.
ISBN-13: 978-1-57113-394-6 (hardcover: alk. paper)
ISBN-10: 1-57113-394-1 (hardcover: alk. paper)
    1. Austen, Jane, 1775–1817—Criticism and interpretation—History.
I. Title.

PR4037.M34 2011
823'.7—dc22

                                                          2010048343

This publication is printed on acid-free paper.
Printed in the United States of America.

This book is dedicated to Sister M. Pacelli Staskiel, OSF, and the Honorable Thomas M. Golden, both gone but still alive in the memory of one who cherished their friendship.

Contents

Acknowledgments

M Y FIRST "thank you" goes to the editorial board at Camden House, and to Jim Walker, for continuing to show faith in my scholarship. I want to thank the two anonymous readers who provided significant suggestions for improvement. While I suspect I will never please both of them fully, I have tried to incorporate their many good ideas into the revised manuscript that is appearing in print. As I have done so often in the past, I want to publicly commend the staff of the Frank A. Franco Library at Alvernia University, especially Roberta Rohrbach, for help in tracking down books and articles from places all around the globe.

Introduction

HOW SURPRISED, AND HOW AMUSED, Jane Austen would have been if she could have known what an immense number of critical works would be devoted to her," writes Jane Aiken Hodge in her 1972 biography of the novelist. " 'Who, me?' one imagines her saying, with one of her occasional grammatical lapses. 'All those books . . .'" (15).

All those books, indeed.

As Claire Tomalin observed in 1997, "Austen has become very big business" (25). Contemporary interest in her rivals that which Britons over the years have shown for members of the Royal Family, or which contemporary fans exhibit toward Hollywood celebrities. Today, nearly two hundred years after Austen's death, dozens of editions of her works are available, often sharing the shelves with popular romance novels and those of the latest "hot" genre, vampire lit. Additionally, as Moyra Haslett noted recently, "coffee-table books about Jane Austen outnumber those for any other English author" (203). High-school and college students frequently find an Austen novel on their literature class syllabus. Academics write treatises about her, while people who have not read much since finishing their formal education buy and read copies of *Pride and Prejudice* or *Sense and Sensibility* so they can discuss them with friends over coffee. In *The Literary 100: A Ranking of the Most Influential Novelists, Playwrights, and Poets of All Time* (2001) Daniel Burt ranks Austen number eighteen among world figures. It is almost certain, however, that a survey of general readers would place her nearer to the top in terms of the contemporary audience she commands. The universality of her appeal has been succinctly summed up by one of her most perceptive critics and editors, Janet Todd: "Nobody can doubt that Jane Austen serves something of the Bible's former function: helping to make a shared community of reference for the literate English-speaker" (*Cambridge Introduction*, 1).

Austen's reputation may seem to be secure today; but has it always been so? If we still believe Edmund Wilson, the answer is a decided "yes." Writing in 1944, Wilson observed that though "there have been several revolutions of taste during the last century and a quarter of English literature," perhaps "only two reputations have never been affected by the shifts of fashion: Shakespeare's and Jane Austen's" (629). But one need only to read in succession David Cecil's *Jane Austen* (1935), Marvin Mudrick's *Jane Austen: Irony as Defense and Discovery* (1952), Marilyn

Butler's *Jane Austen and the War of Ideas* (1975), and Allison Sulloway's *Jane Austen and the Province of Womanhood* (1989) to realize that the novelist's work (and her personality) can be — and have been — interpreted quite differently by critics whose own predilections often influence the way they approach Austen's fiction.

Hence, *Jane Austen: Two Centuries of Criticism* has a twofold purpose. First, of course, it is an attempt to see how Austen has fared as the object of critical inquiry. But second, it is, in postmodern critical terms, intended to gaze at the gazers, to examine the philosophical and critical premises from which critics have approached Austen and her fiction to reveal something of their methods and motives. In this book I try to provide a fair hearing to both sides of what I call the Great Austen Controversy: Was she a conservative or a radical? Did she really believe in the moral values and social structure of Regency England, or was she using her considerable wit and talent for storytelling for subversive purposes?

At the outset, I must offer a cautionary note. While I hope those who have devoted their lives to the study of Austen's fiction will find some benefit in *Jane Austen: Two Centuries of Criticism*, I am aware that a broad survey such as this one is likely to leave specialists feeling that they have learned little new after reading it. My aim, however, is to provide undergraduates, graduate students, and scholars who are not Austen specialists a tool for understanding the reasons for Austen's rise to prominence among English novelists and the uses critics have made of her fiction for advancing their own theories about aesthetic, moral, political, gender, or cultural issues.

The history of Austen criticism might be described metaphorically as beginning with a long series of drips and then suddenly erupting into a raging torrent. In fact, forty years ago Brian Southam found it necessary to apologize for both the paucity and quality of Austen scholarship published during the first fifty years after her death. "There are no masterpieces of criticism in this volume," he says in the introduction to *Jane Austen: The Critical Heritage* (1968). "In many respects the birth and growth of Jane Austen's critical reputation was a dull and long-drawn-out affair" (1). The quality of criticism improved markedly during the next seventy years, as Southam observes in the introduction to his companion study, *Jane Austen: The Critical Heritage, 1870–1940* (1987). But the real explosion in Austen studies began after the Second World War, and there are no signs that it will slow down in the near future. Hence, any attempt to provide in a single book a survey of the criticism of Austen's fiction is sure to suffer from two limitations: First, it will be at best a snapshot in time. Second, it will of necessity consist of summaries and excerpts. That has certainly been the case for me in writing *Jane Austen: Two Centuries of Criticism*. Unquestionably there is danger in the kind of reductive approach I take to the body of Austen criticism. All paraphrase is distortion in some way, and an important goal of anyone attempting to describe the trajectory of Austen studies is to reduce this distortion to a minimum.

My principal focus in *Jane Austen: Two Centuries of Criticism* is on the development of Austen's reputation within the scholarly community. On occasion, however, I have chosen to include popular works to give readers some indication of what the general public was learning about Austen while scholars debated the merits of her fiction. I have restricted my examination to written criticism found principally in books. Of course, most of the commentary on Austen written during the nineteenth century — what little there is — appeared in periodicals designed for a literate general audience with a wide range of interests. One might call these journals popular in the same sense that the *New Yorker*, the *Economist*, the *Saturday Review*, or *Atlantic Monthly* is popular today. By contrast, much of what was written about Austen during the twentieth century was produced by scholars and intended for other scholars, many of whom share a specialized vocabulary, especially after the 1960s.

There are other forms of criticism, of course, and in the case of Austen those have been formidable and noteworthy, especially in the last thirty years. I am referring, of course, to the many adaptations of her novels for movie and television audiences. The process of transposing the written medium for the screen necessarily involves judgment, and during the past three decades a far greater proportion of the general population in England and America (and probably around the globe) has developed its notions of Jane Austen from watching film and video versions of her novels than from reading the works themselves. There are also written adaptations of Austen, fiction and occasionally poetry that attempts to revise, extend, or recast in modern dress the stories Austen tells in her six novels. The box office hit *Clueless* (1995) and the bestselling novel *The Jane Austen Book Club* (2004) are but two examples of hundreds that springboard off Austen's fiction to create new tales, attempting to give viewers or readers the same sensations (usually warm, fuzzy ones) that many people expect to get from the original fiction.

I have opted not to deal in any detail with these forms of criticism for two reasons. First, that terrain has already been covered recently in books I cite in my text; those interested in learning about the effect of visual adaptations or literary recreations will find ample materials already published. Second, in keeping with the principles of the Literary Criticism in Perspective Series, I have tried to produce a study that shows how the traditional profession of literary study affects the reputation of an author over time. Later in the twenty-first century, it may be that distinguishing between written academic criticism and more imaginative forms of interpretation — especially as that practice is being influenced by the Internet — will be largely irrelevant. But for now, the distinction still seems worth making, as Austen's fiction continues to be read and written about within the academic community, ever more so now than in decades past.

Although I make only occasional mention of them, I am also aware of the many reference guides available to scholars and students. A quick sampling should suffice to indicate the focus of these books: Michael Hardwick's *Guide to Jane Austen* (1973), Glenda Leeming's *Who's Who in Jane Austen and the Brontës* (1974), Paul Poplawski's *A Jane Austen Encyclopedia* (1998), and William Baker's rather imposing *Critical Companion to Jane Austen: A Literary Reference to her Life and Work* (2008) provide in some form or other plot summaries, abbreviated critical commentaries, descriptions of Austen's characters, and brief sketches of people important in Austen's life. None is more impressive, however, than Deirdre Le Faye's monumental *A Chronology of Jane Austen and Her Family* (2006), a 776-page volume (mostly small type), listing by date every known event in Austen's life and providing key information on other family members as well. While useful, most of these reference tools assume Austen's status as a major literary figure and do little to advance or change Austen's reputation. Those that provide important critical commentary are discussed in my text.

Also, in order to focus on the general trends in Austen criticism, I have chosen not to discuss at length works that deal with a single novel unless these have implications for shaping Austen's reputation as a whole. The result is that hundreds of articles, notes, and even books about individual works receive little or no notice. I have also tended to ignore casebooks or guides to individual works, although ones that attempt to review or redefine Austen's reputation are included. Useful guides to individual works are certainly plentiful, as a quick survey of titles about any Austen novel will indicate. To take one example from among many: In 1968 David Lodge edited *Jane Austen: Emma: A Casebook* for Macmillan, collecting previously published work and supplementing it with his own commentary on the critical history of the novel. That volume was revised and expanded to include some more recent critical commentary in 1991, a year before David Monaghan's *Emma: Jane Austen* was published by St. Martin's in its New Casebooks series. The essays in Monaghan's collection are all from work published after Lodge's 1968 volume appeared. Paula Byrne's *Jane Austen's Emma: A Sourcebook* (2004) provides some background information and selections from criticism published between 1815 and the end of the twentieth century. Alistair Duckworth's edition of *Emma* in Palgrave's Case Studies in Contemporary Criticism series (2004) appends to the text of the novel a series of essays examining *Emma* from various critical perspectives. Fiona Stafford's *Emma: A Casebook* (2007) collects a number of early influential essays and a handful of poststructuralist readings, as well as a lengthy original essay on the critical history of the novel. And just to be sure teachers would know how to present *Emma* in class, in 2004 the Modern Language Association commissioned Marcia McClintock Folsom to prepare *Approaches to Teaching Austen's Emma* (2004), which also contains a history of criticism about the work, commentary on film adaptations, and essays outlining various viewpoints on the novel. A similar list could be offered for Austen's other fiction as well, although it must be said that there are considerably more guides to *Pride and Prejudice* than to the remaining four novels. But because by design these kinds of books reprint previously published materials or concentrate on individual works, I have foregone discussion of most of them.

I have been fortunate in my search for key texts that *do* help define and modify Austen's reputation to have had available several important bibliographies. Geoffrey Keynes's *Jane Austen: A Bibliography* (1929) was the first scholarly attempt to catalog Austen's published works. Though two-thirds of the volume is given over to descriptions of various printings of original editions, reprints, and collected editions, the remaining section provides a selective listing of criticism. R. W. Chapman's entry on Austen in the *Cambridge Bibliography of English Literature* (1940), reproducing some entries from Keynes book but adding a selected list of materials published after 1928, had value when it appeared and for some years afterwards. The same can be said of his *Jane Austen: A Critical Bibliography* (1953).

Keynes's and Chapman's work was in a sense superseded by David Gilson's *A Bibliography of Jane Austen* (1982), which contains more than eight hundred pages of small print, cataloging original editions, translations, later editions, minor works, letters, dramatizations, continuations, and other fiction based on Austen's work, and a listing of more than eighteen hundred entries describing critical commentary published between 1812 and 1978. Although Gilson's bibliography is only lightly annotated, it remains an indispensable reference tool. A 1997 edition includes new materials and brings Gilson's work forward by fifteen years. Anyone wishing further evidence of Gilson's extensive knowledge of Austen can find it in his *Jane Austen: Collected Articles and Introductions* (1998).

More heavily annotated than Gilson's works, the three bibliographies that Barry Roth had a hand in preparing are also of great value to anyone wishing to trace the history of Austen criticism. The first, coauthored by Joel C. Weinsheimer, *An Annotated Bibliography of Jane Austen Studies, 1952–1972* (1973) covers much of the same ground as Gilson, annotating more than eight hundred entries. The second, *An Annotated Bibliography of Jane Austen Studies, 1973–83* (1985), provides brief descriptions for more than a thousand entries. The third, *An Annotated Bibliography of Jane Austen Studies, 1984–94* (1996), includes annotations for more than thirteen hundred entries. Until his death in 2008 Roth continued his bibliographic work by providing an annual review of scholarship for *Persuasions,* and later *Persuasions On-Line,* journals of the Jane Austen Society of North America. Roth's last article covers 2006.

Of course I am aware that *Jane Austen: Two Centuries of Criticism* is not the first book to trace Austen's reputation over time. The first important attempt to survey Austen's critical reputation is Brian Southam's introduction to his *Jane Austen: The Critical Heritage* (1968), a compendium of excerpts from nineteenth-century sources. In *Jane Austen: The Critical Heritage, 1870–1940* (1987), Southam continues his assessment to the outbreak of the Second World War. Less comprehensive than Southam's two volumes, Judith O'Neill's *Critics on Jane Austen* (1970) excerpts a number of nineteenth-century reviews of Austen's work and a handful of important twentieth-century commentaries. Another more limited attempt is Laurie Harris's chapter on Austen in *Nineteenth-Century Literature Criticism* (1981), a selection of critical statements on Austen's novels published between 1812 and 1979. More extensive in its selection of materials than Southam's work, Ian Littlewood's four-volume *Jane Austen: Critical Assessments* (1998) excerpts not only seminal commentaries from the nineteenth and early twentieth centuries but dozens of late-twentieth-century assessments as well. To assist users, Littlewood groups criticism under broad categories such as biographical background, social background, and studies focused on each of Austen's novels and her juvenilia.

Among studies published during the past two decades, Graham Handley's *Criticism in Focus: Jane Austen* (1992) is similar to the present work in its organization but decidedly shorter and much more eclectic in selecting criticism for commentary. A study quite similar to mine in approach and scope, Reimer Jehmlich's *Jane Austen* (1995), contains an extensive discussion of criticism from 1812 to 1992. Jehmlich's text was published in German, however, and has not been translated into English, thereby limiting its usefulness to those not proficient in German. Juliet McMaster's "Jane Austen as a Cultural Phenomenon," the opening essay in her collection *Jane Austen the Novelist* (1996), provides an informed review of Austen's reputation, discussing the changes in attitudes toward her novels brought on by new critical approaches to fiction, most notably feminism. The recently published *Cambridge Companion to Jane Austen* (2009), edited by Janet Todd and Claire Tuite, contains an entire section — nine essays — on what the editors describe as "Reception and Reinvention," although these essays are organized topically. In a shorter study similar to mine, "Criticism and Institutions: The Conflicted Reception of Jane Austen's Fiction" (1991), Philip Goldstein offers some provocative food for thought about reasons contemporary critics still feel uneasy dealing with what seems like Austen's straightforward conservative vision.

Annika Bautz's *The Reception of Jane Austen and Walter Scott* (2007) concentrates on nineteenth-century commentary on both novelists, although her concluding chapter examines criticism after 1900. Bautz's study bears close affinities to Southam's (*Jane Austen: The Critical Reception*, 1968), but her constant comparison of Austen and Scott help explain how shifts in taste and critical perspectives have affected the reputation of both writers. Anthony Mandal and Southam's *The Reception of Jane Austen in Europe* (2007) fills in a lacuna often present in studies such as my own. Three chapters provide detailed information on Austen's popularity in France. Sixteen additional chapters discuss her appeal in countries across the Continent from Holland to Russia and from Norway to Greece. Finally, Claire Harman's *Jane's Fame: How Jane Austen Conquered the World* (2009 in England, 2010 in America), published while my book was in press, offers detailed and insightful commentary on the growth of Austen's reputation among general readers and the scholarly community. The book is rich in detail and sound in its analysis, but covers the development of scholarly interest in Austen less fully than my study.

A recent study quite similar to mine is Deidre Lynch's *Janeites* (2000), a collection of essays by several Austen heavyweights that examines readership of Austen's novels over the past two centuries. While the essays tend to be more specialized and more theoretically focused than my work, the premises on which Lynch's volume is structured are worth noting, because they are in my view the right foundations for any good reception study of Austen. First, as Lynch acknowledges by quoting Lionel Trilling, there is something "interesting and important" in "the record of adaptations, reviews, rewritings, and appreciations of Austen" that have accumulated since 1811 ("*Emma* and the Legend of Jane Austen," 31). Second, it is less important to try to referee between "faithful and unfaithful readings" than to perceive "the diverse frameworks" in which Austen criticism has been conducted, to understand the "varying motives audiences have had for identifying with or repudiating Austen's example," and to examine "the divergent uses to which such alternative Austens have been put in the literary system and the culture at large" (Lynch, 5). The essays in Lynch's volume go a long way to exploring these crucial issues. However, they do not provide the chronological perspective offered in *Jane Austen: Two Centuries of Criticism*, and for that reason the present book seems justified.

In closing, I want to make some observations about the organization of the chapters in this book. The dividing lines between each of the first five chapters are easy to explain. Chapter 1 covers Austen's reputation during the first century after she died. Chapter 2 surveys critical commentary from the end of the First World War until the publication of F. R Leavis' influential *The Great Tradition: George Eliot, Henry James, Joseph Conrad* (1948), in which Leavis makes the pronouncement that Austen is "the inaugurator of the great tradition of the English novel" (7). Chapter 3 assesses the work of critics during the middle decades of the century, the period when new methods of inquiry — formalism and its stepchild, New Criticism, and psychoanalytic criticism — competed with older forms of criticism — humanism, historical studies, comparative analysis, influence and source studies — for dominance in Austen studies. Chapter 4 provides a snapshot of Austen criticism at an important juncture, the bicentennial of Austen's birth. At this point what had been considered new methodologies as well as older ones were being challenged by critics adopting still newer methods of inquiry — deconstruction, narratology, new historicism, postcolonial studies, and most importantly, feminism. Because feminist studies revolutionized the way we view Austen, I have isolated "early" feminist commentary — that written before 1990 — in a single chapter (chapter 5).

The organization of the next four chapters may be less apparent. One might ask, legitimately I think, "Why a chapter on 'New Theories 1976–1990' (chapter 6) followed by one on 'Traditional Criticism 1976–1990' (chapter 7) followed by two more (chapters 8 and 9) that perform the same kind of analysis but cover the period 1991–2008? Is there some reason for the dividing line being set at 1990?" None, I must confess, but convenience for the reader. I wanted to keep the chapters short enough so that I could give readers a sense of what new theorists were saying during a given period, then let them see what practitioners of traditional methods were doing at the same time.

Additionally, while the first two chapters are for the most part organized chronologically, I believe that once the amount of criticism available for study becomes too great to accommodate a strictly chronological assessment, some further subdivisions are necessary to guide readers through the maze of materials. I have chosen in most cases to devote a separate section in chapters 3 through 9 to books about Austen, and where appropriate to further subdivide these into biographies and critical studies. Usually these appear before discussions of articles and chapters in longer studies that include commentary on Austen. When I believe a shorter study has had influence on longer works, I try to make some mention of that influence when discussing a book, even if my commentary on the shorter work appears later in my text. I also realize that separating books from shorter studies creates a curious taxonomy, especially when one notices that I have subdivided the shorter studies by critical focus or methodology, not by length. But I hope my readers will bear with me as they read through *Jane Austen: Two Centuries of Criticism*, finding it useful to see how Austen has been handled as the principal subject of a critical study or as one point of focus in works that deal with multiple authors or cover broader topics.

Works Cited

Baker, William. *Critical Companion to Jane Austen: A Literary Reference to Her Life and Work*. New York: Facts on File, 2008.

Bautz, Annika. *The Reception of Jane Austen and Walter Scott: A Comparative Longitudinal Study*. London and New York: Continuum, 2007.

Burt, Daniel. *The Literary 100: A Ranking of the Most Influential Novelists, Playwrights, and Poets of All Time*. New York: Facts on File, 2001.

Butler, Marilyn. *Jane Austen and the War of Ideas*. Oxford: Clarendon Press, 1975.

Byrne, Paula, ed. *Jane Austen's Emma: A Sourcebook*. New York and London: Routledge, 2004.

Cecil, David. *Jane Austen*. Cambridge: Cambridge UP, 1935.

Chapman, R. W. "Jane Austen (1775–1817)." *The Cambridge Bibliography of English Literature*, edited by F. W. Bateson, 3:381–84. Cambridge: Cambridge UP, 1940.

———. *Jane Austen: A Critical Bibliography*. Oxford: Clarendon Press, 1953.

Duckworth, Alistair, ed. *Emma*. London: Palgrave, 2004.

Folsom, Marcia McClintock, ed. *Approaches to Teaching Austen's* Emma. New York: Modern Language Association of America, 2004.

Fowler, Karen Joy. *The Jane Austen Book Club*. New York: Putnam, 2004.

Gilson, David. *A Bibliography of Jane Austen*. Oxford: Clarendon Press, 1982. Updated ed., Winchester, UK: St. Paul's Bibliographies; New Castle, DE: Oak Knoll Press, 1997.

———. *Jane Austen: Collected Articles and Introductions*. [England]: D. Gilson, 1998.

Goldstein, Philip. "Criticism and Institutions: The Conflicted Reception of Jane Austen's Fiction." *Studies in the Humanities* 18 (1991): 35–55.

Handley, Graham. *Criticism in Focus: Jane Austen*. New York: St. Martin's, 1992.

Hardwick, Michael. *A Guide to Jane Austen*. Reading, England: Osprey; New York: Scribner's, 1973.

Harman, Claire. *Jane's Fame: How Jane Austen Conquered the World*. Edinburgh: Canongate, 2009; New York: Henry Holt, 2010.

Harris, Laurie, ed. *Nineteenth-Century Literature Criticism*. Detroit: Gale, 1981.

Haslett, Moyra. *Marxist Literary and Cultural Theories*. New York: St. Martin's, 2000.

Hodge, Jane Aiken. *The Double Life of Jane Austen*. London: Hodder & Stoughton, 1972. Issued as *Only a Novel: The Double Life of Jane Austen*. New York: Coward, McCann & Geoghegan, 1972.

Jehmlich, Reimer. *Jane Austen*. Darmstadt: Wissenschaftliche Buchgesellschaft, 1995.

Keynes, Geoffrey. *Jane Austen: A Bibliography*. London: Nonesuch Press, 1929.

Le Faye, Deirdre. *A Chronology of Jane Austen and her Family*. Cambridge; New York: Cambridge UP, 2006.

Leavis, F. R. *The Great Tradition: George Eliot, Henry James, Joseph Conrad*. London: Chatto & Windus, 1948.

Leeming, Glenda. *Who's Who in Jane Austen and the Brontës*. London: Elm Tree Books, 1974.

Littlewood, Ian, ed. *Jane Austen: Critical Assessments*. 4 vols. Mountfield, East Sussex: Helm Information, 1998.

Lodge, David, ed. *Jane Austen: 'Emma' — A Casebook*. London: Macmillan, 1968. Rev. ed., London: Macmillan Education, 1991.

Lynch, Deidre, ed. *Janeites: Austen's Disciples and Devotees*. Princeton, NJ: Princeton UP, 2000.

Mandal, Anthony, and B. C. Southam. *The Reception of Jane Austen in Europe*. New York: Continuum International, 2007.

McMaster, Juliet. *Austen the Novelist: Essays Past and Present*. Basingstoke, Hampshire: Macmillan; New York: St. Martin's, 1996.

Monaghan, David, ed. *Emma: Jane Austen*. New Casebooks. New York: St. Martin's, 1992.

Mudrick, Marvin. *Jane Austen: Irony as Defense and Discovery*. Princeton, NJ: Princeton UP, 1952.

O'Neill, Judith, ed. *Critics on Jane Austen*. London: Allen & Unwin; Coral Gables, FL: U of Miami P, 1970.

Poplawski, Paul. *A Jane Austen Encyclopedia*. Westport, CT: Greenwood Press, 1998.

Roth, Barry, and Joel C. Weinsheimer, comps. *An Annotated Bibliography of Jane Austen Studies, 1952–1972*. Charlottesville: UP of Virginia, 1973.

Roth, Barry, comp. *An Annotated Bibliography of Jane Austen Studies, 1973–83*. Charlottesville: UP of Virginia, 1985.

———, comp. *An Annotated Bibliography of Jane Austen Studies, 1984–94*. Athens: Ohio UP, 1996.

Southam, B. C., ed. *Jane Austen: The Critical Heritage*. London: Routledge & Kegan Paul; New York: Barnes & Noble, 1968.

————, ed. *Jane Austen: The Critical Heritage, 1870–1940*. New York: Routledge & Kegan Paul, 1987.

Stafford, Fiona, ed. *Jane Austen's* Emma*: A Casebook*. Oxford: Oxford UP, 2007.

Sulloway, Alison G. *Jane Austen and the Province of Womanhood*. Philadelphia: U of Pennsylvania P, 1989.

Todd, Janet M. *The Cambridge Introduction to Jane Austen*. Cambridge; New York: Cambridge UP, 2006.

Tomalin, Claire. *Jane Austen: A Life*. New York: Knopf, 1997.

Trilling, Lionel. "*Emma* and the Legend of Jane Austen." Introduction to *Emma*. Boston: Houghton Mifflin, 1957.

Wilson, Edmund. "A Long Talk about Jane Austen." *New Yorker* 20 (June 24, 1944): 70, 72–74, 77–78. Reprinted in *Edmund Wilson: Literary Essays and Reviews of the 1930s–40s*, 620–35. New York: Library of America, 2007.

1: Becoming England's Jane, 1811–1918

IT MAY SEEM UNUSUAL to be covering an entire century of criticism in a single chapter, but I think there are good reasons for this approach. First, until after the First World War, much of what was published about Austen's fiction was more along the lines of appreciation rather than critical commentary. Some of this material is important, of course, in that opinions formed during the nineteenth century influenced judgments made by critics in the twentieth, especially those writing before the rise of New Criticism as a dominant critical methodology. Second, and perhaps even more important, this field has been plowed before. Rather than repeat the excellent work of Brian Southam, I would simply like to refer readers to the lengthy introductions to his *Jane Austen: The Critical Heritage* (1968), which covers Austen's reception to 1870, and *Jane Austen: The Critical Heritage, 1870–1940*, which examines works published before the advent of the Second World War. Additionally, Claire Harman's recent reception study, *Jane's Fame: How Jane Austen Conquered the World* (2009) is also quite useful in describing how Austen remained a popular novelist throughout the nineteenth and into the twentieth century, and Joanne Wilkes's *Women Reviewing Women in Nineteenth-Century Britain* (2010) presents a thorough critique of nineteenth-century reviews of Austen's work by women, supplementing and extending Southam's work considerably.

Nevertheless, a brief summary of critical commentary on Austen during the first century after the publication of *Sense and Sensibility*, her initial foray into print, seems appropriate to set the stage for a more extensive examination of what followed, and why. For most of that time the sparse commentary on Austen's novels was likely to be civil acknowledgments of their merits as polite fiction. Some writers offer unstinted praise for her exceptional wit and insight into the domestic sphere, others seem rather deprecatory in praising her for keeping her focus on that realm rather than tackling grander subjects. While most of these works can hardly be called "criticism" by modern standards, they are nevertheless important because many of the myths about Austen and her fiction that would confound critics well into the twentieth century were established by early commentators. Hence, understanding how Victorian and Edwardian prejudices about Austen shaped popular attitudes is important for appreciating the advances made after the First World War when literary criticism became an important academic discipline.

A glance at the few notices that did appear should dispel any notion that Austen was totally unappreciated. Comments about *Sense and Sensibility* are complimentary. The writer of a notice in the *Critical Review* (1812) calls it a well written, genteel comedy by an author "who displays much knowledge of character" (150), while a brief note in the *British Critic* (1812) suggests that readers — particularly women readers — may benefit from reading this novel because its author presents "sober and salutary maxims for the conduct of life, exemplified in a very pleasing and entertaining narrative" (527). A year later, notices of *Pride and Prejudice* describe it as "far superior to almost all of the publications of the kind which have lately come before us" (*British Critic* [1813], 190) and "very superior to any novel we have lately met with in the delineation of domestic scenes" (*Critical Review* [1813], 324).

Mansfield Park was not reviewed at all, but *Emma* was noticed in several places. A brief notice in the *Gentleman's Magazine* (1816) describes it as not quite as good as *Pride and Prejudice* but still "amusing, if not instructive" (249). More importantly, however, *Emma* was the subject of a lengthy and generally favorable commentary in the prestigious *Quarterly Review* (1816). Although the journal did not give its reviewers by-lines, it was later made public that the author was the famous poet and novelist Sir Walter Scott. Modern students of Austen may be surprised, however, to find the review not as universally gushing as some have made it out to be. Scott praises Austen as one of the best practitioners of the new style in novels that copy nature — viz., those that exhibit qualities of realism absent in so many novels published in the decades before Austen wrote. Her "knowledge of the world, and the peculiar talent with which she presents characters" reminds Scott "of the Flemish school of painting" (197), but he faults her for focusing too much on minor comic characters. Scott's greatest praise for Austen — and the comment most often cited as evidence of his high regard for her — is not in the review, but in an 1826 entry in his journal, where he remarks that Austen's "talent for describing the involvements and feelings and characters of ordinary life is to me the most wonderful I ever met with. The big bow-wow strain I can do myself like any going now, but the exquisite touch which renders ordinary commonplace things and characters interesting," he admits candidly, "is denied to me" (Lockhart [1897], 203). The reading public first learned of Scott's high praise in 1837, when his son-in-law John Gibson Lockhart quoted the better part of the passage in his *Memoirs of the Life of Sir Walter Scott*.

The publication of *Persuasion* and *Northanger Abbey* after Austen died gave the world its first glimpse of the woman behind the novels. In the volume Austen's brother Henry provided a "Biographical Notice" in which he plants the seeds for what many have called the "Jane Austen Myth." Henry makes his sister out to be a kind of domestic saint. "Though the frailties, foibles, and follies of others could not escape her immediate detection," he observes, "yet even on their vices did she never trust herself to comment with unkindness" (Austen, *Persuasion* [2006], 329). Henry Austen's sketch is the *locus classicus* for the idea that, although his sister had read widely and had a tenacious memory, her talent was innate, not learned from reading, imitation, and careful craftsmanship. "Her power of inventing characters seems to have been intuitive, and almost unlimited. She drew from nature," he assures readers, "never from individuals" (330). Henry Austen also provided the world Austen's own description of her methodology. In a postscript to the "Notice," he quotes (not quite accurately) a letter from the novelist to her nephew about the possibility of her using sketches the youngster had written. "What should I do" she says, "with your manly, vigorous sketches, so full of life and spirit? How could I possibly join them on to a little bit of ivory, two inches wide, on which I work with a brush so fine as to produce little effect after much labour?" (331). Apparently the portrait of Austen as a sweet-tempered recluse who wrote novels of limited scope but great insight was one that the family approved, and would try to perpetuate for more than a century.

Notices of the posthumously published novels suggest that Austen's talent was recognized and appreciated, especially when compared to her contemporaries. The *Blackwood's Edinburgh Magazine* (1818) reviewer thought her works deserved more attention than they had received because readers were accustomed to racier material. When tastes change, the writer says, there is no doubt Austen "will be one of the most popular English novelists" (455). The writer of a longer review in the *British Critic* (1818) said essentially the same thing. This review reveals quite clearly, however, what most of Austen's contemporaries were looking for in a novel: not just good writing but good moral instruction. *Northanger Abbey* is praised as worthy of readers' attention, but *Persuasion* is faulted because the reviewer cannot condone "its *moral* [reviewer's emphasis], which seems to be, that young people should always marry according to their own inclinations and upon their own judgment" (301).

The publication of *Northanger Abbey* and *Persuasion* was also the occasion for the first important critical assessment of Austen. Writing for the *Quarterly Review* in 1821, Richard Whately summarizes contemporary opinion and lays out the premises on which her work was being judged. Although his misspells her name throughout, calling her "Miss Austin," Whately insists it is no longer necessary to apologize for Austen — or any other novelist. It is now possible to find in novels guidance for leading a good life, where sound principles are conveyed by example. Whately finds that the moral lessons in Austen's fiction, "though clearly and impressively conveyed, are not offensively put forward, but spring incidentally from the circumstances of the story" (360). Hence, her works "may safely be recommended, not only as among the most unexceptionable of their class, but as combining, in an eminent degree, instruction with amusement, though without the direct effort at the former" (375).

Victorian Appreciations and Depreciations

The Victorians seem to have appreciated Austen's novels while accepting many of the early judgments about her merits and deficiencies. Reverend Whately's sentiments were echoed a decade later by Alan Cunningham, who noted in an 1833 *Athenaeum* essay that "the works of Jane Austen have quietly won their way to the public heart" (773). Cunningham's contemporary Thomas Henry Lister observed in a review of Catherine Gore's *Women as They Are* in the *Edinburgh Review* (1830) that Austen was never as popular as she deserved to be because she was so adept at creating realistic characters that readers did not appreciate her artistry. His final judgment highlights a perceived characteristic about Austen's accomplishment that would dominate criticism for more than a century: "No novelist perhaps ever employed more unpromising materials, and by none have those materials been more admirably treated" (449).

Because the Victorians tended to value novels for their wide scope and intellectual prowess, Austen's stories of quiet country life achieved only a small following, but her admirers were passionate about her work. The highest early praise came from the historian Thomas Babington Macaulay who said that he had no hesitation placing Austen next to Shakespeare among English writers (*Edinburgh Review*, 561). The anonymous essayist writing about Austen in Robert Chambers's *Cyclopaedia of English Literature* (1844) expresses some sadness that her "genuine but unobtrusive merits" have gone largely unnoticed, "though her works are now rising in popular esteem" (2:572). Anne Katherine Elwood also suggests that Austen's "merits are beginning to be properly appreciated" (*Memoirs of the Literary Ladies of England*, 180–81). Elwood approves of Austen because the novelist possesses "every feminine grace and virtue" and is "thoroughly religious and devout" (184) — although Elwood cites no evidence from the novels to prove these points. In his oft-reprinted *Outlines of General Literature* (1849), T. B. Shaw cites Austen's novels as "models of perfection in a new and very difficult species of writing." Although he finds in them "little to inspire strong emotion, nothing to excite wonder or laughter," there is much "admirable good sense, exquisite discrimination, and an unrivalled power of easy and natural dialogue" (479).

The Victorians' penchant for ranking novelists — as well as their gender prejudice — is evident in a number of mid-century assessments. In his *New Monthly Magazine* article on Austen (1852) Francis Jacox automatically relegates her to the second rank among novelists — because "none but a man, of first-rate powers withal, can produce a first-rate novel" (17). Jacox nevertheless admires Austen's ability to create realistic characters and celebrates the moral of her stories. The influential critic David Masson states unequivocally in *British Writers and Their Styles* (1859) that Austen was the best of the previous generation of women novelists. Men love her work, he asserts, and women have only one objection: Austen's novels "reveal too many of their secrets" (189).

However, not every Victorian critic was so kind. John Jeaffreson suggests in *Novels and Novelists from Elizabeth to Victoria* (1858) that Austen's novels are little read, even though it has become fashionable to praise them. Her penchant for painting the "quiet home life of educated people" is a subject Jeaffreson says his contemporaries find "distasteful" (86). More pointedly, the author of "The Progress of Fiction as an Art" in the October 1853 *Westminster Review* — possibly George Eliot, if her biographer Gordon Haight is correct — believes that while Austen succeeded simply because she could accurately describe what she knew best, her works fail to meet the tests of the best fiction, because they fail to elevate the spirit.

Austen's greatest champion during the mid-nineteenth century was G. H. Lewes, a critic who continuously lobbied for a set of standards for judging literature apart from simple appreciation or the tendency to reward efforts at writing about grandiose topics. Still, Lewes's high regard for Austen is a bit surprising, perhaps, since his lifelong companion Marian Evans (the novelist George Eliot) was not particularly fond of Austen's work. Lewes wrote frequently about Austen, and always with great admiration. In an 1847 *Fraser's Magazine* essay he pairs her with Fielding as "the greatest novelists of our age" (687). Five years later, writing in the *Westminster Review* (1852), he calls her "the greatest artist that has ever written, using the term to signify the most perfect mastery over the means to her end" (134). His 1859 *Blackwood's Edinburgh Magazine* essay, "The Novels of Jane Austen," provides a more comprehensive assessment. Lewes uses this article to substantiate his claim that Austen is "an artist of high rank, in the most rigorous sense of the word" (99). He suggests that if "the art of the novelist be the representation of human life by means of a story; and if the *truest* representation, effected by the *least expenditure* of means, constitutes the highest claim of art, then we say that Miss Austen has carried the art to a point of excellence surpassing that reached by any of her rivals" (101). In the "economy of art" she stands with Sophocles, Molière, and Shakespeare (102).

Yet Lewes displays his own predilection for works with grand subjects in his reluctant admission that, while Austen's "genius" is "exceedingly rare," it is "not the highest kind of genius" (103). Austen "did not choose the highest range" for expressing her talents (103). Her "subjects have little intrinsic interest; it is only in their treatment that they become attractive" (107). With a nod toward the literary tastes of his own day, Lewes suggests that the "absence of breadth, picturesqueness, and passion, will also limit the appreciating audience of Miss Austen to the small circle of cultivated minds" (107).[1] Lewes is careful throughout, however, to distinguish taste from criticism, insisting that an artist be judged on technical merits. For him, storytelling is not an essential part of art, so despite her indifferent stories, Austen can still be considered a first-rate artist because her "charm lies solely in the art of representing life and character, and that is exquisite" (109). Finally, he feels compelled (as a good Victorian critic would) to determine Austen's rank among literary figures. "Her place is among great artists, but it is not high among them. She sits in the House of Peers, but it is as a simple Baron." Still, he insists, her fame "must endure. Such art as hers can never grow old, never be superseded" (113).

It is particularly instructive to read Lewes's praise alongside the criticism of his contemporary Julia Kavanagh, a novelist and critic with feminist sensibilities. Kavanagh is among the first to discern in Austen's novels a strain of disquiet beneath the surface sparkle that had captivated so many readers. Although Austen does not portray "the grand, the heroic, the generous, the devoted," Kavanagh says in *English Women of Letters* (1862), "the simply good, the dull, the lively, the mean, the coarse, the selfish, the frivolous, she saw and painted with a touch so fine that we often do not perceive its severity." What is more, Austen possessed a quality even more rare: "she knew where to stop" (190). But Kavanagh is critical of Austen because "the stillness of her books is not natural, and never, whilst love and death endure, will human lives flow so calmly as in her pages" (192). The irony Kavanagh detects in the novels is in her estimation "a fault, and the parent of much coldness" (193). Like others of her generation, Kavanagh acquiesces to the general belief that Austen succeeds in spite of her choice of subjects. It is remarkable that "out of materials so slender, out of characters so imperfectly marked," Austen could "fashion a story." This ability, Kavanagh says, "is her great, her prevailing merit, and yet, it cannot be denied, it is one that injures her with many readers" (232) — because most people want exaggeration rather than modest realism in fiction.

Lewes's and Kavanagh's conclusions are echoed by the distinguished Victorian critic E. S. Dallas, who offers what might be considered the majority opinion on Austen at mid-century. Reviewing George Eliot's *Felix Holt, The Radical* in *The Times* (1866), Dallas says that Austen displays her exceptional talent for weaving a narrative, but George Eliot is superior because she excels with more important subject matter. Similar sentiments are expressed by the anonymous author of "Miss Austen" in the *Englishwoman's Domestic Magazine* (1866), who praises Austen for creating lifelike portraits of people and transporting readers back to an earlier, simpler time. In these comments one senses the stirrings of sentiment that would characterize generations of admirers who would prize Austen's humor and relish her novels as costume dramas without ever perceiving the critical stance she had taken against the foibles and excesses of her age.

James Austen-Leigh's *Memoir* and Its Influence

The first full-length biography of Austen was published by her nephew, James Edward Austen-Leigh, son of Austen's eldest brother James. *A Memoir of Jane Austen* first appeared in 1870, and sales were so good that a second edition was called for a year later.[2] Austen-Leigh had known his aunt — he was the youngest mourner at her funeral — and was certainly qualified to write a memoir. But like a good Victorian biographer he was careful not to delve too deeply into personal matters. Austen-Leigh provides considerable information about his aunt's daily life, describing household furnishings, social schedules, and dining practices. He seems especially interested in establishing the family pedigree, and as a consequence traces the history of Austen's ancestors on both sides of the family.

Austen-Leigh's assessment of Austen's achievement as a novelist reflects his own Victorian values. Although his aunt's society was limited, he says, she "found in her neighborhood persons of good taste and cultivated minds" from whom she drew her characters. As a result, her work is "free from the vulgarity" found in so many novels that seem to stress the value of wealth for its own sake (18). The juvenilia was not yet available for others to judge, of course, but Austen-Leigh assures his readers that his aunt's early efforts tended to be burlesques, and that as she grew older — and presumably wiser — she gravitated toward more realistic fiction while retaining her zest for comedy. Austen-Leigh portrays his aunt as a sort of natural genius who at an early age possessed exceptional insight into character and manners. Roughly half of his book describes the qualities he finds in the novels, but there is only a superficial attempt to get at the mind behind them.

More effort is taken to guard Austen's innermost thoughts. Admitting that many have expressed a wish that Austen's letters be published, Austen-Leigh demurs, explaining that "the materials" in these missives "may be thought inferior to the execution, for they treat only of the details of domestic life." They contain "no notice of politics or public events," no "discussions on literature or other subjects of general interest" (60). With the virtue of hindsight, it easy to criticize Austen-Leigh for his patriarchal attitude; how "details of domestic life" might be a subject "of general interest" seems to escape him. He goes so far as to claim the "politics of the day occupied very little" of Jane Austen's attention, and suggests she ascribed to the same conventional Tory attitudes that others in her family held.

What Austen-Leigh does quite well is solidify the myth of Jane Austen as the lively and kindly unmarried aunt, sacrificing her personal happiness to tend to the welfare of others. Austen-Leigh certainly gave his readers what they wanted. His Jane Austen is the beloved Victorian heroine, possessing exceptional virtue, a lively yet demurring personality, and a strong sense of duty to family. When young, she is twice disappointed in love — Austen-Leigh alludes to her romantic liaisons but gives no names of the men she loved, and makes clear that these relationships were chaste. Doomed to remain unwed, she deals with her disappointment by writing with great insight and jovial resignation. Her work is published anonymously, never allowing her the opportunity to gain recognition for her exceptional talents. Then, like a character in Dickens, she dies too soon, leaving the world to wonder about what she could have accomplished had she lived.

The literary world reacted with great interest to the *Memoir*. Here at last was the story of the mysterious woman whose novels had attracted a small but loyal group of fans for more than half a century. The Victorians were delighted to discover that the woman was as good as any heroine in her books — or any Victorian heroine. Reviews were generally positive, but three commentaries are worth examining in some detail. The first is Juliet Pollock's, which appeared in *St. Paul's Magazine* in 1870. Pollock suggests the appearance of the *Memoir* has created a greater stir among late Victorians than it would have among Austen's contemporaries because the novelist's reputation had grown considerably. Austen's works continue to please those who enjoy gentle ironic commentaries on ordinary life written by a woman who never attempted to exceed her limitations. And although Pollock recommends against a steady and exclusive diet of Austen's fiction because that might lead one to develop a "low estimate of humanity" and starve "the higher imaginative faculties" (639) — she recommends Scott's fiction instead — she notes with approval that Austen's novels still entertain young women and are "pondered over with most attention and most appreciation by men of thought and literary education" (643).

Where Pollock delights in the surface sparkle of Austen's fiction, the novelist and critic Margaret Oliphant, like Julia Kavanagh before her, finds something going on beneath the cheerful façade. In "Miss Austen and Miss Mitford" (1870), an essay prompted in part by the publication of the *Memoir*, Oliphant suggests Austen's determination to write about what she knew is not necessarily a limitation, but instead "throws a certain light upon her character, which is not the simple character it appears at first glance, but one full of subtle power, keenness, finesse, and self-restraint — a type not at all unusual among women of high cultivation, especially in the retirement of the country, where such qualities are likely enough to be unappreciated or misunderstood" (294). Austen-Leigh, she says, unwittingly provides "a passing gleam of light upon the fine vein of feminine cynicism which pervades his aunt's mind. It is something altogether different from the rude and brutal male quality that bears the same name"

(294). More than half a century before D. W. Harding would write what many have considered the most influential essay on Austen's hidden cynical side, Oliphant notes that "the feminine cynicism which we attribute to Miss Austen" includes "a great deal that is amiable, and is full of toleration and patience." However, "it is not charity, and its toleration had none of the sweetness which proceeds from that highest of Christian graces." In fact, she continues, "humankind stands low in her estimation, in short, as a mass. There are a few pleasant young people here and there," but "there is a great deal more amusement to be got out of the mean people, and to them accordingly she inclines" (295). Oliphant insists that "nothing but a mind of this subtle, delicate, speculative temper, could have set before us pictures which are at once so refined and so trenchant, so softly feminine and polite, and so remorselessly true" (296). Oliphant is pleasantly surprised that, given these tendencies, Austen had achieved any following at all. "It is scarcely to be expected," she notes, "that books so calm and cold and keen, and making so little claim upon their sympathy, would ever be popular." Austen's novels belong to "the class which attracts the connoisseur" (304).

While Oliphant may display great prescience in her judgment of Austen's fiction, by far the review of the *Memoir* most often cited by Austen scholars as having influenced the direction of Austen criticism is Richard Simpson's. Writing in the April 1870 issue of the *North British Review*, Simpson asserts that Austen was "a critic who developed herself into an artist" (131). Her "critical faculty" can be seen in "the didactic purpose and even nomenclature of her novels" (131) — by which he means the themes and titles of works such as *Sense and Sensibility* and *Pride and Prejudice* — which are "intended to contrast, and by the contrast to teach something about, the qualities or acts named in the titles" (131–32). Austen may be a superb humorist, as others have noted, but "her humour is only partial" and is always qualified by her "pervading critical judgment" (135). Simpson believes Austen is concerned principally with people in their social aspects. "Man is only known to her" Simpson says (his terminology reminding later readers that political correctness had not yet become commonplace in critical discourse), "not as a solitary being complete in himself, but only as completed in society" (137). At the same time, Austen had "no interest for the great political and social problems which were being debated with so much blood in her day. The social combinations which taxed the calculating powers of Adam Smith or Jeremy Bentham were above her powers" (138).

Although Simpson is analytic and evenhanded in examining Austen's novels, his general conclusion borders on the rhapsodic. "She is neat, epigrammatic, and incisive, but always a lady," he insists. Her career stands as a stellar example for the aspiring artist, because she "shows what patience, perseverance, modest study, and a willingness to keep her compositions for the test of time, could do for a genius not very commanding in its own nature" (152). Might it not be appropriate, he asks, to "borrow from Miss Austen's biographer the title which the affection of a nephew bestows on her, and recognize her officially as 'dear aunt Jane'?" (152). In Simpson's careful study one can discern many of the characteristics of Austen's technique and vision that would become critical commonplaces over the next half-century: her penchant for gentle irony emerging from her critical view of society, her concern for humankind in its social dimension, her deep commitment to craftsmanship. Perhaps it is unfortunate that Simpson ends with that final encomium, because it seems not only to vitiate his studied examination of Austen as a critic and craftsman, but also because it would become the shorthand for describing the attitude of future generations of adoring fans who allow no aspersions to be cast on their "dear Aunt Jane." Although he would not have recognized the term — it was not coined for several decades — Simpson ended his essay by professing to be among the Janeites.[3]

Late Victorian Critical Judgments

Criticism written during the last three decades of the nineteenth century generally reflects the judgments about Austen promulgated by her nephew James Austen-Leigh and supported by Richard Simpson in his influential review of the *Memoir*. Most readers and critics approached Austen with certain presuppositions: she was a naturally gifted artist, a keen observer of ordinary life, at times a gentle satirist, always a congenial humorist. Above all she was someone who, knowing her place both as a woman and artist, never attempted writing about subjects which she did not experience intimately. For the Victorians, this meant she was a pleasant and talented practitioner of a minor form of fiction, the novel of manners — perhaps the best to write in that genre, but certainly not a major literary figure.

These opinions inform a number of late nineteenth-century synopses of Austen's life and career. For example, William Forsyth praises Austen's ability to create characters, especially young women, who reflect the period in which she lived. But women have advanced in stature since Austen's day, he tells his readers in *Novels and Novelists of the Eighteenth Century* (1871); they possess a "greater degree of modesty" than Austen's heroines, and have considerably greater opportunities to display their talents, particularly in "works of charity and benevolence" (337). Austen merits a scant five pages in Jerome Murch's *Mrs. Barbauld and Her Contemporaries* (1877), because, Murch says, "her works never were and never will be highly popular. It requires a cultivated taste to appreciate the rare skills with which the scanty materials of her tales are handled" (22). Leslie Stephen's brief account of Austen's career in the *Dictionary of National Biography* (1885) stresses the novelist's conscious determination to limit herself to treating subjects she knew — "no writer ever understood better the precise limits of her own powers," he insists — but now, seven decades after her death, "all critics agree to the unequalled fineness of her literary tact" (732). Millicent Fawcett's sketch of Austen's career in *Some Eminent Women of Our Times* (1889), a collection of essays she wrote for *The Mother's Companion*, presents Austen as someone who made a virtue of her fate as a woman. "The ordinary, everyday joys and sorrows that form a part of the lives of all of us, were hers," Fawcett says. "But she stands alone, hitherto quite unequalled, for the power of investing with charm and interest these incidents in the everyday life of everyday people" (136).

Margaret Oliphant, however, continued to insist that there was more substance to Austen's fiction than most critics recognized. In *The Literary History of England* (1882) Oliphant calls Austen, Maria Edgeworth, and Susan Ferrier leaders of a revolution in women's fiction. "Female writers had never been wanting," Oliphant says, but they had never been considered equal to men working in the genre. These three ushered in "an entirely feminine strain of the highest character and importance" (207). Oliphant calls Austen "the greatest and most enduring of the three" who "belongs to humanity of all periods" (206). She is particularly impressed with Austen's ability to make art of the domestic sphere, capturing the essence of human nature and creating "delightful" characters. In these aspects of her craft, Oliphant says, "Austen has no superiors, and very few that can be called her peers" (237).

In addition to these brief sketches, several books on the novelist appeared in the closing decades of the century. Unfortunately, most did little to advance critical understanding of Austen's fiction. For example, Sarah Tytler's *Jane Austen and Her Works* (1880) is little more than a reworking of the *Memoir*, a fact somewhat gleefully noted by Austen's great nephew Edward Knatchbull, the first Lord Braeburn, in his introduction to *Letters of Jane Austen* (1884). In addition to providing the world two volumes of Austen's letters, Braeburn gives Austen lovers additional details about family life and history, identifying many of the individuals alluded to in Austen's letters and his cousin's *Memoir*. Of course, Lord Braeburn does little to change the notion of Austen as a prim and retiring spinster. That impression is challenged by another member of the family, Fanny Caroline Lefroy, whose three essays in the *Temple Bar* — "Hunting for Snarkes at Lyme Regis" (1879), "Is It Just?" (1883), and "A Bundle of Letters" (1883) — are intended to dispel the notion that Austen was passionless. Unfortunately, Lefroy's pleas seem to have fallen on deaf ears, and her contributions to Austen scholarship not fully appreciated until the publication of Alice Marie Villaseñor's article on Lefroy in the 2010 issue of *Persuasions On-Line*.

Similarly, in his monograph *Jane Austen's Novels* (1883), British-born, Harvard-educated critic George Pellew challenges the typical description of Austen as "a singular and inexplicable phenomenon without connection to the past" (5), tracing her debts to various literary forebears, particularly Richardson and Rousseau. Pellew demonstrates his perceptivity in suggesting that Austen's novels are reactions against the prevailing trend of sentimentality in fiction. However, he reveals his bias in discussing Austen's handling of moral issues and delineation of character in comments such as "we [late nineteenth-century readers] are interested by the subtle and more elemental conflicts of the soul," whereas in Austen's time "the considerations of a somewhat elementary though conventional civilization were still predominant" (33–34). Austen's women are true to life, he says, "but the world in which they lived, and its interests, were too limited for their full development" (40). Nevertheless, Pellew believes Austen has made "an important contribution to English fiction" by highlighting "the intellectual" side of "the feminine character" so well (43).

Sarah Malden's *Jane Austen* (1889) displays similar bias in its readings of the six major novels. She complains that Colonel Brandon's "decidedly dull" and "disagreeable" account of Willoughby's transgressions in *Sense and Sensibility* is unsuitable fare for the ears of nineteen-year-old Marianne (67), and that there is no reason for *Pride and Prejudice* to be spoiled by the squalid details of Lydia's elopement (106). On the whole, though, the "absoluteness of dainty finish" and "a keen, delicate satire and a humor which is never coarse" (223) make Austen suitable reading for Malden's contemporaries. Malden's critical judgment is worth noting, if only for its place in setting the course for future assessments. She subscribes to the theory that Austen's art improved as she matured. "The motives and actions" of her characters become more complex, "the satire is a little softened," and the feelings her characters express "are more womanly than girlish" (107).

The distinction of writing the first critical biography of Austen goes to Goldwyn Smith, whose *Life of Jane Austen* (1890) combines a recapitulation of the major events of her life, cadged from Austen-Leigh's *Memoir*, with an attempt to provide some systematic critical estimation of her novels. Smith constantly points out parallels between Austen's life and her fiction, but warns against being too speculative in assigning the genesis of fictional incidents to events in the novelist's life. With respect to her achievements, Smith takes what was by the end of the century a conventional view that she excelled in her craft but had willfully limited her scope to maintain her ability to construct believable characters and incidents.

Smith finds Austen can be distinguished from the "group of female novelists of manners" by a "gift of creative power" shared only by giants like Shakespeare, Homer, Cervantes, and Scott (11). Despite this exceptional talent, Smith says, she was reluctant to be identified as an author lest she be seen as "overstep[ping] the limitations of her sex" (34) Such an interpretation suggests something of Smith's paternalistic attitude toward Austen, whom he calls a woman of good sense and propriety, conservative in her politics and her personal life. Although he detects "a flash of something like Radical sympathy" for governesses in *Emma*, Smith is quick to assure his readers that "No other glimmering of the 'Revolt of Woman'" appears anywhere in her fiction (48).

Although Smith attempts to read the novels as portraits of life in Austen's day, he cannot help injecting his own standards of conduct when he finds certain behavior egregious. So Lady Catherine de Bourgh's "autocracy" may have been acceptable in Austen's day, but in Victorian society "her dictatorial insolence would scarcely escape a fall" (86). Similarly, he is outraged that Austen allows Willoughby to defend his decision to marry for money (95). Smith's bias is most notable in remarks about Austen's talents as a realist. He is careful to applaud Austen's talents in that direction while separating her from what he considers the more sordid practitioners of that genre, viz. the naturalists. Commenting on Austen's description of the Price household in *Mansfield Park*, Smith remarks that "there is nothing in Zola more realistic" — but the scene contains nothing of Zola's "repulsiveness" (162–63).

Smith's conclusions reveal something about both the state of critical practice in his day and late Victorian attitudes about Austen. "Criticism is becoming an art of saying fine things," he remarks, "and there are really no fine things to be said about Jane Austen. There is no hidden meaning in her; no philosophy beneath the surface for profound scrutiny to bring to light; nothing calling in any way for elaborate interpretation" (185). Instead, he says, Austen's genius lies in her ability to "make the familiar and commonplace intensely interesting and amusing" (185). On the other hand — a point Smith feels compelled to make — in recommending Austen over "the unwholesome products of sensationalism and the careless manufactures of literary hacks, we do not mean to take a leaf from the crown of those who have dealt with nobler and more entrancing themes" (191). In the final analysis, the "lives and loves" of Austen's characters are but "the lightest of bubbles on the great stream of existence," however bright they might shine (191).

R. H. Hutton's review of Smith's *Life of Jane Austen*, published in the *Spectator* (1890), suggests that Smith's view represented the majority opinion — certainly the male majority opinion — of Austen among late Victorians. Hutton, a respected critic and author of several books on theology, supplements his laudatory comments on Smith's study with his own extensive commentary on Austen's achievement. Hutton believes Austen has enjoyed only limited readership because of the "fineness" and "reduced scale" of her "exquisite pictures" ("The Charm of Miss Austen," 169). This high praise is almost immediately tempered, however, by his observation that Austen's novels present "a selection of all that is most superficially interesting in human life, of all that is most easily appreciated without going very deep, and an exclusion of all that it takes real wear and tear of spirit to enter thoroughly into" (170–71). Hence, Hutton suggests, readers like her because she provides a wonderful way to escape life's real trials. But for those who want literature to "stir them to the very depths and electrify them, or present them with some new mass of facts," Austen will be a disappointment (173).

Studies published shortly after Smith's biography appeared suggest that opinion about Austen's personal and literary qualities was solidifying, and scholars were beginning to flesh out the background of both. The American critic Oscar Fay Adams says in his preface to *The Story of Jane Austen's Life* (1891) that he wishes to present a story of Austen different from that told by his predecessors. He does so by writing more extensively about the settings in which Austen spent her life and quoting liberally from Lord Braeburn's edition of Austen's letters. His attempts at literary criticism are minimal, largely because he believes others have covered the field fairly well. Instead, he attempts to capture the character of the novelist. In his book, Austen emerges as a loving, devoted daughter and sister, a winsome and delightful aunt, and a selfless family member and friend who always put others before herself. Lucy Walford's chapter on Austen in *Twelve English Authoresses* (1892) also concentrates on Austen's life, interjecting comments which reflect appreciation and even admiration for Austen's ability as a writer of humor and lighthearted satire. Catherine Hamilton takes a slightly different approach in *Women Writers: Their Works and Ways* (1892), tracing the rise of Austen's reputation up to the publication of the *Memoir*. Her assessment reflects the late-Victorian attitudes toward Austen's work: "Jane Austen's fame will increase rather than diminish," she says, because her "subtle humour," "delicacy of touch," and "innate perception of character" all "exalt her to the rank of genius" (206). While interesting as reflections of late Victorian attitudes toward Austen, none of these admirers has much to offer in the way of fresh critical commentary.

Somewhere near the turn of the century, however, the reaction against the Victorians began to influence critical commentary on Austen as well. Among precursors of the generation that would become known as the Moderns, Austen was to lose some (but not all) of the unqualified admiration she had begun to receive from the general reading public. In her 1894 *Pall Mall Gazette* article "The Classic Novelist," the poet Alice Meynell contrasts Austen unfavorably with modern writers, finding her overly didactic, far too loose in her use of words that ought to have specific meanings, and generally disdainful of the people about whom she writes. Austen's greatest fault, however, is her concentration on trivial matters. It is permissible, Meynell says, for a novelist to write of "very small matters," but for Austen "love, vengeance, devotion, duty, maternity, sacrifice, are infinitely trivial" (*Second Person Singular*, 63). Her "art is not of the highest quality," but merely "of an admirable secondary quality" (64–65). In a similar vein, James Oliphant begins his brief comments on Austen in *Victorian Novelists* (1899) by celebrating her as the first modern English novelist, but then launches into a discussion of her limitations and faults that almost overshadow what he claims are Austen's notable accomplishments in creating memorable characters and writing realistically about human relationships.

But the most negative assessment at the end of the nineteenth century came from the Irish writer and politician Stephen Gwynn, whose *Cornhill* essay "The Decay of Sensibility" (1899) contains harsh words not only for Austen but for the age in which she lived. Gwynn begins his playful but at times sardonic assessment of women novelists and readers of bygone ages by stating emphatically that "I do not aspire to meet Miss Austen in Paradise. She must have been a most unlovable woman, and I cannot forgive her her ideals, not even for the sake of her dislikes" (*Decay of Sensibility and Other Essays*, 1). While Gwynn's real target is the false sentimentality of women in earlier times — a fault he says that is happily absent in modern females — he takes the opportunity to savage Austen's heroines for possessing too much of the unfortunate quality of "sensibility." "The truth about Miss Austen," Gwynn says, "is that she lived in a morally stupid, confined, narrow-minded society, and disliked her surroundings without feeling any desire to rise out of them" (2). His caustic portrait of Austen raised the ire of one the novelist's ardent admirers, the noted English drama critic Arthur Bingham Walkley. In an essay in *Frames of Mind* (1899) Walkley says Austen is "like the shadow of a great rock in a weary land" (110) and takes issue with Gwynn for his unflattering assessment of her. Walkley also offers a reason why some women do not care for Austen. "Ladies will say anything — especially about other ladies" (107).

One of the amusing ironies in Austen criticism between the middle of the nineteenth century and the First World War is the critics' belief that they would have to struggle to find something new to say. A case in point: Walter Pollock begins *Jane Austen: Her Contemporaries and Herself* (1899) by acknowledging that "so much has been written and so much well written, concerning Miss Austen that there seems to be need for some sort of apology or explanation for putting forth any new volume" (1). But Pollock forges ahead with his own new study, hoping to make clear to any skeptics who might still exist that Austen was not only the most gifted of a group of talented women writers, but was in fact one of the greatest writers England ever produced. Pollock's work demonstrates that the late Victorians were making some attempt to account for Austen's talent and explain why her work had stood the test of time while those of contemporaries more famous in their own day had already faded from the public memory.

Austen's Status in Surveys of Literature

By the 1890s the increasing professionalization of literary studies led to the proliferation of general surveys that in one way or another attempted to position individual writers within various movements or traditions. Most — but not all — present positive assessments of Austen. These critiques are important, because surveys were one way to introduce students and readers to literature and shape the opinions of the next generation of readers.

Perhaps the most influential, and certainly the most prolific critic of the late century, George Saintsbury, helped solidify Austen's reputation in the surveys he produced. In *A History of Nineteenth-Century Literature (1780–1895)* (1896) Saintsbury calls her "the mother of the English novel" (128–29). He takes a hard line with detractors who complain that her fiction is little more than a representation of "the habit of minute and semi-satiric observation natural to womankind" (129). While her work is feminine — a term of deprecation in Saintsbury's day — Austen stands apart from all other women writers in her ability to use irony for artistic purposes. Her special achievement lies in her ability to confine herself to describing ordinary life in such a way as to "extract the characteristics of that life which are perennial and human" (131), and to have developed a style that resonates with succeeding generations. In a chapter on Austen and Scott in *The English Novel* (1913) Saintsbury claims the two writers "dealt the death blow to the notion that the novel was an inferior if not actually discreditable" form of literature (189). In contrast to most of her contemporaries, Austen managed to achieve a narrative art that "duplicate[s] nature" (195). While others may complain about her limited range, Saintsbury insists the "actual things she knew she could do consummately; and she would not risk the production of anything not consummate" (200).

For the late Victorians and Edwardians, comparing Austen with Shakespeare seemed unavoidable. Hence, despite Walter Raleigh's assertion in *The English Novel* (1894) that Austen, like Burney and Edgeworth, wrote only "romance[s] of the tea-table" (255) where the focus is limited to affairs of the heart, he finds some truth in Macaulay's claims that Austen deserves to be compared to Shakespeare. Both, he says, possess a "sameness of artistic impersonality, of serene abstraction from life" (262). Taking the opposing position in *Essays on the Novel* (1897), Adolphus Jack is baffled that a writer of such limited range and philosophical outlook should be "as undisputed as Shakespeare" (278). Austen does not really "increase our knowledge of life" or "enlarge our sympathies" (280); she "is not a master to whom any one would turn to learn about life" (282). Disputing Jack's claim, in *A Short History of Modern English Literature* (1897) Edmund Gosse asserts Austen is "the one prose writer of this period whose genius has proved absolutely perdurable." Although her range is limited, "there is no other English writer who possesses so much of Shakespeare's inevitability, or who produces such evidence of a like omniscience" (295). Gosse repeats these claims (sometimes verbatim) in *English Literature: An Illustrated Record* (Garnett and Gosse, 1903). In that book Gosse raises her to an even higher level of merit, asserting that "among the creators of the world, Jane Austen takes a place that is with the highest and that is purely her own" (91). Another champion of Austen, William James Dawson, claims in *The Makers of English Fiction* (1905) that she "stands for so much in the development of English fiction" (41). Calling her the "supreme mistress of comedy" (42), he applauds her impersonal style and her abilities as a satirist. What is more, Austen displays a sound "criticism of life," a "hatred of shams" and a "quick irony that pierces and exposes them," but at the same time finds in these human shortcomings too many "absurdities" to become seriously irritated with those who display them (42).

In surveys prepared for American students, Austen received mixed reviews. Wilbur Cross, the Yale professor whose *Development of the English Novel* (1899) influenced a generation of American students, calls Austen's fiction one of the best examples of "art for art's sake" (115) because she wrote without concern for publication. Austen's "delicate psychological humor," he says, is akin to "the higher comedy of Shakespeare" (119). Cross sees her contributing to the development of the genre by restoring to the novel "an art and a style, which it once had had, particularly in Fielding, but which it had since lost" (122). The observation is worth noting, since Austen had traditionally been associated with the strand of fiction that ran from Richardson through a series of women novelists more interested in character development than intricate plotting. In her work "there was precisely that selection and recombination and heightening of incident and character that distinguish the comedy of manners from real life" (124), raising it to the level of high art. Richard Burton offers a similar assessment in *Masters of the English Novel* (1909), asserting she is "the best example in the whole range of English literature of the wisdom of knowing your limitations and cultivating your own special plot of ground" (104). Calling her "the literary godmother of Trollope and Howells," Burton says she passes the "supreme test" of a classic: she continues to be read (122). But in *The Evolution of the English Novel* (1900) another American professor, Francis Stoddard, offers a less effusive critique of Austen. Believing, like Matthew Arnold, that literature should be a criticism of life, Stoddard finds Austen a perfect technician but an imperfect artist. Taking *Pride and Prejudice* as his test case for Austen's merit, he says the novel may be "an observation of life," but it is more accurately described as "a satirical criticism of its outer phases, rather than a study of any of its problems" (53). Additionally, the novel presents "a dated society" and "a dated woman, not the woman of all time" (53).

Most notably, it lacks "intensity of interest" because its "perfection is really not the perfection of truth, but the perfection of finish" (57).

Curiously, Austen did not receive unqualified praise in two surveys focused exclusively on women writers. Ethel Wilmot-Buxton's sketch of her in *A Book of Noble Women* (1907) stresses her character, especially her devotion to her family and her powers of observation, while downplaying the work she put into her writing. "She did not make of her writing a serious occupation," Wilmot-Buxton says (111–12), perhaps missing the irony in Austen's frequent observations about the casual approach she took to her work. One might expect a better assessment from the American scholar Clara Whitmore, who observes in the preface to *Women's Work in English Fiction from the Restoration to the Mid-Victorian Period* (1910) that many of the works she considers in her study have fallen into oblivion "from which their intrinsic merit should have preserved them," in large part because "nearly all of the books in literature have been written from a man's point of view" (iii). Indeed, Whitmore challenges some of the notions regarding Austen that had become almost commonplace. She believes Austen deals honestly and with skill in treating relationships between men and women, and insists Austen presents women of real passion — but not the flamboyant, sentimental kind that populate conventional romances. Whitmore believes Austen is not "narrow" in her treatment of character, either; her men and women "furnish as broad a view of humanity as would be obtained by traveling up and down the world" (174). Ultimately, however, Whitmore concludes that Austen was conservative in both her art and her politics — suggesting that, even from a woman's point of view, Austen was hardly out to subvert the status quo.

Whitmore's claims to the contrary, describing Austen as limited in scope had become a critical commonplace by the turn of the twentieth century. Some critics saw this as an advantage, while others considered it a reason for dismissing her as a minor writer. For instance, Harold Williams's sketch of Austen's career in *Two Centuries of the English Novel* (1911) repeats conventional wisdom about her abilities as an observer of the world around her, portraying her as a gentle satirist who was able to draw exceptionally memorable characters in books where the plot is easily forgettable. Laurie Magnus is a bit more daring in his assessment of Austen in *English Literature in the Nineteenth Century* (1909) as a key transitional figure between the eighteenth century and the modern — in this case, Victorian — period. Austen's affinity with the neoclassic age is illusory. She "belongs to the new age and is a foremost exponent of its principles, by the indefeasible right of her conquest of new territories of art" (51). She made the most of the materials she had at hand, finding great variety in what many have considered her limited scope of experiences. Oliver Elton is even more bold. In his *Survey of English Literature, 1780–1830* (1912) Elton says that, though Austen limited her subjects, readers of her novels discover that "her power of selection is so sure" that we forget there is any other world for her to write about (191). The most notable contribution Elton makes, however, is his assessment of Austen's place as a woman writer. She is "representative," he says, of "a type usually inarticulate or incapable of art, which has never, before or after, been able to speak for itself so well" (201) — by which he means women. "She sees her world as men could not see it if they would"; as a result, men feel "disconcerted" by her truthful presentation. Although men "acknowledge her, we do not quite like her, and we quit her — perhaps run away from her — not without relief" (201). At a time when most people — especially men — were still touting Austen as a *safe* writer, Elton's observations seem particularly prescient.

Elton's iconoclastic comments were not often repeated, however. In *History of English Literature from "Beowulf" to Swinburne* (1912) Andrew Lang sees Austen's novels as distinct advances over the work of her predecessors, and while "she never went outside of the life she knew," her art "has the exquisite balance and limit of Greek art in the best period" (539). Even Harold Child, whose essay on Austen in the *Cambridge History of English Literature* (1915) suggests her fiction is part of "the movement towards naturalism and the study of common life and character" (257), believes Austen's achievements must be qualified because she chose to limit her repertoire. Still, despite her few shortcomings and self-imposed limitations, Child says, she "produced novels that came nearer to artistic perfection than any others in the English language" (257) and constructed works in which "character and motive drive the story" (271). But like so many of Austen's critics of his time, Child succumbs to the notion that they are "all alike" (271).

New Biographies and Background Studies

Typical of the kind of biography being done at turn of century is Constance Hill's *Jane Austen: Her Homes and Her Friends* (1901), a work that went through three editions in Hill's lifetime, and was reprinted again in 1977 and 1995 (the last with a lengthy introduction by David Gilson). Hill notes in her preface that Austen admirers find in her an "undefinable charm" that drives them "to follow the author to all the places where she dwelt" and inspires them "with a determination to find out all that could be known of her life and its surroundings" (viii). In some ways, Hill's book might be described as a walk in Austen's footsteps, an appreciation cadged together from previously published sources, family manuscripts and reminiscences, and observations made by the author on personal visits to the places Austen lived or visited in her lifetime. There are loving references made to Austen's manuscripts, her working desk, and her needlework, and the first-person approach Hill employs gives the work a sense of intimacy — as if this were a conversation between good friends who shared a mutual reverence for Austen and her work. There is little of what might be called critical commentary, but rather some consistent attempt to ground in real life the fictional people and places Austen describes in her novels. Hill does offer one particularly insightful observation about the critical tradition to date: Austen's critics, she says, seems to find in her the special qualities each one "looks for in a favourite writer" (262).

Geraldine Mitton's *Jane Austen and Her Times* (1905) also uses the sparse information available about Austen's life as a skeleton on which to construct a rather long study of the period in which Austen lived. Mitton investigates ways Austen's age shaped her outlook, and attempts to determine how she managed to escape becoming time-bound. Mitton confesses to believing Austen was a genius, able to make much of mediocre materials in her quest to get at the heart of human character. In this she was "a pioneer" (88), Mitton insists, advancing fiction beyond the limits set by her predecessors. But Mitton's adherence to late-Victorian standards of literary judgment comes out in her analysis of the novels. The standards by which novelists should be judged, she says, are propriety of subject matter and authenticity in treatment. Mitton is also guilty of falling back on the Victorians' clichéd view of Austen's life and excusing her limited range of subject matter by suggesting that she wrote only about what she knew. Mitton values the "dear Aunt Jane" the late Victorians adored, the happy spinster who led a "sunny, well-occupied" life, "surrounded with the refinements that a sensitive mind appreciates" (324).

A third biography from this period, William Helm's *Jane Austen and Her Country-House Comedy* (1909), is probably best described as a transitional work between the appreciations offered by the Austen family and many Victorians, and the more systematic critical examinations that would follow in the coming decades. Helm is of a generation still interested in the way Austen depicted the fashions and customs of her day. However, he says the aim of his book is "to show Jane Austen as she lives in her writings, and to suggest some at least of the many directions in which those writings may be explored," so that the "comparatively restricted circle" of readers of her fiction might be enlarged (249). Helm considers Austen a neglected classic, and his mission is to reclaim for her a place among England's great authors — something denied her as recently as 1908 when Holbrook Jackson omitted her from discussion in his *Great English Novelists*. Although Helm recognizes that "a lack of 'exciting' qualities" in her work has limited Austen's readership (15), he insists this "absence of almost all the qualities of plot and treatment on which fiction usually depends for success with the public" is actually Austen's "most original characteristic" (107). Instead, her strength lies in her ability as a satirist. The freshness of her portraits of human character transcend the boundaries of time and place, making it possible for readers a century later to appreciate her work in a way they might not savor the more time-bound novels of Scott, Ainsworth, or Bulwer-Lytton.

In 1912 Percy Fitzgerald, perhaps better known for his association with Dickens and his circle, wrote a brief monograph, *Jane Austen: A Criticism and Appreciation*. Based in part on his 1903 essay "Jane Austen's Novels," the book is intended as a guide to help readers appreciate the subtleties of Austen's fiction. Much of it, however, is simply a pastiche of quotations from the novels and other critics that help illustrate the qualities Fitzgerald finds most appealing in Austen's work. Fitzgerald includes some valuable insights into Austen's ability as a satirist, but he has some quirky judgments to offer, such as his claim that Mr. Collins in *Pride and Prejudice* is admirable for his attachment to Lady Catherine De Bourgh. Like many critics of his time, Fitzgerald feels obligated to critique Austen's style by pointing out various grammatical lapses and infelicities of expression.

In 1913, the son and grandson of *Memoir* author James Edward Austen-Leigh continued the Austen family's campaign to manage Jane Austen's reputation by issuing *Jane Austen: Her Life and Letters: A Family Record*. To their credit, William and Richard Austen-Leigh provide a more balanced narrative of the novelist's life based on her letters, family records, local histories, and reminiscences from dozens of people who knew Jane Austen. Like their father and grandfather, however, the authors of the *Family Record* are principally concerned with humanizing Jane Austen — and establishing the credentials of the Austen family as English gentry. Critical commentary on the novels is slight and tends to emphasize strengths. Despite this weakness, the volume does provide readers a more comprehensive look at Austen's life than had yet been made available, even if her descendants still feel compelled to cast her as a long-suffering spinster, pure in thought and action, possessing great genius but never so vain as to let her success as a novelist get in the way of her service to family and neighbors.[4]

In the same year, the publishing house of Macmillan finally included a book on Austen in its "English Men of Letters Series" — not bothering to mention anything about the obvious irony in the series title. One key contribution Francis Warre Cornish makes in *Jane Austen* (1913) is his studied assessment of the trajectory of Austen's reputation to date, celebrating the criticism of recent decades for giving the world a more accurate portrait of the novelist and her work. "The analytical psychology of modern novelists was implicitly present" in her work, he says, "though long unnoticed." It turns out "Austen knew as much about mankind" as many of her successors. Perhaps most importantly, Warre Cornish says, "her vision of the world around her is independent of changes of fashion" (53). Although she has faults — "no remarkable distinction of style," plots "neither original nor striking," an absence of incident, a certain degree of repetitiveness, "little idealism, little romance, tenderness, poetry or religion" — she is worthy to stand "by the side of Molière, unsur-passed among writers of prose and poetry, within the limits she imposed on herself, for clear and sympathetic vision of human character" (235).

Turn-of-the-Century American Views

On the other side of the Atlantic, esteem for Austen had grown steadily throughout the nineteenth century, although there, too, she seemed to be an acquired taste. One who seemed not to have acquired that taste was Mark Twain, who appeared to have a visceral distaste for Austen's fiction and a penchant for telling everyone about it. Typical of his revulsion is his comment in a diary entry made aboard ship in 1896: "Jane Austen's books, too, are absent from this library. Just that one omission alone would make a fairly good library out of a library that hadn't a book in it" (*Following the Equator*, 3:62). Ironically, Twain was on a tour of the Brit-ish Empire at the time.[5]

One of the people to whom Twain fulminated about Austen was nov-elist and editor William Dean Howells. The constant carping must have stung Howells, who championed Austen in numerous essays and helped define the shape of American criticism of her. His *Heroines of Fiction* (1901) reflects the advances in critical commentary over the previous generation's tendency toward appreciation without specificity, while at the same time reveals his own preference for realistic fiction. A decade earlier in *Criticism and Fiction* (1891) Howells had offered brief praise for Austen, claiming the novels of "the divine Jane" are great because "they were honest" — by which Howells means realistic. "Realism is nothing more and nothing less than the truthful treatment of material, and Jane Austen was the first and last of the English novelists to treat ma-terial with entire truthfulness" (38). In *Heroines of Fiction*, Howells calls Austen "the greatest of the gifted women" to write English fiction, "so fine an artist, that we are only beginning to realize how fine she was." In her ability to express personality, construct a narrative, and subordinate incident to character, Howells says, "she is still unapproached in the En-glish branch of Anglo-Saxon fiction" (38). In similar fashion, the re-nowned book collector Henry Bonnell says in *Charlotte Brontë, George Eliot, Jane Austen: Studies in Their Works* (1902) that Austen is a serious and highly talented novelist, worthy of what Bonnell, a man of his times, believes is the highest compliment possible: She should be considered on par with male novelists — because, he says by way of explanation, "a good woman novelist must have something of a man in her," namely "judg-ment and strength," just as a good male novelist must possess something of a woman's sympathy (325).

Henry James was decidedly less enthusiastic about Austen's merits. In a speech delivered in Philadelphia and later published as "The Lesson of

Balzac" (1905), James asserts that Balzac, more than any other novelist, provides great reward to the critic who chooses to study him. To prove his point he contrasts Balzac with several other novelists, including Austen, whom he considers very good — but not up to Balzac's level. At the same time, however, James values Austen's work highly, and is somewhat disappointed at how long it took her reputation to form. Unfortunately, he says, by the turn of the twentieth century her reputation had risen so high that appreciation of her work had become "an eager, active, interfering force which has a great many confusions of apparent value, a great many wild and wandering estimates" clouding a sound judgment of her real value (61). Unfortunately, James's pronouncement that Austen is an "unconscious" artist whose prose is unmetaphorical and whose tendency was to write by instinct without any real understanding of the literary tradition, did little to advance Austen studies. Those who found in James's writings a methodology and a theory of criticism simply did not look for signs of conscious craftsmanship in Austen because The Master had searched for them and found them wanting.

Academics seemed to be less harsh on Austen than James was. William Lyon Phelps of Yale University defends Austen from charges of narrow vision in an introductory essay to an edition of her novels that was reprinted in his *Essays on Books* (1914). Phelps says Austen knew what was happening in Europe but opted not to deal with these matters because they were extraneous to her aims as an artist. He applauds Austen's adherence to high artistic standards, claiming she did not understand what it meant to "write for the market" (145). Unlike many of her contemporaries, Phelps says, Austen never "worked up material" from outside research, but instead drew on her own experience for her plots and characters (146). Austen possesses what Phelps believes is the essential quality of a great artist, the ability to give readers "the *illusion* that we are gazing not on the image, but on the reality" (150). Phelps is also adamant in defending Austen from criticism that she lacks passion. To say her characters lack passion because "not one of them would have sacrificed a principle for its enjoyment, is to make the old error of assuming that only those persons have passions who are unable to control them" (177). Phelps makes similar claims for Austen's talents in *The Advance of the English Novel* (1916), a book assembled from previously published essays, asserting Austen is one of two women (George Eliot being the other) who has risen to the first rank among novelists of all languages.

The Austen Centenary: Retrospective Judgments

The centenary of Austen's death was noticed rather quietly, possibly because England was at the time embroiled in the horrors of the First World War. Brief celebratory articles appeared in several publications like the *Pos-*

itivist Review (by Paul Descours) and the *Book News Monthly* (by Henry Shelley) during 1917, and one by the noted critic J. Cuming Walters in the *Manchester Quarterly* the following year. The *Texas Review* also published H. E. Woodbridge's somewhat longer notice in 1918. *Catholic World* (1917) carried a lengthy tribute titled "Jane Austen and the Comic Spirit" in which the author, Brother Leo [Francis Meehan], calls Austen "England's premier thought-humorist" (754) and notes with approval that her career proves that "the saving sense of humor is not an exclusive masculine possession" (763). In October 1917 the Reverend Montague Summers delivered a lecture on Austen, later published as *Jane Austen: An Appreciation* (1918), in which he recites some of the commonplaces about her sheltered life, sweet temperament, and limited range of interests.

Some centenary publications were a bit more perceptive, however. Stuart Mais reminisces in the *Fortnightly Review* (1917) that he developed an appreciation for Austen only when he began to read her slowly. That is when he discovered she was not the "'Aunt Jane' of the crinoline era" but rather "a genial, kindly yet caustic genius who wrote with her tongue in her cheek" (257). At her best, she displayed sound common sense and brooked no silliness, especially from women. "Compared with her astringent tonic properties," he says, "the satire of Addison or Steele is as barley water to ammonia." At the same time, her work possesses "that unfathomable quality which makes it ring as fresh and true after a hundred years as it did on the day when it was first written" (266).

Unquestionably, however, the most important essay published as part of the centenary observance appeared in the *Quarterly Review* (1917) under the inauspicious title "Jane Austen, ob. July 18, 1817." Reginald Farrer's insightful critique of Austen's fiction was more than a tribute to her greatness — although it must be admitted, Farrer devotes nearly half his essay to answering the commonplace charges against Austen that had accumulated over the previous century. He is comfortable with comparing Austen to Shakespeare, calling them "our two greatest creators" (2). He sings Austen's praises for being "always concerned only with the universal, and not with the particular," and hence never "out of date" (5–6).

Farrer proves to be a keen, careful reader who is able to discern in Austen's fiction qualities that few — sometimes none — had noted before. Although Austen has been praised as a devoted family member, Farrer notes that "nowhere" in her fiction "does she give any picture of united family happiness" (2). She uses her exceptional skill to comment without mercy on the society she sees around her; "only her calm has obscured from her critics the steely quality, the inexorable rigour of her judgment." She stands "aloof from the world," Farrer continues, finding it "on the whole, as silly." She is not interested in changing the world or railing against it; rather, "she simply sets herself to glean pleasure" from the folly of those who affect greatness, sincerity, or passion when they obviously lack those qualities. If she seems cruel, "her anger is but just impatience against the slack thought and ready-made pretences that pass current" in her world (11). Farrer's analysis of the six major novels exposes ways Austen carries out her task of exposing foibles and celebrating the all-too-uncommon virtue of common sense. As she advanced in her career, Farrer continues, her characters become more complex, and she asks readers to love them despite their faults because their good qualities demand our admiration and respect. That Austen is less than gentle in her satire, or that she revels in exploiting the hypocrisy she sees around her without having any higher moral purpose, foreshadows revisions of critical opinion about Austen and her novels that were to follow in the next two decades.

Notes

[1] Lewes may have been influenced in his judgment about Austen's lack of passion by Charlotte Brontë, who wrote to him in 1848 that she was not a fan of Austen. Brontë found her "shrewd and observant" but not "profound" (Wise and Symington 2:179). When Lewes wrote back and said Brontë should learn to appreciate Austen even though she is not a poet, Brontë replied somewhat caustically, "Can there be a great artist without poetry?" (Wise and Symington, 2:180). Brontë's now-famous judgment that "the Passions are perfectly unknown" to Austen was not sent to Lewes, however, but to W. S. Williams, the reader for Smith Elder, publisher of Brontë's *Jane Eyre* (Wise and Symington, 3:99).

[2] James Austen-Leigh's *Memoir* has been variously cited as being published in 1869, 1870, and 1871. In *Personal Aspects of Jane Austen* (1920), Austen-Leigh's daughter Mary Augusta indicates the *Memoir* was published on December 18, 1869. However, in *A Bibliography of Jane Austen* (1982), David Gilson indicates the correct publication date is 1870. The 1871 date refers to a second, expanded edition which contains Austen-Leigh's text and includes the first publication of *Lady Susan*, *The Watsons*, the canceled chapter of *Persuasion*, and extracts from *Sanditon*.

[3] According to Kathryn Sutherland, the prolific late-Victorian critic George Saintsbury coined the term "Janeites" in an 1894 introduction to *Pride and Prejudice* to describe the "growing band of Jane Austen devotees" who felt unquestioning personal love for the novelist and her work (*Jane Austen's Textual Lives*, 9).

[4] In 1989 Deirdre Le Faye, perhaps the most diligent Austen scholar of the late twentieth century, issued an edition of the *Family Record* that updates and expands information provided by Austen's kinsmen. Le Faye's work is discussed in chapter 8.

[5] A good recent critique of Twain's views on Austen is provided by Emily Auerbach (*Virginia Quarterly Review*, 1999). Her essay is reprinted in *Searching for Jane Austen* (2004).

Works Cited

Adams, Oscar Fay. *The Story of Jane Austen's Life*. Chicago: A. C. McClurg, 1891.

Auerbach, Emily. "'A Barkeeper Entering the Kingdom of Heaven': Did Mark Twain Really Hate Jane Austen?" *Virginia Quarterly Review* 75.1 (Winter 1999): 109–20. Reprinted in *Searching for Jane Austen*. Madison: U of Wisconsin P, 2004.

Austen, Henry. "Biographical Notice of the Author." *Northanger Abbey and Persuasion*. London: John Murray, 1817. Reprinted in *Persuasion*, edited by Janet Todd and Antje Blank. Cambridge: Cambridge UP, 2006.

Austen-Leigh, James Edward. *A Memoir of Jane Austen*. London: Richard Bentley, 1870. 2nd ed., expanded, 1871. Reprinted with introduction and notes by R. W. Chapman. Oxford: Clarendon Press, 1926.

Austen-Leigh, Mary Augusta. *Personal Aspects of Jane Austen*. London: John Murray, 1920.

Austen-Leigh, William, and Richard A. Austen-Leigh. *Jane Austen: Her Life and Letters. A Family Record*. London: Smith, Elder 1913.

Blackwood's Edinburgh Magazine. See "Notice of *Northanger Abbey* and *Persuasion*."

Bonnell, Henry H. *Charlotte Brontë, George Eliot, Jane Austen: Studies in Their Works*, 323–475. New York: Longmans, Green, 1902.

Braeburn, Edward Lord (Edward Knatchbull), ed. *Letters of Jane Austen*. 2 vols. London: Bentley, 1884.

British Critic. See "Notice of *Pride and Prejudice*," "Notice of *Sense and Sensibility*," and "Review of *Northanger Abbey* and *Persuasion*."

Burton, Richard. "Realism: Jane Austen." *Masters of the English Novel*, 102–22. New York: Henry Holt, 1909.

Chambers, Robert, ed. *Cyclopaedia of English Literature*, 2:571–72. Edinburgh: William & Robert Chambers, 1843–44.

Child, Harold H. "Jane Austen." *Cambridge History of English Literature*, 12:257–71. Cambridge: Cambridge UP, 1915.

Critical Review. See "Notice of *Sense and Sensibility*" and "Review of *Pride and Prejudice*."

Cross, Wilbur L. "Jane Austen: The Critic of Romance and Manners." *The Development of the English Novel*, 114–24. New York and London: Macmillan, 1899.

Cunningham, Alan. "Biographical and Critical History of the Literature of the Last Fifty Years: British Novels and Romances." *Athenaeum* 316 (16 November 1833): 773–77.

Dallas, E. S. Review of George Eliot, *Felix Holt, the Radical. The Times*, 26 June 1866, p. 6.

Dawson, William J. *The Makers of English Fiction*, 38–52. New York: Revell, 1905.

Descours, Paul. "The Centenary of Jane Austen." *Positivist Review* 25 (1917): 180–84.

Elton, Oliver. *A Survey of English Literature, 1780–1830*, 191–201. London: Edward Arnold, 1912.

Elwood, Anne Katherine. *Memoirs of the Literary Ladies of England, From the Commencement of the Last Century*, 2:174–86. London: Henry Colburn, 1843.

Farrer, Reginald. "Jane Austen, *ob.* July 18 1817." *Quarterly Review* 228 (1917): 1–30.

Fawcett, Millicent. *Some Eminent Women of Our Times: Short Biographical Sketches*, 136–44. London: Macmillan, 1889.

Fitzgerald, Percy. *Jane Austen: A Criticism and Appreciation*. London: Jarrold & Sons, 1912.

———. "Jane Austen's Novels." *Gentleman's Magazine* 295 (1903): 399–413.

Forsyth, William. *The Novels and Novelists of the Eighteenth Century*. London: John Murray; New York: D. Appleton, 1871.

Garnett, Richard, and Edmund Gosse. *English Literature: An Illustrated Record in Four Volumes*, 4:91–97. London: William Heinemann; New York: Macmillan, 1903.

Gentleman's Magazine. See "Notice of *Emma*."

Gilson, David. *A Bibliography of Jane Austen*. Oxford: Clarendon Press, 1982.

Gosse, Edmund. *A Short History of Modern English Literature*. London: Heinemann, 1898.

Gwynn, Stephen. "The Decay of Sensibility." *Cornhill* n.s. 7 (1899): 18–30. Reprinted in *The Decay of Sensibility and Other Essays and Sketches*, 1–33. London and New York: John Lane, The Bodley Head, 1900.

Hamilton, Catherine J. *Women Writers: Their Works and Ways*, 191–206. London: Ward, Lock, Bowden, 1892.

Harding, Denys Wyatt. "Regulated Hatred: An Aspect of the Work of Jane Austen." *Scrutiny* 8 (1939–40): 346–62. Reprinted in *Regulated Hatred and Other Essays on Jane Austen*, edited by Monica Lawlor, 1–26. London and Atlantic Highlands, NJ: Athlone Press, 1998.

Harman, Claire. *Jane's Fame: How Jane Austen Conquered the World*. Edinburgh: Canongate, 2009; New York: Henry Holt, 2010.

Helm, William H. *Jane Austen and Her Country-House Comedy.* London: Eveleigh Nash, 1909.

Hill, Constance. *Jane Austen: Her Homes and Her Friends.* London and New York: John Lane, 1901.

Howells, William Dean. *Criticism and Fiction,* 73–77. New York: Harper; London: Osgood, McIlvane & Co., 1891.

———. *Heroines of Fiction,* 1:37–78. London and New York: Harper & Bros., 1901.

Hutton, R. H. "The Charm of Miss Austen." Review of Goldwyn Smith's *Life of Jane Austen.* Spectator 64 (1890): 403–4. Reprinted in *Brief Literary Criticisms,* 168–74. London: Macmillan, 1906.

Jack, Adolphus A. *Essays on the Novel as Illustrated by Scott and Miss Austen.* London and New York: Macmillan, 1897.

Jackson, Holbrook. *Great English Novelists.* London: R. Richards, 1908.

Jacox, Francis. "Female Novelists, No. I: Miss Austen." *New Monthly Magazine* 95 (May 1852): 17–23.

James, Henry. *The Question of Our Speech: The Lesson of Balzac: Two Lectures.* Boston: Houghton Mifflin, 1905.

Jeaffreson, John Cordy. *Novels and Novelists, From Elizabeth to Victoria,* 2:84–87. London: Hurst and Blackett, 1858.

Kavanagh, Julia. "Miss Austen's Six Novels." *English Women of Letters: Biographical Sketches,* 188–236. Leipzig: Tauchnitz, 1862; London: Hurst & Blackett, 1863.

Knatchbull, Edward. See Braeburn, Edward Lord.

Lang, Andrew. *History of English Literature from "Beowulf" to Swinburne,* 536–40. London: Longmans Green, 1912.

Lefroy, Fanny Caroline. "A Bundle of Letters." *Temple Bar* 67 (1883): 258–88.

———."Hunting for Snarkes at Lyme Regis." *Temple Bar* 57 (1879): 391–97.

———. "Is It Just?" *Temple Bar* 67 (1883): 270–84.

Leo, Brother [Francis J. G. Meehan]. "Jane Austen and the Comic Spirit." *Catholic World* 106 (1917–18): 752–63.

Lewes, George Henry. "The Lady Novelists." *Westminster Review* n.s. 2 (1852): 129–41.

———. "The Novels of Jane Austen." *Blackwood's Edinburgh Magazine* 86 (1859): 99–113.

———. "Recent Novels: French and English." *Fraser's Magazine* 36 (December 1847): 687.

Lister, Thomas Henry. Review of Catherine Gore, *Women as They Are.* *Edinburgh Review* 53 (July 1830): 448–51.

Lockhart, John Gibson. *Memoirs of the Life of Sir Walter Scott.* 7 vols. Edinburgh: R. Cadell, 1837–38. Single-volume abridgment, *The Life of Sir Walter Scott,* edited by R. H. Hutton. Philadelphia: J. D. Morris & Co., 1897.

Macaulay, Thomas Babington. "The Diary and Letters of Mme D'Arblay." *Edinburgh Review* 76 (January 1843): 561–62.

Magnus, Laurie. *English Literature in the Nineteenth Century,* 49–52. London: Andrew Melrose; New York: Putnam, 1909.

Mais, Stuart P. B. "The Centenary of Jane Austen." *Fortnightly Review* 108 (1917): 257–66.

Malden, S. F. *Jane Austen.* Famous Women Series. London: W. H. Allen & Co., 1889. Boston: Roberts Bros., 1889.

Masson, David. *British Novelists and Their Styles,* 188–89. London: Macmillan; Boston: Gould and Lincoln, 1859.

Meynell, Alice. "The Classic Novelist." *Pall Mall Gazette* 58 (16 February 1894): 4. Reprinted in *The Second Person Singular and Other Essays,* 62–67. London: Oxford UP, 1921.

"Miss Austen." *Englishwoman's Domestic Magazine* 3rd ser. 2 (1866): 237–40, 278–82.

Mitton, Geraldine E. *Jane Austen and Her Times.* London: Methuen, 1905.

Murch, Jerome. *Mrs. Barbauld and her Contemporaries.* London: Longmans, Green, 1877.

Notice of *Emma. Gentleman's Magazine* 86 (September 1816): 248–49.

Notice of *Northanger Abbey* and *Persuasion. Blackwood's Edinburgh Magazine* n.s. 2 (May 1818): 453–55.

Notice of *Pride and Prejudice. British Critic* 41 (February 1813): 189–90.

Notice of *Sense and Sensibility. British Critic* 39 (May 1812): 527.

Notice of *Sense and Sensibility. Critical Review* n.s. 4.1 (February 1812): 149–57.

Oliphant, James. *Victorian Novelists,* 14–30. London: Blackie & Son, 1899.

Oliphant, Margaret. *The Literary History of England,* 3:203–50. London: Macmillan, 1882.

———. "Miss Austen and Miss Mitford." *Blackwood's Edinburgh Magazine* 107 (March 1870): 294–305.

Pellew, George. *Jane Austen's Novels.* Boston: Cupples, Upham & Co., 1883.

Phelps, William Lyon. *The Advance of the English Novel.* New York: Dodd, 1916.

———. "Jane Austen." *Essays on Books,* 129–77. New York: Macmillan, 1914.

Pollock, Juliet. "Jane Austen." *St. Paul's Magazine* 5 (March 1870): 631–43.

Pollock, Walter H. *Jane Austen: Her Contemporaries and Herself: An Essay in Criticism*. London: Longmans, Green, 1899.

"The Progress of Fiction as an Art." *Westminster Review* n.s. 4 (1853): 342–74.

Raleigh, Walter. *The English Novel*, 253–75. London: John Murray. New York: Scribner, 1894.

Review of *Northanger Abbey* and *Persuasion*. *British Critic* n.s. 9 (March 1818): 293–301.

Review of *Pride and Prejudice*. *Critical Review* 4th ser., no. 3 (March 1813): 318–24.

Saintsbury, George. *A History of Nineteenth Century Literature (1780–1895)*. London: Macmillan, 1896.

———. "Scott and Miss Austen." *The English Novel*, 189–210. London: J. M. Dent, 1913.

Scott, Walter. Unsigned review of *Emma*. *Quarterly Review* 14 (March 1816): 188–201.

Shaw, T. B. *Outlines of English Literature*, 479–80. Philadelphia: Blanchard & Lee, 1849.

Shelley, Henry C. "Centenary of Jane Austen's Death." *Book News Monthly* 35 (1917): 397–99.

Simpson, Richard. Review of James Edward Austen-Leigh, *A Memoir of Jane Austen*. *North British Review* 52 (April 1870): 129–52.

Smith, Goldwyn. *Life of Jane Austen*. Great Writers Series. London: Walter Scott, 1890.

Southam, B. C., ed. *Jane Austen: The Critical Heritage*. London: Routledge & Kegan Paul; New York: Barnes & Noble, 1968.

———, ed. *Jane Austen: The Critical Heritage, 1870–1940*. New York: Routledge & Kegan Paul, 1987.

Stephen, Leslie. *Dictionary of National Biography*, 1:731–32. London: Smith, Elder, 1885.

Stoddard, Francis H. *The Evolution of the English Novel*. New York and London: Macmillan, 1900.

Summers, Montague. "Jane Austen: An Appreciation." *Transactions of the Royal Society of Literature of the United Kingdom* 2nd ser. 36 (1918): 1–33.

Sutherland, Kathryn. *Jane Austen's Textual Lives: From Aeschylus to Bollywood*. Oxford and New York: Oxford UP, 2005.

Twain, Mark [Samuel Langhorne Clemens]. *Following the Equator*. 3 vols. New York: Doubleday & McClure, 1897.

Tytler, Sarah [Henrietta Keddie]. *Jane Austen and Her Works.* London: Cassell, Petter, Galpin, 1880.

Villaseñor, Alice Marie. "Fanny Caroline Lefroy: A Feminist Critic in the Austen Family." *Persuasions On-Line* 30.2 (Spring 2010).

Walford, Lucy Bethia. *Twelve English Authoresses,* 65–81. London: Longmans, Green, 1892.

Walkley, Arthur B. *Frames of Mind,* 107–12. London: Grant Richards, 1899.

Walters, J. Cuming. "Jane Austen: A Centenary Tribute." *Manchester Quarterly* 148 (October 1918): 295–311.

Warre Cornish, Francis W. *Jane Austen.* English Men of Letters series. London: Macmillan, 1913.

Whately, Richard. Review of *Northanger Abbey* and *Persuasion. Quarterly Review* 24 (January 1821): 352–76.

Whitmore, Clara H. *Women's Work in English Fiction from the Restoration to the Mid-Victorian Period,* 157–78. New York and London: G. P. Putnam's Sons, 1910.

Wilkes, Joanne. *Women Reviewing Women in Nineteenth-Century Britain.* Aldershot, England: Ashgate, 2010.

Williams, Harold H. "Jane Austen (1775–1817)." *Two Centuries of the English Novel,* 132–48. London: Smith, Elder, 1911.

Wilmot-Buxton, Ethel Mary. *A Book of Noble Women,* 207–17. London: Methuen, 1907.

Woodbridge, H. E. "Jane Austen." *Texas Review* 3 (1917–18): 195–207.

2: Modernist, Humanist, and New Critical Approaches, 1918–1948

IN RUDYARD KIPLING'S "The Janeites" (1924), a humorous fictional account of Austen's influence, a group of soldiers discusses the comfort
they get from reading her work. "It's a very select society," one of them
remarks, "an' you've got to be a Janeite in your 'eart, or you won't have
any success" in understanding her. "You take it from me," the soldier
says, "there's no one to touch Jane when you're in a tight place" (*Debits
and Credits*, 173). That Austen could appeal to soldiers in the trenches
during the First World War as well as to women and schoolgirls speaks
volumes about the range of readers she attracted. By the end of the war
she was unquestionably considered a major figure in the English literary
tradition. Precisely what to make of her, however, began to be the central
question occupying scholars who recognized the appeal she had for millions of readers who valued her novels for their fairy-tale quality, and for a
more discriminating group who found in her work a critique of the social
order she represented so faithfully.

Early Post-War Criticism, 1918–1930

One of the first scholars to devote a considerable portion of his career to a
study of Austen was R. Brimley Johnson. Johnson published an edition of
Austen's works in 1906. In *The Women Novelists* (1918) Austen figures
prominently in his summation of the merits of the group he calls "The
Great Four": Fanny Burney, Austen, Charlotte Brontë, and George Eliot.
Johnson believes Austen has spoken "the last word for all women for all
time" (66). He is particularly struck with her fine sense of humor and her
ability to poke fun at people without ridiculing them. The judgments
Johnson offers, however, are not much advanced over the critics he
quotes liberally who applauded Austen for her technical effort while being
pleased to assign her to what was obviously a lesser realm of importance
— domestic fiction. Johnson repeats much of his praise for Austen, along
with his view of the sources of her genius, in his lengthy preface to *Jane
Austen: A French Appreciation* (1924), a translation of Léonie Villard's
study, which he had arranged to have published (and which he abridged
notably).[1] His own *Jane Austen* (1927), reissued three years later as *Jane
Austen: Her Life, Her Work, Her Family, and Her Critics* (1930), is a pas-

tiche of essays that explore various aspects of Austen's fiction. As he does in his 1918 study, Johnson advances the theory that Austen's first three novels were essentially adaptations of works by Fanny Burney, while the last three were wholly her own creation.

The American professor Oscar Firkins thought enough of Austen to write a book about her, but did not seem to be able to make up his mind about her status as an artist. His *Jane Austen* (1920) seems influenced by Jamesian ideas about fiction, although he does not admit as much anywhere in the narrative. Yet at the same time he cannot disguise his American bias against Austen's treatment of matters concerning social class. Firkins believes she was most unfortunate to have been born too close to the eighteenth century, in that its literature affected both her tastes and her manner of expression. He finds her presentation of character clichéd, tied too closely to her predecessors' penchant for creating abstractions. Additionally, Firkins believes Austen's decision to limit herself to writing about what she knew has serious negative consequences. "There is no politics, no literary or aesthetic life, no supernaturalism" in her novels, he says, "no sex-radicalism, no class problems, almost no landscape, almost nothing of the *corpus* or physical order of life, no low-life portraits, scant domesticity, no moral experience, no vestige of religious sentiment." Firkins's observation on this remarkable lack of range is certainly curious: "I doubt if any such concourse of negatives, any such wealth of privations, can be attributed to any other novelist of superlative capacity" (210).

One might have thought that the combination of James Austen-Leigh's 1870 *Memoir* and the more lengthy 1913 biography by his son and grandson would have been the last the family might have to say about the novelist, but in 1920 Austen-Leigh's daughter, Mary Augusta Austen-Leigh, felt compelled to compose yet another tribute, *Personal Aspects of Jane Austen*. The book attempts to supplement accounts by others in her family as a means of answering what Mary Augusta calls "misperceptions" concerning the novelist's life. Specifically, she wants to counter hints that Jane Austen had a limited outlook on life or was a social snob. Austen-Leigh traces the novelist's many connections to social communities in which she lived, explains how her education broadened her horizons, and emphasizes Austen's interest in, and understanding of, public events occurring far from the isolated village of Steventon.

The targets of Austen-Leigh's ire are those among the Moderns who dared to criticize the novelist. Quoting from a critic who claims Austen's letters "do not suggest the uneasiness attached to the possession of a soul — as we moderns understand it," Austen-Leigh blasts back that she is "thankful" her great aunt "did not possess its 'uneasiness,' for had she done so, we could never have possessed works such as those she has left to the world" (37). She is exceedingly disturbed by critics who infer from Austen's letters and novels that all was not well at Steventon when young

Jane was growing up. Such psychologizing has no basis in fact, Austen-Leigh assures her readers; one need only read Austen's work carefully, she says, to see how wrong such a judgment is. In Austen-Leigh's opinion, *real* lovers of Austen turn to her novels again and again as "beguilers of trouble and companions in mirth," discovering that they "even seem to grow with our growth and strengthen with our strength" (63).

Like Austen-Leigh, Arthur Walkley, who took on Stephen Gwynn in 1899 for his deprecatory remarks about Austen, was still defending Austen during the 1920s, although his critical approach retains late-Victorian standards of critical judgment. In "Jane's Prejudices," a brief note in *More Prejudice* (1923), he makes her a champion of democratic values, claiming she is "prejudice[d] against rank," impatient with "the social hierarchy of her day," and particularly harsh on those who act "too ostentatiously like" aristocrats (27). In like fashion, J. B. Priestley's comments on Austen in *English Humour* (1929) stress the novelist's great "variety of feminine humour" (116) and defend his claim that Austen is a master of irony and detachment. And although Orlo Williams's commentary on *Emma* in *Some Great English Novels: Studies in the Art of Fiction* (1926) displays affinities with newer critical approaches to fiction, he begins his commentary on Austen with a cantankerous critique of modern society, which he sees as essentially different from Austen's more sedate community of yesteryear. "Young people to-day display their glands or their libidos and button up their brains" (159), Williams complains. Perhaps because he prefers the older society, Williams prefers what he calls Austen's quiet comedy, admiring her ability to capture everyday life, which "is not continuously suffused by great issues or inspired by overwhelming emotions" (161).

Of course, new critical methodologies had not taken hold completely by the end of the 1920s, as Augustus Ralli's "The Home-Land of Jane Austen" (1927) illustrates. In his essay Ralli argues that home life is the source of Austen's genius and that an essential component of her outlook on life is a deeply religious dimension. The pursuit of happiness ends well only for those who "face facts" and "manage" their "worldly business" in such a way as to demonstrate a love for "the life of the spirit — the spirit that knows nothing of death" (89). Clara Linklater Thomson's *Jane Austen: A Survey* (1929) is typical of another type of criticism that flourished during the 1920s: the extended source study. Thomson says she is most interested in showing how Austen was influenced by Burney and Radcliffe, but her book looks at a wide variety of influences: family, friends, and reading (especially eighteenth-century novelists, essayists, and poets). After carefully reviewing each of Austen's novels to reveal specific influences, Thomson provides an assessment of Austen's methods that reveal the ways her techniques, especially her use of dialogue and narrative, depend on the drama with which she was so familiar.

In addition to the professional critics and amateur admirers, a number of distinguished novelists expressed their opinion of Austen during these post-war years. Among those who admired her was E. M. Forster, who begins his 1924 review of R. W. Chapman's new edition of the novels with the confession, "I am a Jane Austenite, and therefore slightly imbecile about Jane Austen." She is, he says, "my favourite author," one he could "read and re-read" with his "mouth open" and his "mind closed" (*Abinger Harvest*, 148). Forster refers to her almost reverentially in *Aspects of the Novel* (1927), a book that reproduces his series of Clark Lectures given that year at Cambridge University. One can almost imagine him raising his voice to exclaim to his audience, "How Jane Austen can write!" (116). Unlike Dickens, he says, "she never stooped to caricature," instead offering her readers a series of "highly organized" characters who "function all around" (114), supplementing her stories by introducing a number of minor figures who, though "apparently simple and flat," carry out their function without calling undue attention to themselves (117). One not quite so taken with Austen's talents, however, was Ford Madox Ford, who says in *The English Novel* (1930) that she is outside the mainstream of the English literary tradition, and that searching her work for clues to the progress of English fiction is a fruitless exercise. D. H. Lawrence was even more derogatory, calling her an "old maid" and claiming she represents all that is "English in the bad, mean snobbish sense of the word" (*Apropos of Lady Chatterley's Lover*, 58).

R. W. Chapman and the Oxford
Edition of Austen's Novels

Undoubtedly the first important Austen scholar to emerge in the twentieth century was R. W. Chapman. Born in 1881, he studied in Edinburgh before going to Oxford in 1902, completing his degrees and remaining there as a teacher. In 1913 he married Katherine Metcalfe, who in the previous year had completed a new edition of *Pride and Prejudice* from a copy of a first edition she owned. Initially the two planned to work jointly on an edition of all of Austen's work, but Metcalfe opted to take up duties as a wife and mother while her husband forged ahead with the project. Chapman's scholarly investigations were interrupted by the First World War, during which he served in the Army, but after the war he came back to Oxford, took a position at the Clarendon Press, and continued his own research. Had he not continued his work on Austen, Chapman might still be remembered as an influential editor and publisher. Austen scholars, however, are forever indebted to him for producing the first scholarly editions of her novels, which appeared in 1923. The full title of Chapman's project suggests its scope: "The novels of Jane Austen;

the text based on collation of the early editions, by R. W. Chapman. With notes, indexes and illustrations from contemporary sources."

Chapman did not write extensively about Austen, perhaps because he spent so much of his time editing her work. He did engage in a brief controversy with H. W. Garrod, whose 1928 article "Jane Austen: A Depreciation" prompted Chapman's "Jane Austen: A Reply to Mr. Garrod" (1931). Chapman's 1948 Clark Lectures were based on a collection of essays and notes he had been preparing for several decades. Published as *Jane Austen: Facts and Problems* (1948), the book is a hybrid of biographical study, background investigation, and literary criticism. It is true that much of the scholarly information Chapman provides had appeared in other places, and his critical analysis seems rooted in early-century humanist approaches to literary study. Yet Chapman's commentary is valuable for the insight it provides into the methods he used when preparing his definitive edition of Austen's novels.

Although late-century critics would register complaints about the lack of precision and irregular nature of Chapman's critical apparatus, Austen scholars continue to cite the Chapman edition as the "official" text of her work. Chapman's work has even greater significance when considered in light of the history of textual editing. "Chapman's was the first scholarly edition of any English novelist — male or female — to appear," Claudia Johnson observes in *The Cambridge Companion to Jane Austen* (1997). Johnson points out that Chapman "treated Austen's novels with a scrupulousness customarily reserved for classical authors" at that time (218).[2]

Virginia Woolf and Early Feminist Assessments

Although its blossoming was four decades away, one most influential cultural trends that began to germinate after the First World War was the modern feminist movement. Its impact on Austen criticism was to be the single most important factor in revising Austen studies during the twentieth century. Hints of modern feminist criticism of Austen can be seen in the work of several women who wrote about her after the First World War. Prominent among them was the novelist and essayist Virginia Woolf. To be accurate, however, it must be acknowledged that Woolf's feminism is modified by her decidedly Modernist view of Austen's achievements. In "How It Strikes a Contemporary" (1923), Woolf says with irony and deliberate playfulness, "honestly, the shock of the comparison between past and present is at first disconcerting. Undoubtedly there is a dullness in great books. There is an unabashed tranquility in page after page of Wordsworth and Scott and Miss Austen" (*The Common Reader*, 237). These writers "refuse to gratify those senses which are stimulated so richly by the moderns; the senses of sight, of sound, of touch — above all, the sense of the human being, his depth and the variety of his perceptions, his complexity, his confusion, his self, in short." What *does* characterize works by Austen and her contemporaries is a "natural conviction that life is of a certain quality." They are "certain that what they write about their age will be true for all time" (238). Because Austen believed in the enduring values about which she wrote, the "little grain of experience once selected, believed in, and set outside herself, could be put precisely in its place" and transformed "by a process which never yields its secrets to the analyst, into that complete statement which is literature" (239).

In essays about Austen collected in *The Common Reader* (1925), Woolf provides a summary of Austen's accomplishments. Beneath the surface finish of Austen's novels, she says a "much deeper emotion" lies buried. Austen "stimulates us to supply what is not there." The "trifle" Austen offers "expands in the reader's mind and endows with the most enduring form of life scenes which are outwardly trivial. Always the stress is laid upon character" ("Jane Austen," 139). The careful reader finds beneath the surface animation and meticulous realism "a deeper pleasure, an exquisite discrimination of human values" (139). Austen knew her own strengths and she used them wisely, Woolf continues, and refused to let herself wander off to deal with subjects for which she was not fitted to write. "The balance of her gifts was singularly perfect. Among her finished novels there are no failures" (143). Had she lived, Woolf speculates, Austen would have gone beyond the limits she set for herself in her early works. There are hints in *Persuasion* that Austen was coming to a more mature understanding of the nature of romance — and a better realization that there was less certainty in the world than she exhibited in her earlier fiction. As a result, Woolf says, she would have written less comedy, but more insightful character studies. Her satire "would have been more stringent and severe. She would have been the forerunner of Henry James and of Proust" (145).

Although Woolf is not openly feminist in her interpretation of Austen, she does exhibit a willingness to treat Austen's work with the same level of seriousness normally accorded the leading male writers — something that was still a novelty even in the postwar period. However, during the years between the World Wars there appeared two other critiques of Austen's career that could be loosely described as feminist, although Marjory Bald insists in *Women Writers of the Nineteenth Century* (1923) that hers is not "in any sense a 'feminist' treatise," but one that instead considers Austen and other writers as "remarkable human beings" (v). Still, Bald's assessment of Austen reveals a certain ambivalence toward an author who cannot "be regarded as a herald of the coming age" (1), but who, rather, looks back with fondness on the one that preceded her. Bald calls Austen "a connoisseur of human nature — a collector of fine quaint specimens" (5). And while she has "sufficient proper pride to uphold the virtues of her own sex" (24), Bald says, "from the standpoint of the 'woman's movement,' Jane Austen is sadly out of date" (25).

Ida O'Malley is much kinder (and perhaps more perceptive) in her judgment of Austen in *Women in Subjection: A Study of the Lives of English-women before 1832* (1933), a politically charged examination of the condition of women before the Victorian Age. While O'Malley, too, recognizes qualities in Austen that align her with more conservative forces in society, she celebrates her as important to the women's movement for two reasons: "She described the cage" in which women were imprisoned by the patriarchy, and "in doing so she showed qualities which were not expected of the canary" (243). Although all of Austen's heroines eventually conform to the outward conventions of society, O'Malley insists that Austen believed a woman "could always keep her own soul free and must do so at the cost of everything" (269).

Critical Assessments 1931–1940

During the 1930s favorable reactions to Austen's fiction dominated critical commentary. For example, John Bailey's *Introductions to Jane Austen* (1931), essays he had written for a 1927 edition of Austen's novels, makes no excuses for Austen's limitations and finds few faults, concluding that "no one has ever been a more acute observer" of life as "seen by those who walk its middle paths every day" (22). In *The Novel in English* (1931) Grant Knight says she is to be appreciated for her "calmness" (152), her irony, and her ability to capture the essence of life in the English countryside and give it universal significance. However, he suggests "it is not for the plot that one will read Jane Austen" (153). On the other hand, Knight believes Austen "so dignified the comedy of manners that it has ever after been the chosen field for the greatest number of English novelists" (159). Stating the case more metaphorically in *Reflections and Memories* (1935), John Squire describes Austen as "the quiet sunset of the great day of eighteenth-century prose" (255). This judgment is carried forward in his dismissal of her failure to deal with anything outside her own circle. Although she might not have been in touch with the larger world, her "powers of observation, of criticism, of expression" were "truly extraordinary" (255). Squire is certain that, "as far as she goes," she is "perfection" (262). Besides, he asserts, "her range of subject was her own business: at any rate nobody can complain about her treatment of it" (267). Additionally, she was "the English Lady at her apex; a perfect specimen who spoke for her whole intelligent class — and with not too much mercy for the rest" (260).

Some criticisms of Austen's limitations persisted, however. Robert Lovett and Helen Hughes's *The History of the Novel in England* (1932), a book designed to "bring out the relation of the novel to the interests and attitudes of successive ages, of which it has been the product," finds her technically proficient but severely limited in scope, doing nothing to help her readers learn about "the more intimate relations between men and women" or the larger social and political issues of her day (170). Similarly, in *The Art of the Novel from 1700 to the Present Time* (1933), Pelham Edgar expresses his appreciation for Austen's abilities, but is less enthusiastic about her talents than many of his predecessors. To say that either her "ideas or their expression" possess a "Shakespearean quality" is to "render her a disservice." Instead, he says, she is more like Chaucer, possessing "playful malice and sympathetic irony" (93). Continuing the line of criticism that rates Austen a master technician but a lightweight in the realm of intellectual acumen, Edgar says she "recognized in herself no aptitude for general ideas, and no impulse in the direction of social or political problems" (94). She is "not prone to analysis," by which he means the kind of psychoanalytical exploration he sees modern novelists (and critics) employing. In another mixed assessment, Virginia Moore complains in *Distinguished Women Writers* (1934) that Austen's works contain "no passion, no crime, no violence of any kind," nor any religious ideas. Austen's "classic restriction of theme has led," she says, "to a controversy in taste" (101). Moore means, of course, that not everyone will approve of the kinds of novels Austen writes, even if she is acknowledged to be a master at creating interesting characters. Hence, Moore's judgment perpetuates the notion that Austen is an acquired taste with limited appeal.

One of the last truly harsh assessments of Austen's artistry published before the Second World War is Norman Collins' critique in *The Facts of Fiction* (1932). Influenced by his own assumptions about literature and gender relations, Collins offers a most unflattering portrait of the novelist, criticizing both her intellect and her talents. He begins with an observation clearly intended as a compliment: "She is perfectly feminine in her range of experience," but "in her competence of reporting feminine experience," she is "perfectly masculine" (108). Still, Collins finds Austen all too narrow and obtrusive. To regard her as "one of the great masters of fiction" requires one "sooner or later" to "make excuses for her" (109). Instead, Collins calls for a "discerning appreciation" of Austen, one which recognizes that "her plots are childlike where they are not absurd" and her prose "among the most unmusical in the language." She had no gift for creating setting. She "could not draw a man that is recognizable as other than the sort of man an unmarried woman sees." Even more limiting is her ability to portray strong emotions. "She knew passion as the canary knows the cat," Collins snipes, "as something to be avoided" (110). Instead, she is "obsessed by money" (112). Those reading her fiction a century after it was published can only regard it as "a chapter in the domestic and marital economics of a system that has been supplanted" (113). Ironically, some of Collins's criticisms would be described as Austen's particular strengths by a later generation of scholars, especially cultural critics.

On the other hand, a good example of what many critics were saying about Austen at this time can be found in Ernest Baker's discussion of her work in *The History of the English Novel* (1935). Tracing her heritage back to Fielding and Richardson, and recognizing the influence of Fanny Burney (especially in the early works), Baker acknowledges the limited range of society about which she wrote, but immediately says "she knew the middling classes" thoroughly and "for her such a strip of society was a world in itself in the range and diversity of character that it enfolded" (59). She does not "preach a doctrine or illustrate some moral theorem" (92–93), but instead serves as a "critical observer, an interpreter of what actually goes on" in the society she depicts. She is thoroughly "anti-romantic" (120), but still possesses a sense of idealism tempered by the realization that people must make compromises to live in the everyday world. Though he considers Austen a superb craftsman, Baker is not reticent about criticizing her when she fails in her craft, as evidenced by his critique of the ending of *Sense and Sensibility* or her portrayal of the Crawfords in *Mansfield Park*. Minor flaws notwithstanding, Baker proclaims Austen a major figure in the history of the English novel, one who has made a profound contribution to English letters.

An even more zealous advocate for Austen is David Cecil, whose 1935 Leslie Stephen Lecture at Cambridge, published in that year as *Jane Austen*, makes the case for her as one of the finest novelists of all time. Combining techniques of formalist criticism with traditional British concerns for a writer's morality and social consciousness, Cecil enumerates the reasons that, despite what some have described as the narrow scope of her fiction, Austen actually produced novels of universal appeal. It is, he says "the triumph of her craft" (7) that first strikes a reader. Because she chose to write about a limited segment of human experience, she could explore it deeply and imbue her characters and situations with a sense of realism seldom matched by practitioners of the genre. Deftly managing to unite her imaginative vision with reality, she adopts the stance of a gentle satirist that allows her to shape the "heterogeneous tangle" of reality into "an orderly unity" that is art (18). "At her best," Cecil says, "she keeps the balance between fact and form as no other English novelist has ever done" (20).

But Cecil insists it is not merely in technical merit that Austen excels. Though her characters are seen only in "their private aspect," her novels "have a universal significance" because this relationship is far from superficial (23). Furthermore, she "realizes the psychological organism that underlies speech and manner" (24) and has a sound "understanding of the moral nature of man" (25) — by which Cecil means humankind. As a consequence, her characters are at once highly individualized and "universal types" (31). Austen's appreciation for the sensible side of living, and the need for certain civilities, sets her apart in Cecil's view from the more puritanical (but secretly licentious) Victorians who followed her. The "considered intellectual foundation" on which her novels are built makes Austen's books "far more serious than their surface appearance would lead us to expect." These "quiet comedies of country life," Cecil says, "propound fundamental problems of human conduct" (41).

Two other studies from the same period reflect how Austen criticism was beginning to be influenced by new critical theories — in this case, feminism and psychological criticism. Mona Wilson, author of *Jane Austen and Some Contemporaries* (1938), sees Austen as an early feminist, linking her with Mary Wollstonecraft. Wilson focuses on Austen's views of education for women, especially education in literature. What Wilson discovers in reading the novels is that Austen, much better read than most critics acknowledge, includes beneath the dazzling surface of her novels a consistent theme — that "woman is, or should be, a rational being" (34). Wilson finds this thesis as radical in its time as any pronouncement made by the more visibly iconoclastic Wollstonecraft. In "The Myth in Jane Austen" (1939) Geoffrey Gorer applies the methods of Freudian psychology to explain the intense interest readers have in Austen's novels despite their seemingly narrow focus. Gorer insists that it is neither Austen's mastery of technique nor her powers of observation that account for this phenomenon. There are "profounder reasons" (91) that explain much about Austen's psyche and those of her ardent disciples, the Janeites. Gorer posits that Austen was somewhat repelled by the Gothic and Romantic literature popular in her youth. She was "temperamentally unable to feel" the kind of "violent emotions" found in these works, and "as a realist, did not believe they were genuine" (92). Yet her own "myth," he says, is motivated by deep unconscious feelings. All of Austen's major works feature "the girl who hates and despises her mother and marries a father-surrogate." This formula is not new, Gorer admits, but it seems to fit nicely as an explanation for the power of Austen's novels. Additionally, "for the psychoanalyst, there will be little cause for surprise at the ease with which most of her readers so passionately identify with her heroines" (94–95). Austen's novels should be read as dreams (a convenient Freudian maneuver) in which "we can clearly trace the gradual working out and alteration of Austen's attitudes toward the members of her family constellation" (96–97). By "reworking her fantasies" Austen was able to uncover "the hidden motives behind the too warm, too loving family relationships which circumscribed her" (98). All of her novels reflect in some way her cries "against her starved life, and the selfishness of the father and sisters [*sic*] on whose account it had been starved" (98).

Biography between the Wars

Despite the scarcity of primary source documents, biographers were busy during the 1930s attempting to extrapolate details of Austen's life from her fiction or embellish the few facts known about her with extensive commentary on the age in which she lived. David Rhydderch's *Jane Austen: Her Life and Art* (1932) is a kind of transitional work, bridging the space between Victorian and Edwardian appreciations and the more rigorous scholarly studies that would follow just a few years after Rhydderch's book appeared. To his credit, Rhydderch makes good use of available resources, constructing his work from the letters and other (slim) materials published at the time. But his style is reminiscent of decades gone by rather than a signal of those to come, and his bias apparent not only in the recitation of details about Austen's life, but especially in his critique of the novels. His Jane Austen is both an unblemished maiden and a first-rate novelist, hardly subject to criticism, as he reveals in introducing his discussion of her artistry and methods: "You need not search with diligence to discover her beauties," he says, "but to inhale the incense which patient contact alone can communicate, you must stoop like a votary" (115). Rhydderch writes passionately about Austen's ability to transform the people and places she knew into the imaginary world of her novels. His defense of her treatment of love — which he admits she handles without any of the trappings of romantic passion — suggests where his own predilections lie. He even justifies her treatment of the clergy: "It was not the clergy, but the men who happened to be clergymen she derided" (231). He closes with an extended tribute to the novelist whose works, though underappreciated during her lifetime, now stand "cheek by jowl with the masters of our tongue." Her "appreciation of the usual," he asserts boldly, "is an art that can never grow old" (241).

Less extensive and less informative than Rhydderch's book, Guy Rawlence's *Jane Austen* (1934) relies heavily on the 1870 *Memoir* and subsequent publications by Austen's descendants, as well as Austen's letters, to construct a brief biography that provides the outline of her life but little criticism of the fiction. In fact, no novel receives more than two paragraphs of critical commentary. Instead, Rawlence attempts to make sense of Austen's character and temperament, answering implied charges that she was somewhat cynical and heartless in her feelings for, and dealings with, others. Similarly, Isabel Clarke's sketch of Austen in *Six Portraits* (1935), heavily dependent on memoirs published by the Austen-Leighs, repeats many of the familiar stories of Austen as dutiful daughter and devoted sister, interested in publishing and exceptionally talented but always willing to subordinate her interests to those of her family.

Margaret Lawrence's *The School of Femininity* (1936) offers a decidedly different view of Austen. Lawrence begins with a discussion of "a pattern of thought" among women writers beginning in the nineteenth century, when "women for the first time in history upon a large scale are saying their particular say about themselves, about men, and about life as it treats them separately and together with men" (xii). Her readings of Austen's novels, lacking any scholarly apparatus but detailed in dealing with the texts, focus on issues of importance to women, most notably the necessity for a young woman to marry in order to achieve social and financial security. Caught up in the trend toward psychological criticism, Lawrence cannot resist developing a portrait of the novelist from her fiction. After all, she insists, "novelists sit down to do just one thing — to portray themselves. This has been psychologically proven so many times that it is almost unnecessary to state it as a premise for investigation" (48–49). By examining her heroines, Lawrence says, we can infer what the novelist herself was like. She may well have been "catty" and "irritable" (50) — or not — but what is certain is that "underlying all the satire" there is a "profoundly fatalistic" portrait of "life as she saw it for women." Lawrence believes that Austen herself had been "disappointed" in life, and that she uses her novels as a means of displacing her own disappointments (56).

There is bias of a different kind in Beatrice Kean Seymour's *Jane Austen: Study for a Portrait* (1937), a work written to eradicate the idea of Austen as the "Essential Spinster." Seymour insists Austen "had a tolerance for things and people almost modern in its sweep" (9). Despite what others have said about the lack of documentation concerning Austen's life and work, she says, there is sufficient information from which to make judgments. The problem has been that too many wrong inferences have been drawn from her letters and from memoirs written about her. Austen was neither cold nor unemotional, Seymour claims, nor was she aloof from what was happening in the wider world. While admitting that Austen frequently draws one-dimensional male characters, Seymour finds her delineations of women exceptionally true-to-life, frequently seeing Austen's heroines as thinly veiled self-portraits. Where Seymour might be considered most controversial is in her defense of the novelist's decision to limit her scope to country life, which Seymour says was motivated not by Austen's lack of knowledge regarding wider political and social questions, but by her wish to escape "a world which did not bear thinking about" (251). Austen deliberately turns her back on the tragic aspects of human life to celebrate its more uplifting side, including romance. Hence, Seymour says in a direct attack on her own postwar world, "in a society that has enthroned the machine-gun and carried it aloft into the quiet heavens," there will always be readers who turn to Austen's novels "with an unending sense of relief and thankfulness" (255).

Austen Light and Dark: The Criticism of Elizabeth Jenkins, Mary Lascelles, and D. W. Harding

If the publication of James Austen-Leigh's 1870 *Memoir* can be viewed as the first watershed in Austen criticism, the second surely occurred in the space of three years just as the nations of Europe began their second bloody conflict of the century. Between 1938 and 1940 three studies by British scholars provided models for future biographical and critical commentary that helped shape Austen studies for decades to come. The first to appear was Elizabeth Jenkins's *Jane Austen: A Biography* (1938). In the opinion of most Austen specialists, Jenkins's work is the first truly scholarly biography of the novelist. Certainly she does a better job than previous biographers of relating details of Austen's life. Jenkins uses Austen's letters as well as those of family and friends to weave the story of the novelist's quiet and seemingly uneventful life, expanding to discussions of the cultural, social, and political milieu only when appropriate. Her narrative is interrupted, however, by long passages of literary criticism where her shrewd insights significantly advance our understanding of the novelist's aims and methods.

As a result, scholars had for the first time a comprehensive biography based on a methodology that had become accepted by the academic community. In it one reads of Austen's friendships (especially her devotion to her sister Cassandra), her tastes in fiction and poetry, her genuine love for the social scene in which she participated actively, and her emergence as the sprightly and devoted aunt who was the favorite of dozens of nieces and nephews. Without engaging in too much speculation, Jenkins handles the matter of Austen's love affairs with sympathy, but insists these are not the direct autobiographical basis for any of the novelist's fictional creations. Similarly, she is careful to explain how Austen works from her experience to shape her fiction, avoiding the tendency toward *roman a clef*. Throughout, Jenkins remains aware that she is writing for a modern audience that might be put off by Austen's adherence to, and apparent approval of, the class system that postwar England was coming to question in the 1930s. Jenkins's discussion of the differences between Austen's heroines and modern women, interspersed throughout her narrative, provides a perceptive commentary on the situation in which women found themselves then — and in the present. While not a feminist, Jenkins is on the verge of discovering the subtle protest that lies beneath the surface portrait of Austen's narrative — but she shrinks from challenging openly the received opinion that Austen was a supporter of the society she depicts in her fiction.

Perhaps the most significant contribution Jenkins makes to critical studies of Austen is her challenge of the myth that Austen's career shows "two periods of great fertility" divided by "a mysterious gap of eight years" (130–31). Some have marveled at how perceptive Austen must have been to have written a novel like *Pride and Prejudice* when she was barely an adult. Others have made much of this "eight years' silence" (131). But Jenkins says those who look for meaning in this silence are misreading the facts of Austen's life. While it is true she composed the first versions of three novels before moving to Bath, and then wrote her other novels nearly a decade later, the intervening years were spent on other projects and on revising the earlier works. In fact, Jenkins says, the published versions of both *Sense and Sensibility* and especially *Pride and Prejudice* display the hand of a mature artist who has reshaped the work of her youth into a perceptive study of relationships and self-discovery.

In a lengthy commentary on Austen's reluctance to seek the public eye, Jenkins insists the novelist was right to stay out of the limelight, because most women writers were dismissed as ephemeral. Austen has been able to grow in popularity, Jenkins says, precisely because she was not affected by the fads of her age, and her work has a quality of readability, largely derived from close perception of essential human qualities not masked by excessive attention to detail, that make her attractive to readers "who have not only time but mental energy to read" (349). Jenkins ends on what must in retrospect be seen as a curious, even ironic, note about the potential for Austen's status among critics in future times: "This is not an age favourable to the development of aesthetic genius," she says with an obvious note of regret. In her view, criticism seems to be moving into the grasp of "those who think that a good picture can be painted only if the artist's political view accord with theirs, and that it is only possible to write a good novel provided the author follows the rules they have laid down" (349). Four decades later, a revision in critical judgments — about Austen and many others — would occur precisely because political and artistic standards would be applied by a new group of theorists.

The second in this trio of important commentaries is Mary Lascelles's *Jane Austen and Her Art* (1939), generally considered the first important modern critical study of Austen's fiction. While not a slave to the dicta laid down by the formalists, evidence of their critical principles is everywhere in her work. However, concerned that some contemporary critics have denigrated the value of narrative, Lascelles believes "it is surely time to look into the story-teller's peculiar problems" (v). She concentrates on Austen's "art" by studying the novelist's "use of language" and the methods she uses to solve "the narrator's peculiar problems" (vi). Though Lascelles had published earlier articles on Austen's work, *Jane Austen and Her Art* was to establish her as one of the century's most influential Austen critics, and further solidify Austen's reputation as one of the most gifted, careful craftspersons ever to write fiction.

The first quarter of *Jane Austen and Her Art* deals with Austen's life, but Lascelles does not merely repeat the novelist's biography from previously published sources. Instead, interested in the relationship between a novelist's life and the production of fiction, she examines events to determine how they may have influenced Austen as a writer. For example, her commentary on Austen's reading explains how what she read influenced what — and how — she wrote. "Allusions to books run like an undercurrent through Jane Austen's writing" (49), Lascelles says, but most of Austen's literary references are indirect. Austen worked in an atmosphere where people read and reacted to novels, Lascelles says, and her writing reflects her adoption of some conventions but her clear rejection of others. A minimalist who clearly disliked "unnecessary elaboration of sentence structure" (88), Austen provides only a few key details about people or places to ground them in her work. There is, Lascelles insists, steady development in her techniques of presenting character and situation — a phenomenon often missed by those dazzled by her early novels. Lascelles believes Austen rewrote constantly to make her characters "*communicative*" — Lascelles's emphasis — "in a natural and probable manner" (101).

In a lengthy discussion of Austen's narrative art, Lascelles details the ways Austen solves the problems a novelist faces in getting readers to become interested in both character and story. Acknowledging that some critics have expressed "a profound and more reasoned discontent" about Austen's work, a "distrust of the range and depth" of her imagination, "an apprehension lest her vision may be limited in such a way as to be falsified" (119–20), Lascelles lays out a detailed argument to explain how Austen is consistent and brilliant in expressing a "constant tranquil preference for a true over a false vision of life, particularly with regard to ideas of happiness" (120). Austen does limit herself, Lascelles concedes, not only in her subject matter but in her narrative patterns. Within those narrow confines, however, she is exquisitely accurate in presenting a portrait of life and a value system that is both authentic and highly probable. Austen's major achievement lies in her ability to communicate with readers "through the consciousness of her people" (198) and through her handling of what Lascelles calls "aspect" (198) — the facility to create a range of characters about whom readers have varying degrees of information. Lascelles believes Austen solves the problem of "the relationship between story-teller and reader" (208) by carefully controlling point-of-view, and also by relating her tales through the consciousnesses of characters who are sympathetic but not perfect. Thus, readers are allowed to maintain some distance from them and not become too emotionally involved in their stories. What makes Austen's art appealing and transcendent of its own time, Lascelles concludes, are her "close and genial relationship with the familiar, daylight world," her "scrupulous fidelity to the evidence at her disposal," her "mastery of her chosen methods of representation," and her intuitive understanding of "her reader's capacity for response" (218).

If Lascelles sees Austen and a purveyor of sweetness and light, D. W. Harding provides a provocative counter argument for Austen as the angry young woman with a decidedly black view of society. Although others, notably Julia Kavanagh, Richard Simpson, and Reginald Farrer, had hinted that Austen's novels were not the gentle comedies most people took them to be, Harding's "Regulated Hatred: An Aspect of the Work of Jane Austen" (1940) provided the impetus for a revision of opinion in academic circles about the novelist's intentions in her fiction. Harding argues persuasively that there is a kind of simmering discontent in Austen's novels that peeks through in isolated places within her narratives. The notion that her works "provided a refuge for the sensitive when the contemporary world grew too much for them" and that she "succeeded admirably in expressing the gentler virtues of a civilized social order" (5) is "a seriously misleading impression" (6). Instead, "her books are, as she meant them to be, read and enjoyed by precisely the sort of people whom she disliked; she is a literary classic of the society which attitudes like hers, held widely enough, would undermine" (6). Harding says it is possible to see Austen being severely critical, even spiteful and fearful, of certain types — represented in the novels not only by figures such as Mr. Collins, Lady Catherine de Bourgh, and Mr. Elton, but also by Mrs. Bennet and Mrs. Bates — while recognizing that the furtherance of her society depends on the acceptance and tolerance of such people. Austen's heroines cannot totally reject them — and neither could the novelist, who was forced to live in a community populated by individuals whose values she abhorred. However, he continues, rather than being satires with an avowedly didactic intent, Austen's novels are really a way for her to be sensitive to the crudeness and complacency of so many around her while somehow resisting the values these people espoused. The novels became for her a means of "unobtrusive spiritual survival," allowing her to refrain from "open conflict with the friendly people around her whose standards in simpler things she could accept and whose affection she greatly needed" (12). When one reads her novels in this light, Harding argues, they become not escapist fantasies but allies "against things and people which were for her, and still are, hateful" (25).

Although Harding spent most of his professional career as a psychologist, he did manage to write a dozen essays on Austen, most notably "Jane Austen and Moral Judgment" in Boris Ford's *From Blake to Byron* (1957) and "Jane Austen: Character and Caricature" in B. C. Southam's *Critical Essays on Jane Austen* (1968). All of his later work reinforces Harding's notion that Austen was a great but conflicted novelist who used her writing as a means of accommodating herself to the society that treated people like her so badly. None, however, had the impact on Austen studies that his 1940 essay did in revising critical opinion about the novelist. There is but a short step from Harding to the more extended commentaries of Marvin Mudrick and others who would transform the gentle spinster into a savage assailant on dominant social values.

The "Canonization" of Austen in English Studies

In summarizing Austen's accomplishments in *The Patterns of English Fiction* (1942), Gordon Gerould says that she amply "merits the steadily mounting fame that has been coming to her through the generations" (166). A "watermark" of sorts in Austen's rise to international prominence, if not among academics then certainly among lovers of her novels worldwide, was the establishment in 1940 of the Jane Austen Society. Dorothy Darnell, a longtime devotee of Austen's fiction, believed that other lovers of Austen would be happy to support efforts to obtain Chawton Cottage, Austen's residence for the last eight years of her life. Darnell wanted to see the building converted into a museum. She sought assistance from university professors, businessmen, politicians, and homemakers in forming a group for this purpose. Creating such an organization in the midst of the worst war in recorded memory might have seemed foolhardy, but Darnell was undaunted, and her efforts eventually paid off. In 1949 Chawton Cottage was opened to the public, and has since been a kind of Mecca drawing the literary and the curious.[3] The Jane Austen Society grew rapidly and eventually included branches in England and similar societies abroad. In 1967 the Society sponsored publication of *Collected Reports of the Jane Austen Society 1949–1965*; similar volumes followed in 1977 and 1989. These included summaries of the Society's activities, reprints of addresses delivered to the members at their annual meeting, and numerous illustrations of memorabilia associated with Austen and her circle.

Much of the credit for Austen's rise to fame among British scholars goes to the husband-and-wife team of Cambridge professors F. R. and Q. D. Leavis, whose writings and teaching influenced a generation of Cambridge students and scholars worldwide to regard Austen as one of the truly great English novelists. Both ascribed to the philosophy that great novelists possess the Arnoldian quality of "high seriousness" that sets their work apart from lesser writers. The conviction that Austen was such a writer informs Q. D. Leavis's extended assessment of her work. Beginning in 1941, Leavis published a series of articles on Austen in *Scrutiny*, the journal she and her husband founded in 1932. Appearing in separate parts under the general title "A Critical Theory of Jane Austen's Writings" (1941–45), Leavis's analysis is intended to put to rest what was then the prevailing opinion of Austen as a natural genius and a retiring, lovable spinster who enjoyed poking gentle fun at the foibles of her neighbors. Leavis attacks the problem on two fronts, demonstrating how Austen carefully and constantly revised her earlier work to shape it into final form for publication. At the same time, following Harding's lead, she explains how Austen's comic stance is far from universally benign, but instead is intended to expose the shortcomings of a society to which she remained curiously attached.

Much of "A Critical Theory of Jane Austen's Writings" is devoted to textual analysis because, Leavis says, by understanding how Austen produced her novels one can come to understand her mastery of the techniques of the genre in which she worked. Leavis believes all of Austen's mature work has its origins in the juvenilia she wrote to entertain her family, or in earlier, often unfinished sketches that she reworked into what would become her six finished novels. The one to which most attention is paid is *Mansfield Park*, a work Leavis calls a "turning point" in Austen's career (*Collected Essays*, 124) and which she describes in a 1958 introduction to an edition of the work as "the first modern novel in England" (*Collected Essays*, 167). In "A Critical Theory" Leavis engages in a bit of rather ingenious textual analysis to demonstrate how *The Watsons*, a novel begun while Austen was living at Bath but never finished, was the basis for *Emma*, and how Austen's early fragment *Lady Susan* became *Mansfield Park* — positing that a now-lost epistolary narrative existed as a transitional document between the earlier sketch and the 1813 novel. Leavis believes all of Austen's novels are "palimpsests through whose surface portions of earlier versions" frequently protrude (*Collected Essays*, 65). What comes through constantly in Leavis's examination of Austen's work is her clear belief that Austen "was not an inspired amateur" but rather "a steady professional writer who had to put in many years of thought and labour to achieve each novel" (65).

Leavis's commentary notwithstanding, there still remained no consensus in Britain or America on what really made Austen so special to lovers of happy romance *and* so meaningful to those who saw her as a stern social critic — though some certainly tried. The American critic Edward Wagenknecht writes appreciatively of Austen in *Cavalcade of the English Novel* (1943), pointing out that her limited life experience seemed not to be a barrier to the production of important fiction that reflects a strong moral sense. In *The Later Women Novelists, 1744–1818: The Female Pen* (1947), an early and sometimes overlooked feminist revaluation of women's fiction, British scholar Bridget MacCarthy focuses on the importance of irony in Austen's fiction. American man of letters Edmund Wilson praises her (albeit somewhat chauvinistically) in a 1944 *New Yorker* piece as being "almost unique among the novelists of her sex in being deeply and steadily concerned, not with the vicarious satisfaction of emotion" nor "the skillful exploitation of gossips," but instead, "as the great masculine novelists are, with the novel as a work of art" (632).

A few, like Samuel Chew, continued to emphasize her limitations. Chew writes in *A Literary History of England* (1948) that although Austen's style is characterized by delicate precision and balance and a "seeming simplicity which often masks subtlety" (1205), her lack of knowledge about finance, political power, and money places her work in shadow when compared with that of acknowledged masters such as Tolstoy or Dostoevsky. Going even farther in his criticism, Richard Aldington claims in *Jane Austen* (1948) that Austen is limited largely by her inability to express passion, and that her attitude toward sex "is as unreal, mercenary and gross as that of a modern divorce court" (17).

But for at least two decades, the Leavises' work would set the tone for critical study of Austen's novels. While Q. D. Leavis concentrates on Austen's mastery of her art, F. R. Leavis puts forward Austen as a moralist of the first rank who uses her considerable artistic talents to advance a moral position about society. Leavis begins his influential (and controversial) 1948 study *The Great Tradition: George Eliot, Henry James, Joseph Conrad* with the pronouncement that "the great English novelists are Jane Austen, George Eliot, Henry James, and Joseph Conrad — to stop for the moment at that comparatively safe point in history" (1). Although Leavis concentrates on only the last three, he does offer some insightful observations about Austen in his introductory chapter, where he establishes her place as "the inaugurator of the great tradition of the English novel" (7). While he acknowledges that other writers might be important historically, he limits inclusion in this "great tradition" to those few who "not only change the possibilities of the art for practitioners and readers," but also "are significant in terms of the human awareness they promote: an awareness of the possibilities of life" (2). Leavis insists Austen's aesthetic concerns cannot be separated from the "moral significance" of her fiction. "Without her intense moral preoccupation" with certain problems of life, he says, "she wouldn't have been a great novelist" (7).

Notes

[1] As Noel King explains in "Jane Austen in France" (1953), Austen had enjoyed readership across the Channel almost immediately, but by the end of the nineteenth century her popularity had waned. In 1914 Kate and Paul Rague's brief appreciation, *Jane Austen*, reintroduced French readers to her fiction. However, its appearance raised little attention in Britain. By contrast, Léonie Villard's *Jane Austen: Sa Vie et Son Oeuvre, 1775–1817* (1915), drew criticism from the Austen-Leigh family for what they considered its error-prone sketch of the novelist's life and Villard's sometimes unflattering assessments of Austen's artistry. A decade later, Louis Cazamian wrote a favorable assessment of Austen in *Histoire de la Litterature Anglaise* (1924), calling her work "more truly psychological than that of Richardson" (994) and "infused with the spirit of classicism in its highest form" (995).

[2] A more extensive discussion of the Chapman edition can be found in Kathyrn Sutherland's *Jane Austen's Textual Lives: From Aeschylus to Bollywood* (2005).

[3] In a thought-provoking essay on the ways Austen has been appropriated for various ideological causes, Deidre Lynch argues in "At Home with Jane Austen" (1996) that the establishment of the Jane Austen Society in 1940 and concurrent efforts to preserve Chawton Cottage were actually part of the "war effort," activities undertaken to solidify the concept of "Englishness" in a nation that needed to know that their sacrifices were worth the price they were paying (159–61). Lynch sees this as one of many efforts undertaken during the twentieth century to make Austen the property of the masses, usually done by stressing the cozy domestic aspects of her fiction. A longer narrative about Darnell's project and the founding of the Jane Austen Society can be found in Claire Harman, *Jane's Fame* (2009), 177–82.

Works Cited

Aldington, Richard. *Jane Austen*. Pasadena, CA: Ampersand Press, 1948.

Austen-Leigh, James Edward. *A Memoir of Jane Austen*. London: Richard Bentley, 1870. 2nd ed., expanded, 1871. Reprinted with introduction and notes by R. W. Chapman. Oxford: Clarendon Press, 1926.

Austen-Leigh, Mary Augusta. *Personal Aspects of Jane Austen*. London: John Murray, 1920.

Austen-Leigh, William, and Richard A. Austen-Leigh. *Jane Austen: Her Life and Letters. A Family Record*. London: Smith, Elder, 1913.

Bailey, John Cann. *Introductions to Jane Austen*. London: Oxford UP, 1931.

Baker, Ernest A. *The History of the English Novel*. Vol. 6, *Edgeworth, Austen, Scott*, 57–121. London: H. F. & G. Witherby, 1935.

Bald, Marjory A. *Women Writers of the Nineteenth Century*, 1–27. Cambridge: Cambridge UP, 1923.

Cazamian, Louis, and Émile Legouis. *Histoire de la Litterature Anglaise*. 2 vols. Paris: Hachette, 1924. English ed., *A History of English Literature*, translated by Helen D. Irvine and W. D. MacInnes, 1:944–97. London: J. M. Dent, 1926–27; New York: Macmillan, 1929.

Cecil, David. *Jane Austen*. Cambridge: Cambridge UP, 1935.

Chapman, R. W. "Jane Austen: A Reply to Mr. Garrod." In *Essays by Divers Hands, being the Transactions of the Royal Society of Literature of the United Kingdom* n.s. 10 (1931): 17–34.

———. *Jane Austen: Facts and Problems*. Oxford: Clarendon Press, 1948.

———, ed. *The Novels of Jane Austen: The Text Based on Collations of the Early Editions*. 5 vols. Oxford: Clarendon Press, 1923.

Chew, Samuel C. *A Literary History of England*, edited by Albert C. Baugh, et al., 4:1200–1206. New York: Appleton Century Crofts, 1948.

Clarke, Isabel C. *Six Portraits*, 93–134. London: Hutchinson, 1935.

Collected Reports of the Jane Austen Society, 1949–1965. London: Dawson, 1967.

Collected Reports of the Jane Austen Society, 1966–1975. Folkestone: Dawson, 1977.

Collected Reports of the Jane Austen Society, 1976–1985. Overton, Hampshire: Jane Austen Society, 1989.

Collins, Norman. "Jane Austen's Unheavenly World." *The Facts of Fiction*, 104–15. London: Gollancz, 1932.

Edgar, Pelham. *The Art of the Novel from 1700 to the Present Time*, 93–116. New York: Macmillan, 1933.

Firkins, Oscar W. *Jane Austen.* New York: Henry Holt, 1920.

Ford, Ford Madox. *The English Novel: From the Earliest Days to the Death of Conrad.* London: Constable, 1930.

Forster, E. M. *Aspects of the Novel.* London: Edward Arnold, 1927.

———. "Notes on the English Character." *Atlantic Monthly* 137 (1926): 30–37. Reprinted in *Abinger Harvest*, 3–14. London: Edward Arnold, 1936.

———. Review of *The Novels of Jane Austen. Nation* 34 (5 January 1924): 512. Reprinted in *Abinger Harvest.* London: Edward Arnold, 1936.

Garrod, H. W. "Jane Austen: A Depreciation." In *Essays by Divers Hands, being the Transactions of the Royal Society of Literature of the United Kingdom* n.s. 8 (1928): 21–40.

Gerould, Gordon. *The Patterns of English and American Fiction: A History.* Boston: Little, Brown, 1942.

Gorer, Geoffrey. "The Myth in Jane Austen." *Life and Letters Today* 21 (May 1939): 38–44. Reprinted in *American Imago* 2.3 (1941): 197–204. Reprinted in *Five Approaches to Literary Criticism*, edited by Wilbur S. Scott, 91–98. New York and London: Macmillan, 1962.

Harding, Denys Wyatt. "Character and Caricature in Jane Austen." In *Critical Essays on Jane Austen*, edited by B. C. Southam, 83–106. London: Routledge & Kegan Paul, 1968; New York: Barnes & Noble, 1969.

———. "Jane Austen and Moral Judgment." In *From Blake To Byron*, edited by Boris Ford, 51–59. Harmondsworth: Penguin, 1957.

———. "Regulated Hatred: An Aspect of the Work of Jane Austen." *Scrutiny* 8 (1939–40): 346–62. Reprinted in *Regulated Hatred and Other Essays on Jane Austen*, edited by Monica Lawlor, 1–26. London and Atlantic Highlands, NJ: Athlone Press, 1998.

Harman, Claire. *Jane's Fame: How Jane Austen Conquered the World.* Edinburgh: Canongate, 2009; New York: Henry Holt, 2010.

Jenkins, Elizabeth. *Jane Austen: A Biography.* London: Gollancz, 1938.

Johnson, Claudia L. "Austen Cults and Cultures." *The Cambridge Companion to Jane Austen*, edited by Edward Copeland and Juliet McMaster, 211–26. Cambridge and New York: Cambridge UP, 1997.

Johnson, R. Brimley. *Jane Austen*. London: Sheed & Ward, 1927. Reprinted as *Jane Austen: Her Life, Her Work, Her Family, and Her Critics*. London and Toronto: J. M. Dent & Sons; New York: E. P. Dutton, 1930.

———. *The Women Novelists*, 66–130. London: W. Collins & Sons, 1918.

King, Noel J. "Jane Austen in France." *Nineteenth-Century Fiction* 8 (1953–54): 1–26.

Kipling, Rudyard. "The Janeites." *Story-Teller* (May 1924): 139–50. Reprinted in *Debits and Credits*, 147–74. London: Macmillan, 1926.

Knight, Grant C. *The Novel in English*, 150–59. New York: Richard C. Smith, 1931.

Lascelles, Mary. *Jane Austen and Her Art*. Oxford: Clarendon Press, 1939.

Lawrence, D. H. *Apropos of Lady Chatterley's Lover*. London: Mandrake Press, 1930.

Lawrence, Margaret. *The School of Femininity*, 32–59. New York: Frederick Stokes, 1936.

Leavis, F. R. *The Great Tradition: George Eliot, Henry James, Joseph Conrad*. London: Chatto & Windus, 1948.

Leavis, Q. D. "A Critical Theory of Jane Austen's Writings." *Scrutiny* 10 (1941–42): 61–87, 114–42, 272–94; *Scrutiny* 12 (1944–45): 104–19. Reprinted in *The Englishness of the English Novel*. Vol. 1 of *Collected Essays*, edited by G. Singh, 61–146. New York: Cambridge UP, 1983.

———. "Introduction to *Mansfield Park*." London: Macdonald, 1958. Reprinted in *The Englishness of the English Novel*. Vol. 1 of *Collected Essays*, edited by G. Singh, 161–94. New York: Cambridge UP, 1983.

Lovett, Robert M. and Helen S. Hughes. *The History of the Novel in England*, 165–71. Boston: Houghton Mifflin, 1932.

Lynch, Deidre. "At Home with Jane Austen." In *Cultural Institutions of the Novel*, edited by Deidre Lynch and William B. Warner, 159–92. Durham, NC: Duke UP, 1996.

MacCarthy, Bridget G. *The Later Women Novelists, 1744–1818: The Female Pen*, 235–81. Cork, Ireland: Cork UP; Oxford: Blackwell, 1947.

Moore, Virginia. *Distinguished Women Writers*, 97–107. New York: E. P. Dutton, 1934.

O'Malley, Ida B. *Women in Subjection: A Study of the Lives of Englishwomen before 1832*. London: Duckworth, 1933.

Priestley, J. B. *English Humour*, 116–25. London: Longmans, Green, 1929.

Rague, Kate, and Paul Rague. *Jane Austen*. Paris: Bloud & Gay, 1914.

Ralli, Augustus. "The Home-Land of Jane Austen." *Critiques*, 67–92. London: Longmans, Green, 1927.

Rawlence, Guy. *Jane Austen*. Great Lives series. London: Duckworth, 1934.

Rhydderch, David. *Jane Austen: Her Life and Art*. London: Jonathan Cape, 1932.

Seymour, Beatrice Kean. *Jane Austen: Study for a Portrait*. London: Michael Joseph, 1937.

Southam, B. C., ed. *Critical Essays on Jane Austen*. London: Routledge & Kegan Paul, 1968; New York: Barnes & Noble, 1969.

Squire, John Collins. "Jane Austen." *Reflections and Memories*, 254–73. London: Heinemann, 1935.

Sutherland, Kathryn. *Jane Austen's Textual Lives: From Aeschylus to Bollywood*. Oxford and New York: Oxford UP, 2005.

Thomson, Clara Linklater. *Jane Austen: A Survey*. London: Horace Marshall & Son, 1929.

Villard, Léonie. *Jane Austen: Sa Vie et Son Oeuvre, 1775–1817*. Saint-Étienne: Société Anonyme de l'Imprimerie Mulcey, 1915. English ed., *Jane Austen: A French Appreciation*, translated by Veronica Lucas. London: Routledge & Sons, 1924.

Wagenknecht, Edward. *Cavalcade of the English Novel*, 142–51. New York: Holt, Rinehart & Winston, 1943.

Walkley, Arthur B. "Jane's Prejudice." *More Prejudice*, 26–30. London: Heinemann, 1923.

Williams, Orlo. *Some Great English Novels: Studies in the Art of Fiction*, 149–78. London: Macmillan, 1926.

Wilson, Edmund. "A Long Talk about Jane Austen." *New Yorker* 20 (24 June 1944): 70, 72–74, 77–78. Reprinted in *Edmund Wilson: Literary Essays and Reviews of the 1930s–40s*, 620–35. New York: Library of America, 2007.

Wilson, Mona. "Jane Austen 1775–1817." *Jane Austen and Some Contemporaries*, 1–42. London: Cresset, 1938.

Woolf, Virginia. "How It Strikes a Contemporary." *Times Literary Supplement*, 25 April 1923. Reprinted in *The Common Reader*, 231–41. 1st series. New York: Harcourt, Brace, Jovanovich, 1925.

———. "Jane Austen." *The Common Reader*, 134–45. 1st series. New York: Harcourt, Brace, Jovanovich, 1925.

3: The Zenith of Formalist and Humanist Criticism, 1949–1974

B Y THE END OF THE SECOND WORLD WAR, Austen's reputation had become firmly established, so it is not surprising to find a marked increase in the study of her fiction during the next thirty years. Concurrently, during the postwar period New Criticism became a dominant mode of critical inquiry for examining fiction. Applying techniques of New Criticism to realist fiction had always posed something of a challenge, since the assumption was that the approach worked better when applied to lyric poetry than for the more socially connected genre of the novel. A look at essays by the respected American critic Mark Schorer gives some insight into how these principles could be applied to Austen's novels. In his 1949 essay "Fiction and the Matrix of Analogy" Mark Schorer uses *Persuasion* to demonstrate how critics might give the novel the same kind of attention they had devoted to poetry in the past twenty years. The important first step, he says, is to treat fiction as "a literary art," a representation of life which is open to analysis of "the structure of the image" (539). His detailed examination of Austen's final novel concentrates on repeated words and patterns of imagery that reveal Austen's interests, making it clear that *Persuasion* is "a novel in which sensibility is subdued to property" (543). Schorer also published an essay in the *Kenyon Review* that was used as the introduction for Houghton Mifflin's *Pride and Prejudice* (1956), and contributed introductions for an inexpensive edition of Austen's novels published by Dell between 1959 and 1962, indicating that his method of critical inquiry was widely available to — and undoubtedly influenced — instruction in high-school and college classrooms for years.

Schorer's emphasis on form can be seen in his remarks on *Emma* in a 1959 *Literary Review* essay. The novel has "a double theme," he says, "but in no other" of Austen's works "has the structure been raised so skillfully upon it" (61). The novel contains "four movements," or "four intermeshing blocks" (65). Schorer explains how these major movements (a symphonic metaphor) or blocks (an analogy drawn between literature and architecture) display Emma's "diminution" in the social scale and her concurrent "growth" in "the moral scheme" (67). In this case, as in the readings by many of Schorer's contemporaries, the analysis of structure leads to the revelation of the novel's moral *schema*.

Understanding Schorer's approach provides some insight into what was certainly the dominant mode of critical inquiry, especially in America. At the same time, however, Austen criticism during the middle decades of the twentieth century was clearly affected by the back-and-forth between formalists and practitioners of other forms of criticism, especially humanists and moralists. A good example of how humanists and moralists viewed Austen during this period can be found in the work of the Columbia scholar Lionel Trilling. Associated with the politically liberal New York intellectuals, Trilling brought to literary criticism a firm belief that literature had a social mission and that the critic's job is not simply to discover a work's artistic merits but to uncover its moral stance. While not a major figure in Austen studies, his teaching and writing had great influence on a number of other scholars who wrote more extensively about Austen. When writing directly about her, Trilling looks for what might be called the enduring moral value of her work. His introduction to *Emma* in the Riverside Edition of the novel (1957), reprinted in *Encounter* in the same year, highlights the variety of approaches critics have taken in assessing the merits of Austen's work. Austen has come to be identified with traditional femininity, Trilling says, and readers tend to love her or hate her. While Trilling is not willing to subscribe to the unqualified adulation of the Janeites, he does find there is something to be said for their reaction to the novels. Austen suggests that there is a chance for the world to be better, he says, if only people would rely on their intellect and wits rather than their emotions to guide them in life. About *Emma* Trilling is particularly insightful — perhaps even prescient of the kind of criticism that would follow two decades later — when he notes that the title character possesses "the peculiar reality of moral life that self-love bestows." This laudable quality is normally found in male protagonists, he claims, but Emma is able to assert her own sense of self-worth rather than content herself with achieving her identity "by the reflected moral light of men" (38).

The following review of criticism published between the end of the Second World War and the middle of the 1970s illustrates the back-and-forth between critics who stress the importance of aesthetic qualities as the principal gauge for determining the value of Austen's fiction and those who look for broad moral and social themes as a means of explaining her greatness. After reading it, one might well come away understanding that virtually everyone thought highly of Austen — but there was often stark disagreement about why we should consider her a novelist of the first rank.

Summary Judgments in Literary Histories

The trajectory of critical judgments about Austen can be seen in a number of "histories of the novel" that appeared after the war. Arnold Kettle's discussion of Austen in *An Introduction to the English Novel* (1951), an early Marxist analysis of her fiction, pays tribute to her talents but considers her conservatism a serious limitation on her achievement. Focusing on *Emma*, Kettle says that as realist fiction the novel has much to recommend it; Austen teaches abstract lessons about marriage by allowing readers to experience actual courtship and marriage. But *Emma* is seriously flawed by the unconscious class-based assumptions about the inherent value of the society that aggrandizes heredity and money as inherently good. Another critic with Marxist leanings, Annette Rubinstein, stresses in *The Great Tradition in English Literature from Shakespeare to Shaw* (1953) Austen's radical, alienist position within her social milieu. Rubinstein finds Austen increasingly committed to her personal values and standards, and increasingly critical of those esteemed by the society in which she lived. There is also a strong hint of feminism in Rubinstein's critique. She is dismissive of critics (mostly male) who object to Austen's rather commercialized presentation of love and marriage, insisting that by "reading between the lines" one can discover Austen's "unsparing analysis" of society "beneath the imperturbable surface" (374).

Just where Austen stood in the history of the development of fiction remained a matter for debate. Many characterized her as the last of the eighteenth-century novelists. Diana Neill's brief synopsis of Austen's career in *A Short History of the English Novel* (1951) paints her as a staunch anti-Romantic. Perpetuating the notion that Austen was "immune from the great movements of her time" (147), Neill says the novelist was truly comfortable with the society she portrays and content to mock its excesses. In Neill's view the published novels are decidedly consistent in presenting a critique of Romanticism — because Austen revised her earlier work extensively to erase any trace of Romantic tendencies. Walter Allen echoes Neill's sentiments in *The English Novel: A Short Critical History* (1954). Though he laments the fact that Austen's contemporaries did not recognize her "revolutionary" accomplishments (113), he insists that, in her outlook, Austen was "an eighteenth-century moralist" (115) whose "formal ordering" of her materials constituted her "criticism of life" (114). So, too, in his four-volume *A Critical History of English Literature* (1960) David Daiches describes Austen as a strong moralist and "the greatest of all the novelists of manners" (3:743). Refusing to link her with contemporaries captivated by the spirit of Romanticism, Daiches says her novels portray "an eighteenth-century world in its habits, tastes, and appearances" (744). But Lionel Stevenson claims in *The English Novel: A Panorama* (1960) that Austen broke from her predecessors by helping to reorient the novel away from treatments of the fantastic back toward realism. She was essentially conservative in her own life, though, coming from "the social class that was most obstinately opposed both to new ideas and to unseemly displays of emotion." Her works express "the very essence of the eighteenth century — its sense of permanent social and moral standards, its suspicion of uncontrolled emotion or imagination, its precise observation of immediate fact" (186). But Stevenson reveals himself a man of his own time in his comments about what he considers a common thread running through all of Austen's novels: the treatment of women's issues. Austen was so narrowly focused on these matters that she could not discuss men without women present in a scene. But he assures his readers this narrowed focus "serves actually to enhance her particular effect, for each story is kept strictly in the focus upon the feminine character" — after all, women "naturally would have no insight into male conversations" (189).

In contrast to Allen, Stevenson, and Daiches, Frederick Karl places Austen at the head of his list of nineteenth-century writers in *An Age of Fiction: The Nineteenth-Century British Novel* (1964). He believes she shares many characteristics of the writers who followed her in the succeeding decades. Austen began her career at a time when the position of social prominence held by the landed gentry, a group characterized by inherited wealth and titles, was being challenged by "a new kind of gentleman: the genteel man of attainments" (15). Austen's heroines "desire a kind of equality" denied their predecessors, Karl says, and they want "romantic love as well" (16). Karl's readings of the novels stress their "profundity and breadth" (27), and he is clearly interested in the larger themes that inform Austen's work. However, despite Austen's support for what he sees as new social parameters, Karl thinks she was a champion of stability — both material and emotional. Harrison Steeves echoes Karl's judgment, concluding his *Before Jane Austen: The Shaping of the English Novel in the Eighteenth Century* (1965) with an exploration of the influence of eighteenth-century writers on Austen's work. Steeves calls Austen "the first *modern* English novelist," depicting life as twentieth-century readers might understand it. She is also the first to "free herself from conventions that had limited the novel in both matter and form" and filled the genre with "heavy and pretentious prose" (4).

Books on Austen, 1950–1974

The number of books devoted exclusively to Austen increased markedly during this period. Three early studies seem to carry forward settled opinion about the novelist. Margaret Kennedy's *Jane Austen* (1950) provides nothing new in her reading of the novels, but her assessment of Austen's role as a comic novelist — and not a satirist — counters the position taken by Harding and others who claim Austen was a savage critic of society. Sylvia Townsend Warner's short pamphlet *Jane Austen* (1951) in the Longman's Writers and Their Work series represents Austen as "a completely worldly artist" (7), born at the right age when celebrating the worldly was acceptable.

In 1952, however, there appeared a work that was to affect judgments of Austen for at least the next three decades, and whose influence on critics continues into the twenty-first century: Marvin Mudrick's *Jane Austen: Irony as Defense and Discovery* (1952). For decades a majority of critics celebrated "dear Aunt Jane" as the champion of old-fashioned Tory values, a beacon of reason writing at the height of the Romantic movement. Mudrick's portrait of Austen suggests instead that she is critical of stale conventions, inherent hypocrisies, and reliance on economic status as a measure of personal worth. Armed with the tools of psychology and formalism, and perhaps influenced by the postwar *zeitgeist* that tended to celebrate writers who were alienated from their society, Mudrick produced a work of criticism that allowed Austen to keep her place among the great novelists while turning upside down the reasons for according it to her.

The general premise of *Jane Austen: Irony as Defense and Discovery* is that Austen spent most of her time subverting the values she supposedly upheld, and that she used irony as a means of distancing herself from her material. Mudrick's claim that Austen was the only woman writer "to oppose the tide of feminine sensibility in the novels of the time" (17) puts him at odds with earlier critics such as R. Brimley Johnson and Mary Lascelles, who insist Austen had a deep love for the existing social order and for middle-class virtues. He is also frustrated with the systematic — and for him, wrongheaded — criticism of Q. D. Leavis, whose articles on Austen purport to offer a comprehensive account of her artistry. To support his thesis, Mudrick offers close readings of individual novels, concentrating on functionality, complexity, and the ability to create interest. One of his most important contributions to Austen scholarship is his careful reading of the juvenilia, where he finds the seeds of Austen's social criticism and discovers the novelist "clear[ing] her imagination of everything except the socially seen and heard, the actual, immediate, ironically vulnerable forms of the bourgeois world" (25). The published novels, he says, display advances in technique and social vision. In *Pride and Prejudice* Austen draws characters without sentimentality and yet makes them interesting as individuals. This novel, he says, is principally about power — the power to make choices in a world where so much is determined by conventionality and economic necessity. *Mansfield Park* is a "severely moral" novel which Mudrick finds disappointing, largely because it contains no irony. By contrast, in *Emma*, a novel displaying "an uncomplex and immediate art," full of "wit, irony, light laughter shining in a triumph of surface" (181), Austen returns to a mode of writing that suits her admirably. By contrast, in *Persuasion* the irony is muted, and for the first time "personal feeling" is introduced everywhere, pervading character and setting and "complicat[ing] the moral climate" (218).

Throughout his study, Mudrick claims Austen uses irony as a means of shielding herself from some of what might have been the hurtful consequences of becoming involved and engaged in contemporary society. Even in her earliest works, he says, "she is steadily wary, she must keep her distance from the threat of contact, above all from the ultimate commitment of sex" (25). In all her earlier work she shies away from dealing directly with passionate relationships between the sexes. She would like to have written about such affairs, Mudrick says, but to do so would have forced her to expose her own feelings about love — something she simply could not bring herself to do. Only in *Persuasion* does she exhibit any tendency to identify with the emotions she presents in her heroine, "discard[ing] the shield of irony" (240). Mudrick says the novel is "crucially different" (228) from its predecessors and signals what would certainly have been a new direction for Austen's fiction had she lived.

The immediate impact of Mudrick's study can be seen in Andrew Wright's *Jane Austen's Novels: A Study In Structure* (1953). In the introduction to his book, Wright calls Mudrick's work "the best recent study of Jane Austen," although "sometimes wrong-headed" (vii).[1] What Wright objects to is what he calls Mudrick's reductive use of the term irony. As a corrective, Wright devotes considerable effort to defining the term in a way that makes Austen's fiction seem decidedly more complex than it appears in Mudrick's analysis. Wright explains how Austen's novels can be read on three levels: first as "local" works, illustrative of eighteenth-century country life; second "as broad allegories" commenting on various human virtues and defects; and finally on the "ironic level," in which the "incidents, situations, and characters" are "symbolic rather than allegorical" (16). Concentrating on point-of-view, characterization, and dramatic irony, Wright identifies six different approaches Austen uses in presenting character and situation: an objective account, indirect comment, direct comment, the insertion of maxims (the "universal truths" made famous in the first line of *Pride and Prejudice*), the dramatic mode, and interior disclosures. Wright also describes ways Austen modifies the rhetorical tradition of the eighteenth-century to support her ironic vision. In contrast to those who had begun to find Austen cold and detached, Wright believes her "profound vision" of human nature is essentially comic: "she laughs at man [meaning humankind], but only because she takes him seriously." As with any great ironist, "the more she perceives the less she understands"; or perhaps, Wright says, "the more she understands, the more she is perplexed by the contradictions she finds" (171–72).

Another book less controversial than Mudrick's but also frequently cited by later critics, is Howard Babb's *Jane Austen's Novels: The Fabric of Dialogue* (1962). Expanding on the argument he had made in a 1958 *Kenyon Review* article, Babb offers an analysis of dialogue in all of Austen's novels to illuminate her mastery of the form of fiction. "Austen's dialogue actually reveals her characters in depth," Babb says, "and shows them engaged in the most fundamental activities of personality" (5–6). In dialogue, "characters define themselves" (28), and it is in her characters that readers have the greatest interest. Therefore, Babb says, appreciating her handling of dialogue provides "a sharpened insight" into her art (viii).

The conflict in critical circles generated by Mudrick's contentious description of Austen's personality and methods prompted Robert Liddell to undertake what he describes as a balanced study of Austen's novels, because "the serious criticism of Jane Austen has lately suffered from separatism" (xi). *The Novels of Jane Austen* (1963) argues against popular myths about Austen that paint her as a gifted amateur who underwent a long silence but showed no real development over her career. Wanting to "push this rubbish on one side" (xii), Liddell offers readings of each major work that trace its composition history and comment on Austen's techniques of characterization and major themes. Liddell's tendency to focus on the fiction with little reference to Austen's life is typical of criticism of the period that aims principally at helping readers get a sense of Austen's artistry and accomplishments.

An ongoing concern of critics during the 1950s and 1960s was in an artist's use of tradition, and a number of studies of Austen's work address that issue. For example, in *Jane Austen: A Study in Fictional Conventions* (1964) Henrietta Ten Harmsel studies the way Austen uses the conventions of fiction established in the eighteenth century. Acknowledging that earlier critics saw Austen burlesquing many of these conventions, Ten Harmsel argues that Austen's novels are highly dependent on those of her predecessors, and that literary conventions are often used with serious purpose in her work. Austen's achievement, which sometimes obscures the importance of these conventions, is to have transformed them using four principal techniques: "realism, gradually developing character [as opposed to static characters], variety of function, and irony" (36). While her fiction seems radically different from that of her predecessors, when one looks carefully at each novel one discovers the novelist using stock characters, themes, and situations.

Austen's technique is also the subject of Wendy Craik's *Jane Austen: The Six Novels* (1965), an examination relying on "comparison and analysis" (3) to study of all six of Austen's novels. Craik embarks on close readings that reveal what she identifies as a linear pattern of increasing complexity of technique and mastery of form. In her view *Northanger Abbey* is a clever but flawed satire. *Sense and Sensibility* is an excellent first attempt at serious social commentary, but not nearly so technically polished as *Pride and Prejudice*, a novel in which Austen advances in handling character and stating her principal theme indirectly: "the moral weight of material and financial matters in personal affairs" (64). Craik believes Austen reprises the mood of *Sense and Sensibility* in *Mansfield Park*, but expands her vision to create a portrait of the "breakdown and the subsequent reform of a whole highly organized society" (92). *Emma*, Austen's "best and most misunderstood work" (125), reveals further advances in the novelist's ability to create realistic and psychologically convincing characters within a tightly structured yet plausible plot. Craik is not able to continue her argument for steady advance in artistic ability when examining *Persuasion*, but she manages to explain away what she considers some of the novel's artistic faults by suggesting it was not really ready for publication when Austen died. In a companion piece, *Jane Austen in Her Time* (1969), Craik foregoes textual analysis in favor of extended discussions of historical and social background to help readers approach Austen's novels "with the understanding the author assumes [they] will possess" (Preface). In this book Craik focuses on life in Regency England, providing readers extensive information about both the commercial pursuits of the middle classes and the various forms of entertainments and diversions they enjoyed. To keep the focus on Austen, Craik excerpts or summarizes key scenes from the novels to illustrate how much Austen depends for effect on readers' knowledge of the subtleties of her society. Much more than in her earlier study, Craik seems insistent that only by reading the novels as sociological documents can readers of a later age appreciate the larger, universal issues with which Austen deals.

The work of one of the most distinguished American champions of Austen, Princeton scholar A. Walton Litz, provides an excellent example of the way her work was treated by critics at the height of formalism's popularity as a critical approach to fiction. *Jane Austen: A Study of Her Artistic Development* (1965) is a well-argued and well-researched critique of the techniques Austen uses to create works that Litz says revolutionized the practice of novel-writing. Austen was "the first 'modern' English novelist," he says, and her fiction is really "an act of criticism that places the history of the eighteenth-century English novel in perspective and foreshadows the course of much nineteenth-century English fiction." More importantly, "many of the narrative principles formulated by James and Forster are implicit" in the "mature work" of this "supremely conscious artist" (3).

Litz notes that the trend in the past two decades to emphasize Austen's "control of language and mastery of ironic exposure," an approach that tends to present her "as a radical dissenter" with "subversive" aims, is too limiting (v). By analyzing her techniques "with an examination of the moral and literary backgrounds of the novels" (vi), Litz offers what he believes is a more satisfying and more accurate view. He also wishes to refute some of the claims about Austen made by those who view her as aloof and judgmental. Litz believes Austen had genuine affection for the people and customs she pokes fun at in her novels, but she was also a strong believer in the need for individuals to find ways to express themselves *as* individuals, a stance that often led to conflict. Hence, at the heart of her mature fiction attentive readers will find "a tension between two fundamental attitudes which may be called, for want of better terms, neoclassicism and romanticism," the former embodying society's claims on people, the latter the claims of the individual (116). Litz devotes a good deal of attention to techniques of composition, focusing on Austen's use of dialogue and description, irony, and point-of-view to reveal her themes rather than dictate them to her readers. To Austen's credit, Litz says, she did not repeat herself in later works, instead exploring the relationship of setting to theme in ways not evident in earlier novels. And although *Persuasion* is but another variation on "one of Jane Austen's most persistent themes, the perils of the free spirit in its search for social identity," Austen makes Anne's situation even more precarious by refusing to give her heroine any confidantes with whom to share her feelings and test her hypotheses about proper perceptions and behavior. The unfinished fragment *Sanditon*, Litz says, contains strong evidence of how much Austen had been influenced by the Romantic poets. Although unfinished and flawed in some respects, this fragment reveals that "Austen was still exercising those critical powers which had made her artistic career a process of continuous development and discovery" (169).

However, it is good to remind ourselves that the notion of "traditional" criticism at this time differed significantly from its current definition. Litz's study is an example of what critics of the 1960s would have considered the "new" approach to fiction. More typical of what was then considered "traditional" is Norman Sherry's *Jane Austen* (1966), a volume in the Literature in Perspective Series edited by Kenneth Gross. In the preface to Sherry's book, Gross calls for a return to "traditional" methods of literary study because, he says, in recent years too many critics had taken to "exploring slender ramifications of meaning, exposing successive levels of association and reference, and multiplying the types of ambiguity into seventy times seven." By contrast, Gross says, books like Sherry's aim at giving "a straightforward account of literature and writers" in which "critical jargon is as far as possible avoided" (5). Sherry does a creditable job of fulfilling those goals, describing the literary background to Austen's fiction, offering brief assessments of the six major novels, examining Austen's limitations and strengths as a writer (emphasizing her talent for characterization), and commenting on various topics such as marriage and morals. While he does steer clear of the jargon that characterized certain popular approaches, he devotes considerable space to exploring the ramifications of Austen's use of irony, a favorite pastime of the New Critics.

Although certainly more in tune with critical trends of the times, Joseph Wiesenfarth's *The Errand of Form* (1967) is in large part an extended qualification or refutation of earlier critical readings of Austen's novels. Finding that the tendency in recent criticism has been to read Austen's fiction through a single critical lens, Wiesenfarth promises a more eclectic approach, choosing to enter discussion of each of the six major works by examining a critical crux that has puzzled or irritated other scholars. But he makes clear from the outset his own belief in the primacy of formalist studies as the means of understanding a novel as a work of art. "Every meaning in a novel exists in a formal structure," he says, "and every separate detail of the structure as well as the structure as a whole is necessarily meaningful" (viii). The eclecticism promoted by Wiesenfarth is evident in Avrom Fleishman's *A Reading of 'Mansfield Park': An Essay in Critical Synthesis* (1967). This book initiated a trend in Austen criticism: the publication of entire books about a single novel. The sophistication of literary analysis, augmented by the emergence of what were then new theories of criticism, was principally responsible for the change. In his critique of *Mansfield Park* Fleishman attempts what he describes as a comprehensive reading of the novel, choosing not to privilege one approach but instead attempting to explain how techniques of formalism, psychological criticism, Marxism, sociological examination, and other methods of analysis all help reveal a novel's meaning or illuminate some aspect of the novelist's artistry. Before long, monographs dealing with a single Austen novel began appearing regularly, and the approaches taken by their authors reveal the diversity of opinion that Austen's work continued to generate.

Despite the dominance of formalist studies in America, British critics tended to be more comfortable with methods promoted by critics like the Leavises, who stressed the social and moral dimensions of Austen's fiction. That approach informs Cambridge graduate Yasmine Gooneratne's *Jane Austen* (1970), part of a Cambridge University Press series intended to introduce serious readers to important literary figures. Employing what series editor Robin Mayhead calls "the methods associated with Cambridge" (v), Gooneratne offers detailed readings of Austen's letters, juvenilia, and the major novels to dispel the notion that Austen is "a harmlessly amusing purveyor of romantic social comedy" (7). While one might question the necessity for challenging a thesis that critics had been disproving for half a century, Gooneratne does point toward new critical views of Austen in her examination of Austen's critique of society. "Jane Austen's tone," she says, "is exquisitely poised between ironic detachment and protest at the immorality and injustice of accepted social values" (7). And although Gooneratne insists that interpretation is a personal matter for readers — who should not be swayed too much by critics of any ilk — her own discussions hint at the kind of revaluation feminists were already beginning to undertake.

In another study applying the Cambridge method, *Jane Austen and Her Predecessors* (1966), Frank Bradbrook follows up on the observation of F. R. Leavis, his mentor at Cambridge, that "in her indebtedness to others" Austen "provides an exceptionally illuminating study of the nature of originality" (Leavis, *Great Tradition*, 5). Bradbrook sets out to trace the sources that shaped Austen's view of life and art, operating from the premise that "though the exact extent of Jane Austen's reading can never be known," it is "probably more comprehensive than has been suspected" (139). He examines the influence exerted on Austen by periodical literature, advice books, moral treatises, sermons, and writings on the picturesque, especially the work of William Gilpin. In writing about the influence of poetry and drama, he cites the special, albeit indirect, influence of Shakespeare, as well as the Restoration dramatists. By far the longest section of Bradbrook's study focuses on the debt Austen owes to novelists who preceded her. Bradbrook concludes in a rather Arnoldian fashion that the study of Austen's "relationship to her predecessors" allows us to "see how she gathered together all that was best in the literature of the past that she knew" (137). Using the literary tradition as an apt complement to her direct exposure to "ordinary human experience," Austen creates in her novels "a 'criticism of life'" (138).

Three other studies reflect the ongoing interest of scholars in source study and Austen's use of language. Kenneth Moler's *Jane Austen's Art of Allusion* (1968) examines the novelist's borrowings, showing particular interest in the skill she employs "to revivify them and make them her personal possessions" (1). Studying her use of allusions is important, Moler says, because Austen is by nature drawn to parody and satire, two forms that frequently comment on earlier literature. Moler claims that by understanding the use of allusion one can apprehend meaning — which in Austen's case always has moral overtones. Kenneth Phillips's *Jane Austen's English* (1970) explores in great detail Austen's vocabulary, sentence structure, and modes of address. Phillips believes that, while working with the language of her time, which was influenced by the eighteenth-century predilection for abstraction, Austen still manages to create "a perfect vehicle for her purposes; a style that, like its creator, is still, perhaps, underrated" (15). Similarly, Norman Page's *The Language of Jane Austen* (1972) argues that the "triumph" of Austen's novels is "to a large extent a triumph of style." Austen's "greatness," he observes, "lay in exploiting the distinctive strengths of the English language as she found it, and in resisting some of the influences which were at work to change it" (9). Page circles back over the novels to consider Austen's recurring use of specific words, her careful attention to syntax, her exceptional, almost revolutionary use of dialogue, and even her use of epistolary methods of moving her narrative forward. However, this is no mere catalog of stylistic devices. Page consistently links Austen's methods to her aims, which he finds decidedly moral, although disguised behind a mask of comedy and wit. And while Page suggests that Austen's influence on her immediate successors was not strong, a careful analysis such as his proves she possessed a "dual quality as a traditionalist and innovator" (187).

While books on Austen's style often ignore or minimize the controversy over her view toward society, the question was still on the mind of a number of critics. Nowhere is the reaction against the subversive Jane Austen more clearly and forcefully expressed than in Alistair Duckworth's *The Improvement of the Estate* (1971). Duckworth takes on those who would read Austen as ironic or spiteful, suggesting instead that her fiction presents a consistent portrait of a social and moral order that is essentially good. In his view critics such as Harding, Mudrick, and even Schorer are misguided when they read her fiction as an attack on the social order. The six novels exhibit what he calls a "consistent thematic unity" grounded in Austen's portrayal of "the estate" — which Duckworth interprets not simply literally, but metaphorically as well, suggesting the term means for Austen "society as a whole, a code of morality, a body of manners, a system of language" (ix) which exists to provide a framework in which people can express their individuality in a myriad of acceptable ways as long as they do not cross over the boundaries which circumscribe the system. What is more, he says, the individual is free to help "improve" the "estate," to help others and society as a whole become more genteel and more moral. Reading her novels as outgrowths of the eighteenth-century tradition of providential fiction, Duckworth explains how Austen's heroines are often tested by disruptions in the social order, and how their actions (and their growing awareness of the proper roles of self and society) help restore balance within the social estate. Throughout, he is consistent in asserting that, far from being modern in its critique of the social order, at most "Jane Austen's fiction is intermediate" (25), standing between the faith-based society of the neoclassic age and the *angst*-driven world of the Victorians and moderns (24–25).

Jane Nardin also challenges the stance taken by proponents of the subversive Austen, claiming in *Those Elegant Decorums: The Concept of Propriety in Jane Austen's Novels* (1973) that their interpretation of Austen is too reductive. Austen was not simply a cynic attacking society, Nardin argues, but neither was she the stern moralist other critics have made her out to be. In Nardin's view, "irony and morality are far from being irreconcilable elements in her work." She is "basically an affirmative novelist" who uses irony as the "yardstick by which she measures the adequacy of moral positions in her work" (2). The problem is not with Austen, Nardin says, but with critics who find in her works "a simple, dogmatically endorsed moral code, incompatible with her complex ironic vision" (10). Concentrating on a few key words that Nardin claims have subtly nuanced meanings for Austen, Nardin offers extended readings of individual novels to explain how Austen uses the concept of propriety as a kind of moral touchstone. Austen's greatness, she suggests, lies principally in her ability to offer insight into human nature by establishing relationships between outward behavior and inner character.

Of course, not everyone felt it necessary to take sides in the debate over the purpose of Austen's satire. Lloyd Brown argues in *Bits of Ivory: Narrative Technique in Jane Austen's Fiction* (1973) that many previous critics have erred in attempting to fit her "protean materials" into "one exclusive thesis or another" (3). He promises to do much more, offering readers a detailed examination of seven aspects of her fiction that he claims demonstrate the close alliance between language or form and meaning. But he ends up sounding much like Duckworth and Nardin in his commentary on Austen's style, which he says she viewed as essential to communicating meaning and establishing a moral hierarchy. His detailed analysis of Austen's ironic diction, imagery, parody, and symbolism, as well as her use of conversation, letter-writing, and dialogue are all aimed not simply at noting her technical skill in achieving verisimilitude but also — and more importantly — in molding various literary conventions into forms that contain significant moral truths. Those truths reflect an intellect firmly grounded in the eighteenth century, Brown says, influenced by the great moral philosophers of the age and by literature that supports traditional values in the face of new fads that challenge time-tested precepts about conduct and morality. There is no hint of rebellion in the Austen that Brown presents to readers of his critique of her fiction.

Darrel Mansell's *The Novels of Jane Austen* (1973) seems to steer clear of the controversy over Austen's relationship to her society, focusing instead on her technical abilities to create character, incident, and theme. Mansell is interested primarily in ways Austen manipulates plots and characters to serve a single purpose: to dramatize the heroine's "course of psychological reformation" (ix). Concentrating on this single, overriding theme, Mansell offers extended analyses of the six novels, focusing equally on Austen's techniques for plotting, methods of narration (including irony and indirect discourse), and character development. Austen subordinates everything to the development of her heroine's recognition of "facts" from false impressions about herself or others. "The heroine's consciousness is always the organizing centre" of Austen's novels, and characters, events, even objects are "placed around her primarily for the purpose of defining her" (53). Furthermore, Mansell says, Austen's fiction contains numerous improbabilities — claims for her achievements as a supreme realist notwithstanding — and as she advanced in her career these improbabilities became more prevalent. Austen is a masterful artist, Mansell concludes, sure of the plan she lays out for each of her novels and adept at making all the pieces fit with little wasted effort.

Biographies

As one surveys books about Austen written during this period, however, it soon becomes apparent that concern for explaining technical merits has squeezed out interest in biography. Although a number of articles appeared during the 1950s and 1960s fleshing out the scant details of Austen's life, few full-length biographies were published, and those that did seem to have had little influence on subsequent study of the novelist's life. Kathleen Freeman's biography *T'Other Miss Austen* (1956) adopts the notion popularized by David Cecil of the "two Austens," the dutiful daughter and the consummate artist, but adds a psychological twist. Freeman claims Austen was in a sense possessed by a *daimon* that drove her to write, influencing her relationships with family and friends and shaping her vision of society. Constance Pilgrim's *Dear Jane: A Biographical Study of Jane Austen* (1971) is actually an extended argument attempting to prove that Austen's great novels were all inspired by the secret love of her life, a man she met in the late 1790s who died before the two could ever declare their love publicly. Reading something like a "G-rated" version of studies intended to reveal the identity of Jack the Ripper, *Dear Jane* lays out the case for Austen's liaisons with John Wordsworth, a young naval officer and brother of the poet, who died at sea in 1805. Deftly selecting passages from the fiction and extant letters, Pilgrim weaves a fascinating story of a relationship that she claims inspired many of the characters and incidents in Austen's novels, especially *Persuasion*, which she claims is boldly autobiographical. This kind of sleuthing would certainly appeal to fans of Austen who for two hundred years have been convinced that a young woman of great literary talent must be inspired by a lover. However, lacking any direct evidence, Pilgrim is forced to make her argument on conjecture alone, presenting a scenario not even hinted at by earlier biographers. Serious scholars apparently found her case tenuous; as a consequence, she seems to have been ignored by subsequent biographers.

Jane Aiken Hodge's *The Double Life of Jane Austen* (1972), published in the United States as *Only a Novel: The Double Life of Jane Austen* (1972), seems to have fared a bit better. Like Freeman, Hodge argues that Austen led two lives, one as the dutiful daughter, sister, and middle-class country woman whose life was a model of eighteenth-century values, the second as an author devilishly subversive of these same values. As Hodge acknowledges in her Preface, her book is highly derivative and full of background to situate Jane Austen's life within the context of late Georgian and Regency England during a period that witnessed the rise of the middle class and the minor gentry, of which Austen's family were members. Hodges's aim is to tease out Austen's personality from details in her fiction to supplement what can be known with certainty from her correspondence. She is determined to correct what she sees as the misguided notion that Austen was "a born old maid" (38), or a snob, or — *contra* Charlotte Brontë — that she lacked the ability to write with passion.

Hodge suggests writing was Austen's way of compensating for the demands she faced in the social position into which she was thrust by her position in her family and community. As an author she was able to ignore the restraints placed on her by society. But Hodge also attributes Austen's decision to write for publication to a form of mid-life crisis in which she felt she needed to publish as a means of asserting her self-worth. This kind of guarded speculation appears throughout Hodge's biography. There are glimmers of a feminist perspective throughout Hodge's book, although others writing at the same time would be more direct in reading Austen through the lens of feminism. Nevertheless, *The Double Life of Jane Austen* provided a new generation of fans with a concise appreciation of an author who by now was recognized as not only a proponent but also a keen critic of conservative moral and social values.

Essays and Chapters on Austen

In addition to dozens of books on Austen and her fiction, hundreds of shorter essays appeared in journals and other studies. A sampling provides some indication of the way Austen's fiction was used by critics at mid-century to examine broader literary and social topics. Some of these were designed to reach a large audience, like Dorothy Van Ghent's *The English Novel: Form and Function* (1953). Intended as a textbook and guide for those wishing to understand "eighteen classical novels" (vii), Van Ghent's study includes a lengthy discussion of *Pride and Prejudice*. Approaching it "as a work of art" (viii), Van Ghent examines Austen's style, techniques of characterization, and some of the major themes. Van Ghent finds it necessary to admit that Austen's novels "offer no contiguity with modern interests," but she insists they deserve attention anyway because Austen demonstrates "artistic mastery" of her limited materials (99). Among Van Ghent's more interesting observations — one that certainly looks forward to cultural studies that would follow several decades later — is that the society Austen depicts is dominated by materialist concerns, and that the task of the heroine is to rise above this milieu and seek to establish meaningful personal relationships not based purely on economics.

The Irish writer Frank O'Connor made Austen a centerpiece of his series of lectures at Harvard in 1953–54, publishing his remarks first in the *Yale Review*, then in *The Mirror in the Roadway* (1956). Treating Austen's works as precursors to the modern novel, O'Connor finds she was prescient in composing fiction as she did, since her way and not Scott's became the dominant form of novel-writing in succeeding decades. O'Connor believes Austen "had a fanatically serious approach to the different problems of verisimilitude in fiction" and a "profound respect for the art she practiced" (*Mirror in the Roadway*, 22). Furthermore, she possessed a "formidable critical intelligence" (24), but she had a penchant for establishing distance from her characters through the use of humor and irony. This tendency O'Connor attributes to psychological causes;

she had an innate fear "of the violence of her own emotions" (25), and that fear drove her to become a moralist, subduing imagination to judgment. O'Connor says that is why *Mansfield Park*, a novel high in judgment, is a failure, while novels like *Pride and Prejudice* and *Emma*, where Austen's imagination is allowed some free play, are masterpieces.

Where O'Connor leans toward psychological analysis, Columbia University scholar Douglas Bush calls for study of Austen from a different perspective. Bush points out in "Mrs. Bennet and the Dark Gods: The Truth About Jane Austen" (1956) that anthropological (mythic) critics seemed to have largely ignored her. But Bush says there ought to be such studies, because her work has an "essential affinity with Melville and Kafka" (20). Concentrating on *Pride and Prejudice*, he demonstrates how mythic patterns underlie the social comedy operating on the surface level. Understanding these patterns gives readers an even greater appreciation for Austen's achievement. In fact, Bush says, "the subject of archetypal myth in Jane Austen needs a book," and while he has no plans to provide one, he is certain some other critic will take up the challenge (26).

Meanwhile, more conventional assessments of Austen's novels appeared in great number, including two in Robert Rathburn and Martin Steinman's *From Jane Austen to Joseph Conrad* (1958). In "The Background of *Mansfield Park*" Charles Murrah discusses the setting and other supporting devices in the novel. Alan McKillop's "Critical Realism in *Northanger Abbey*" reads the novel as "the comprehensive result of Jane Austen's early reactions to excesses in prose fiction" within the literary tradition she inherited (35). Another good example of conventional analysis is Leo Kirschbaum's essay on *Pride and Prejudice* in *Twelve Original Essays on Great English Novels* (1960). Influenced by critics such as Trilling, Kirschbaum concentrates on Austen's portrait of characters bound by social conventions and largely dependent on economic forces for their sustenance. He argues that Austen was not blindly supportive of a world she regarded as "frozen into immobility" (85), yet at the same time she seems unwilling to expose fully the complex personalities of her main characters. To do so, Kirschbaum says, would have required Austen to abandon her "polite, general, impersonal style" for "a kind of poetry." But Austen "chose not to be a poet," and hence failed to penetrate into the deepest recesses of her own characters' being (84). In *The Shaping Vision: Imagination in the English Novel from Defoe to Dickens* (1966), Robert Donovan uses techniques of close reading to critique *Mansfield Park*, a work he says others have faulted for its "bald didacticism" (155). Donovan thinks the work has been misread, especially by David Cecil. He insists Austen's examination of individuals and society in this novel is consistent with the critiques she offers in other works.

Representative of the growing sophistication of analyses of Austen's rhetoric, style, and technical ability are four examples selected from dozens published during the 1960s. In his influential book *The Rhetoric of Fiction* (1961), Wayne Booth describes Austen as "one of the unquestionable masters of the rhetoric of narration" (224). In *Emma* she tackles the problem of presenting a heroine who has many potentially dangerous faults but who is at the same time someone with whom Austen wants readers to sympathize. Booth provides a close reading of the text to explain how Austen achieves this balance, creating what he calls the "double vision" of the heroine: "our inside view of Emma's worth and our objective view of her great faults" (256). A second study, Albert Cook's *The Meaning of Fiction* (1960), uses Austen's work to explain how the technical device of irony, particularly irony of statement and dramatic irony, can be employed to reveal the author's meaning. Austen's talents as a stylist are celebrated in Percy Marshall's *Masters of the English Novel* (1962), which describes her ability to create life-like characters. A fourth critique, Philip Waldron's "Style in *Emma*" in John Colmer's *Approaches to the Novel* (1967), continues the line of criticism that emphasizes the close relationship between Austen's style and her moral vision. Waldron's technical discussion of her use of nouns, lack of metaphor and imagery, use of generalization, lack of particularity, and employment of contrast and balance in sentence structure all demonstrate that, to appreciate Austen's novel, it is necessary to have a "precise idea" of what Austen thought was "appropriate, natural, and 'right' in style" (60).

A question of interest to critics since early in the century, whether plot or characterization is the primary driver for creating interest in a novel, continued to engage the attention of Austen scholars. In what may seem like a reversal of received opinion — that Austen's plots are thin but her characterization strong — Charles Walcutt's commentary on Austen's *Pride and Prejudice* in *Man's Changing Mask: Modes and Methods of Characterization* (1966) demonstrates that plot determines characterization. Walcutt believes Austen achieves a perfect balance between plot and character in *Pride and Prejudice*, accepting as given "a society firmly and rock-solidly based on status, manners, education, which in turn all rest on wealth" (72), but at the same time makes clear to readers that achieving happiness and being good involves more than just possessing wealth.

Two studies focusing on Austen as a satirist are representative of ways formalists approached this aspect of Austen's writing. David Demarest's "*Reductio ad Absurdum*: Jane Austen's Art of Satiric Qualification" (1965) suggests that her satire is more complex than earlier critics have noted. Influenced by eighteenth-century satirists, Austen is constantly qualifying her criticism, suggesting that one must be willing to "tolerate and somehow accept the unreason" that warrants censure (53–54). For Austen, "neat logical systems on the one hand and passive amoral acceptance of life on the other are both inadequate responses" to the experiences one confronts in society (68). There is need for a certain irony, of course, in holding positions of judgment and tolerance simultaneously; this is what Demarest finds in Austen's fiction. In a second study of Austen's techniques of satire, Ronald Paulson argues in *Satire and the Novel in Eighteenth-Century England* (1967) that Austen uses satire as a tool for achieving her larger purpose, which is to write about the importance of self-discovery. Paulson offers a fairly detailed analysis of *Pride and Prejudice*, as well as observations on other novels, to show how Austen amalgamates the techniques of Richardson and Fielding. She takes her "concern for conscience and the inner workings of the heroine's mind" from the former, while borrowing the "mode of expression — irony" from the latter. Paulson says that throughout Austen's work satire is sublimated and replaced by a concern for realism. Hers is a new kind of realism, however; it is "a careful description of how society operates" without regard for the larger forces that make society the way it is (306).

At the same time Booth and others were writing about Austen's style and Paulson and Demarest about her satiric techniques, practitioners of humanist criticism were also publishing essays on Austen's fiction. In fact, G. Armour Craig's "Jane Austen's *Emma*: The Truths and Disguises of Human Discourse" is one of fifteen essays in Reuben Brower and Richard Poirier's essay collection *In Defense of Reading* (1962), a book designed to challenge some of the new critical methodologies or ground them in more traditional methods of literary study. Craig provides a reading of *Emma* that takes into account not only the techniques Austen employs to develop her comedy, but also the historical context — in this case, the influence of the Napoleonic wars which, though never mentioned, place "strong pressure" on the "small community" about which Austen writes (238). In the same volume editor Poirier's "Mark Twain, Jane Austen, and the Imagination of Society," offers a thoughtful commentary explaining why Twain had such an aversion to Austen's work. On one level, Poirier admits, Twain (as well as Emerson and Henry James) had an extreme aversion to novels of manners. Yet there is more to the story. These American writers "tend to see a necessary division between a part of us that we express by accommodation to social systems, and another, more admirable" part of human personality that "exists in the imagination only" (284). Austen, on the other hand, saw no such division. Poirier's comparison of Austen's Emma and Twain's Huck Finn is an ingenious exposition of what mainstream critics of the mid-century could produce in ferreting out psychological, social, and moral themes from works of fiction by analyzing literary techniques.

In another humanist reading, Elizabeth Drew links *Emma* with Thackeray's *Vanity Fair* in *The Novel: A Modern Guide to Fifteen English Masterpieces* (1963), calling Austen and Thackeray novelists in "the humanist tradition" (8). In Austen's fiction, what happens *to* characters is not as important as what occurs *in* them. Concerned with exposing the "moral and social design" of *Emma* (103), Drew provides a close reading that explains the importance of Emma's journey toward self-awareness. Christopher Gillie, too, finds Austen's work useful in discussion the role of fiction as a means of allowing readers to experience life. Gillie's premise in *Character in English Literature* (1965) is that literature makes what is initially perceived as alien come to be known and understood through the experience of reading. Discussing *Emma* in a chapter he titles "The Heroine Victim," Gillie suggests Emma's growth toward mature self-knowledge is made evident to readers through her interactions with other characters whose life experiences are quite different from hers.

From time to time philosophers have contributed to the discussion of Austen's achievement. In 1966 Gilbert Ryle published "Jane Austen and the Moralists," a study intended to demonstrate from a philosopher's point of view that Austen was a moralist not simply in the generic sense, but in what Ryle calls "the thick sense." He claims Austen wrote as she did "partly from a deep interest in some perfectly general, even theoretical questions about human nature and human conduct" (*English Literature and British Philosophy*, 168). Constructing his argument along the lines of a philosophical proof, Ryle mines the novels for examples of these concerns, distinguishing between some of the surface moralizing in the tales and the "abstract, ethical themes" that emerge from almost every work (176). Ryle finds the source of Austen's outlook in eighteenth-century moral philosophy, particularly the work of Lord Shaftesbury, whose ideas and vocabulary are mirrored in her fiction.

Interest in Austen's ideas about religion did not stimulate as much discussion during the 1950s and 1960s as they would in succeeding decades, but two studies reveal that the topic did remain of interest to scholars. In *The Novel in the Victorian World* (1967), an examination of the growing importance of religious questions as a subject for novels in the nineteenth century, William Marshall argues that Austen's novels present "a characteristic mixture of traditional Christian value and eighteenth-century rationalism" (49). However, the view of Austen as a Christian moralist is challenged by Laurence Lerner in his provocative and at times iconoclastic *The Truth Tellers* (1967), a study of "the view of man and the moral attitudes that inform the work" of three writers "who compel us to reconsider our view of man" (11). What Austen shares with George Eliot and D. H. Lawrence, he says, is a compulsion to "tell the truth" (83) about life as they see it. Lerner habitually challenges received opinion about Austen as both a thinker and writer, boldly asserting that "Jane Austen the novelist did not believe in God" (23), but was intensely interested in human conduct and values as they exist in the society around her. Her comedies are filled with the stresses caused by conflicts between normative behavior and the individual's growing awareness of right conduct.

The propensity of critics following the lead of the Leavises or the Chicago Humanists to value novels of high seriousness on occasion produced what some might consider skewed assessments of Austen's work. For example, R. S. Crane, leader of the Chicago Humanists during the middle decades of the century, writes in his essay on *Persuasion* in *The Idea of the Humanities* (1967) that despite its comic tones, the novel is "a serious work — serious ethically no less than artistically" (287). Although it has neither a stated moral nor even an overt thesis, Crane says, this "novel of personal relations" (287) is a "serious comedy" (289). Perhaps it was in reaction to criticism such as this that Benjamin Whitten observed in 1974 that, of late, "Jane Austen criticism has tended to be burdened with grave thematic studies that almost entirely ignore the crucial fact that all the novels are comic in intent" (4).

Murray Krieger's commentary on Austen in *The Classic Vision: The Retreat From Extremity* (1971) might seem to give some credence to Crane's observations, however, as he elevates comedy to a level of importance equal to tragedy. Krieger uses the term "classic" as a contrast to "tragic," a concept he explored at length in *The Tragic Vision: Variations on a Theme in Literary Interpretation* (1960). Krieger sees the classic and tragic as two master metaphors describing the work of literary artists. Simply put, he finds the tragic vision emphasizing strong individuality and a determination toward extremes in human behavior, while the classic — some might call it comic — vision stresses a retreat from extremes into the security of community. Predictably, Krieger finds Austen a classic novelist in these terms. In fact, he believes she is one of those who takes the "communal sense too much for granted" (221). His reading of her work exposes the way she forces readers to accept the values of community over individual freedoms. Austen's careful craftsmanship is employed strenuously, he says, to insure that end. Ultimately, Austen's characters express a "diminished sense of serious freedom" (225). Even a character like Elizabeth Bennet in *Pride and Prejudice*, who clearly possesses the "critical intelligence" to recognize the limitations and deficiencies of her world, must ultimately accept its premises and subdue her individual proclivities to social harmony (241).

Krieger's judgment would have been received sympathetically by Lionel Trilling, whose *Sincerity and Authenticity* (1972) explores the changes in what he called "the moral life" of humankind over time (1). Trilling concentrates on what he considers a relatively recent phenomenon — one dating back only four hundred years — the idea of "sincerity," which he defines as "a congruence between avowal and actual feeling" (2). The philosophical ground for Trilling's literary study is a concept borrowed from Hegel, who uses the terms *honest soul* and *disintegrated consciousness* to describe the two kinds of relationships that exist between one's values and actions. Trilling believes Austen is passionately concerned with what he calls "the sentiment of being" (73), a devotion to some noble idea that shapes one's life and drives one's behavior. He finds in *Mansfield Park* the best example of Austen's depiction of that commitment to noble ideals. Fanny Price is Austen's most noble heroine because she searches for what is categorically noble, not succumbing to some form of dialectic to determine what is relatively best. Some readers are put off by the novel, Trilling admits, because they balk at "its impercipient and restrictive moralism, its partisanship with duty and dullness, its crass respectability." Actually, he says the novel is an "affront" to "an essential disposition of the modern mind" with its tendency toward "the dialectical mode of apprehending reality" (79). The process of education for the heroine, in this and in other Austen novels, is toward discovering categorical truths about love and life.

Malcolm Bradbury admits in *Possibilities: Essays on the State of the Novel* (1973) that he, too, is interested to an extent in the cultural and social dimensions of fiction, but insists that what is "essential to criticism" (ix) is the "reading of individual texts and the consideration of larger questions of structure and style" (x) that permit comparison of works. Bradbury insists that Austen's novels are "verbal constructs" (57), consciously made to create an illusion of reality. Her job, as Bradbury sees it, is "to create and complexly to connect a society and a moral life" (57). What he finds particularly impressive is Austen's ability to create very different people within the confines of the limited society she depicts. A study contemporaneous with Bradbury's that explains how Austen manages to exhibit her creative talents in such confined space is John Halperin's *The Language of Meditation* (1973). Halperin examines what he calls "meditation scenes" in novels by Austen, Eliot, Meredith, and James. Arguing that this scene, which presents a moment in which the heroine becomes aware of her true relationship to a man with whom she is romantically involved, reveals to readers something "about the novel in which it appears and about the author who wrote it" (10). In Austen's novels, when considering carefully the interplay between the heroine's perception and that of the omniscient narrator, one glimpses the epistemological process at work. As the heroine comes to see how her imagination has led to misperceptions of herself and others, she develops a better appreciation for both. The conclusion is clear: to achieve maturity and attain real happiness Austen's heroines must subordinate their imagination to "empirical data" (47). For Halperin, Austen is always insistent on the subordination of the imagination to logic.

The continuing divergence of opinion regarding Austen's contribution to the development of the novel can be seen by juxtaposing two studies published in the 1970s. Ioan Williams asserts in *The Realist Novel in England: A Study in Development* (1974) that, despite Austen's conservatism, which kept her from understanding new ideas about reality and human relationships being explored by her contemporaries, the Romantics, she had an important place in the development of the realist novel, being "nothing short of revolutionary" in transforming both subject and treatment, bringing the novel "down to the scale of actuality" (12). By contrast, in *English Comedy: Its Role and Nature from Chaucer to the Present* (1975) Allan Rodway has a decidedly less grandiose notion of Austen's importance. Writing about the nature of Austen's comedy, he notes with some apprehension her tendency toward didacticism, prompted he thinks by her dependence on "the acceptance of social patterns" as givens for judging the behavior of her characters (186). Rodway considers her a minor comic writer, technically talented but less cosmic in her reach and less condemning of those who violate social norms than the great comic geniuses of the past.

Casebooks and Essay Collections

Taking advantage of Austen's growing popularity as a featured novelist in high school and college courses, in the 1960s publishers of educational texts all over the globe began issuing handbooks and study guides to Austen's work. Indian students pursuing university degrees could find help in preparing for examinations in works such as B. R. Mullik's *Jane Austen* (1957) and *Jane Austen's 'Emma'* (1960) in the Critical Studies for M.A. and B.A. Students of English Literature in Indian Universities series. Hulton Educational Publications produced a series of guides for British students. Typical of these books is Sidney Farrar's brief *Jane Austen: "Northanger Abbey"* (1962), which informs students that "the real study of a good novel will increase the reader's knowledge of his fellow men and his understanding of their nature" (1). Farrar sketches Austen's career, describes the writing and publication of *Northanger Abbey*, surveys characters that appear in the book, provides a synopsis of the plot, prints selected passages that students can use to test their memory of the text, and lists twenty sample examination questions — all in fewer than sixty pages. Like Farrar's book, Jack Dalglish's *"Pride and Prejudice": Jane Austen* (1962) presents a sketch of Austen's life, comments on style, plotting, and characterization, and offers a more detailed analysis of a single chapter of the novel. His attitude regarding Austen is made clear at the outset: "Jane Austen is a great English novelist," he says, because in her work the novel is used to "explore and expose human relationships and situations significantly" (3). Her supposed limitations should not deter students from appreciating the highly moral nature of her fiction because she is someone who can teach us about life. Similarly, K. M. Lobb's volume on *Pride and Prejudice* (1962), part of another series designed to prepare British students for examinations on Austen's work, provides a brief summary of Austen's life, commentary on the novel, and sample examination questions. Lobb is even more detailed in describing Austen's limitations, but like Dalglish he insists that within them she is "almost un-equalled"; she is a "great English novelist" and a master of satire (4).

During the 1960s and 1970s publishers also began to profit from the growing interest in Austen by issuing collections of previously published work about the novelist and her fiction. William Heath's *Discussions of Jane Austen* (1961) collects critical commentary beginning with the novelist's correspondence with J. S. Clarke, the Prince Regent's librarian, and in-cludes excerpts from reviews by Scott and Whately, Charlotte Brontë's deprecatory judgment, Reginald Farrer's revaluation, and a dozen twen-tieth-century assessments. Ian Watt's *Jane Austen: A Collection of Critical Essays* (1963) in Prentice-Hall's Twentieth Century Views series brings together essays by noted and influential Austen critics, among them Vir-ginia Woolf, Edmund Wilson, Rueben Brower, Marvin Mudrick, Mark Schorer, Arnold Kettle, Lionel Trilling, and D. W. Harding. The volume on *Pride and Prejudice* in Prentice-Hall's Twentieth-Century Interpreta-tions series, edited by Elliot Rubenstein and issued in 1969, includes ten essays or excerpts from longer studies by influential scholars like Dorothy Van Ghent, Brower, Walton Litz, Mary Lascelles, and Andrew Wright.

A slightly different type of collection, Brian Southam's 1968 *Critical Essays on Jane Austen* brings together work by a number of important writers — some Austen specialists, others not — to examine topics that seem broader than ones typically considered by critics interested princi-pally in Austen's technical achievements. The editor deserves some special mention, too. If R. W. Chapman was the most influential Austen scholar of the first half of the twentieth century, Southam has some right to claim that distinction for the second half (although it might be argued that he should share the distinction with Deirdre Le Faye). His first book, *Jane Austen's Literary Manuscripts* (1964), immediately won acclaim from Austen scholars for its meticulous attention to the novelist's existing manuscripts and for the critical commentary that introduces them. Even before this book appeared, Southam had shown his bravado by taking on the doyen of Austen critics at Cambridge, Q. D. Leavis, in "Mrs. Leavis and Miss Austen: The 'Critical Theory' Reconsidered" (1963), an article that challenges Leavis's assumptions about the composition of *Mansfield Park* and *Pride and Prejudice*. Southam suggests that, *contra* Leavis, there is decidedly less correspondence between the novelist's life and the figures she presents in her fiction. More than forty years later in 2001, Southam would bring out a new edition of *Jane Austen's Literary Manuscripts* and include a revised version of his 1963 essay as an appendix. In some ways, however, Southam reveals his own critical bias in the introduction to *Critical Essays on Jane Austen*. While acknowledging Austen's mastery of form, he expresses some annoyance at her self-imposed limitations in sub-ject — but at the same time suggests she has much to offer readers in her concerns with moral issues.

Typical of the guidebooks published during this time are those by F. B. Pinion and Christopher Gillie. Pinion's *A Jane Austen Companion* (1973) provides plot summaries of the major and minor fiction, a brief biography, and a useful glossary of people and places that appear in Austen's work. Pinion's brief critical commentaries seem influenced by a rather Arnoldian take on Austen's achievements. The "most significant characteristic" of Austen's fiction, Pinion says in the preface, "is her insistence on the fallibility of judgment in human relationships." Tracing that theme throughout her novels, Pinion suggests it is "a key to much in Jane Austen's art and its appreciation by the reader" (xii). Christopher Gillie's *Preface to Jane Austen* (1974) in the Longman Prefaces to Literature series gives students (and many scholars as well) background helpful in gaining a greater appreciation of Austen's work. Though traditionalist in his own approach, Gillie highlights important changes in critics' views of Austen during the nineteenth and twentieth centuries. He suggests that, over time, the original image of "Jane Austen the tranquillizer for the overstressed" has been replaced by (in the words of Laurence Lerner's 1972 study) "Jane Austen the 'truth teller'" (ix). Gillie believes Austen has been influential in forming the "modern consciousness" (xii), which he describes as an alert awareness of the self.

Harbingers of Change

The foregoing discussion emphasizes the mainstream of Austen criticism during the middle decades of the century. Toward the end of the 1960s, however, there were signs that critics of Austen's work, influenced by emerging political and social trends that were reshaping ways of looking at literary works, were beginning to shift their approach. For example, in his 1969 Clark Lectures at Trinity College, Cambridge (published the following year as *George Meredith and English Comedy*), V. S. Pritchett challenges one of the heretofore sacrosanct notions about Austen's work: that it is somehow timeless because it is not linked to her age. Pritchett recognizes that "our perfect novelist of comedy, Jane Austen, is often presented as an example of the felicity of living in a small, cosy [*sic*] world, with one's mind firmly withdrawn from the horror outside." He believes nothing could be farther from the truth. "I think of her as a war-novelist, formed very much by the Napoleonic wars, knowing directly of prize money, the shortage of men, the economic crisis and the change in value of capital" (28). From Pritchett is it but a small step to the New Historicists and cultural critics who would revise significantly notions of Austen as a cheery novelist of manners or an artist divorced from the age in which she lived and wrote.

Similar revisionist thinking was going on about Austen's portraits of women, especially their ability to negotiate their way in a male-dominated society. Of course, it was not uncommon as late as the 1960s to run across comments like those of W. L. Renwick in *English Literature 1789–1815* (1963) that Austen refrained from dwelling on male characters because she wished to be considered a lady, and "ladies do not intrude on the privacy of gentlemen" (91). Sylvia Myers leans a bit more toward the feminist camp in her brief but provocative "Womanhood in Jane Austen's Novels" (1969). But one of the first truly different judgments of Austen is offered by Hazel Mews in *Frail Vessels: Woman's Role in Women's Novels* (1969), an early feminist assessment of women's fiction. Mews approaches Austen's work with what appears to be mixed feelings. She was "far from revolutionary," Mews admits, but she was also far from being the demure lady who shied away from controversy. Detailed portraits of men are not important to Austen because her chief reasons for writing have little to do with how men act and feel. Her heroines develop and embody both self-awareness and self-discipline, making them admirable in themselves even if they do not seem willing to break more radically from the chains of the patriarchy.

Patricia Beer's comments on Austen in *Reader, I Married Him* (1974) also reflect a change in direction for critical analysis of her fiction. Beer examines Austen's novels as part of a longer study of ways "women and their situation" were portrayed by women writers in nineteenth-century English novels (ix). As a reader of novels, Beer enjoys Austen immensely. But as a feminist, she finds Austen wanting. Her women are all bent on marriage, Beer observes, and it seems to her that Austen is satisfied with the limited options available to women in her society. From time to time, Beer says, there are "hints" that Austen is "dissatisfied with the traditional status of women" (46), but the novelist undercuts any truly revolutionary actions on the part of her heroines. "As far as the Woman Question is concerned," Beer says, "Austen could well be described as a latent socialist who helps to make capitalism work" (46). The heroines fight their battles alone, without any true community of sisters to aid them. Fortunately, they seldom get into any real difficulties, as Austen avoids serious issues like childbirth (and its high mortality rate) and even rape. Beer concludes — with what seems like a note of disappointment — that there is no outright "conflict between Jane Austen's ideals for women and her basic acceptance of a male-dominated society," only "some sort of stress and ambivalence" that readers — especially those sympathetic to feminist causes — "must enjoy without asking for more" (82–83).

Another important shift in methodology can be seen in the work of David Lodge, one of the first English critics to stress the importance of new critical theories as a means of understanding Austen. The first half of his *Language of Fiction: Essays in Criticism and Verbal Analysis of the English Novel* (1966) is a lengthy analysis of "important issues concerning the nature of literature and the principles of criticism" (ix). Against the backdrop of this extensive review of theoretical principles on which criticism is based, Lodge undertakes an examination of a handful of works, including *Mansfield Park*, traditionally considered the most enigmatic of Austen's novels. His careful explication reveals how Austen uses language to manipulate readers "to endorse a system of values with which we have no real sympathy at all" (95). Austen gets readers to accept what is clearly a rather rigid moral code by applying values (negative or positive) to certain words, then associating those words with characters whose behavior leads us to make judgments about them. By eventually siding with some figures and rejecting others, readers end up in the paradoxical position of supporting a code of behavior and morality that, on its surface, seems much too stultifying when considered in the abstract. Lodge's approach foreshadows the work of narratologists and even hints at the importance that deconstructionists place on the indeterminacy of meaning.

New methodologies for providing close textual readings also characterize Stuart Tave's *Some Words of Jane Austen* (1973), a book intended to say "a few central things" about Austen by taking "a few of her words" and extrapolating to develop an understanding of "the meaning and definition of her world" (xi). Concentrating on Austen's heroines, Tave explains how she uses language that is at once precise and allusive to shape her characters and reveal her own value system. He makes a virtue of the novelist's limitations, insisting that "the more valuable way to approach her novels is not through the list of all the mighty matters and all the odd corners that she omits" (33). The "world" she presents her readers is "full," Tave insists, and it "has all the parts it needs and all of them are fully given to use as far as they are needed" (34). Her supposedly simple stories are actually clear portraits of "the actions of men and women in common life." Her novels are essentially similar because she has managed to deal with issues that transcend time and instead concentrate on matters essential to men and women in any social setting. "In that sense," Tave says, "hers is a timeless world, where life repeats and renews itself in each well-lived individual life" (34).

Like the work of Lodge and Tave, Joseph Kestner's *Jane Austen: Spatial Structure of Thematic Variations* (1974) pushes the boundaries of conventional critical analysis. Kestner's book is one of the earliest extended studies of Austen's fiction to pay homage to European theorists whose work would influence the course of literary criticism, especially in America, in the last three decades of the twentieth century. Kestner explains in his introduction that he relies on the aesthetic criticism of Georges Poulet, Paul de Man, and Tzvetan Todorov in creating what he calls a "special reading" (2) of Austen's novels. His aim is to understand each novel as a "single spatial unit" (3). To do so he examines six recurring themes: "improvement," "intimacy," "concealment," "imagination," "silence," and "shyness" (4). However, once Kestner gets past his own theoretical introduction, he becomes increasingly more interested in demonstrating how Austen's solves the "problem of reconciling matter (diversity) and form (unity) in a single organic whole, the novel" (5). Kestner's reliance on important Continental thinkers to underpin his approach and judgments is indicative of the trend in Austen criticism toward the use of new critical theories to interpret her fiction.

An even more intriguing commentary on the possibility for new directions in critical inquiry is offered by Karl Kroeber in *Styles in Fictional Structure* (1971), a work that is at once a summation of mid-century formalist technique and a signal of what was on the critical horizon. Krober examines ways "strictly aesthetic systems" provide "coherence to the development of a particular kind of work of art" — fiction (4). Krober uses Austen's novels, along with those of Charlotte Brontë and George Eliot, as evidence in larger discussions about the way words, imagery, point of view, narrative, and dialogue function as devices for distinguishing one novelist's work from another, and for tracing influence from earlier to later writers. The "chief quality" of Austen's language, Kroeber says, is its "transparency"; "it works to clarify the obscure," he says, "which often involves the revelation of complexities within apparent simple relationships" (79). What is important about Austen for Kroeber may be lost on his readers, however, because she is but a means to a larger end. Kroeber's real aim is to provide a new mode of critical analysis, built along the lines adopted by his colleagues in the sciences, who routinely set forth their work as interim steps toward understanding large, complex theories about the way the world works. By contrast, Kroeber admits somewhat dejectedly, modern literary criticism is simply "separatist, egocentric, and committed to perfection" (181–82). What he wants to see is a movement among literary critics that promotes cooperative ventures, honest exploration, and some real humility in recognizing that their conclusions could be wrong. To date, however, Kroeber's suggestions seem to have had little impact on the way we do our business in the academic world of literary studies.

The change in direction hinted at by the critics cited above was a signal that the older order of critical inquiry was passing, as a new generation of readers and critics began to appropriate Austen for their own uses. That trend is lamented by one of Austen's strongest supporters of the first half of the century, the American cultural critic Lionel Trilling. In the posthumously published "Why We Read Jane Austen" (1976), Trilling considers the impact that reading Jane Austen has on students in the 1970s. Over the years, Trilling says, he has observed the change in her reputation. Originally celebrated as "dear Jane" by people Trilling is sure Austen would have despised, she now seems to have "been delivered from their deplorable adulation" into "the charge of scholars and critics of the most enlightened and energetic kind" (206). The irony in his tone is intentional, because what he has discovered is that students in his own classes enjoy reading Austen — but not for the reasons contemporary scholars think they should. Instead, they tend to express an interest in her work similar to that exhibited by anthropologists examining other cultures.

Notes

[1] Not everyone was so evenhanded in judging Mudrick's contributions. Some of the comments about his treatment of Austen border on the vitriolic. His status among Austen scholars may have been summed up best by Judith Wilt, who refers to him in her 1981 essay "Jane Austen's Men: Inside/Outside 'The Mystery'" as "the Black Knight of Austen criticism" (70).

Works Cited

Allen, Walter. *The English Novel: A Short Critical History*, 113–26. New York: E. P. Dutton, 1954.

Babb, Howard S. "Dialogue with Feeling: A Note on *Pride and Prejudice*." *Kenyon Review* 20 (1958): 203–16.

———. *Jane Austen's Novels: The Fabric of Dialogue*. Columbus: Ohio State UP, 1962.

Beer, Patricia. *Reader, I Married Him*, 45–83. London: Macmillan; New York: Barnes & Noble, 1974.

Booth, Wayne. "Point of View and Control of Distance in *Emma*." *The Rhetoric of Fiction*, 243–66. Chicago: U of Chicago P, 1961.

Bradbrook, Frank W. *Jane Austen and Her Predecessors*. Cambridge: Cambridge UP, 1966.

Bradbury, Malcolm. "Persuasions: Moral Comedy in *Emma* and *Persuasion*." *Possibilities: Essays on the State of the Novel*, 55–78. London: Oxford UP, 1973.

Brown, Lloyd W. *Bits of Ivory: Narrative Techniques in Jane Austen's Fiction*. Baton Rouge: Louisiana State UP, 1973.

Bush, Douglas. "Mrs. Bennet and the Dark Gods: The Truth about Jane Austen." *Sewanee Review* 64 (1956): 591–96. Reprinted in *Engaged and Disengaged*, 20–26. Cambridge, MA: Harvard UP, 1966.

Cook, Albert. "Modes of Irony: Jane Austen and Stendhal." *The Meaning of Fiction*, 38–63. Detroit: Wayne State UP, 1960.

Craig, G. Armour. "Jane Austen's *Emma*: The Truths and Disguises of Human Discourse." In *In Defense of Reading: A Reader's Approach to Literary Criticism*, edited by R. A. Brower and Richard Poirier, 235–55. New York: E. P. Dutton, 1962.

Craik, Wendy Ann. *Jane Austen in Her Time*. London: Thomas Nelson & Sons; New York: New York UP, 1969.

———. *Jane Austen: The Six Novels*. London: Methuen; New York: Barnes & Noble, 1965.

Crane, Ronald S. "Jane Austen: *Persuasion*." *The Idea of the Humanities and Other Essays Critical and Historical*, 2:283–302. Chicago and London: U of Chicago P, 1967.

Daiches, David. *A Critical History of English Literature*, 3:743–65. London: Secker & Warburg, 1960.

Dalglish, Jack. "*Pride and Prejudice*": *Jane Austen*. Notes on English Literature. Oxford: Basil Blackwell, 1962.

Demarest, David P., Jr. "*Reductio ad Absurdum*: Jane Austen's Art of Satiric Qualification." *Six Satirists*. Carnegie Series in English, No. 9, 51–68. Pittsburgh: Carnegie Institute of Technology, 1965.

Donovan, Robert A. "*Mansfield Park* and Jane Austen's Moral Universe." *The Shaping Vision: Imagination in the English Novel from Defoe to Dickens*, 140–72. Ithaca, NY: Cornell UP, 1966.

Drew, Elizabeth. *The Novel: A Modern Guide to Fifteen English Masterpieces*, 95–110. New York: Dell, 1963.

Duckworth, Alistair. *The Improvement of the Estate: A Study of Jane Austen's Novels*. Baltimore and London: Johns Hopkins UP, 1971.

Farrar, Sidney. *Jane Austen: "Northanger Abbey."* Guides to English Literature. London: Hulton Educational Publications, 1962.

Fleishman, Avrom. *A Reading of "Mansfield Park": An Essay in Critical Synthesis*. Minneapolis: U of Minnesota P, 1967.

Freeman, Kathleen. *T'Other Miss Austen*. London: Macdonald, 1956.

Gillie, Christopher. "The Heroine Victim." In *Character in English Literature*, 117–24. London: Chatto & Windus, 1965.

———. *A Preface to Jane Austen*. London: Longman, 1974.

Gooneratne, Yasmine. *Jane Austen*. Cambridge: Cambridge UP, 1970.

Halperin, John. *The Language of Meditation: Four Studies in Nineteenth-Century Fiction*, 19–50. Ilfracombe, England: Stockwell, 1973.

Heath, William, ed. *Discussions of Jane Austen*. Boston: D. C. Heath, 1961.

Hodge, Jane Aiken. *The Double Life of Jane Austen*. London: Hodder & Stoughton, 1972. Issued as *Only a Novel: The Double Life of Jane Austen*. New York: Coward, McCann & Geoghegan, 1972.

Karl, Frederick R. *An Age of Fiction: The Nineteenth Century British Novel*. New York: Noonday Press, 1964. Reprinted as *A Reader's Guide to the Nineteenth-Century British Novel*. New York: Octagon, 1972.

Kennedy, Margaret. *Jane Austen.* London: Arthur Baker, 1950.

Kestner, Joseph. *Jane Austen: Spatial Structure of Thematic Variations.* Salzburg: Institut für Englische Sprache und Literatur, 1974.

Kettle, Arnold. *An Introduction to the English Novel,* 1:90–104. London: Hutchinson's University Library, 1951.

Kirschbaum, Leo. "The World of *Pride and Prejudice.*" In *Twelve Original Essays on Great English Novels,* edited by Charles Shapiro, 69–85. Detroit: Wayne State UP, 1960.

Krieger, Murray. *The Classic Vision: The Retreat from Extremity in Modern Literature,* 221–43. Baltimore and London: Johns Hopkins UP, 1971.

———. *The Tragic Vision: Variations on a Theme in Literary Interpretation.* New York: Holt, Rinehart, Winston, 1960.

Kroeber, Karl. *Styles in Fictional Structure: The Art of Jane Austen, Charlotte Brontë and George Eliot.* Princeton, NJ: Princeton UP, 1971.

Leavis, F. R. *The Great Tradition: George Eliot, Henry James, Joseph Conrad.* London: Chatto & Windus, 1948.

Lerner, Laurence. *The Truthtellers: Jane Austen, George Eliot, D. H. Lawrence.* London: Chatto & Windus; New York: Schocken Books, 1967.

Liddell, Robert. *The Novels of Jane Austen.* London: Longmans, Green, 1963.

Litz, A. Walton. *Jane Austen: A Study of Her Artistic Development.* London: Chatto & Windus; New York: Oxford UP, 1965.

Lobb, Kenneth M. *Jane Austen: "Pride and Prejudice."* Guides to English Literature. London: Hulton Educational Publications, 1962.

Lodge, David. *Language of Fiction: Essays in Criticism and Verbal Analysis of the English Novel,* 94–113. London: Routledge & Kegan Paul; New York: Columbia UP, 1966.

Mansell, Darrel. *The Novels of Jane Austen: An Interpretation.* London: Macmillan, 1973.

Marshall, Percy. *Masters of the English Novel.* London: Dennis Dobson, 1962.

Marshall, William H. *The World of the Victorian Novel,* 37–72. New York: A. S. Barnes; London: Thomas Yoseloff, 1967.

McKillop, Alan D. "Critical Realism in *Northanger Abbey.*" In *From Jane Austen to Joseph Conrad,* edited by Robert Rathburn and Martin Steinman, 35–45. Minneapolis: U of Minnesota P, 1958.

Mews, Hazel. *Frail Vessels: Woman's Role in Women's Novels from Fanny Burney to George Eliot.* London: Athlone Press, 1969.

Moler, Kenneth L. *Jane Austen's Art of Allusion.* Lincoln: U of Nebraska P, 1968.

Mudrick, Marvin. *Jane Austen: Irony as Defense and Discovery.* Princeton, NJ: Princeton UP, 1952.

Mullik, B. R. *Jane Austen.* Studies in Novelists for M.A. and B.A. Students of English Literature in Indian Universities, 2. New Delhi: S. Chand & Co., 1957.

———. *Jane Austen's "Emma."* Critical Studies for M.A. & B.A. Students of English Literature in Indian Universities, 14. New Delhi: S. Chand & Co., 1960.

Murrah, Charles. "The Background of *Mansfield Park.*" In *From Jane Austen to Joseph Conrad,* edited by Robert Rathburn and Martin Steinman, 23–34. Minneapolis: U of Minnesota P, 1958.

Myers, Sylvia H. "Womanhood in Jane Austen's Novels." *Novel* 3 (1969–70): 225–32.

Nardin, Jane. *Those Elegant Decorums: The Concept of Propriety in Jane Austen's Novels.* Albany: State U of New York P, 1973.

Neill, S. Diana. *A Short History of the English Novel.* London: Jarrolds, 1951; New York: Macmillan, 1952. Rev. ed., New York: Collier; London: Collier-Macmillan, 1964.

O'Connor, Frank [Michael Donovan]. "Jane Austen and the Flight from Fancy." *Yale Review* 45 (1955–56): 31–47. Reprinted in *The Mirror in the Roadway,* 17–41. New York: Knopf, 1956.

Page, Norman. *The Language of Jane Austen.* Oxford: Basil Blackwell, 1972.

Paulson, Ronald. *Satire and the Novel in Eighteenth-Century England,* 291–306. New Haven and London: Yale UP, 1967.

Phillips, Kenneth C. *Jane Austen's English.* London: Deutsch, 1970.

Pilgrim, Constance. *Dear Jane: A Biographical Study of Jane Austen.* London: William Kimber, 1971.

Pinion, F. B. *A Jane Austen Companion: A Critical Survey and Reference Book.* London: Macmillan, 1973.

Poirier, Richard. "Mark Twain, Jane Austen, and the Imagination of Society." In *In Defense of Reading: A Reader's Approach to Literary Criticism,* edited by R. A. Brower and Richard Poirier, 282–309. New York: E. P. Dutton, 1962.

Pritchett, V. S. *George Meredith and English Comedy.* London: Chatto & Windus; New York: Random House, 1970.

Rathburn, Robert, and Martin Steinman, eds. *From Jane Austen to Joseph Conrad.* Minneapolis: U of Minnesota P, 1958.

Renwick, William L. *English Literature, 1789–1815.* Vol. 9 of *The Oxford History of English Literature,* edited by F. P. Wilson and Bonamy Dobrée, 89–100. Oxford: Clarendon Press, 1963.

Rodway, Allan. *English Comedy: Its Role and Nature from Chaucer to the Present Day*, 182–201. London: Chatto & Windus, 1975.

Rubenstein, Elliot L., ed. *Twentieth Century Interpretations of "Pride and Prejudice": A Collection of Critical Essays*. Englewood Cliffs, NJ: Prentice-Hall, 1969.

Rubinstein, Annette T. "Jane Austen." *The Great Tradition in English Literature from Shakespeare to Shaw*, 1:328–74. New York: Citadel Press, 1953.

Ryle, Gilbert. "Jane Austen and the Moralists." *Oxford Review* 1 (1966): 5–18. Reprinted in *English Literature and British Philosophy: A Collection of Essays*, edited by S. P. Rosenbaum, 168–84. Chicago: U of Chicago P, 1971.

Schorer, Mark. "Fiction and the 'Matrix of Analogy.'" *Kenyon Review* 11 (1949): 539–60.

———. "The Humiliation of Emma Woodhouse." *Literary Review* 2 (1959): 547–63. Reprinted in *The World We Imagine: Selected Essays*. New York: Farrar, Straus, & Giroux, 1969.

———. "Pride Unprejudiced." *Kenyon Review* 19 (1956): 72–91.

Sherry, Norman. *Jane Austen*. With preface by Kenneth Gross. Literature in Perspective Series. London: Evans Brothers, 1966.

Southam, B. C. *Jane Austen's Literary Manuscripts: A Study of the Novelist's Development Through the Surviving Papers*. London: Oxford UP, 1964. Rev. ed., London: Athlone, 2004.

———. "Mrs. Leavis and Miss Austen: The 'Critical Theory' Reconsidered." *Nineteenth-Century Fiction* 17 (1962–63): 21–32.

———, ed. *Critical Essays on Jane Austen*. London: Routledge & Kegan Paul, 1968; New York: Barnes & Noble, 1969.

Steeves, Harrison Ross. *Before Jane Austen: The Shaping of the English Novel in the Eighteenth Century*. New York: Holt, Rinehart, & Winston, 1965; London: Allen & Unwin, 1965.

Stevenson, Lionel. *The English Novel: A Panorama*, 185–93. Boston: Houghton Mifflin; London: Constable, 1960.

Tave, Stuart M. *Some Words of Jane Austen*. Chicago and London: U of Chicago P, 1973.

Ten Harmsel, Henrietta. *Jane Austen: A Study in Fictional Conventions*. The Hague: Mouton, 1964.

Trilling, Lionel. "*Emma*." *Encounter* 8.6 (June 1957): 49–59. Reprinted in *Beyond Culture: Essays on Literature and Learning*. New York: Viking, 1965.

———. *Sincerity and Authenticity*, 72–83. London: Oxford UP; Cambridge, MA: Harvard UP, 1972.

————. "Why We Read Jane Austen." *TLS* 5 (March 1976): 250–52. Reprinted in *The Last Decade: Essays and Reviews 1965–1975*, edited by Diana Trilling, 204–25. New York: Harcourt Brace Jovanovich, 1979.

Van Ghent, Dorothy. *The English Novel: Form and Function*, 99–112, 346–59. New York: Holt, Rinehart & Winston, 1953.

Walcutt, Charles C. "Jane Austen's Minuet: *Pride and Prejudice.*" *Man's Changing Mask: Modes and Methods of Characterization in Fiction*, 71–90. Minneapolis: U of Minnesota P, 1966.

Waldron, Philip. "Style in *Emma.*" *Approaches to the Novel*, edited by John Colmer, 59–70. Edinburgh: Oliver & Boyd, 1967.

Warner, Sylvia Townsend. *Jane Austen*. Writers and Their Work Series. London: Longmans, 1951. Rev. ed., London: Longmans, 1957.

Watt, Ian, ed. *Jane Austen: A Collection of Critical Essays.* Twentieth Century Views. Englewood Cliffs, NJ: Prentice-Hall, 1963.

Whitten, Benjamin. *Jane Austen's Comedy of Feeling: A Critical Analysis of "Persuasion."* Ankara: Hacettepe UP, 1974.

Wiesenfarth, Joseph. *The Errand of Form: An Assay of Jane Austen's Art.* New York: Fordham UP, 1967.

Williams, Ioan. "The Novels of Jane Austen: Conservatism and Innovation." *The Realist Novel in England: A Study in Development*, 12–24. London: Macmillan, 1974.

Wilt, Judith. "Jane Austen's Men: Inside/Outside 'The Mystery.'" In *Men by Women*, edited by Janet Todd, 59–76. New York: Holmes & Meier, 1981.

Wright, Andrew H. *Jane Austen's Novels: A Study in Structure.* London: Chatto & Windus, 1953.

4: The Austen Bicentenary, 1975 (and Beyond)

B Y 1975, THE TWO HUNDREDTH ANNIVERSARY of her birth, Austen had become a major figure in the canon of English literature. As one might expect, the bicentennial was a time of great activity among critics. Individual articles, special issues of journals, and several books appeared offering new readings of individual works, assessments of Austen's reputation, and speculations about the future of Austen studies. Most significantly, though, one can see in work published coincident with the bicentenary that the division over Austen's politics that had begun during the 1930s had become the principal focus of critics by this time. A quick review of commentary published in 1975 shows that Austen continued to be celebrated as both a conservator of traditional values and a champion of subversive causes. Before turning to a more detailed examination of ways those applying new theoretical models of criticism effected a radical revisioning of Austen's fiction, the bicentennial seems a good place to pause to get a snapshot of the critical landscape as new critical methods began to replace more time-honored ones.

Anniversary Collections

In 1975 the critical landscape was inundated with anniversary collections. John Halperin, emerging as a new voice in Austen studies, served as editor of the Cambridge University Press volume *Jane Austen: Bicentenary Essays*. The contributors' list reads like a Who's Who in twentieth-century Austen studies. Essays prepared especially for this volume provide a snapshot of the state of Austen criticism — from one point of view. All share in the belief that Austen was a consummate artist, a supporter of Tory values, and a believer in the rights of women *within* the confines of the society of her time. Though it appeared a year later, Juliet McMaster's *Jane Austen's Achievement* (1976), a collection of papers from a bicentennial conference, is similar to Halperin's book in that contributors celebrate the novelist's "keen intellect, significant vision, and impeccable artistry" (xiii). In most instances, critics such as Walton Litz, Barbara Hardy, Lloyd Brown, and Alistair Duckworth work the same critical vein they mined in other studies. A clever entry by George Whalley on Austen as poet — both literally and metaphorically — provides some inkling of new approaches to her work, but the preponderance of the collection supports both technical and ideological assumptions developed and largely accepted during the earlier decades of the century.

Both the journals *Studies in the Novel* and *Nineteenth Century Fiction* produced special numbers devoted to Austen. The ten essays in *Studies in the Novel* explicate individual works or discuss important matters of background, such as the role of charity or the place of the gentry in Austen's fiction, and summarize the history of Austen criticism during the past century. *Nineteenth Century Fiction*'s celebratory issue is an eclectic collection in which some essayists explore topics already well covered (manners, morals, heroines), while others focus on specific novels (although only four of the six major works are discussed in detail). A few provide fresh interpretations based on emerging new theories of literature and reading. The concluding essay provides insight into the motives of some of Austen's detractors and suggests why people like D. H. Lawrence and H. W. Garrod are misguided in their criticisms of her. If there is a unifying thread to these works, editor Alexander Welsh says, it lies in the essayists' common interest in challenging the notion that Austen presents a "stable, unhistorical vision of society." The trend of recent criticism, including the contributions to this volume, is to explore "the seams and edges of Austen's fabric" (*NCF*, 253).

Hoping to examine those seams and edges more closely, contributors to Joel Weinsheimer's *Jane Austen Today* (1975) confront "the fundamental problem of assessing Jane Austen's achievement," which Weinsheimer says involves "an examination of both the novels themselves and the methods of interpretation and evaluations we apply to them" (viii). Thus a traditionalist like Duckworth takes on implications for Austen studies of deconstruction and other theories emerging from France, while Juliet McMaster remains grounded in traditional modes of viewing Austen's work in her essay on Austen as a didactic novelist. Every essayist demonstrates a keen awareness of what has already been said about Austen, and displays exceptional skill in evaluating the merits of received opinion in the hopes of charting — or at least glimpsing — the future direction of Austen studies.

Even *The Wordsworth Circle* participated in the celebration, although its contribution did not appear until Fall 1976. In a special issue on Austen, essayists concentrate on what guest editor Gene Ruoff calls the "neglected issue" of Austen's place in literary history, especially "the possible grounds of her relationship to the major tendencies and other major writers of her era" (289). Some contributors examine Austen's fiction in relation to the tradition of the Romantic novel or to the writings of feminists such as Mary Wollstonecraft, while others provide more general assessments of her relationship to English Romanticism and the wider Romantic movement. The common thread running through all these essays is the insistence that, to be truly appreciated for her accomplishments, Austen must be read in historical context.

Books on Austen Issued in 1975

Several books appeared in this bicentennial year. Douglas Bush's *Jane Austen* (1975) in the Masters of World Literature series is a general survey of her career intended for students. Its importance lies in its being readily available and often highly recommended by teachers who had been trained in the 1950s and 1960s when Bush was a major figure in literary criticism. Hence, Bush's celebration of Austen's conservative outlook and her achievements as a promoter of the status quo was more likely to become "accepted wisdom" by students of the period. Bush begins by asserting that Austen's growing popularity in the twentieth century is due "less to interest in her finely unobtrusive craftsmanship" than to her "humorous and serious insight into the character and the personal relations" of "ordinary people of the upper middle class" (xi–xii). Throughout his critique, Bush takes pains to deflate the lofty claims of critics who press for the seriousness of Austen's work in favor of the humor she employs and the gentle irony that permeates the novels. Bush applauds her for her classic vision, seeing her as contributing to the support of "a scale of values which had age-old experience and authority behind it." Her simple scenes of families in country villages "embodied Burkean principles of traditional wisdom, stability, and order" (196). For Bush, Austen is the only truly classical novelist in English fiction.

David Devlin's *Jane Austen and Education* (1975) is typical of thematic studies published during the middle decades of the century. Devlin concentrates on a specific aspect of Austen's fiction to explain how understanding her aims and methods in handling this topic offer significant insight into her works as a whole. "Education" for Devlin means the process by which Austen's heroines and often other characters "come to see clearly themselves and their conduct, and by this new vision or insight become better people" (1). Tracing Austen's ideas to the work of Locke, Devlin examines several of Austen's early attempts at fiction to demonstrate how she employs Lockean principles in shaping her stories, highlighting points at which Austen seems to break from eighteenth-century ideas about human nature, specifically ones espoused by the Earl of Shaftesbury, to whom other critics have insisted she is heavily indebted.

Brian Southam's 1975 pamphlet *Jane Austen* replaced Sylvia Warner's earlier contribution to the Longman Writers and Their Work series, and the differences between the two become obvious even on a cursory reading. Where Warner's is a thoughtful appreciation of Austen's talent, Southam's is a well argued critical evaluation of Austen's technical merit and her vision of the world about which she writes. Noting that she appeals to both scholars and general readers, Southam warns that her surface realism can be deceptive. Her "detailed account" of the "manners and fashionable pursuits" of Regency England "is the descriptive groundwork for a highly analytical portrait of the age, which in turn conveys an implication of the deeper processes of change in early nineteenth-century society and in the individual's understanding of himself and the world around him" (5–6). Southam makes a virtue of Austen's decision to leave out larger social and political issues from her fiction. "One of Jane Austen's major achievements in the novels," he says, "is to have captured the total illusion of the gentry's vision, the experience of living in privileged isolation" from the world around them (8). But Austen does not totally ignore the world outside this closed circle, he claims, citing several examples from the novels where hints and allusions to that world crop up. Perhaps because he is already attuned to issues being raised by feminist critics, Southam sees a second major achievement as Austen's ability to present "an account of society from the woman's point of view." Her heroines' "predicament" is to be "born into a world which values them for their marriageability, where the culmination of womanhood is to be a wife and mother, where their lives are regulated by the artificial ideals of polite femininity" (12). The novels "provide us with a historically accurate picture of a society under stress, its values and its groups in a state of change" (31). Southam says Austen sets "a high value on self-knowledge and each of the novels can be analyzed in terms of the heroine's progress along this path. But self-knowledge on its own is not enough"; it must be complemented by "a second kind of knowledge, knowledge of our duty in life" (41).

In *A Reading of Jane Austen* (1975) Barbara Hardy attempts to rescue Austen from what she believes are unfair criticisms of Austen's artistic talents and her attitudes regarding the role of the individual in society. Hardy begins by asserting that Austen created a revolution in novel-writing by making use of "the flexible medium," which she defines as "a capacity to glide easily from sympathy to detachment, from one mind to many minds, from solitary scenes to social gatherings" (14). The bulk of Hardy's study explains how Austen employs this technique in her six major novels, providing examples of Austen's ability to deal with passion and feeling, handle multiple methods of narration that suit the aims she sets for herself in each of her novels, create social groups whose interactions reveal something about the values Austen finds admirable (or not), and use narrative voice to express her own opinions and comment on social and moral values. Hardy takes issue with critics who claim Austen is a satiric writer, or who fault her for being uninterested in expressions of feeling. One of the more notable observations Hardy makes concerns Austen's handling of property and possessions. Austen saw a kind of symbiotic relationship between the environment and her characters, using places and objects symbolically to signify something about the people who live in and possess them. Few critics before Hardy would have ascribed such significance to environment.

Surprisingly, only one major biography appeared at the time of the bicentenary, and that too came out in the following year. Joan Rees's *Jane Austen: Woman and Writer* (1976) emphasizes Austen's place in her family, which Rees says occupied most of her time. Aiming her study at readers less interested in critical controversies surrounding Austen's novels than in the woman who wrote them, Rees concentrates on relating the facts of Austen's life as they are known from letters and other documentary evidence. She skirts most areas of controversy taken up by other biographers, glibly accepting that the politician Warren Hastings was only godfather of Jane's cousin Eliza de Feuillide, commenting little on Cassandra's character or her role in shaping her sister's memory, and relating the circumstances surrounding Jane's various love affairs with tact and brevity. In her view, Austen lived by the precept she gave to her fictional heroines: there could be no good marriage unless it were founded on love, and unfortunately for Austen, she never received a proposal from anyone she found worthy of loving. Rees is quick to point out how much Austen was influenced by the literary tradition (in response, perhaps, to the lingering idea that she was unlettered), and was quite aware of the larger political and social issues that shaped her age. She also defends the novelist from various charges regarding her biting wit and sarcasm, challenging Virginia Woolf's contention that Austen would be a difficult guest to entertain and refuting claims that she was a snob at heart. Calling her "a stoic Christian" (192), Rees insists Austen's novels reflect a strong sense of morality and conventional (if sometimes unexpressed) Christian virtues. Although perhaps not worshipful, Rees believes Austen lived a life that was, in almost every sense, beyond reproach.

When she does speak of Austen's fiction, Rees adopts the attitude of critics who emphasize the highly moral nature of Austen's work. Her brief critiques stress Austen's fascination with the theme of maturation and self-discovery. Not hesitant to rank the novels, Rees praises the juvenilia for the promise it shows; claims *Sense and Sensibility* deserves higher praise than it has received from earlier critics; and considers *Pride and Prejudice* a delightful comic masterpiece. While acknowledging that *Emma* is Austen's crowning achievement from a technical and thematic standpoint and praising both *Northanger Abbey* and *Persuasion*, Rees seems most insistent on rescuing *Mansfield Park* from what she considers the unjust criticism that has stemmed from critics' annoyance with the moral stance Austen takes in the novel. This is the work, Rees insists, that establishes Austen's claim to being "a very great novelist" (152). But Rees suggests that Austen achieved her status in part because she decided to remain simply dear Aunt Jane, placing Rees at odds with the most important movement in Austen studies emerging at the time — the appropriation of Austen by feminist critics, who were discovering in her work a (sometimes hidden) wellspring of rebellion against the patriarchy she was ostensibly supposed to be supporting.

Marilyn Butler: A Strong Conservative Voice

Unquestionably, the most important book published during the bicentenary year — and one of the most influential ever to appear — was Marilyn Butler's *Jane Austen and the War of Ideas* (1975). If Alistair Duckworth laid out in *The Improvement of the Estate* the case for Austen as morally and aesthetically conservative, Marilyn Butler completed the task with great force and unusual stridency in rebuking those who claimed the novelist was a revolutionary. Butler begins by insisting that Austen can be understood only within the context of the age in which she wrote, and that twentieth-century attempts to extract her from that milieu do injustice to her accomplishments. In the first half of her study, Butler provides an extended analysis of the intellectual furor created by the rise of sentimentalism, examining the contributions of important figures like Henry Mackenzie, Samuel Johnson, William Godwin, and Maria Edgeworth to a debate which Butler says Austen knew of and cared about. Butler is careful to trace the reaction to this new way of viewing humankind through a number of writers that Austen admired, and whose work she echoes in novels that all belong "to a movement that defines itself by its opposition to revolution" (122).

As a consequence, Butler's readings of individual novels reflect ways Austen displays her aversion for revolutionary ideas. Working from the premise that Austen's "manner as a novelist is broadly that of the conservative Christian moralist of the 1790s" (164), Butler focuses on showing how Austen establishes clear moral grounds for judging her characters, and assessing how successful she is in achieving her moral ends through artistic means. "Austen's method of presentation," Butler says at the conclusion of her study, "is meant to explode the sentimentalists' claim that subjective experience is the individual's whole truth" (293). But Austen does not always employ those methods as skillfully as she might have, and Butler is not averse to criticizing her when she seems unable to realize her aims either through faulty craftsmanship or mishandling of her materials. That seems to have been the case, Butler suggests, in the creation of Elizabeth Bennet, who seems a bit too revolutionary for Butler's liking — and, she claims, for Austen's as well. On the other hand, Butler suggests, Fanny Price is an over-correction and does not quite carry the burden placed on her by her creator — to be an example of moral virtue and a figure who can win readers' sympathy. The one novel where everything comes together, Butler says, is *Emma*. In this novel Austen gives readers sufficient insight into Emma's character to make them understand where she goes wrong and why she eventually triumphs by accepting society's norms for herself and others. Butler has significant problems with *Persuasion*, however, because she finds Austen consistently revealing too much of Anne Elliot's inner self and generating sympathy for her as an individual.

Although Butler can be hard on Austen occasionally, she is always harsh with those who promote the idea of Austen as a revolutionary or subversive artist. Her introductory chapter lays out the case against critics such as Harding, Mudrick, and even Lionel Trilling, whose liberal view of society and literature makes him unable to read Austen correctly. In fact, Butler's chapter on *Pride and Prejudice* is a running critique of the opposition. Here her method of challenging what she considers a wrong-headed view of Austen's fiction is best exposed, as she answers point-by-point claims made by Samuel Kliger in a 1947 article that Elizabeth is Austen's "revolutionary heroine" (198). Butler insists that "the more one examines the novel the more difficult it becomes to read into it authorial approval of the element in Elizabeth which is rebellious" (203). The same might be said of all of Butler's readings, which are aimed at demonstrating beyond a shadow of a doubt that Austen is "conservative in a sense no longer current." Her "preconceived and inflexible" morality leads her to identify errors firmly, even in figures one might be predisposed to like (298).

It is difficult to overestimate the importance of Butler's work. For more than thirty years it has been the most frequently cited critical study of Austen's fiction. Not everyone has admired it — in fact, some have been infuriated by it. But as Edward Neill notes in the introduction to *The Politics of Jane Austen* (1999), Butler's "magisterial scholarship in the period and the disarming clarity of her exposition enacted a 'paradigm shift' in the study of Austen which has subsequently been challenged as well as developed, but has continued to set the terms of the debate" about the novelist's aims in her fiction (3–4).

Works Cited

Bush, Douglas. *Jane Austen*. Masters of World Literature Series. New York: Macmillan, 1975.

Butler, Marilyn. *Jane Austen and the War of Ideas*. Oxford: Clarendon Press, 1975.

Devlin, David D. *Jane Austen and Education*. London: Macmillan, 1975.

Duckworth, Alistair. *The Improvement of the Estate: A Study of Jane Austen's Novels*. Baltimore and London: Johns Hopkins UP, 1971.

Halperin, John, ed. *Jane Austen: Bicentenary Essays*. Cambridge: Cambridge UP, 1975.

Hardy, Barbara. *A Reading of Jane Austen*. London: Peter Owen, 1975.

Kliger, Samuel. "Jane Austen's *Pride and Prejudice* in the Eighteenth Century Mode." *University of Toronto Quarterly* 16 (1946–47): 357–70.

McMaster, Juliet, ed. *Jane Austen's Achievement*. London: Macmillan, 1976.

Neill, Edward. *The Politics of Jane Austen*. New York: St. Martin's, 1999.

Nineteenth-Century Fiction 30.3 (December 1975). Special Issue on Jane Austen.

Rees, Joan. *Jane Austen: Woman and Writer*. London: Robert Hale; New York: St. Martin's, 1976.

Southam, B. C. *Jane Austen*. Writers and Their Work Series. London: Longman, 1975.

Studies in the Novel 7.1 (Spring 1975). Special Issue on Jane Austen.

Warner, Sylvia Townsend. *Jane Austen*. Writers and Their Work Series. London: Longmans, 1951. Rev. ed., London: Longmans, 1957.

Weinsheimer, Joel C., ed. *Jane Austen Today*. Athens: U of Georgia P, 1975.

Wordsworth Circle 7.4 (Autumn 1976). Special Issue on Jane Austen.

5: The Feminist Revolution in Austen Studies, 1976–1990

ANYONE EXAMINING THE HISTORY of critical studies in the English-speaking world during the past half-century would quickly recognize the significant influence feminism has had in revising opinions of both male and female writers. However, looking back at the 1960s and 1970s in 2010 one might concede that "feminism" is but one of many new critical lenses through which the work of novelists have been examined. Hence, I think it would be permissible in most studies such as this one to include "Feminist Criticism" as a subheading under "New Theoretical Approaches." But in the case of Austen, the importance of feminist critics in revising the way we look at her fiction has been so significant, and the number of feminist critiques so extensive, I believe it is valuable to highlight the influence feminists have had on Austen studies before proceeding to review the work of those practicing other new critical methodologies, or those who remain wedded to more traditional approaches.

Since the nineteenth century, feminists seem to have had a love-hate relationship with Austen. As early as 1848 Charlotte Brontë was complaining that she wrote without passion. Julia Kavanagh, who detected a hint of the feminist outlook in Austen's satire, still objected to her as being something of a cold fish. So perhaps it is not surprising that the new wave of feminists who burst onto the scene in the 1960s would have the same mixed reactions to Austen's work. After all, Austen's novels were — on the surface at least — fairy tales that seemed to reinforce the values of the patriarchy: young heroines, no matter how unruly and independent, eventually had to find husbands if they were to live happily ever after. Perhaps that is why Kate Millett makes no mention of Austen in *Sexual Politics* (1970), one of the most influential books to emerge from the new feminist movement.

Only five years later, however, the critical landscape seems to have changed markedly. References to Austen abound in Patricia Meyer Spacks's *The Female Imagination* (1975), an analysis of the unique ways "the life of the imagination emerges in the work of women writing prose directly as women" (6). Spacks claims Austen "define[s] in fictional terms the delicate emotional balancing point on which women must poise between commitment to others and preservation of their selves" (106). Unlike more radical feminists who often have little good to say about the apparent acquiescence of Austen's heroines to their conventional roles in society, Spacks believes that for these fictional women marriage is not simply an acceptable compromise. Instead, it becomes a conscious "relinquishment or subdual of their childishness" (115) — a way to demonstrate maturity. Austen's heroines begin as real adolescents and grow to womanhood during the course of the novels. In Spacks's view, Austen's fiction demonstrates that "female adolescence" can be "a time of development, not of giving up" (134). Similarly, in *Literary Women* (1976), an assessment of women whose works she believes have lasting value as literature, Ellen Moers links Austen's work to the early feminist tradition, evidenced by Austen's concern for the economic basis of society and women's dependence on men in that milieu. Moers thinks Austen is right to focus on marriage as a means of securing women's futures, and the emphasis Austen places on money is a sign of hard-nosed realism. No wonder, Moers says, people like Emerson found her vulgar, because she was speaking truth to the power of the patriarchy.

Whatever their motives, feminist critics were responsible for the explosion in criticism of Austen after 1970. Her fiction (and her life) became the subject of dozens of books. These are grouped together in a single section below, because each is an attempt to provide a systematic and comprehensive assessment of Austen's work from a feminist perspective. Additionally, during the 1970s and 1980s commentary on one or more of Austen's novels is included in feminist investigations of important questions of gender and gender relationships. These critiques often produce contextualized discussions of Austen's novels that examine their relationship to fiction by other women. While it is impossible in the space of this chapter to review the hundreds of essays published during this fifteen-year period that employ techniques of feminist criticism in examining Austen's fiction, a sampling of such studies provides insight into the widely ranging attitudes of feminist critics regarding the extent to which Austen is truly representative of a tradition that challenges or subverts the notion of patriarchy. They also reveal feminist critics' interest in topics such as women's power (or more appropriately, powerlessness) in a patriarchal society, the concept of sisterhood, and the role of the woman writer in shaping the novel as a literary genre.[1]

Books About Austen

Books by two American feminists lay out the case for Austen as a feminist novelist. The first, Julia Prewitt Brown's *Jane Austen's Novels: Social Change and Literary Form* (1979), is an extended defense of Austen — and by extension, all women writers who focus on domestic issues. Brown wants to turn on its head the critical tradition that seeks to patronize Austen by celebrating her technical accomplishments while dismissing the importance of her chosen subject, the experience of women's everyday lives. Brown says Austen "gave meaning to domesticity for the first time in English fiction," demonstrating "the cultural significance of marriage and family" (1). Her novels are great art *and* important social documents, because in them Austen demonstrates that the lives of her heroines "are proportionate to the complex presentation of their personalities and situations" (4). Rather than being merely highly finished comedies of manners, the novels provide "a foreground of social and moral change, conceived with an irony that ultimately reflects its tensions" (5).

In analyzing Austen's treatment of marriage and family, Brown points out the misguided notions of critics who refuse to consider domesticity an appropriate topic for a great artist. She provides an insightful examination of marriage as it existed — and changed — in Austen's time. She also insists that while the novelist "was not particularly tradition-directed," the "society she wrote about was" (21). Although keenly aware of the importance of the individual's need to operate within social boundaries, Austen did not simply accept as givens the laws, customs, and social norms of her society. Rather, Brown says, Austen's "very intent is to illustrate their functions, reveal their strengths and weaknesses, essentially explain or criticize their presence" (24). The tools Austen employs in her critique of society are irony and satire, structuring her works as either ironic comedies or works of satiric realism. Brown's detailed readings explain how Austen uses these methods to reveal the importance of marriage and domestic relations for women who can be independent spirits and hold personal values that sometimes push the limits of convention or highlight the shortcomings of accepted social norms. In Austen's work domestic issues do not occupy "a corner of the world" (155) but are at the center of it. She is important in women's history because, building on the tradition of the novel in delineating "female consciousness" (156), she became the first major woman author to "reveal the influence and importance of women in her class" and "articulate the unspoken-for values of her sex" (157). Until Austen — and for a time afterwards — female consciousness remained relegated to the by-ways of history, including literary history. Only in the twentieth century, Brown says, have Austen and her literary sisters been rescued from relative oblivion as serious forerunners of the modern feminist movement.

In the second major study by an American feminist, *In the Meantime: Character and Perception in Jane Austen's Fiction* (1980), Susan Morgan provides a rationale for revising the notion that Austen was a conservative writer. Instead of making her out to be a subversive feminist, however, Morgan offers readings of the novels that demonstrate her affinity with the Romantics. To appreciate the Austen canon, one must recognize that "Austen's subject" in all her fiction is "the problem of perception"; to recognize this "provides a unified interpretation of her work and illuminates it in areas until now considered obscure" (3). Morgan challenges the notion that Austen is principally a novelist of manners or is concerned primarily with matters of education, two theories that do not account adequately for the complexity of the six major works. Morgan also takes pains to point out the weaknesses of readings that emphasize Austen's conservative viewpoint and present her as a novelist of intellect, while acknowledging that she was influenced by the dominant ideology of her times. One of the particular strengths of Morgan's critique is that it allows her to get beyond having to judge the novelist and her characters in terms of morality. "One of the fascinations of Austen's fiction," she notes, "is that she distinguishes the problem of perception from that of individual fallibility and moral improvement." Austen *is* an artist of the everyday — something Morgan sees as a major strength, because "in our everyday lives most of the confusion and doubts which are not self-inflicted have to do with not being able to see into other people" (191–92). Watching others grapple with the problem of perception is what gives readers a continual sense of pleasure from Austen's fiction.

Somewhat surprisingly, in *Jane Austen: Feminism and Fiction* (1983) British critic Margaret Kirkham seems to go even farther than Brown or Morgan in developing a strong case for Austen as a conscious feminist. The surprising aspect of this judgment is that it comes from a British scholar, since the notion of Austen as an extreme radical seemed to find more favor with Americans. Kirkham argues that Austen was steeped in the tradition that produced Mary Wollstonecraft, intensely concerned with establishing the rights of women to be treated as men's equals both socially and intellectually. She insists that criticisms such as the "slightness" of Austen's subject matter can be dismissed out of hand if her work is seen "in the context of eighteenth-century feminist ideas" (xi). In addition to explaining how Austen's version of this brand of rationalist feminism works to shape her fiction, Kirkham wishes to expose the weaknesses of her own contemporaries (especially Marilyn Butler) who insist on Austen's essentially conservative nature. Kirkham's commentary on the novels relates "Austen as literary artist and innovator to her declared position as feminist moralist and critic of fictional tradition" (xvii). After explaining how the feminist controversy influenced Austen, she traces carefully and cleverly the feminist voice and vision that emerges from the fiction.

Kirkham concludes with an equally insightful and somewhat ingenious explanation of the reasons Austen's feminism had not been discovered earlier. There was, she explains, no adequate understanding of eighteenth-century feminism before the 1970s. Additionally, whatever inklings of feminism Austen's first readers might have discovered in her work were systematically suppressed by critics, most of whom were bent on preserving her reputation as a proper lady and conservative moralist. It is now possible, Kirkham concludes, to see Austen for what she really was — a feminist sympathizer who uses irony to launch a scathing critique of her own society for anyone capable of reading beneath the surface of her highly polished stories. And *only* if one understands how feminism shaped Austen's work, Kirkham concludes, can one really appreciate it.

LeRoy Smith, one of the first men to deal with feminist issues concerning Austen, is decidedly less strident in his portrait of her in *Jane Austen and the Drama of Woman* (1983). Rejecting both the notion that Austen was essentially conservative and the more radical view of her as a subversive, Smith looks for a way to reconcile these competing views. He is convinced that Austen was keenly aware of the problems women faced in a patriarchal society and that her protest against this treatment exists in her novels. He believes, however, that one can better appreciate her work if one sees "the woman's quest for freedom and the preservation of her selfhood" in her novels as "an intense version of human experience in general" (9). "At the heart of Austen's fiction," he says, "is the quest for freedom: each man or woman's wish to choose his or her own acts and thereby become a person" (28). Austen is dismayed by the restrictions she sees placed on women, and her novels explore the problems women encounter in contemporary society. But she does so, Smith insists, to provide a positive resolution to social strictures by seeing the world as a place where "the growth of sensitivity and candor points the way to mutual understanding, respect, and accommodation between her male and female principals" (45).

In contrast to Smith's more mediated stance, Alison Sulloway takes the notion of Austen as extremist radical about as far as anyone in *Jane Austen and the Province of Womanhood* (1989). Somewhat curiously, this position is actually a departure from the more centrist stance she takes in her 1986 article "Jane Austen's Mediative Voice," in which she argues that Austen is actually a "conscious mediator" (193) between those who simply accepted notions about women's inherent inferiority and proponents of women's equality and right to independence. In her book, however, Sulloway seems determined to highlight Austen's radical qualities. Interested primarily in explicating the nature of Austen's fiction, Sulloway posits that Austen and other women of her generation were writing a new kind of satire, essentially different from that produced by men of the Augustan age. This "satire of the outsider" (xiii) displays subtle (and sometimes not-so-subtle) rebellion against prevailing ideas that women were by nature subservient, sinful, and not particularly bright. In this feminist and (unacknowledged) Foucaldian critique of Austen's fiction, Sulloway stresses the novelist's continual attack upon the privileged in the voice of the oppressed. She ranges freely among the novels to find examples of what she considers Austen's principal theme, tracing the intellectual and cultural background of the controversy surrounding the nature and social role of women, which percolated between 1780 and 1820, to show how keenly

Austen was aware of this debate and how strongly she sided with the radicals. All of Austen's work contains "not only themes of women's potential evolution," but also "themes of the Wollstonecraftian revolution" (49). Sulloway believes Austen has hidden herself in her heroines, and that their story is both hers and that of her sisters. But she has done this with great discretion, Sulloway insists — so great, in fact, that "only now have a few readers begun to recognize the explosive qualities embedded in her fiction" (xvii).

Given her rather bold assertions, one might expect some discomfort with Sulloway's argument, especially from the more moderate feminists outside America. The Australian critic Jocelyn Harris, generally a supporter of feminism, suggests in her 1993 review of *Jane Austen and the Province of Womanhood* that there is much good to learn in Sulloway — but that her failure to acknowledge precisely what she borrows from some earlier feminist critics and where she disagrees leaves one wondering just how original her contribution to Austen studies really is. Perhaps the strongest rebuke came from the British scholar Deirdre Le Faye, who was generally critical of the entire feminist revision in Austen studies. In her *Review of English Studies* (1993) review Le Faye suggests Sulloway simply is not well read in Austen studies, nor a good reader of Austen. "Jane Austen intended her books to be clear reflections of the society she lived in," Le Faye says, "mirrors that were neither distorting nor tinted with grey." The thought that she meant them to be "subversive timebombs so heavily disguised as to pass unrecognized by any of her contemporary reviewers or readers" is ludicrous (115).

Finally, one book among the dozens written during this period deserves special mention. If Marilyn Butler's *Jane Austen and the War of Ideas* represented the conservative response to early feminist, postmodern, and radical revaluations of Austen's achievements, certainly Claudia Johnson's *Jane Austen: Women, Politics and the Novel* (1988) is the most important feminist rebuttal to Butler's argument. Johnson, who would go on to earn an international reputation in feminist studies, demonstrates in her first book that she possesses an independent spirit, a keen intellect, and an exceptional talent for amassing information to support a complex argument. *Jane Austen: Women, Politics and the Novel* openly challenges the critical tradition that celebrates Austen as a safe novelist. Johnson directs particularly harsh remarks at the work of R. W. Chapman, whose edition she says seems to be "animated by an impulse markedly more antiquarian than scholarly" (xvi). She believes Chapman has done even worse damage to Austen's reputation by treating her as a conduit for the conservative ideology of her time rather than granting her "her dignity" and acknowledging her as "a warrior of ideas" (xviii). But Johnson is not much happier with critics who celebrate Austen as a subversive, largely because many of them attribute her iconoclasm to emotional instability.

Johnson applies a historical approach to Austen's fiction in order to "reconceptualize the stylistic and thematic coherence" of her work and explain its relationship with "a largely feminist tradition of political novels" (xix). She calls for a gendered response to Austen's work, since gender mattered much to Austen's contemporaries. Johnson insists Austen was a careful and professional novelist (not a dilettante or unconscious artist) who wanted her work to be taken seriously. Hence, she had to be careful not to appear radical; but at the same time she was too keen an observer of society not to be affected by the inequities she saw around her, especially when it came to women's position in society. Austen was skeptical of conservative ideology, Johnson says, but she had to express her skepticism obliquely. To avoid charges of radicalism she employed techniques such as irony, double plotting, contrast (especially between overtly doctrinaire precepts and lived experiences), and especially the use of "unempowered characters — that is, women" (xxiv) as the centers of her narratives.

Johnson pays special attention to the relationship of Austen's novels to political fiction written by women who were her older contemporaries, suggesting that in some ways Austen relies on these works in her narratives. Johnson's readings of Austen's early fiction stress that they are "exercises in stylistic and generic self-consciousness" rather than "expressions of personal belief" (31). *Northanger Abbey* is a highly charged political text that "clarifies and reclaims" gothic conventions "in distinctly political ways" (34). The powerlessness of females in gothic fiction is "transferred to the daytime world of drawing room manners" (37). Similarly, *Sense and Sensibility* is a "dark and disenchanted novel" that exposes the seamy underside of the principal icons of conservative ideology, "property, marriage, and family" (49). Johnson admits that *Pride and Prejudice* is more conservative and less reformist than other works, but even in this novel Austen allows conservative principles to succeed only when the upholders of the status quo prove worthy. In fact, Johnson says, *Pride and Prejudice* is a "provisional experiment" with established forms of social order "in order to transform them into the purveyors of ecstatic personal happiness" (93).

Although many critics have had great problems making sense of *Mansfield Park*, Johnson manages to point out the weaknesses of their interpretations while offering a reading that stresses the novel's political subtext. Austen's aim in this work, Johnson says, "is to turn the conservative myth sour" (97). There is in *Mansfield Park* only an appearance that "conservative ideologies have it their way." Austen permits this only so conservative figures can "discredit themselves with their own voices" (120). *Emma*, too, has presented a problem for traditionalist critics, because Emma Woodhouse alone among Austen's heroines does not need a man to complete her life. But the marriage of Emma and Knightley is clearly unconventional; it is apparent from the text, Johnson says, that they will continue to operate in their separate spheres, making their wedding a union of friends rather than a capitulation of the heroine to patriarchal demands. Several years later, in an appendix to *Equivocal Beings: Politics, Gender and Sentimentality in the 1790s* (1995), Johnson offers a reading of *Emma* that "diminish[es] the authority of male sentimentality, and reimmasculat[es] men and women alike with a high sense of national purpose" (191). In the novel, Johnson says, Austen "disdains not only the effeminacy of men, but also the femininity of women" (202), promoting instead a common-sense approach to relationships that offers both sexes equal status as rational beings.

Johnson says near the end of *Jane Austen: Women, Politics and the Novel* that *Persuasion*, a novel which also explores the possibilities of female independence, shows most clearly signs of Austen's movement away from conservative principles. Despite this trend, Johnson insists Austen was no radical. At a time when the structure of the family and the place of women in society were important topics in social debate, Austen adopts a middle ground: cautious in recommending change, but clearly not a staunch advocate for maintaining the patriarchal hegemony that kept women subordinate and dependent.

Studies of Power Relationships

Austen's role in shaping women's consciousness about power relationships in a patriarchal society is the subject of quite a few studies during this period. A truly influential commentary on this topic appears in Sandra Gilbert and Susan Gubar's *The Madwoman in the Attic: The Woman Writer and the Nineteenth-Century Literary Imagination* (1979), an exploration of strategies women writers used to operate in a tradition formed and dominated by men. Gilbert and Gubar explore how Austen uses recurrent "images of boundaries and enclosures," tropes common in the work of women living at different times and working in different genres. They contend these "self-imposed novelistic limitations" help Austen "define a secure place" as a writer, "even as she seemed to admit the impossibility of actually inhabiting such a small space with any degree of comfort." But they believe Austen thought it necessary for women, whom she considered "too vulnerable in the world at large," to "acquiesce in their own confinement" (108). Because she seems to be willing to subjugate herself and her gender, Austen seems *safe* for male readers, who see her as a supporter of traditional social norms. But Gilbert and Gubar note that women, too, are among the worst offenders in celebrating Austen's willingness to accept this second-class position for women in society.

Gilbert and Gubar see Austen in a different light. "Although she has become a symbol of culture" — meaning traditional, patriarchal culture — "it *is* shocking how persistently Austen demonstrates her discomfort with her cultural inheritance, specifically her dissatisfaction with the tight place assigned women in patriarchy and her analysis of the economics of sexual exploitation" (112). Austen is "centrally concerned with the impossibility of women escaping the conventions and categories that, in every sense, belittle them" (113). Gilbert and Gubar notice in Austen's early fiction "her alienation from her culture" (117). Further, they believe Austen was suspicious "about the effect of literary images of both sexes" and resorts to "parodic strategies to discredit such images" (119). But because she appears on the surface to follow patriarchal cultural norms in her fiction, her "revolt against the conventions she inherited" (119–20) has gone almost unnoticed.

Along the same lines, In *The Dilemma of the Talented Heroine* (1978) Susan Siefert examines a number of nineteenth-century fictional heroines who do not seem to fit prevailing stereotypes of the "ideal woman" — the passive, intellectually feeble female that needs a man's protection and guidance. Siefert is interested in exploring how these women reconcile their personal aspirations with the demands of a society that does not acknowledge or value them. She discovers that two of Austen heroines — Elizabeth Bennet and Emma Woodhouse — seek "an acceptable compromise between their individual aspirations and societal expectations" (7). Judith Lowder Newton's *Women, Power, and Subversion: Social Strategies in British Fiction, 1778–1860* (1981) also examines literature that deals with ways women exert power within a patriarchal society. Focusing on the relationships between the sexes and the economic aspects of *Pride and Prejudice*, Newton concludes that Elizabeth Bennet is able to achieve some level of power and independence only by separating herself from the dominant values of her society.

How Austen depicts men in these relationships has been a topic of interest to feminists, although there is not always agreement about what the novelist hoped to accomplish in her handling of "maleness." For example, Judith Wilt's provocative essay "Jane Austen's Men: Inside/Outside 'The Mystery'" (1981) examines several of Austen's male characters, particularly the Handsome Stranger who has strong appeal for women. Through these figures and others, she says, Austen attempts to capture the special *angst* that characterizes maleness, the drive to be somebody, and explains how Austen's women are drawn to (or repelled by) her male figures. In *Women Writing About Men* (1986), Jane Miller explores Austen's treatment of father figures in her novels. Noting that men play an important role in women's fiction, Miller cautions that "the men in women's novels are not just men, but men seen from a woman's perspective" (3). Miller's readings stress the importance of fathers as authority figures, and catalog the many shortcomings Austen finds in these men whom her heroines look to as role models for future husbands who might provide security (and perhaps even love) in a world that offers them few prospects for independent living. "That dependence, which was economic, political, so-cial, physical and emotional is spelled out in painful detail in Jane Austen's novels," Miller says (47). The "tension which permeates the novels lies in the contrast between the realities of marriage and family life, boredom and ugliness, lack of privacy and lack of stimulation, and the merry wassail of those brief months of a woman's life during which everything seems possible and which will end in failure or a wedding" (61). This hardnosed portrait of Austen directly contradicts the view of critics who consider Austen a genial supporter of conventional values. "To read Jane Austen's novels as realistic *and* optimistic," Miller says, "is willfully to skate over the sense she gives of the constraints on women, the ignominies involved in any decision they make" (71). The same argument is made by Julie Shaffer, who presents Austen as a subversive writer in Arthur Marotti's *Reading with a Difference: Gender, Race, and Cultural Identity* (1986). In her essay ("Not Subordinate: Empowering Women in the Marriage Plot") Shaffer argues that Austen, Maria Edgeworth, and Fanny Burney all use the conventional marriage plot as a device to challenge what Ma-rotti describes as "repressive ideas of femininity" (9).

The feminist move to revise the concept of heroism informs Lee Ed-wards's examination of the female hero, *Psyche as Hero: Female Heroism and Fictional Form* (1984). In a chapter entitled "Heroes into Heroines," she explores ways Austen's protagonist in *Emma* exhibits characteristics of the hero within the context of social comedy. Acknowledging that the con-cept of the hero is a male construct, Edwards is interested in showing how female heroes like Emma challenge the equation of heroism with aggres-sive behavior, subvert "patriarchal structures," and level "hierarchy's end-less ranks" (5). The very notion of comedy as defined by Northrop Frye, Edwards says, privileges the male in the quest to create community. That is why Emma, a female cast as hero in a conventional comedy, is "too big" for the plot of the novel (65). Throughout, her "heroic potential is negatively realized" (70), and while Austen makes readers "feel the cor-rectness" of Emma's marriage to Knightley, the "terms" of the heroine's happiness "negate rather than fulfill Emma's original aspirations" (71).

Elizabeth Sabiston comes to a decidedly different conclusion about *Emma* in *The Prison of Womanhood: Four Provincial Heroines in Nineteenth-Century Fiction* (1987), another study of strong idealistic young women. Sabiston comes down harshly on Austen's Emma Woodhouse, calling her "the prototype of the creative provincial, self-deceived and mentally blind who, in trying to rise above her society, often merely reinforces its values" (3). In a novel Sabiston describes as a kind of *bildungsroman*, Emma learns that her ideals are often dashed by reality. However, Emma's stum-bles are gently comic rather than tragic, and ultimately she does manage to shape her own future, even if it involves making certain compromises to the dominant ideology of her age.

In another examination of the status of women in marriage, "*Pride and Prejudice* and the Belief in Choice: Jane Austen's Fantastical Vision" (1984), Cynthia Caywood argues that the novel is both a tragedy and fantasy — tragic in revealing what life was really like for women in Austen's time, fantastic in proposing a heroine whose story can only be described as fantasy. In the novel, Caywood says, Austen "systematically demolishes a number of socially approved stereotypes of ideal feminine behavior and virtue" and "questions the value of traditional female accomplishments" (32). While readers may be satisfied with the happy ending, the novel suggests the impossibility of this kind of happiness ever being achieved in Austen's real world, where women were continually oppressed by social convention.

Kate Fulbrook's contribution to editor Susan Roe's *Women Reading Women's Writing* (1987), a book intended to redress some of the excesses of feminist criticism, also stresses the comic nature of Austen's writing while still insisting on its essentially subversive nature. The thesis of Fulbrook's "Jane Austen and the Comic Negative" is that what makes Austen most interesting as a woman writer is her ability to use the comic as a means of social critique. Fulbrook says Austen "turns her hostility on the complacencies of power in both its cruel and hypocritical manifestations with a cynical irony that evidences a rare understanding of the roots and ends of power" (42). Austen creates a world in which women and men can be equals and where love rather than economy determines happiness. This is a radical vision for Austen's day — and for the present as well, Fulbrook argues, since she is certain that, despite some advances, many women are in much the same position in the late twentieth century as they were in Austen's time, dependent on men for their survival.

Susan Fraiman's "The Humiliation of Elizabeth Bennet" in *Refiguring the Father: New Feminist Readings of Patriarchy* (1989) is a decidedly radical feminist reading of *Pride and Prejudice* in a collection of essays designed to "explore the father figure as a shifting multiple field of tropes and practices that must be reconstructed and deconstructed" (x) in order for women to get beyond stereotypes that contribute to their continuing oppression within a patriarchal society. Fraiman reads *Pride and Prejudice* as a novel in which the "paternity" of Mr. Bennet over Elizabeth is replaced by that of Darcy, "with a subsequent loss of clout for Elizabeth" (168). Elizabeth's "progress" through the novel can be seen as a "gradual devaluation" and "humiliation" (169). Fraiman believes all of Austen's women suffer in the patriarchy — even intelligent ones like Elizabeth Bennet. And although the title of Judith Mayne's *Private Novels, Public Films* (1988) might suggest a focus on film adaptations of novels, such is not the case in her treatment of *Pride and Prejudice*. Instead, informed by feminist and Marxist theories of patriarchy and economics, she offers a succinct analysis of the private and public spheres in which Austen's characters operate, concentrating on the limitations of Austen's women to influence their own destinies. Those limitations — and much more — are the subjects of Grant Holly's "*Emma*grammatology" (1989), a reading of *Emma* informed by Lacanian theories regarding reality, gender relationships, and the possibilities of closure. Acknowledging that the traditional way of examining Austen's art is to discuss her novels "in terms of moral realism" (42), Holly demonstrates how it is possible to see the novel resisting such interpretation and refusing to be reduced to simplistic terms that permit a coherent reading.

Commentaries on Sisterhood

Austen's depiction of women's relationships with other women has been as important to feminists as her portrayal of power relationships. That interest is paramount to Nina Auerbach in *Communities of Women* (1978). Auerbach discusses Austen's fiction as part of a larger examination of "communities of women," where codes of behavior and values — often unstated but nevertheless powerful as motivators for action and belief — operate to help women establish their identities independent from the roles in which men have traditionally cast them. Concentrating on *Pride and Prejudice*, Auerbach analyzes Austen's reaction to these communities and to matriarchy as she perceives it imaginatively. Auerbach's conclusions contain disturbing notes for those who look upon Austen with some affection. In dealing with "direct female power," she says, Austen's novels are "most equivocal" (50). The resolution and happy ending come only when Mrs. Bennet's ineffectual blunderings in trying to shape her daughters' futures are taken over by Darcy, the "acknowledged center of power in the novel" (52). In the end, the "female community of Longbourn, an oppressive blank in a dense society, is dispersed with relief in the solidity of marriage" (55).

One of the most important statements on Austen's view of women's relationships with other women is Janet Todd's in *Women's Friendship in Literature* (1980). Based in part on her earlier article "Female Friendship in Jane Austen's Novels" (1977), Todd's first scholarly book immediately established her as an important new voice in Austen studies. Over the next thirty years she would become a major international figure in the field, going on to write groundbreaking criticism and edit numerous works by and about Austen, including the new Cambridge edition of the novelist's works in 2005–2009. In *Women's Friendship in Literature* Todd investigates the "form and ideology" inherent in "the literary phenomenon of female friendship" (1). Her analysis of *Mansfield Park* and *Emma* suggests that Austen is hesitant to delve too deeply into this topic. She avoids it altogether in *Mansfield Park*, Todd says, and although she defends the idea of equal social friendships between women in *Emma*, she truncates any discussion of it rather than explore what in her age may have been considered an awkward topic to handle with frankness.

A curious twist on the power of sisterhood is offered by Rachel Brownstein in *Becoming a Heroine: Reading About Women in Novels* (1982). Brownstein is interested in exploring what might be called the concept of *heroineship* — what it means to be a heroine in novels that focus principally on female protagonists. Consequently, quite a few of the works she discusses are domestic novels built around the marriage plot. In her chapter on Austen, Brownstein explains how her heroines are ostensibly freed from stale conventions by their superior intellect or self-awareness, but at the same time constrained by the society in which they live. While Brownstein does not view Austen as a mother of the modern feminist movement, she does point to some ways in which the novelist turns on its head the notion that women are interesting only in the years when they are marriageable but not yet wed. And while Austen's heroines find they "must separate from other women" in order to achieve self-realization and self-actualization, Brownstein notes that eventually the heroine in every Austen novel "must also learn that she is like her sisters and her mother" (99).

The heroine's relationships with family members also generated critical interest among feminists. The mother-daughter bond provides the framework for Susan Peck MacDonald's "Jane Austen and the Tradition of the Absent Mother" (1980). MacDonald argues that Austen is driven to create heroines with absent mothers not because of "the impotence or unimportance of mothers," but rather from "the almost excessive power of motherhood" (58). Leaving the daughter alone or with inadequate surrogates to help her make the transition from girlhood to adulthood places her in a position where she must learn, often painfully, from trial and error to make her place as a woman in the world. How the sister bond played out for Austen in real life is discussed in Susan Sniader Lanser's essay on the relationship between Jane and her sister Cassandra in *The Sister Bond: A Feminist View of a Timeless Connection* (1985). Lanser stresses the close ties between the two women and the influence of that relationship on Austen's fiction, going so far as to assert that "the combined state of singlehood and sisterhood clearly provided the material situation that made Jane Austen's literary career possible" (59).

Feminist Genre Studies

Feminists also took up the question of Austen's place in literary history — specifically, the heretofore underreported history of women's role in the development of the novel. Hence, Austen figures in Anthea Zeman's *Presumptuous Girls* (1977), a feminist-inspired discussion of what Zeman calls the serious woman novelist — to be distinguished from the popular or romantic woman novelist. Serious women novelists, she says, "made it [their] business to depict the state of play" in the age during which they wrote (2). They are "not engaged in secret revolutionary work" (2), but instead are exploring new possibilities for women while chronicling contemporary limitations. Zeman sees Austen and others like the Brontës, Gaskell, Woolf, and Lessing as proffering advice to women who want to break with convention but achieve what was (or is) possible for them.

The work of three critics writing during the 1980s can serve as examples of the way Austen's contributions to the development of fiction were being viewed by British feminists. In *Sex and Subterfuge: Women Novelists to 1850* (1982), Eva Figes argues that Austen's contribution to the evolution of the novel as an art form lay in her ability to bring a degree of realism to the genre that had hitherto been lacking. Austen turned to her advantage many of the apparent limitations that novelists had experienced in portraying women as heroines. Breaking from the tradition of the passive heroine created by many of her predecessors, Austen created young women who were actively engaged in shaping their own destinies and who were in possession of a degree of common sense that earlier heroines seemed to lack. Although not radically feminist in her assessments, in *Women in the English Novel, 1800–1900* (1984) the poet and critic Merryn Williams goes out of her way to argue that Austen was a "free spirit" who "delighted in using her mind, and she could not endure any relationship between two people who were not mentally equal" (52). Most of Austen heroines, she says, seem to delight in intellect and independence — but notes with some disappointment that heroines who follow in Victorian novels are more like Fanny Price, "with her headaches, her shrinking-violet nature and her willingness to let other people form her mind" (52). A third British scholar, Jane Spencer, says in *The Rise of the Woman Novelist* (1986) that Austen is an inheritor of the didactic tradition. Hence, in several of her novels she is concerned with the way her heroines learn from others to accept their proper role in society. Although this could be seen as a rather conservative reading, especially from one whose intent is to "contribute to the feminist project of uncovering women's history" (viii), Spencer asserts that, despite her links to the didactic tradition, Austen was able to expand and deepen "the fictional presentation of human character" (177).

The American view of Austen as a feminist figures prominently in discussions included in Mary Anne Schofield and Cecilia Macheski's *Fetter'd or Free? British Women Novelists, 1670–1815* (1986), a collection of essays examining the relationship of individual women novelists to the conventions of their age. Were they bound by them, ask the editors and contributors, or were they "free to invent a female rhetoric, to express a self-hood, and to develop economic independence[?]"(1) In looking at Austen, Linda Hunt suggests her heroines defy fictional conventions, largely because Austen was committed to principles of realism. Gary Kelly argues that, in exploring relationships between self and society, Austen shows tendencies toward reform of social conventions to accommodate individual development and expression. Although she was not a radical, Kelly says, Austen demonstrates in her fiction that the novel could serve as a political tool; in this, she "revolutionized the potential of the novel as an instrument of ideological warfare" (304). Irene Taylor sees Austen as a visionary who recognized that, in a world where work and service rather than land and lineage would determine a person's value, "the problems and possibilities facing English women were paradigmatic of those that faced England itself" (428).

Two other books by American critics suggest, however, that there was not a monolithic "American feminist" view of Austen. In *Tradition Counter Tradition: Love and the Form of Fiction* (1987), an examination of the marriage plot in English and American fiction, Joseph Allen Boone explains how Austen balances competing ideological forces, but ultimately asserts a conservative position that marriage is both inevitable and good. Although her heroines are allowed great freedom, they are always contained within an ordered society. "Austen creates the illusion of an ordered world that is contained and complete," Boone says, "and insofar as her text reproduces this ideology, she stops short of questioning the necessity of marriage as the primary ordering desire of society itself" (96). However, Linda Hunt suggests in *A Woman's Portion: Ideology, Culture, and the British Female Novel Tradition* (1988) that Austen struggles to reconcile her commitment to psychological realism with the ideal of femininity she inherited from her culture. Hunt believes Austen found much to admire in the elevation of woman's rational capacity; her works emphasize the possibility of women's contributing to society rather than remaining in subservient and dependent roles. Austen's heroines are complex creations, not stereotypes, Hunt insists; they increase readers' interest and challenge some of the negative stereotypes about women.

Blended Methodologies

One of the principal characteristics of many critical arguments written by feminists was the tendency to blend theoretical approaches in discussing Austen's fiction, combining, for example, feminism with Marxist or new methods of psychological criticism to produce more nuanced readings. Mary Poovey employs that strategy in *The Proper Lady and the Woman Writer* (1984), a study of what Poovey calls a bourgeois construct, the Proper Lady, an ideal that demanded women be "decorous and domestic" (vii). Poovey's intent in this book is to "examine the shadow the Proper Lady casts across the careers" of Austen and other women writers "who became professional authors despite the strictures of propriety" (x). She describes Austen as a kind of mediator between conservative and radical extremes. Living in an age when the dominant, male-directed ideology suddenly seemed open to challenge, Austen chose to question patriarchal attitudes without falling into open rebellion, as Mary Wollstonecraft did. Instead, Poovey says, Austen's posits the existence of "separate spheres" (238), public and private. In the private sphere women can be self-assertive and work "in the service of moral reform" (240). Austen recognized that traditional expectations for women, embodied in the concept of propriety, were in great need of reforming — but she did not want to destroy the existing social order completely. Hence, Poovey argues, she "turned her creative energies to the reformation of propriety in the hope of finding within its codes an acceptable form for a woman's desires and a reinforcement for the social order she cherished" (241–42).

However, no hint of Austen's occupying a middle ground is present in Judith Weissman's Marxist-feminist reading of Austen in *Half Savage and Hardy and Free: Women and Rural Radicalism in the Nineteenth Century Novel* (1987). Weissman considers Austen part of the "radical tradition of resistance" (8), one of the writers who defended the rural economy against the encroachments of capitalistic industrialism and urbanism. She challenges the idea that Austen was conservative and unconcerned with larger political issues, claiming the novelist has much in common with "the Romantic radicalism" of the nineteenth century (65). In commenting on individual novels, Weissman considers *Mansfield Park* an attack on the corruptions introduced by urban society, and *Emma* a Wordsworthian idyll in which the stable rural society is challenged by outsiders. But Austen's Romantic tendencies are best seen in *Persuasion*, where she creates in Anne Elliot "a new and Romantic heroine" (73). Sadly, it seems to Weissman, in moving away from rural England, Anne gives up "a life with powers and duties" (75) for one in which she might be forced to play a subordinate and limited role.

Austen is also viewed as a fighter for women's rights by Nancy Armstrong in *Desire and Domestic Fiction: A Political History of the Novel* (1987), one of the first critical studies to apply Foucaldian insights to the study of women and literature. Armstrong offers a highly charged political reading of the rise of the novel and suggests that women writers actually exerted real power in creating the idea of the middle class and its values through the medium of domestic fiction. "The rise of the novel," Armstrong says, "hinged upon a struggle to say what made a woman desirable" (4–5), and this quality transcended class boundaries. Linking the history of British fiction with the empowering of the middle classes, Armstrong insists that "the history of the novel cannot be understood apart from the history of sexuality" (9). In a lengthy critique of *Emma* Armstrong explains how, by limiting her subject, Austen is able to create an enclosed world in which social relations and domestic relations are conflated — and control of language becomes a form of power.

In a chapter on Austen in *"Catching the Drift": Authority, Gender, and Narrative* (1988) Laura Tracy applies tools of psychology in combination with those of feminism and narrative theory to examine Austen's fiction. Interested in "the effect of psychoanalytic transference in fiction" (3), Tracy presents a critique of Austen's work in which the novelist's unacknowledged commitment to the dominant ideology of her day is gradually undermined as her career progressed. What Tracy finds particularly intriguing is that most of Austen's novels produce in readers "the sort of intense reactions normally reserved for real people in the real world." This phenomenon Tracy describes as "countertransferrence," the kind of response some analysts make to patients' tales when they create their own narratives from the details provided to them. This happens, Tracy says, because of Austen's "use of an overwhelmingly authoritative and didactic narrator," which generates in readers the same response "originally provoked by authority figures encountered in early childhood" (134). In the early novels Austen appears to use this technique to impose a dominant, patriarchal ideology on readers. But as her career progressed, and especially in *Persuasion*, Austen "hinted at the presence of an irony undetected by her contemporaries" (141). In creating Anne Elliot Austen finally demonstrates a "conscious appreciation of the structure of dominance and subordination she had unconsciously transferred into her earlier work" (186). As a consequence, Tracy concludes, *Persuasion* is Austen's only real feminist novel.

Susan Morgan seems to disagree with this conclusion, finding all of Austen's fiction feminist in intent if not explicit in its discussion of matters most important to women in their relationships with men. In a provocatively titled chapter on Austen in *Sisters in Time: Imagining Gender in Nineteenth-Century British Fiction* (1989)—"Why There's No Sex in Jane Austen's Fiction"— Morgan explains how Austen deals with sexual matters without mentioning them directly. She argues that "the radical premise in Austen's novels that distinguishes them so essentially from previous novels and makes them the original ancestors of so many later novels is that plot is not a threat to character, life not an assault on self." Austen does not feel threatened by sex in the way earlier novelists were, nor does she feel obligated to define her characters primarily in terms of their roles as sexual objects. The "absence of sex in Austen's work represents neither a moral absolutism nor an historical conservatism nor a psychological limitation," Morgan insists. Instead, it "represents a literary innovation" and "a political innovation" as well (50). Her novels revise the pattern of "male dominance and female vulnerability," most visible in *Emma* but present in other works as well (51). Furthermore, Austen's fiction "establishes a link between, indeed an interfusion of, women and creativity — not as inspiration but as creators," making creativity "a feminine value" (55).

The same theme recurs in British novelist Margaret Drabble's introductions to editions of Austen's novels published in 1989 by Virago Press, the highly successful feminist publishing house. Taken collectively, Drabble's essays represent the studied critique by a respected novelist on the work of a fellow practitioner. The six introductions blend criticism and appreciation effortlessly, and while Drabble casts a feminist's eye on the text, she lets each novel determine the focus of her analysis. Her general assessment of Austen's achievement is best summed up in her observation on *Pride and Prejudice*: "In the Lukácsian sense, Austen, like Balzac, portrays her own society so faithfully that she preserves it as a valid object for later historical analysis" (xii).

Karen Chase tries to solve the problem of Austen's place in feminist literary history in a provocative and thoughtful essay, "'"Bad" Was My Commentary': Propriety, Madness, Independence, in Feminist Literary History" (1989). Chase chooses as her test case *Mansfield Park*, a novel that had already proven particularly problematic for feminist critics. It is hard to deny, Chase acknowledges, that the heroine seems passive and acquiescent to the demands of the society in which she lives. As a result feminists cannot seem to reconcile the fact that "our great novelistic matriarch" could "celebrate a prig" and "enshrine the loyal daughter of patriarchy" (14). Chase argues for a re-interpretation of Fanny based on observations made by Marilyn Butler in *Jane Austen and the War of Ideas*, in which Butler reads the novel as a conservative critique marred by Austen's attempt to use Fanny's consciousness as a vehicle for delivering that judgment. However, Chase argues, what Butler sees as "the fatal fissure" actually points to "an essential disjunction between values and experience" (15). Chase sees Austen's authorial commentary attempting to shape readers' opinions of Fanny in order to circumscribe any sense that Fanny might be limited by her eventual marriage — the only viable option available to her. To see her simply as a prig, Chase continues, is to ignore her feelings, her subjectivity, and her lived experience, which at times runs counter to the moral categories the novel seems to prescribe.

In *Desire and Truth: Functions of Plot in Eighteenth-Century Novels* (1990) Patricia Meyer Spacks employs contemporary theories of narratology with a keen feminist sensibility to examine Austen's canon as the endpoint in a study of "the kinds of truth" (2) conveyed by fiction written during the long eighteenth century. Focusing on the "viability of power as a principle of social organization" (3) and positing that desire is a gendered concept, Spacks reveals the tensions in novels created by the different ways men and women of this period approached writing and reading fiction. After exploring several earlier works which illustrate her notion that eighteenth-century novels can be categorized by the competing drives for power or intimacy, Spacks explains how Austen and Scott managed to resolve these apparently contradictory tendencies. Using *Sense and Sensibility* and *Mansfield Park*, she demonstrates how Austen handles power relationships in a more subtle way than any of her predecessors — with such subtlety, in fact, that many critics have been baffled about whether she intends to uphold conventional values or challenge them. "Austen consistently *describes* the subordination of female to male," Spacks says, "but I am not so sure she *affirms* it" (224). Her real achievement lies in her ability to "demonstrate [the] rich fictional possibilities" inherent in the "double awareness of power and community as simultaneous if conflicting human impulses" (237).

Finally, Janis Stout's discussion of Austen in *Strategies of Reticence* (1990) makes use of an earlier feminist strategy — one that both later feminists and cultural critics alike would challenge — of linking women regardless of historical period in a sisterhood of subjection and oppression. This approach allows her to consider Austen as a "contemporary" of a trio of twentieth-century American women. Following Wayne Booth's delineation of rhetorical strategies employed to influence readers (in *The Rhetoric of Fiction*, 1961) Stout focuses on "silences and reticence as consciously or unconsciously chosen strategies for effect" (viii). Although Stout admits Austen did not directly influence the other writers she studies, she is the "fountainhead of the strategically reticent style in the novel as we know it" (ix). Stout's review of Austen's novels points out the abundance of "elusive or incomplete conversational interchanges" that "invite the reader's imaginative involvement," making readers "cocreators in the dynamics of the text" (26).

Tempering and Challenging Feminist Readings

As feminist criticism was beginning to blossom, a few critics mounted a kind of old-fashioned defense of the distinction between the sexes and the importance of recognizing different spheres in which men and women excelled. Austen's fiction receives extended treatment in A. O. J. Cockshut's *Man and Woman: A Study of Love and the Novel* (1977), in which he examines Austen's commentaries on jealously and rivalry for affections, the role of the mentor for the young woman, and the sometimes competing influences of rationality and passion. However, Cockshut's analysis of the way English novelists including Austen have dealt with this topic appears somewhat dated, perhaps even reactionary. In a somewhat more subtle dissent, Jean Kennard argues in *Victims of Convention* (1978) that to fully appreciate Austen and other women novelists it is first necessary to distinguish between "literary conventions" and "sociological truths" (10). In her analysis of Austen's novels she concentrates on various literary conventions employed by the novelist in structuring her work. One receiving considerable attention is the motif of having the female protagonist forced to choose between two suitors, a situation which inevitably forces the heroine to make some compromise in opting for one over the other. This conventional format works particularly well for Austen, Kennard says, because she "expects all of her characters — not just her women — to accept some limitations on their personalities for the sake of the social structure" (23).

Reacting to feminist criticism that attempts to remake Austen into a radical or subversive writer, in *The "Occult" Experience and the New Criticism: Daemonism, Sexuality, and the Hidden in Literature* (1986) Clive Bloom offers a reading of *Mansfield Park* that attempts to "reconsider Austen's conservatism" in order to "see her radicalism as one that ultimately upholds that conservatism" (12). Heavily influenced by theories of narratology, his examination reinforces the notion that Fanny Price serves as a preserver of traditional moral and cultural values. And in *The Ladies and the Mammies: Jane Austen and Jean Rhys* (1983) Selma James, who describes herself as a feminist but not a literary critic, tries to get beyond what she believes are misconceptions about Austen created by the critical establishment who read her for what she should be saying. As a counter, James offers close readings that analyze Austen's feminist sensibilities but at the same time reveals her limitations. James's ability to glean the revolutionary aspects of Austen's fiction from her overtly conservative portrait of her society and women's place in it make this brief sketch useful in identifying Austen's true relationship to the feminist tradition in literature.

Notes

[1] For more detailed studies of the early feminist reaction, consult: David Monaghan, "Jane Austen and the Feminist Critics" (1979); Christine Marshall, "'Dull Elves' and Feminists: A Summary of Feminist Criticism of Jane Austen" (1992); and Julia Prewitt Brown, "The Feminist Depreciation of Austen: A Polemical Reading" (1990).

Works Cited

Armstrong, Nancy. *Desire and Domestic Fiction: A Political History of the Novel.* New York: Oxford UP, 1987.

Auerbach, Nina. *Communities of Women: An Idea in Fiction.* Cambridge, MA: Harvard UP, 1978.

Bloom, Clive. "Sexuality in Jane Austen's Fanny, and *Mansfield Park.*" *The "Occult" Experience and the New Criticism: Daemonism, Sexuality, and the Hidden in Literature,* 12–26. Brighton, Sussex: Harvester P; Totowa, NJ: Barnes & Noble, 1986.

Boone, Joseph A. "Narrative Structure in the Marriage Tradition: Paradigmatic Plots of Courtship, Seduction, and Wedlock." *Tradition Counter Tradition: Love and the Form of Fiction*, 65–137. Chicago: U of Chicago P, 1987.

Booth, Wayne. *The Rhetoric of Fiction*. Chicago: U of Chicago P, 1961.

Brown, Julia Prewitt. "The Feminist Depreciation of Austen: A Polemical Reading." *Novel* 23 (1990): 303–13.

———. *Jane Austen's Novels: Social Change and Literary Form*. Cambridge, MA: Harvard UP, 1979.

Brownstein, Rachel W. "Getting Married: Jane Austen." *Becoming a Heroine: Reading About Women in Novels*, 79–136. New York: Viking, 1982.

Butler, Marilyn. *Jane Austen and the War of Ideas*. Oxford: Clarendon Press, 1975.

Caywood, Cynthia. "*Pride and Prejudice* and the Belief in Choice: Jane Austen's Fantastical Vision." In *Portraits of Marriage in Literature*, edited by Anne C. Hargrove and Maurine Magliocco, 31–37. Macomb: Western Illinois UP, 1984.

Chapman, R. W., ed. *The Novels of Jane Austen: The Text Based on Collations of the Early Editions*. 5 vols. Oxford: Clarendon Press, 1923.

Chase, Karen. "'"Bad" Was My Commentary': Propriety, Madness, Independence in Feminist Literary History." In *Victorian Connections*, edited by Jerome J. McGann, 11–30. Charlottesville: UP of Virginia, 1989.

Cockshut, A. O. J. *Man and Woman: A Study of Love and the Novel, 1740–1940*, 54–72. London: Collins, 1977.

Drabble, Margaret. "Introduction." *Emma*, by Jane Austen, v–xix. London: Virago Press, 1989.

———. "Introduction." *Mansfield Park*, by Jane Austen, v–xvii. London: Virago Press, 1989.

———. "Introduction." *Northanger Abbey*, by Jane Austen, v–xvii. London: Virago Press, 1989.

———. "Introduction." *Persuasion*, by Jane Austen, v–xvi. London: Virago Press, 1989.

———. "Introduction." *Pride and Prejudice*, by Jane Austen, v–xvi. London: Virago Press, 1989.

———. "Introduction." *Sense and Sensibility*, by Jane Austen, v–xviii. London: Virago Press, 1989.

Edwards, Lee R. "Heroes into Heroines: The Limits of Comedy in *Emma, Jane Eyre*, and *Middlemarch*." *Psyche as Hero: Female Heroism and Fictional Form*, 62–103. Middletown, CT: Wesleyan UP, 1984.

Figes, Eva. "The Supremacy of Sense." *Sex and Subterfuge: Women Novelists to 1850*, 76–112. London: Macmillan, 1982.

Fraiman, Susan. "The Humiliation of Elizabeth Bennet." In *Refiguring the Father: New Feminist Readings of Patriarchy*, edited by Patricia Yeager and Beth Kowaleski-Wallace, 168–87. Carbondale and Edwardsville: Southern Illinois UP, 1989. Reprinted in *Unbecoming Women: British Women Writers and the Novel of Development*, 59–87. New York: Columbia UP, 1993.

Fulbrook, Kate. "Jane Austen and the Comic Negative." In *Women Reading Women's Writing*, edited by Sue Row, 37–57. New York: St. Martin's, 1987.

Gilbert, Sandra M. and Susan Gubar. *The Madwoman in the Attic: The Woman Writer and the Nineteenth-Century Literary Imagination*, 107–83. New Haven, CT: Yale UP, 1979.

Harris, Jocelyn. Review of Alison Sulloway, *Jane Austen and the Province of Womanhood*. *Eighteenth-Century Studies* 27.1 (Autumn 1993): 186–93.

Holly, Grant I. "*Emma*grammatology." *Studies in Eighteenth-Century Culture* 19, edited by Leslie Ellen Brown and Patricia Craddock, 39–51. East Lansing, MI: Colleagues Press, 1989.

Hunt, Linda C. "A Woman's Portion: Jane Austen and the Female Character." *A Woman's Portion: Ideology, Culture, and the British Female Novel Tradition*, 17–48. New York: Garland, 1988.

James, Selma. *The Ladies and the Mammies: Jane Austen and Jean Rhys*. Old Market, Bristol, England: Falling Wall Press, 1983.

Johnson, Claudia L. *Jane Austen: Women, Politics, and the Novel*. Chicago: U of Chicago P, 1988.

———. "'Not At All What a Man Should Be': Remaking English Manhood in *Emma*." *Equivocal Beings: Politics, Gender, and Sentimentality in the 1790s: Wollstonecraft, Radcliffe, Burney, Austen*, 191–204. Chicago: U of Chicago P, 1995.

Kennard, Jean E. "Jane Austen: The Establishment." *Victims of Convention*, 21–45. Hamden, CT: Archon Books, 1978.

Kirkham, Margaret. *Jane Austen: Feminism and Fiction*. Totowa, NJ: Barnes & Noble, 1983.

Lanser, Susan Sniader. "No Connections Subsequent: Jane Austen's World of Sisterhood." In *The Sister Bond: A Feminist View of a Timeless Connection*, edited by Toni A. H. McNaron, 51–67. New York: Pergamon Press, 1985.

Le Faye, Deirdre. Review of Alison Sulloway, *Jane Austen and the Province of Womanhood*. *Review of English Studies* 44 (February 1993): 115–16.

MacDonald, Susan Peck. "Jane Austen and the Tradition of the Absent Mother." In *The Lost Tradition: Mothers and Daughters in Literature*, edited by Cathy Davidson and E. M. Broner, 58–69. New York: Ungar, 1980.

Marshall, Christine. "'Dull Elves' and Feminists: A Summary of Feminist Criticism of Jane Austen." *Persuasions* 14 (1992): 39–45.

Mayne, Judith. "Two Narratives of Private and Public Life." *Private Novels, Public Films*, 40–67. Athens: U of Georgia P, 1988.

Miller, Jane. *Women Writing About Men*. New York: Pantheon, 1986.

Millett, Kate. *Sexual Politics*. Garden City, NY: Doubleday, 1970.

Moers, Ellen. *Literary Women: The Great Writers*. New York: Doubleday, 1976. London: W. H. Allen, 1977.

Monaghan, David. "Jane Austen and the Feminist Critics." *Room of One's Own: A Feminist Journal of Literature and Criticism* 4.3 (1979): 34–39.

Morgan, Susan. *In the Meantime: Character and Perception in Jane Austen's Fiction*. Chicago: U of Chicago P, 1980.

———. "Why There's No Sex in Jane Austen's Fiction." *Sisters in Time: Imagining Gender in Nineteenth-Century British Fiction*, 23–55. Oxford: Oxford UP, 1989.

Newton, Judith L. *Women, Power, and Subversion: Social Strategies in British Fiction, 1778–1860*. Athens: U of Georgia P, 1981.

Poovey, Mary. *The Proper Lady and the Woman Writer: Ideology as Style in the Works of Mary Wollstonecraft, Mary Shelley, and Jane Austen*. Chicago: U of Chicago P, 1984.

Sabiston, Elizabeth Jean. "'Emma's Daughters': A Study in Isolation and Creativity." *The Prison of Womanhood: Four Provincial Heroines in Nineteenth-Century Fiction*, 18–41. New York: St. Martin's, 1987.

Schofield, Mary Anne, and Cecilia Macheski, eds. *Fetter'd or Free? British Women Novelists, 1670–1815*. Athens: Ohio UP, 1986.

Shaffer, Julie. "Not Subordinate: Empowering Women in the Marriage Plot in the Novels of Fanny Burney, Maria Edgeworth, and Jane Austen." In *Reading with a Difference: Gender, Race, and Cultural Identity*, edited by Arthur F. Marotti, et al., 21–44. Detroit: Wayne State UP, 1986.

Siefert, Susan. *The Dilemma of the Talented Heroine: A Study in Nineteenth-Century Fiction*. St. Albans, VT: Eden Press, 1978.

Smith, LeRoy. *Jane Austen and the Drama of Woman*. New York: St. Martin's, 1983.

Spacks, Patricia Meyer. *The Female Imagination: A Literary and Psychological Investigation of Women's Writing*. New York: Knopf, 1975. London: Allen & Unwin, 1976.

———. "'The Novel's Wisdom': Austen and Scott." *Desire and Truth: Functions of Plot in Eighteenth-Century English Novels*, 203–34. Chicago: U of Chicago P, 1990.

Spencer, Jane. "Reformed Heroines: The Didactic Tradition." *The Rise of the Woman Novelist: From Aphra Behn to Jane Austen*, 140–80. New York: Basil Blackwell, 1986.

Stout, Janis P. "What They Don't Say: Conversational and Narrative Withholdings in Austen's Novels." *Strategies of Reticence: Silence and Meaning in the Works of Jane Austen, Willa Cather, Katherine Anne Porter, and Joan Didion*, 24–65. Charlottesville: UP of Virginia, 1990.

Sulloway, Alison G. "Jane Austen's Mediative Voice." In *Nineteenth-Century Women Writers of the English-Speaking World*, edited by Rhoda B. Nathan, 193–99. New York and Westport, CT: Greenwood Press, 1986.

———. *Jane Austen and the Province of Womanhood*. Philadelphia: U of Pennsylvania P, 1989.

Todd, Janet. "Female Friendship in Jane Austen's Novels." *Journal of the Rutgers University Libraries* 39 (1977): 29–43.

———. *Women's Friendship in Literature*. New York: Columbia UP, 1980.

Tracy, Laura. "Jane Austen: Letting Go." *"Catching the Drift": Authority, Gender, and Narrative Strategy in Fiction*, 133–87. New Brunswick, NJ: Rutgers UP, 1988.

Weissman, Judith. "Jane Austen: Loving and Leaving." *Half Savage and Hardy and Free: Women and Rural Radicalism in the Nineteenth-Century Novel*, 47–75. Middletown, CT: Wesleyan UP, 1987.

Williams, Merryn. "Jane Austen." *Women in the English Novel, 1800–1900*, 44–52. New York: St. Martin's, 1984.

Wilt, Judith. "Jane Austen's Men: Inside/Outside 'The Mystery.'" In *Men by Women*, edited by Janet Todd, 59–76. New York: Holmes & Meier, 1981.

Zeman, Anthea. *Presumptuous Girls: Women and Their World in the Serious Woman's Novel*. London: Weidenfeld & Nicolson, 1977.

6: Austen among the Theorists, 1976–1990

IT SHOULD COME AS NO SURPRISE to find a sharp spike in Austen criticism beginning in the 1970s even without the significant contributions of feminist critics. In fact, the explosion of feminist criticism may have masked advances in Austen studies brought about by critics approaching her work from a variety of other new approaches. Between 1970 and 1990 more than three hundred doctoral candidates wrote dissertations either focused exclusively on Austen or containing large sections devoted to analysis of her work. While most commentary produced after the mid-1970s reflects the influence of feminists, many practitioners of other new critical theories found Austen's fiction fertile ground for their analyses. This chapter offers an overview of the kinds of work being done by critics employing new tools such as theories of narratology, new psychology, sociological studies, Marxism, and new historicism.

Structural Criticism, Deconstruction, and Narratology

Many second-generation structuralists, narratologists, and even poststructuralists writing about Austen after 1970 used their analyses to explore larger issues involving the writing and study of fiction. A sampling of studies illustrates this trend nicely. In *Expositional Modes and Temporal Ordering in Fiction* (1978) Meir Sternberg focuses on Austen's ability to control her readers' response to characters and delay their judgments about moral issues through a technique he calls "anticipatory caution" (129). Sternberg explains how Austen's conscious decisions regarding the timing of exposition and the temporal ordering of events allow her to keep readers interested in her principal figures while giving them the pleasurable sensation of coming to conclusions about these characters gradually. Derek Brewer's discussion of Austen's novels in *Symbolic Stories: Traditional Narratives of the Family Drama in English Literature* (1980) concentrates on "the play of the pattern of fantasy within the naturalistic world of the novel" (148). Brewer finds "at the heart of Jane Austen's supremely novelistic novels" an "interesting variant of the traditional pattern" that concerns "the irredeemable awfulness of mothers and the need to improve and capture a father-figure" (149). Austen employs the Cinderella story in her works to dramatize the struggles of heroines who must face hard choices and numerous obstacles before landing a prince who possesses distinctly paternal qualities.

In a study of structural patterning in Austen's fiction, *Jane Austen: Structure and Social Vision* (1980), David Monaghan concentrates on what he calls the "formal social occasion" (1) as a touchstone for entering Austen's novels to determine what the novelist is aiming at in her portraits of society. In his view, Austen's portrayal of "social rituals" (1) makes it clear how finely attuned she was to her own age. Initially committed to the values of the landed gentry, Austen uses the various social positions of her characters "to demonstrate her thesis that the fate of society depends on the ability of the landed classes to live up to their ideal of concern for others, and on the willingness of other groups to accept this ideal" (7). For Monaghan, not only do manners equal morals; group settings are the crucible in which Austen's characters test their individual understanding of their social and moral obligations, and learn by their experiences. Over the course of her career, Austen's faith in the landed gentry was generally eroded. This is why, Monaghan argues, an early novel like *Pride and Prejudice* seems artistically unified, while *Emma*, which he calls her "greatest formal achievement" (142), takes a more skeptical stance toward the class she had once venerated. If *Persuasion* seems not to be unified, he says it is because Austen was coming to realize that "the social order which it had been the business of her literary career to explore and vindicate" was "falling apart" (162).

Although his emphasis in *Jane Austen: Structure and Social Vision* is on formal devices, Monaghan is primarily a social critic, concerned with the way the social fabric contributes to and is represented in Austen's novels. That point is made even more clearly in the 1981 collection of essays he edited, *Jane Austen in a Social Context*. In this important book Monaghan assembles work from some of the most important contemporary Austen critics in order to demonstrate how the dominant ideologies in Austen's time deeply influenced her work. Hence, "the more accurately the critic can reconstruct Jane Austen's world, the more clearly he is likely to see the macrocosmic significance of the tiny events she describes" (3). Although Monaghan himself believes Austen was essentially conservative, he allows his contributors to take both sides in this debate, and the essays by Nina Auerbach, Ann Banfield, Marilyn Butler, Jan Fergus, Christopher Kent, Jane Nardin, LeRoy Smith, Patricia Meyer Spacks, Tony Tanner, and Monaghan himself attest to the difficulties inherent in trying to uphold either viewpoint consistently.

The continuity of methodology between structuralists of different generations is evident in John Odmark's *An Understanding of Jane Austen's Novels: Character, Value and Ironic Perspective* (1981). Though Odmark admits the influence of Karl Kroeber's *Styles in Fictional Structure* on his work, his book also reveals the influence of emerging theories of narratology and authorship. He rejects at the outset the aesthetic approach to Austen's fiction, claiming that an understanding of the novels' historical context is imperative for right reading. Interested in exploring the relationships between the author and her texts and the novels and their readers, Odmark concentrates on points of view — both the "technical point of view" — the "means used by the author to structure the reader's experience" — and the "real point of view" — the "author's norms and values as well as his assumptions about his reading public as these norms, values and assumptions are manifest in the text" (xiv–xv). Understanding these distinctions helps one read Austen's fiction correctly — something Odmark says most critics have failed to do, especially those who champion her as a critic of her society. When one understands the context in which she wrote, it becomes clear that Austen's ironic stance is intended not to suggest that the values of her society should be rejected; instead, irony is meant "to guide the reader, usually along with the heroine, in learning to perceive and discriminate among grades of moral quality" (183).

The appearance in 1981 of a remarkable first book by D. A. Miller introduced Austen scholars, and the critical community at large, to a strong new voice in literary studies. In *Narrative and its Discontents*, Miller, educated at Yale and well-schooled in new critical theories, examines the work of Austen, George Eliot, and Stendhal as examples of what he calls traditional novels in which the author struggles with problems of closure. In these works, he says, the novelist's "ambition extends beyond resolving the particular issues of the story at hand to removing the very conditions under which a story is possible" (x)— conditions that, by their very nature, are narratable because they seem to continually generate possibilities that can be narrated. His close readings of Austen's fiction are intended to isolate instances when Austen's control over her narrative becomes discernible, as she exercises judgments about characters and values to drive her narrative toward the point where there is simply nothing left to tell, in the process cutting off those narrative strands that conflict with her own moral viewpoint. Miller says that in Austen's case, "what motivates the narratability of a story coincides with what the novelist strongly disapproves of," and "what motivates closure is associated with her most important official values" (xiv).

In another study focused on issues of narratology and communication, *Worlds from Words* (1981), James Phelan uses Austen's *Persuasion* as a test case for examining the validity of — and ultimately undermining — Jacques Derrida's and J. Hillis Miller's theories of deconstruction, which posit that all texts are ultimately indeterminate and that no ground exists in language for fixing meaning. Continuing his study of Austen in *Reading People, Reading Plots* (1989), Phelan offers a critique of *Pride and Prejudice* that stresses the mimetic aspects of Austen's heroine. Challenging thematic readings that in his view privilege one aspect of Elizabeth

Bennet's character and ignore others, Phelan explains how the complexity of Austen's heroine makes her appealing as a possible person while at the same time permits readers to see her as functioning to advance certain themes that Austen wishes to highlight in the novel.

The idea of what "realism" means in describing Austen's work was called into question by Elizabeth Ermarth and Claudia Brodsky. In *Realism and Consensus in the English Novel* (1983), an examination intended to identify the elements common to novels conventionally classified as realist and to "denaturalize" the "premises of realism," Ermarth contends that "realistic conventions are not immutable, eternal, grounded in the nature of things," but instead are "grounded in collective assertion and are limited historically" (xiii). Her discussion of Austen's novels focuses principally on the novelist's narrative methods, noting the radical shift in Austen's social vision between *Emma*, which celebrates community, and *Persuasion*, which values detachment. In *The Imposition of Form: Studies in Narrative Representation and Knowledge* (1987) Brodsky uses Austen's novels to explore what she calls the function and limits of irony in realist fiction to explain why, despite "material, societal, and literary-historical change," Austen's "representationally limited narratives continue to bring about an experience in reading coincident with our experience, whatever its particulars, of 'real life'" (147).

Finally, the works of two other American critics serve as good examples of how an understanding and appreciation of Austen's art could be enhanced by new methods of critical study. Andrew Wright's brief but provocative *Fictional Discourse and Historical Space* (1987), a study of novels as narratives defined by their historical contexts, searches for connections between Austen's *Emma* and E. M. Forster's *Howard's End* to demonstrate how great literature can transcend its own age while simultaneously being rooted in it. The writings of Michel Foucault, Frederic Jameson, and Hayden White seem to guide his critique, which is both a study of the historical process and an analysis of narrative strategies. A second critic, John Dussinger, also demonstrates exceptional ability to employ new critical methodologies to the study of Austen's fiction. His "'The Language of Real Feeling': Internal Speech in the Jane Austen Novel" (1988) presents an analysis of Austen's use of "free indirect discourse" (97). Dussinger believes one can see in Austen's employment of this technique some of her more experimental and radical qualities in handling language and narrative. Following Bakhtin, Dussinger argues that Austen's exceptional diversity of style is the source of both her comedy and her morality — and that her moral stance is not as clearly conservative as others have judged it to be. In *In the Pride of the Moment: Encounters in Jane Austen's World* (1990), Dussinger again shows that he is well versed in a number of new theoretical approaches and intent on a blended approach to critiquing Austen's fiction. Employing sociologist Erving

Goffman's play-theory of social interaction, Dussinger concentrates on "Austen's art of coloring narrative and dialogue to render a character's point of view within carefully arranged encounters" (3). His sophisticated and exceptionally detailed analysis is intended to overturn the "familiar view that Austen's novels are stylistically polished but lack in substance." Austen, he says, gives such weight to the everyday that her works are worthy of comparison with "the worldly metaphysics of such modern thinkers as Heidegger and Sartre" (16).

At this point, before proceeding to examine other new critical approaches to Austen's fiction, I should acknowledge that the work of narratologists and deconstructionists was not met with universal approbation. While American critics tended to celebrate these new readings, many British scholars seemed less ready to adopt such radical revisions of the critical enterprise, and hence were less willing to accept conclusions about Austen's fiction put forth in such studies. The split can be seen in the reaction to Dussinger's book. Most American reviewers gave Dussinger high marks, although Joseph Wiesenfarth (1991) challenged Dussinger's claim of originality regarding the significance of Austen's treatment of domestic life. A number of other reviewers admitted that Dussinger's prose is dense and his argument at times hard to follow, but the majority seem to agree with Catherine Park, who says in her *English Language Notes* review (1994) that Dussinger undertakes "boldly and controversially" to "read Austen's fiction as both mimetic and textual, psychological and semiotic," creating a "critical method that alternates between but does not thereby radically divide models of mind, text, and the creative process" (81). British scholars seemed to take a notably different position, suggested most forcefully in Deirdre Le Faye's assessment in *Review of English Studies* (1993): *In the Pride of the Moment* is "unfortunately so over-written in the polyphonic academic jargon" that "its theme nearly becomes lost in the jungle of verbiage" (116).

Sociological Studies

While critics writing during the first half of the twentieth century relied implicitly on sociological theory as a basis for exploring Austen's fiction, beginning in the 1970s those employing sociological studies were more forthright in acknowledging their debt and in many cases more systematic in following the methodologies developed by theorists in that field. Such is the case in Terry Lovell's "Jane Austen and Gentry Society" in *Literature, Society and the Sociology of Literature* (1977). Lovell's work explores Austen's attitudes toward the gentry, explains what it really meant for her to be a conservative in her own day, and examines her role as a woman writing in an age that set strict limits on women's participation in public matters. David Grylls's *Guardians and Angels: Parents and Children in*

Nineteenth-Century Literature (1978), a sociological investigation of fiction and poetry reflecting the "growth of childhood independence and the decay of parental power" (11) over the course of the nineteenth century, compares Austen's treatment of parent-child relationships with that of Charles Dickens. Austen, Grylls says, is "profoundly pre-Romantic" (130) in her view of children as needing education and reform. Her work reveals her "consistent approval of filial duty and parental authority" (130) — but her treatment of individual young women and their parents demonstrates the complexity of such relationships as children grow to maturity. In *Society in the Novel* (1984), a study positing that the "function of a fictional social order is to represent some outside world" (ix), Elizabeth Langland demonstrates how Austen creates "a balance between individual needs or perceptions and social forms and values which justified regarding her fiction as a watershed in the formal treatment of society in the novel" (25). The society Austen presents in her novels "serves as a formal center of values by which worthy characters rise, and unworthy are identified, in our estimation" (44). If this society is not to be mistaken for the world in which readers live, it is intended as a close parallel so that Austen's novels become critiques of the real world.

The reflection of social concerns in Austen's novels is also discussed in George Levine's *Darwin and the Novelists: Patterns of Science in Victorian Fiction* (1988). Including her in this study may seem curious, since Austen was not a Victorian and her work seems to contain little about science. But Levine is interested in explaining the pervasiveness of science as a cultural discourse by examining the work of writers not directly influenced by scientific writing. Acknowledging that Austen's novels are "distant" from "science and theology," Levine says they nevertheless "reflect the assumptions and possibilities also present in the natural-theological predispositions of pre-Darwinian science." He finds *Mansfield Park* a useful test case to explain what "a novel outside the aura of Darwinism" looks like. Through the keen observer Fanny Price, Austen "works out tensions between the stable vision of a world governed by the principles of natural theology and the destabilizing vision of Darwin's" (56). Levine challenges recent readings of *Mansfield Park* that find the book's strengths in the "disruptive forces" (58). Austen, he insists, is essentially a conservative who believes that life is by nature ordered and designed, and her heroine is a defender of the old order against the forces of disruption.

Austen's novels even serve as the basis for an extensive anthropological assessment of courtship and marriage in Richard Handler and Daniel Segal's *Jane Austen and the Fiction of Culture: An Essay on the Narration of Social Realities* (1990). Using a variety of postmodern techniques of analysis drawn from both literary theory and anthropology, the authors find Austen's novels fertile ground for understanding the society in which she lived and wrote. Further, they conclude that she was decidedly ahead of her time in recognizing the inconsistencies and inadequacies of the social construct of marriage, and that she delighted in pointing out the problems inherent in the dominant values of her society. Unfortunately, this interdisciplinary study was hailed by a number of reviewers but condemned by others who thought the authors' playfulness and failure to recognize adequately the fictive nature of Austen's work made their book of limited value to scholars in either of the disciplines at which it was directed.

Marxist and New Historicist Readings

The dividing line may sometimes be difficult to discern between the sociological and political readings described above and those of critics who take a more avowedly Marxist approach in their analysis of Austen's work. Still, it seems appropriate to single out a handful of works to illustrate how Marxists and New Historicists approached her fiction, since their readings tend to be formed by ideological perspectives that differ (at least in theory) from those that shape the work of critics like Langland, Evans, Levine, or Handler and Segal. For example, Lillian Robinson melds her revolutionary brand of feminism with Marxist ideology in *Sex, Class, and Culture* (1979) to create a framework for examining literature and society. Her intriguing commentary on *Pride and Prejudice* in a chapter she provocatively titles "Why Marry Mr. Collins?" is less literary criticism than a critique of the social and political standing of women about whom Austen wrote. For Robinson, Austen is not quite a full-fledged revolutionary; rather, she is a "restrained but exact social revolutionary, accepting a co-equal hegemony of gentry and bourgeoisie and upholding the daring, fundamentally bourgeois custom that human worth is not a matter of birth but of individual merit, of culture" (180). In Robinson's caustic analysis of bourgeois society, Austen is given credit for exposing some of the evils of both the landed gentry and the rising middle class. But Robinson takes pains to point out the hidden assumptions and values on which that society is based. Embodied in what Robinson calls "the central contradiction in Jane Austen's work" is the "tension between the ideal of marriage for love and the social reality of gentry life" (199).

In "Community and Morality: Towards Reading Jane Austen" (1981) the noted Marxist critic David Aers insists that those who continue to represent Austen as a consummate artist detached from contemporary concerns or as a moralist espousing fixed principles of behavior are doing her work disservice. Following the lead of Marilyn Butler but revising her conclusions to produce a more radical Marxist reading, Aers points out ways in which Austen reveals herself as a Tory ideologue who "closes up her imagination against critical alternatives." As a consequence, Aers says, her works "fail to transcend the narrow limitations of her historical class" (136). Igor Webb reaches a similar conclusion in *From Custom to Capital:*

The English Novel and the Industrial Revolution (1981), a study that extends what he describes as "the holistic tradition of historical and cultural Marxist criticism" (10) of Georg Lukács, Lucien Goldman, and Raymond Williams to a study of novels written in the late eighteenth and early nineteenth centuries. Austen's novels, Webb says, are a defense of "the *idea* of the landed system" (112) and traditional concepts of family and marriage which were being threatened by upheavals in society caused by the Industrial Revolution. Webb cites examples from history, politics, and cultural studies to demonstrate how Austen operates (perhaps unwittingly on occasion) to support the oppressive political and social system of which she was a part.

While not openly Marxist, John Vernon's *Money and Fiction: Literary Realism in the Nineteenth and Early Twentieth Centuries* (1984) shares affinities with Marxist criticism in its focus on the economic basis of society. Vernon employs the work of Foucault and other contemporary theorists to examine ways money becomes both a commodity and a metaphor that reshapes community and society during the nineteenth century. In a chapter he titles "The Breaking Up of the Estate: *Persuasion*" — an obvious reference to Duckworth's *The Improvement of the Estate* — Vernon demonstrates how Austen's last completed work is in some ways the first modern novel because in it Austen acknowledges that money, rather than land, has become the basis for obtaining status in society. She was aware of the social transformation going on in her society, Vernon says, where land was becoming less a place of refuge and stability and more a commodity available for those with enough money to purchase it and thereby gain visible proof of their social status.

R. S. Neale's reading of *Mansfield Park* in *Writing Marxist History* (1985) stresses what he believes is Austen's "perception of the plight of the dominant class under threat" (87). In the novel Austen explores themes of individual alienation within a society dominated by capitalist ideology. Much of the essay combines literary criticism with explanations of economic theory that, in Neale's view, help place the novel culturally as a text that questions, but ultimately does not condemn, the dominant ideology of its age. That interdisciplinary approach may seem quite acceptable, even preferable, to many scholars and students of the twenty-first century, but in 1985 it posed some problems within academe, as Neale playfully notes in describing the difficulties he had in trying to get his work published in a scholarly periodical. "'Not social history,' said a journal of social history. 'Not literary criticism,' said a journal of literary criticism" (87).

Mary Evans's brief monograph *Jane Austen and the State* (1987) provides an overtly political reading of the Austen canon, organized thematically around issues such as property, patriarchy, and the role of the state in human affairs. Asserting at the outset that Austen's novels are "brilliant discussions of the issue of personal behaviour within the context of capitalist social relations" (ix), Evans offers a leftist assessment of the Austen canon that paints Austen as a radical who insists that individual behaviors can shape the social order, and that capitalism, while exceedingly tempting, need not be the only means of organizing society. Evans claims that Austen realized before Marx or Freud that "people construct the world" — whether for good or for ill (86). She was, Evans says, a firm believer that the "strictures of the state" cannot make individuals good; only constant commitment to "the values of mutuality" can create "a society worth living in" (87). In like fashion, David Musselwhite's "Return to *Mansfield Park*" (1987), grounded in the theoretical work of Félix Guattari and Ernesto Laclau, reads *Mansfield Park* as a novel concerned with power relationships in which "a would-be hegemonic class appropriates to itself the popular democratic mobilizations of the masses" (4). Edward Ahearn provides a similar systematic Marxist critique of *Pride and Prejudice* in *Marx and Modern Fiction* (1989), highlighting problems of class, particularly as it is defined by money, in a society witnessing the shift in power from the landed gentry to a middle class that increasingly relied on capital as a means of attaining social status and power. Ahearn also points out the condition of women in that society, noting how Austen — a radical despite the surface conservatism that seems to emerge from a casual reading of her fiction — accurately and sensitively describes the plight of her heroines in a society where women were seen as little more than a form of property that might increase the estates of their husbands.

Less overtly Marxist, James Thompson in *Between Self and World: The Novels of Jane Austen* (1988) offers a systematic new historicist analysis of Austen based principally on the theory of the novel espoused by Georg Lukács, modified by the work of Frederic Jameson and amplified by that of Raymond Williams. What Lukács's "Marxist analysis" provides, Thompson says, is a "totalizing explanation" to the study of Austen's work, situating it in historical context and revealing the ideology that informs it. Marxist overtones are everywhere as Thompson attempts to "historicize Austen's language" and "the feeling expressed in it, by examining emotion in Austen's fiction in the light of a wide range of historical circumstances, social and economic as well as literary" (5). One of his aims is to dispel the idea that Austen's moralism and insight into human emotion is universally valid for all times and places, while at the same time disproving the notion that her ironic stance is motivated by personal concerns. Arguing that Austen's use of language is "essentially Romantic" (15), Thompson explores her concept of language as a means of conveying emotions, specifically those arising from private experience, which he says is characteristic of the novel as a genre.

Psychological Criticism

Although it might be argued that there is considerably less psychological criticism written about Austen and her fiction than that devoted to the life and work of, say, Dickens or Lawrence, there is no doubt that her fiction (and to a lesser extent, her life) has sparked some interest among psychological critics inspired by post-Freudian and neo-Freudian theories. This is not to ignore some of the early attempts to psychoanalyze her and her work, such as Clarissa Rinaker's "A Psychoanalytical Note on Jane Austen" in a 1936 issue of the *Psychoanalytical Quarterly*, or Helen Corsa's "A Fair but Frozen Maid: A Study of Jane Austen's *Emma*" in a 1969 number of *Literature and Psychology*. But certainly the most extensive attempt to provide a psychological reading of the fiction is Bernard J. Paris's *Character and Conflict in Jane Austen's Novels: A Psychological Approach* (1978). Paris was the leading proponent of Third Force Psychology as a tool for literary criticism. The theory had been developed by German psychologist Karen Horney (and popularized in America by Abraham Maslow) as an alternative to Freud's theories regarding personality. Horney argued that it was not necessary to go back to childhood to interpret personality and motivation in order to understand adult behavior. Literary critics found this theory adaptable for analyzing fictional characters, who by definition have no previous life to influence their behaviors. In his book on Austen, Paris employs Horney's principles to study characters in the novelist's fiction. His work systematically analyzes the conflicts he sees emerging from the novels — conflicts not only within and between fictional characters, but between those characters and the novelist herself. Dismissing as erroneous the idea that the novels possess some form of organic unity, Paris analyzes what he calls "powerful unrecognized tensions between form, theme, and mimesis" (13). Because Austen's characters are highly mimetic and seem to possess motivations of real people, Paris believes the novels can best be understood by applying tools of psychology to reveal the hidden motivations behind their actions. Using the theories of Northrop Frye to analyze the comic structure of Austen's work, Paris shows how, by explaining characters' motivations in terms Horney popularized, he can make sense of the fiction *and* at the same time expose some of the "conflicts" in Austen's own personality (11).

As one might expect, given Paris's critical bias, his discussions of individual figures are peppered with observations such as "*Emma* is the story of a young woman with both narcissistic and perfectionistic trends" (73) and "Elizabeth becomes the central figure in [Darcy's] psychic life" (138). Much of his analysis is suggestive of earlier critical commentary on the novels, and he admits that he has been influenced by critics who have seen Austen as an ironist and a subversive. But in his final chapter, "The Authorial Personality," Paris develops a detailed psychological portrait of

Austen based on her handling of characters in her fiction. He believes Austen's personality "contains a mixture of perfectionist, detached, and self-effacing values," and she is successful in presenting "a wide range of psychological types" because of "her own inner conflicts" (198). While it may not be inappropriate to derive some sense of an author from her works, one may come away from Paris's assessment of Austen feeling that he has extrapolated too much from the fiction. What is certain is that his contemporaries and many who came after him pursued other lines of argument in trying to explain Austen's aims and methods in her works.

Three other studies deserve mention as examples of how psychological critics have approached Austen's work. The first, although traditional in its methodology, is rather curious for its choice of subjects. In her discussion of teenage girls coming to maturity in *Female Adolescence: Psychoanalytic Reflections on Works of Literature* (1986), Katherine Dalsimer focuses on Austen's last novel, *Persuasion*, with its twenty-seven-year-old heroine. Believing that it is possible to gain a real appreciation for what happens to girls during their adolescent years by reading literature, Dalsimer examines a handful of novels with teen heroines or adults, like Austen's Anne Elliot, who are vexed by problems that formed in adolescence and linger into their adult lives. *Persuasion*, Dalsimer says, "masterfully renders the internal processes of development" that all young girls undergo, processes that "remain constant in spite of profound historical and cultural change" (114).

David Holbrook also offers a more traditional philosophical and psychological analysis of Austen's fiction in *The Novel and Authenticity* (1987), a study comparing novels to psychological case studies and suggesting they can be read as "the record of a quest for the realization of the self" and "the search for the authenticity of being" (17–18). Focusing on *Mansfield Park*, Holbrook claims that this novel, like all of Austen's fiction, provides readers particular pleasure in watching the characters become aware, "often in pain and distress," of what it means "to be true to the deepest promptings of their hearts" (22). He argues that *Mansfield Park* "very largely made the English novel possible, because of its author's deeply religious moral gravity and authenticity, and her belief that a principled woman is credible" (56).

Phyllis Ralph's *Victorian Transformations: Fairy Tales, Adolescence, and the Novel of Female Development* (1989) includes commentary on Austen's work in a study of the use of fairy tale motifs heavily influenced by psychological theories of development. Accepting the notion that many of Austen's novels display structures akin to fairy tales, particularly the Cinderella myth, Ralph argues that these archetypal patterns move the meaning of her fiction "beyond the social and into the realm of the universal mythic experience of growth and development" (60). Using *Mansfield Park*, *Persuasion*, and *Pride and Prejudice* as her examples, Ralph demonstrates the "basic similarity between Austen's novels and fairy tales," particularly as they deal with "the growth and development on the part of the female protagonist" (84).

Reader-Response Criticism

A good example of how Austen's work has been read by practitioners of reader-response criticism can be found in Michael Steig's *Stories of Reading: Subjectivity and Literary Understanding* (1989). In this sweeping survey of ways readers can approach texts and derive appropriate but sometimes diverse or even conflicting readings, Steig includes a discussion of *Mansfield Park*, the novel he calls Austen's most problematic. With acknowledgment to a number of his predecessors who have offered perspectives for understanding this novel, Steig suggests it can best be appreciated by resisting the desire to find unity in its parts, and instead accept that it is an open form susceptible to multiple interpretations.

Informed by "modes of reading provided by literary theory" (3), John Allen Stevenson's *The British Novel, Defoe to Austen: A Critical History* (1990) includes a discussion of *Emma* that focuses on Austen's treatment of courtship, analyzing the technical problem Austen faces by creating three pairs of lovers already joined in some way at the beginning of her narrative. This creates a challenge for her, Stevenson says, because she must find ways to delay their final unions throughout the course of the tale without losing credibility with her readers.

Finally, while Austen's books continued to be popular in high-school and college classrooms, the difference in the reaction of students at the end of the century from that of their predecessors prompted Walter Gibson to write of his experiences in "Contrarieties of Emotion; Or, Five Days with *Pride and Prejudice*" (1990). In the essay Gibson relates how he manages to get undergraduates to respond to Austen's novel by focusing on the ironic quality of the language. The book opens their eyes to "the perils of taking language at face value" (118). One of the larger themes of *Pride and Prejudice*, Gibson says, is "to watch out for language," especially in contemporary society "where we recognize anew the disparity between word and thing" (119).

The Limits of Theory?

How far could new theories and new technologies take the study of Austen's fiction? Perhaps as far as the digital universe, if one is to believe J. F. Burrows. His *Computation into Criticism: A Study of Jane Austen's Novels and an Experiment in Method* (1987) uses the computer as a critical tool in evaluating Austen's fiction, taking advantage of new computer-generated methods of tabulating occurrences of individual words to construct an elaborate mapping of Austen's usage. Concentrating on what he calls articles, prepositions, and the like, Burrows makes the claim that *"from no other evidence* than a statistical analysis of the relative frequencies of the very common words, it is possible to differentiate sharply and appropriately among the idiolects of Jane Austen's characters and even to trace the ways in which an idiolect can develop in the course of a novel" (4). Although it may appear at first glance more technical than most Austen scholars might wish, Burrows's study is not simply a statistical tabulation; instead, he uses statistics to demonstrate how, by a close reading of individual words, it is possible to learn a great deal about Austen's characters.

Less jarring to traditional literary sensibilities than Burrows, but no less committed to the importance of new theories, are the contributors to Janet Todd's *Jane Austen: New Perspectives* (1983). One after another, notable Austen scholars such as Joel Weinsheimer, David Monaghan, Marvin Mudrick, Margaret Kirkham, Jane Nardin, and Todd herself, along with a dozen others whose work had already achieved acclaim in critical circles, examine individual novels and the Austen canon as a whole. No critical viewpoint is privileged, and one can find in this book historicist, psychoanalytic, and feminist readings offered as appropriate ways of approaching Austen's fiction. Todd believes such an eclectic collection is necessary because, "if the novels give license to careful, particular readings, they also warn against the quick judgment and inappropriate analysis" (2). The essays in *Jane Austen: New Perspectives* demonstrate that, even if they disagree, critics of Austen can find much to say about her work regardless of the approach they choose to take in dissecting it.

And in what might be described as a counter-thrust against deconstructionist and other readings of literature as self-contained "texts," Wayne Booth's *The Company We Keep: An Ethics of Fiction* (1988) insists that stories — including Austen's novels — have value and interest for readers as commentaries on their own lives. Booth is very resistant to ideological appropriations of Austen, and he makes his point emphatically in a discussion of *Emma* in which he explains how conventions of form shaped Austen's fiction. These conventions, he insists, demand certain moral stances, one of which was the contrived happy ending. Because Austen wanted to make *Emma* an "effective novel" for her first readers, she was led into "conventional patterns of desire that she quite obviously did not herself embrace uncritically" (431). Through her deft handling of narration, however, Austen is able to critique the fairy-tale quality of her story and question the adequacy of such outcomes. But Booth admits "it is reassuring to discover" that in 1988 "most of what we learn by asking the questions raised by feminist criticism" tends to "leave Jane Austen looking perhaps even greater than she did before" (435).

Works Cited

Aers, David. "Community and Morality: Towards Reading Jane Austen." In *Romanticism and Ideology: Studies in English Writing, 1765–1830*, edited by David Aers, Jonathan Cook, and David Punter, 118–36. Boston: Routledge & Kegan Paul, 1981.

Ahearn, Edward J. "Radical Jane and the Other Emma." *Marx and Modern Fiction*, 31–75. New Haven, CT: Yale UP, 1989.

Booth, Wayne C. "Doctrinal Questions in Jane Austen, D. H. Lawrence, and Mark Twain." *The Company We Keep: An Ethics of Fiction*, 421–82. Berkeley: U of California P, 1988.

Brewer, Derek. "Mainly on Jane Austen." *Symbolic Stories: Traditional Narratives of the Family Drama in English Literature*, 148–67. Totowa, NJ: Rowman & Littlefield, 1980.

Brodsky, Claudia J. "Austen: The Persuasions of Sensibility and Sense." *The Imposition of Form: Studies in Narrative Representation and Knowledge*, 141–87. Princeton, NJ: Princeton UP, 1987.

Burrows, J. F. *Computation into Criticism: A Study of Jane Austen's Novels and an Experiment in Method*. Oxford: Clarendon Press, 1987.

Corsa, Helen S. "A Fair but Frozen Maid: A Study of Jane Austen's *Emma*." *Literature and Psychology* 19 (1969): 101–24.

Dalsimer, Katherine. "Late Adolescence: *Persuasion*." *Female Adolescence: Psychoanalytic Reflections on Works of Literature*, 113–38. New Haven, CT: Yale UP, 1986.

Dussinger, John A. *In the Pride of the Moment: Encounters in Jane Austen's World*. Columbus: Ohio State UP, 1990.

———. "'The Language of Real Feeling': Internal Speech in the Jane Austen Novel." In *The Idea of the Novel in the Eighteenth Century*, edited by Robert Uphaus, 97–115. East Lansing, MI: Colleagues Press, 1988.

Ermarth, Elizabeth. "Jane Austen's Critique of Distance." *Realism and Consensus in the English Novel*, 144–77. Princeton, NJ: Princeton UP, 1983.

Evans, Mary. *Jane Austen and the State*. New York: Tavistock, 1987.

Gibson, Walter. "Contrarieties of Emotion; Or, Five Days with *Pride and Prejudice*." In *Conversations: Contemporary Critical Theory and the Teaching of Literature*, edited by Charles Moran and Elizabeth F. Penfield, 114–19. Urbana, IL: National Council of Teachers of English, 1990.

Grylls, David. *Guardians and Angels: Parents and Children in Nineteenth-Century Literature*, 111–32. London: Faber & Faber, 1978.

Handler, Richard, and Daniel Segal. *Jane Austen and the Fiction of Culture: An Essay on the Narration of Social Realities*. Tucson: U of Arizona P, 1990.

Higbie, Robert. *Character and Structure in the English Novel.* Gainesville: U of Florida P, 1984.

Holbrook, David. "The Novel and Moral Concern: *Mansfield Park.*" *The Novel and Authenticity,* 21–59. Totowa, NJ: Barnes & Noble, 1987.

Kroeber, Karl. *Styles in Fictional Structure: The Art of Jane Austen, Charlotte Brontë and George Eliot.* Princeton, NJ: Princeton UP, 1971.

Langland, Elizabeth. "Social Contexts for Judgment of Austen." *Society in the Novel,* 25–44. Chapel Hill: U of North Carolina P, 1984.

Le Faye, Deirdre. Review of John Dussinger, *In The Pride of the Moment. Review of English Studies* 44 (February 1993): 115–16.

Levine, George. "*Mansfield Park*: Observation Rewarded." *Darwin and the Novelists,* 56–83. Cambridge, MA: Harvard UP, 1988.

Lovell, Terry. "Jane Austen and Gentry Society." In *Literature, Society, and the Sociology of Literature,* ed. Francis Barker et al., 118–32. Colchester: U of Essex P, 1977.

Miller, D. A. "The Danger of Narrative in Jane Austen." *Narrative and Its Discontents: Problems of Closure in the Traditional Novel,* 3–106. Princeton, NJ: Princeton UP, 1981.

Monaghan, David. *Jane Austen: Structure and Social Vision.* Totowa, NJ: Barnes & Noble, 1980.

———, ed. *Jane Austen in a Social Context.* Totowa, NJ: Barnes & Noble, 1981.

Musselwhite, David E. "Return to *Mansfield Park.*" *Partings Welded Together: Politics and Desire in the Nineteenth-Century English Novel,* 16–42. London and New York: Methuen, 1987.

Neale, R. S. "Zapp Zapped: Property and Alienation in *Mansfield Park.*" *Writing Marxist History: British Society, Economy, and Culture since 1700,* 87–108. New York: Basil Blackwell, 1985.

Odmark, John. *An Understanding of Jane Austen's Novels: Character, Value, and Ironic Perspective.* Oxford: Basil Blackwell, 1981; Totowa, NJ: Barnes & Noble, 1981.

Paris, Bernard J. *Character and Conflict in Jane Austen's Novels: A Psychological Approach.* Detroit: Wayne State UP, 1978.

Park, Catherine. Review of John Dussinger, *In The Pride of the Moment. English Language Notes* 31.3 (March 1994): 79–81.

Phelan, James. "Determinate and Indeterminate Value in the Linguistic System: J. Hillis Miller and the Language of *Persuasion.*" *Worlds from Words: A Theory of Language in Fiction,* 117–52. Chicago: U of Chicago P, 1981.

———. *Reading People, Reading Plots: Character, Progression, and the Interpretation of Narrative.* Chicago: U of Chicago P, 1989.

Ralph, Phyllis C. "Jane Austen: Precursor of the Victorians." *Victorian Transformations: Fairy Tale, Adolescence, and the Novel of Female Development*, 59–85. New York: Lang, 1989.

Rinaker, Clarissa. "A Psychoanalytical Note on Jane Austen." *Psychoanalytical Quarterly* 5 (1936): 108–15.

Robinson, Lillian S. "Why Marry Mr. Collins?" *Sex, Class, and Culture*, 178–99. Bloomington: Indiana UP, 1978.

Steig, Michael. "Making *Mansfield Park* Feel Right." *Stories of Reading: Subjectivity and Literary Understanding*, 157–79. Baltimore: Johns Hopkins UP, 1989.

Sternberg, Meir. "The Rhetoric of Anticipatory Caution: First Impressions in 'First Impressions' and the Poetics of Jane Austen." *Expositional Modes and Temporal Ordering in Fiction*, 129–58. Baltimore: Johns Hopkins UP, 1978.

Stevenson, John Allen. "*Emma*: The New Courtship." *The British Novel, Defoe to Austen: A Critical History*, 110–28. Boston: Twayne, 1990.

Thompson, James. *Between Self and World: The Novels of Jane Austen*. University Park: Penn State UP, 1988.

Todd, Janet, ed. *Jane Austen: New Perspectives*. New York: Holmes & Meier, 1983.

Vernon, John. "The Breaking up of the Estate: *Persuasion*." *Money and Fiction: Literary Realism in the Nineteenth and Early Twentieth Centuries*, 42–64. Ithaca, NY: Cornell UP, 1984.

Webb, Igor. *From Custom to Capital: The English Novel and the Industrial Revolution*. Ithaca, NY: Cornell UP, 1981.

Wiesenfarth, Joseph. Review of John Dussinger, *In The Pride of the Moment. Nineteenth Century Literature* 46.3 (December 1991): 408–11.

Wright, Andrew. "The Emergent Woman." *Fictional Discourse and Historical Space*, 44–73. New York: St. Martin's, 1987.

7: Traditional Criticism, 1976–1990

THE EXPLOSION OF CRITICISM of Austen's fiction based on new approaches to literary study may have pushed more traditional forms of criticism to the side, but by no means did these disappear from the critical landscape. Textual studies, biographies, and various forms of "old-style" formal and aesthetic analysis, as well as a healthy collection of humanist commentaries, continued to be published during the 1970s and 1980s. Many of these, however, reflect the influence of recent theoretical studies, especially feminist critiques of Austen's fiction, even when that debt is unacknowledged. Only occasionally after 1970 does a critic willfully ignore, or specifically reject, the work of theorists in advancing our understanding of Austen's fiction.

Biographies

Three important biographical studies appeared during the 1980s that revised received opinion about Austen The first to appear, John Halperin's *The Life of Jane Austen* (1984), caused Austen lovers notable discomfort. The idea of Austen as the spiteful spinster, first fleshed out by D. W. Harding and later delineated more fully by Marvin Mudrick, found another champion in Halperin, who demonstrates in exhaustive detail that the novelist was "a woman of many moods" (ix). The "moods" Halperin stresses, however, are ones that cast Austen in a decidedly negative light. If there is a way to summarize Halperin's view, it might be that he sees Austen as a girl from a family whose means were not quite sufficient to provide her the financial security and social prospects she felt she deserved. Unable to find a suitable marriage partner, she decided to vent her spleen by exposing the foibles and injustices of the social order that left her unmarried all her life.

Little that Halperin published on Austen in the decade before his biography appeared gave anyone an inkling that he would take this approach. Most of his earlier essays deal with technical issues. And to be fair, much of *The Life of Jane Austen* could be classified as typical of critical biographies, in that Halperin recites carefully the facts of Austen's life and offers extended analysis of her fiction, discussing key themes and describing techniques used to create characters and plots. In the opening pages of his biography, however, Halperin challenges the traditional view of Austen, fostered carefully by her family, that she was flawless. And while he does not go as far as Mark Twain or D. H. Lawrence in savaging her, he devotes considerable attention to her letters and novels to expose what her family experienced but kept secret: "her wit, her irony, her cold-blooded judgment, her irreverence, her occasional malice" (54). From her earliest juvenilia, Halperin says, Austen emerges as a "confirmed parodist and cynic" (35) who possesses the essential qualities of the satirist: she is both "serious and angry" (37). As she grew, she became even more confirmed in that stance — because "one does not," Halperin observes, "become less cynical with the passage of time" (50).

Halperin finds in almost every novel some autobiographical trait, stronger in some, less prevalent in others. *Sense and Sensibility* is "bleak and black and nasty" (84) because it was written when Austen was "in a foul mood" (85). *Northanger Abbey* reveals that, at the time it was composed, Austen was "in a bittersweet mood" and the novel emerges as "a correspondingly mixed *genre*" (101). It has been easy, he says, for critics to see elements of Austen in the heroine of *Pride and Prejudice,* but Fanny Price in *Mansfield Park* "is as much a part of Jane Austen's personality as Elizabeth Bennet" (235). While *Emma* and *Persuasion* are less autobiographical, Halperin suggests that the "bitterness of Anne Elliot" in Austen's final novel might be an expression of her "own bitterness of spirit" during what he calls her dark years, the period from 1801 to 1810 (133). There is further evidence of Austen's inability to become emotionally engaged with her fictional creations in her perfunctory endings, in which the novelist substitutes third-person narration for more dramatic methods of displaying the ultimate union of her heroines with worthy suitors.

It is principally in Austen's letters, however, that Halperin finds the strongest evidence of her vitriol: "One does have the feeling, reading Jane Austen's letters, that the milk of human kindness was often kept in the larder, and the tea served with lemon" (79). For example, Austen's carping comments on matters such as the necessity of attending balls is seen as containing "a note of sexual desperation" (82). She seems to take pleasure in criticizing everyone but Cassandra, her favorite correspondent — and the person who clearly had a hand in destroying any correspondence that might have detracted from the image of Jane as a woman in possession of a saintly demeanor. But Halperin manages to read into off-handed comments and ironic barbs elements of a personality far different from the one described in Henry Austen's brief biographical note of 1817 or James Edward Austen-Leigh's 1870 *Memoir.* Halperin also suggests that a close look at the family history provides further evidence of Austen's waspish demeanor. Although four of her brothers married and some had many children, only one named a daughter after her. This may help us understand, Halperin says, "exactly how 'difficult' a character the novelist really was, and how uncongenial some of her brothers may have found her" (219).

Curiously, having spent so much time trying to knock Austen off the pedestal built for her by previous critics and admirers, Halperin ends with a discussion of the novelist's final months in which her behavior is, in his estimation, nothing short of heroic. She refused to be a difficult patient — something she had seen others become in their final days, and something she had witnessed in her mother for all her lifetime. Instead, this "tough-minded woman" refused to "bend or bow easily under affliction," demonstrating "enormous strength" in meeting death with resignation and resolution to persevere until the very end (350).

Halperin's portrait of Austen as a caustic, frustrated spinster generated reams of critical commentary, most of it negative, on both sides of the Atlantic. Halperin soon replaced Marvin Mudrick as the most hated figure in Austen criticism. Reviewing the book in *Novel: A Forum in Fiction* (1986), Carolyn Heilbrun says that while Halperin's biography has some merit, she thinks he brings too much male stereotyping to his view of Austen, especially when writing about her not marrying. Jo Ann Citron begins her review in *Women's Review of Books* (1985) by saying, "I can imagine Janeites burning effigies of John Halperin all over North America" (15), and adding her own highly critical assessment: "Often outrageous speculation takes the place of justifiable inference," spurred by Halperin's "fundamental misogyny" (16). British scholar Deirdre Le Faye is even more dismissive, claiming in her *Review of English Studies* (1986) review that "there is nothing to praise in this book and much to deplore" (426).

In 1987 Park Honan, author of a well-received biography of Matthew Arnold, brought out *Jane Austen: Her Life*, a work he claims is the first to make use of "a wealth of Austen family manuscripts" since the publication of William and Richard Austen-Leigh's 1913 memoir of their ancestor and the 1938 biography by Elizabeth Jenkins. Honan's aim is "to show Jane Austen's life as intimately and completely as our new data and the rich, existing manuscript material will allow" (preface). Honan adeptly weaves together a comprehensive and cohesive portrait from the many manuscript sources he consulted, and along the way offers some insightful criticism of Austen's fiction. Like a number of other biographers, he finds the source for the novels in the details of Austen's life, and in the adventures and mishaps of various family members and friends. Even more than most previous biographers, he fills in background about the family and provides extensive information about the larger social and political context of the decades during which Austen lived. At times Honan's penchant for cataloging the adventures of Austen's brothers (especially Frank) and her cousin Eliza, the Comtesse de Feuillide, extends the narrative more than one might expect. There is reason for these digressions, and many others besides, however; Honan wants *his* readers to understand how, despite Austen's own profession that she was content to work on a small canvas and concentrate on people in isolated country villages, larger social and political events helped shape her fiction in ways most critics have not noticed. At the same time, Honan is convinced that Austen's seemingly realistic works have much more in common with children's stories and folklore than has hitherto been acknowledged.

As a critic Honan demonstrates on more than one occasion the propensity to be provocative. He argues that events such as the American and French revolutions are integrated into the fiber of Austen's texts, and the Napoleonic Wars form a backdrop for a number of the novels. In most cases, Honan says, Austen's ostensibly simple love stories are actually political tracts aimed at promoting social and cultural values in an age of serious unrest. Like Mudrick, Honan is interested in the juvenilia and early novels for what they reveal about Austen's development as a novelist. *Lady Susan*, he says, is "more subversively anti-social than critics understand" (101). *Sense and Sensibility* is simultaneously Austen's first real foray into "the small scope genteel women have in society" and an inquiry into "the nature of love itself" (102). In *Northanger Abbey*, the last of her apprentice works, Austen developed her ability at narrative in this critique of the gothic.

Turning to the novels of Austen's maturity, Honan finds *Pride and Prejudice* to be "concerned with the problem of the individual's freedom within needful traditions and restrictions of society" (295). The novel is not simply a comedy of young love, however. "It reminds us of society's economic basis," Honan insists, "and just as it attracts philosophers and economists, so it appeals to critics in an era of feminism and semiotic theories, post-structuralism and Derrida's deconstruction" (320).

Writing of *Mansfield Park*, Honan discovers among other themes "the failure of Tory families to train their children as responsible inheritors" (334). The major issue with which Austen deals in this novel, however, is "education, or the discipline and training of the feelings" (338). *Emma*, which Honan considers Austen's best novel, is about perception and control — or the lack of both — and exhibits the novelist's mastery of form in handling details and advancing the narrative while revealing something of her heroine's strengths without making readers reject her for her faults. Like other critics before him, Honan sees Austen breaking new ground in both *Persuasion* and the unfinished *Sanditon*. What is most refreshing about Honan's analysis, however, is his ability to read these novels at the margins, highlighting the function of minor characters and drawing attention to the many allusions that give the novels their particular density and sense of realism.

Honan's work was well received by Austen scholars. In her *Modern Philology* review (1989) Susan Morgan praised his clever, imaginative recreations of events and his solid research, dubbing the book "a blessed event" (191). Writing in *Modern Language Studies* (1989) Deborah Kaplan called it "an innovative contribution to the more than a century old

Austen biography industry" (90). Kaplan is especially pleased to see that Honan "respects female identity and domestic experience" as valuable (91). Stuart Tave is also generous in praising the work, but wonders aloud in his review for *Novel: A Forum on Fiction* (1989) whether Honan's book is too long and filled with excessive details about people other than Austen.

The research behind works like Halperin's and Honan's was soon to be eclipsed by the efforts of one of the most tenacious and dedicated Austen scholars ever to take up study of the novelist. Deirdre Le Faye joined the Jane Austen Society in the mid-1960s but did not become intensely fascinated with the Austens until a decade later. As she explains in the Introduction to *Jane Austen: A Family Record* (1989), beginning in the 1970s she set out to learn "anything and everything which has any kind of bearing upon the life of Jane Austen and her family" (ix). That quest led to the production of a dozen books ranging from brief biographical studies to editions of Austen's letters and at least one novel — as well as a Jane Austen Cookbook and Jane Austen Quiz Book. Le Faye's first major publication on Austen, *Jane Austen: A Family Record*, is actually an expanded version of the 1913 *Jane Austen: Her Life and Letters. A Family Record*, originally compiled by Austen's grandnephew William Austen-Leigh and his son Richard. But Le Faye's work is more than an updated edition. The descendants of the novelist provided Le Faye access to family papers, including a copy of the 1913 book which Richard Austen-Leigh had been using as a base text for a planned revision, annotating it and stuffing it with notes and other documents. Austen-Leigh never completed this expanded edition, but Le Faye benefited immensely from his collection work. Combining this information with her own extensive research, Le Faye produces in *Jane Austen: A Family Record* an essentially new biography of the novelist, one that offers readers exceptional details about the Austens and explains how family life played such an important role in shaping Austen's fiction. While it is light on literary criticism, *Jane Austen: A Family Record* became an instant reference and source book for scholars interested in tracing the relationship between Austen's life and works.

Books Focused Principally on Austen

The continuing appearance of books about Austen employing well established critical methodologies attests to the enduring popularity she enjoyed among scholars who were conservative in their critical practice — and sometimes in their political outlook as well. Not surprisingly, many stress the moral qualities of her fiction and her tendency to support the values of the society of which she was a part. Among the most tradition-based studies is David Cecil's *A Portrait of Jane Austen* (1978). Although it appears to be a new study of Austen's fiction, Cecil says in the preface that the critical judgments he expressed in 1935 have remained virtually unchanged — and they are reproduced almost verbatim in the new book. The *Portrait* is longer, however, expanded by the addition of dozens of photographs and lengthy biographical commentary. Cecil feels this review of Austen's life is important for the generation of young readers and scholars who might not appreciate the milieu in which she lived and worked. Too often, he laments, he "come[s] across critics who discuss [Austen] and her view of life and character as if they were those of a contemporary of their own. The result is a portrait comically misleading" (6). So much for timeless appeal or New Criticism.

To be fair to Cecil, however, by the 1970s many critics had again begun to stress the importance of historical context in understanding fiction. Among the first books to deal with Austen's novels from this new historical perspective is Warren Roberts's *Jane Austen and the French Revolution* (1979). The title is somewhat misleading, in that it suggests a more narrow focus than Warren actually employs. He is interested in exploring the impact on Austen's fiction of the ideology introduced by the French Revolution and similar movements toward democracy and change. What is fascinating about Austen, Roberts says, is that while she chose "not to discuss directly the events that so disturbed her world," she "incorporated many of her responses to those events in her writing," introducing in the novels "a tension that reflects and indeed is part of the history of her time" (7). Roberts concentrates on four key issues: the political environment, England's involvement in the Napoleonic wars, religion (especially Evangelicalism), and feminism. He finds that, while Austen is generally positive toward social change, on some issues she could be decidedly negative — and one such issue is feminism, which Roberts says was associated in her mind with extreme radicalism. Perhaps, though, it helps explain why twentieth-century feminists had such difficulty bringing Austen into the fold with other nineteenth-century writers whose works are more clearly harbingers of the movement.

Another critic who argues for the moral qualities of Austen's fiction is Peter De Rose, whose *Jane Austen and Samuel Johnson* (1980) traces the novelist's debt to Johnson on such matters as imagination, marriage, suffering, self-discipline, the emotions, and self-knowledge. Such a study is needed at this time, De Rose says, because much criticism of recent decades has posed questions about Austen's work that display a "failure to recognize the way Johnsonian morality informs Jane Austen's art" (10). De Rose argues that "morality" is "an inseparable part of Jane Austen's artistic achievement" — and that understanding Austen's "Johnsonian heritage" can make readers aware of "the appreciable differences between" Austen's view of human nature and "our post-Darwinian, post-

Freudian perceptions of man in his ethical relativity and seemingly illimitable possibilities" (115–16).

Though less forceful than De Rose in professing Austen's conservative nature — possibly because she sees Austen as a tacit supporter of feminism — Jan Fergus argues in *Jane Austen and the Didactic Novel* (1983) that a strain of didacticism underlies all of Austen's fiction. It is easy to see why earlier critics may have missed or underplayed this element of her novels, Fergus says, because Austen "rejects most of the literary conventions associated with the doctrine" of didacticism practiced by her predecessors (5). Nevertheless, Austen "manipulates her readers' responses to didactic and moral ends" (6). The extent of her didactic impulse is best seen in the early novels, where she had not yet mastered subtleties of narrative that mask her aim to instruct. Fergus explains how the didactic impulse is present in the later fiction as well, where Austen's "desire to educate the judgment and sympathy of readers" is carried out in "increasingly more sophisticated and effective methods for realizing her intentions" (149). Part of what Austen wanted to teach was the value of human relationships, according to John Hardy, whose *Jane Austen's Heroines: Intimacy in Human Relationships* (1984) offers a careful study of six heroines, stressing each one's "individual awareness" of herself and the potential for happiness that lies in establishing a genuine, intimate relationship with another person (xii). Only by coming to know herself — independent of the social conventions that often define her actions — can the heroine engage in "mutual responsiveness" (xv) with the man she marries.

In the midst of a new wave of criticism that was revising views of Austen, Tony Tanner's *Jane Austen* (1986) seems like something of a throwback to an earlier age. The well-respected and frequently quoted authority on Austen admits in this collection of essays that he finds most new readings that paint Austen as a critic of dominant eighteenth-century ideology "misleading or wrong" (5). There has also been an unfortunate tendency, he says, to "privatize" her works, ignoring their wider social implications (13). Though she does expose faults in her society, Tanner says, she is principally concerned with larger moral issues that transcend her own age. One should not be surprised to find in Tanner's *Jane Austen* many similarities to criticism of the previous two decades. The book is actually a collection of essays he had published during the previous twenty years, supplemented by new pieces that flesh out a complete assessment of Austen's fiction. By his own admission, Tanner is less interested in furthering scholarship than in providing a consistent reading of the Austen canon that stresses the importance she places on communication — both the communication that occurs between characters in the novels, and her own ability to communicate with readers.

Another traditional assessment of Austen's work is Michael Williams's *Jane Austen: Six Novels and Their Methods* (1986). If one really wishes to appreciate Austen's accomplishments, Williams says, one must examine her techniques without applying any particular theoretical lens, because methodology often predetermines conclusions. In what resembles a reader-response assessment, Williams explores two related issues: "the means employed by the novelist to shape the material of the novel," and the "kinds of responses which the reader makes to the novel" (2). Admitting that his approach is not new, Williams concentrates on ways Austen's various techniques affect readers as they read individual novels. Doing so, he says, allows one to see how each is unique in both the questions it asks about people and society and the answers it delivers. In contrast to Williams's sweeping assessment of the Austen canon, Ivor Morris's *Mister Collins Considered: Approaches to Jane Austen* (1987) uses a single character from a single novel as "a means of perspective through which the motivation of many characters may be reviewed." This method, Morris says, allows readers to gain "fresh insights" into the quality of all of Austen's writing (viii).

In *Romance, Language and Education in Jane Austen's Novels* (1988) Laura Mooneyham attempts to account in a single theory for previous claims that Austen's novels are chiefly about romance, or education, or morality. Mooneyham says that language and its power lie at the heart of Austen's novels; only when people first master the vocabulary of morality can they become moral actors. The education of the heroines in Austen's fiction takes place first by having them learn to speak correctly — to forego self-centered expression in favor of true communication. The conflicts in Austen's novels, the stuff of which her romances are made, occur because of the "moral, intellectual and linguistic opposition" between heroine and hero. Mooneyham's critique of Austen's fiction demonstrates how this educative process works for almost all of Austen's heroines. She admits this pattern seems absent from *Sense and Sensibility*, but claims this is why the novel has always appeared weak and unsatisfactory to critics.

Just how much Austen was influenced by religious impulses has been a matter of debate since the early nineteenth century, with some critics offering compelling arguments for her essentially Christian outlook and others for her fundamental secularism. Gene Koppel analyzes this issue in *The Religious Dimension of Jane Austen's Novels* (1988), arguing that the moral stance Austen adopts in her fiction cannot be separated from its religious roots. Disputing the position taken by Gilbert Ryle that Austen is a secular moralist, Koppel demonstrates how in all her novels, but especially in the final three, Austen reveals a "sophisticated kind of religious consciousness" (1). It is possible to explain this phenomenon by appealing to traditional notions of religion, Koppel says, but it is more satisfying to trace the complex patterns of the religious impulse implanted in Austen — perhaps unconsciously — by the revolutionary ideas about religion that were emerging in her century. Koppel offers a modern religious interpretation, relying heavily on the work of Catholic theologian Leslie Dewart, to explain how Austen attempted to reconcile traditional religious ideology with her awareness of "the increasing possibility that we live in a contingent" and perhaps "meaningless universe" (110).

One of the most sophisticated and complex influence studies produced during the later decades of the century is Jocelyn Harris's *Jane Austen's Art of Memory* (1989). In this systematic assessment of the novelist's use of other authors, Harris explains Austen's imaginative genius by identifying the works which inspired each of her novels and showing how Austen transformed both ideas and rhetorical strategies from philosophers, dramatists, and fellow novelists into her own fiction. For each of Austen's novels Harris identifies one or more principal sources: Locke's philosophical writings inspire *Northanger Abbey*, Richardson and Milton provide the sparks for *Sense and Sensibility*, *Pride and Prejudice*, and *Mansfield Park*, Shakespeare for *Emma*, and "the whole range of English literature from Chaucer to Coleridge" for *Persuasion* (213). Harris argues persuasively in this exercise in intellectual history that "to know [Austen's] reading is to understand her better" (x).

Finally, the extent to which Austen's stock had risen by the closing decades of the century is evidenced in J. David Grey's *Jane Austen's Beginnings: The Juvenilia and Lady Susan* (1989), a collection of more than a dozen essays by some of the leading Austen scholars at the time, giving serious consideration to Austen's earliest attempts at story-telling. Contributors find in these fragments and short tales much that make them entertaining reading in their own right, and suggest that careful study of these works can reveal much about the growth of Austen's talents as a writer.

Studies of Theme, Influence, and Technique

By the 1970s commentary on Austen's novels became almost *de rigeur* for any critic writing studies of the eighteenth or nineteenth century novel. Her work had become a kind of touchstone against which movements and writers could be measured. Bernard Harrison uses her in this way in "Muriel Spark and Jane Austen" (1976). In this essay Austen's works exemplify traditional novels that allow Harrison to demonstrate some of the difficulties readers have in coming to grips with Spark's unconventional fiction. The novelist Vladimir Nabokov also offers some comparative judgments in *Lectures on Literature* (1980), a posthumous collection compiled from his lecture notes by Fredson Bowers. Nabokov admired Austen greatly, and in his course on literature at Cornell regularly included *Mansfield Park* among the list of required readings. Nabokov considered Austen a great novelist but not, perhaps, one of the greatest. Certainly *Mansfield Park* is a fine novel, Nabokov says, "a fairy tale" story full of "exquisite needlework" but not a "violently vivid masterpiece" like *Madame Bovary* or *Anna Karenina* (10).

More common, though, were essays that looked directly at Austen's work to determine the themes Austen addresses, the values she wishes to affirm, or the conventions she uses to create her fiction. Hence, one can discover analyses like that of Hoyt Trowbridge, who claims in *From Dryden to Jane Austen: Essays on English Critics and Writers 1660–1818* (1977) that no one has yet systematically "attempted to define [Austen's] values explicitly" and "examine them as a coherent system of ideas" (275). Trowbridge offers a hierarchical list of values at work in the novels —"intelligence, morality, feeling, beauty, and worldly condition (rank and fortune)" (276) — and using *Pride and Prejudice*, demonstrates how these values shape Austen's characters and guide readers' judgments of them. Understanding this value system allows readers to appreciate the "seriousness of subject and implication" that makes Austen's work "something that engages our sympathy and concern" (290). In a similar kind of study, *The English Novel: Defoe to the Victorians* (1977), David Skilton claims Austen's "*forte* was to reveal the ethical basis of everyday life"; she was exceptionally successful in "demonstrating" life's "psychological and social mechanisms" (81). As a craftsperson, her "greatest contribution" to the development of the novel lay in her ability "to exploit existing techniques of fictional speech and narrative in order to achieve her subtle analyses of character and society as economically as possible" (86). Sadly, Skilton laments, Austen's genius was not recognized by the Victorians, whose "habit of analyzing prose fiction principally in terms of subject matter" caused her to be relegated to the status of a minor figure (89). A third study of the development of the novel, Ira Konigsberg's *Narrative Technique in the English Novel: Defoe to Austen* (1985), ends with a discussion of Austen because, Konigsberg says, she stands at the terminus of the period of the novel's growth from infancy to early maturity. Konigsberg believes Austen's techniques are guided by moral and aesthetic goals. His reading of *Pride and Prejudice*, which he calls "the paradigmatic novel" (213), emphasizes Austen's mastery of language and rhetorical technique. He insists, however, that Austen is not an unlettered genius but an inheritor of a long tradition in fiction that she modified and improved.

Playing off F. R. Leavis's notion of a "great tradition" in English literature, in *Comic Faith: The Great Tradition from Austen to Joyce* (1980) Robert Polhemus focuses on eight works that display "comic faith": a union between comedy and religious faith that he believes can be traced through the comic tradition in English fiction. In writing of Austen, Polhemus concentrates on *Emma* because "nothing about [Austen] is more important or more original than the comic vision and the sense of humor that *Emma* shows" (24). The novel presents a form of ideal society in which there exists a perfect "blend of comic perception and ethical sensibility" (24). Polhemus's careful reading demonstrates that Austen is at once a keen observer of life, a superb ironist, and a novelist in whose fiction "comic concern for one individual woman includes comic concern for society" (59).

The notion that Austen was a comic genius is challenged in one of the more controversial readings of her fiction, P. G. M. Scott's *Jane Austen: A Reassessment* (1982). Scott is a hard critic to classify; like many new theorists, especially narratologists and deconstructionists, he is interested in "terms such as 'author' or 'authorial intention,'" but his reading of Austen "is different from those hitherto expounded — sometimes drastically different" (9). In fact, he takes on both sides of the Austen debate, finding fault with those who see her as a champion of her society and those who believe she is its harshest critic. "It is quite easy," he says, "to make out an image of Austen's work as a repository of dark insights and bitter feelings lapped under the clever handling of a comic surface. And quite false." But neither is she genial. "With her we have a keenly critical intelligence which is also more than just critical — censorious and frustrated" (34–35). Scott believes Austen is one of those artists who "produces something other or deeper than he or she probably consciously intended" (43), and one of the few who "have so looked at reality, at life as it actually is and people as they are, undistorted, unromanticized." Few writers, furthermore, possess Austen's "degree of moral realism" or her ability to "turn a light so searching into the human heart" (35). Adopting such a thesis (one that makes Austen more akin to Hawthorne than Fielding), he goes on to suggest a more radical realignment of the importance and value of individual novels: the fragmentary *Lady Susan* "a fully accomplished and important piece of fiction" (23), *Northanger Abbey* "not a very interesting book" (37), *Pride and Prejudice* little more than a delightful comedy, *Emma* essentially "a nasty book" (62–63), *Sense and Sensibility* a sound critique of society, *Mansfield Park* and *Persuasion* masterpieces in which Austen looks firmly and frankly at society, pointing out its weaknesses but ultimately accepting it for all its faults. Scott's final judgment turns on its head the notion that one must understand Austen's world to appreciate fully her accomplishments as a novelist. "The world of the artist's work and that of his [*sic*] actual life have too many crucial differences in their constitution, for information about one greatly to illuminate the achievement of the other." Therefore, he says, the "privacy of the artistic life should be absolute" — otherwise, readers simply become confused with questions of biography rather than those raised by the texts themselves (203). Perhaps, as he suggests about Austen, Scott was saying more than he realized, as his position would be one that New Critics, deconstructionists, and others engaged in the practice of semiotics would find appealing.

Austen's achievement as a realist is highlighted in George Levine's *The Realistic Imagination: English Fiction from Frankenstein to Lady Chatterley* (1981), in which Levine offers a reaction to current trends in criticism that privilege deconstruction, stressing the mimetic nature of much nineteenth-century English fiction. Levine argues that "nineteenth-century realistic fiction tends to be concerned with the possibility of accommodation to established power" (24). His reading of Austen's novels demonstrates how Austen approached this sensitive yet compelling topic. Austen was responsible, Levine says, for giving English fiction "its second full start (after Defoe, Richardson, and Fielding)." Rebelling against popular trends that preferred the Gothic and other forms of Romantic literature, Austen "sought primarily to make words conformable to reality, and particularly the reality of social action" (35). Her art "tests Romantic energies against the pragmatic and ordering values of a fully civilized society" (36). Her real innovation, Levine says, lies in the creation of "voice." Consistently ironic, Austen "speaks to us in a voice that authorizes itself by virtue of its clarity, its invulnerability to illusions, its directness and economy" (67).

The variety of traditional approaches still employed during this period can be seen in a snapshot of Austen criticism published during the mid-1980s. In *The Chain of Becoming: The Philosophical Tale, the Novel, and a Neglected Realism of the Enlightenment* (1983), Frederick Keener explains how Austen appropriated elements of the philosophical tale in creating her works. In *Fictions of Romantic Irony* (1984) Lillian Furst conducts an extensive analysis of techniques Austen uses to create a sense of irony in *Pride and Prejudice*. While acknowledging that irony is an important tool employed by Austen to criticize social and moral norms, Furst concludes she is "an essentially gentle ironist, knowing, good-humoured, benign and composed" (66). Lori Hope Lefkovitz also stresses Austen's use of irony. Lefkovitz's critique of *Persuasion* in *The Character of Beauty in the Victorian Novel* (1987) argues that Austen provides an ironic twist in presenting Anne Elliot as not beautiful on first sight. The novel proceeds to demonstrate that beauty consists of more than physical appearance. One learns to appreciate true beauty, Lefkovitz says, by making distinctions among women (and men) based on attributes of character as well as appearance.

In "Jane Austen's Accommodations," an essay in *The First English Novelists: Essays in Understanding* (1985), Alistair Duckworth explores ways Austen accommodates her own ideas about the realities of a single woman in society with the demands of her readers for a certain kind of fiction. Her novels are "subtle and complex negotiations with the facts of her social experience, as these may be accommodated to inherited fictional traditions" (227–28). Duckworth describes a number of the accommodations Austen makes in reconciling the conflict between acceptance of the social status quo and her appreciation of a woman's plight. Similarly, in *The Civilized Imagination: A Study of Ann Radcliffe, Jane Austen, and Sir Walter Scott* (1985), David Cottom examines Austen's fiction as the product of, and reaction to, established norms of aesthetics and decorum that were under attack at the time she was writing. Cottom concludes that Austen was not necessarily conservative in her outlook but aware of the precarious place women held in society. Hence, he says, "an accurate reading of Austen demands that fewer assumptions be made about her personal psychology and more attention paid to the disguises, silences, and submissions demanded by the society she portrayed in her novels" (87).

Finally, in what could be described as a follow-up to his 1980 volume *Comic Faith*, in 1990 Robert Polhemus pursued the topic of romantic love in *Erotic Faith: Being in Love from Jane Austen to D. H. Lawrence*, a volume that once again places Austen's fiction in a position of prominence. Arguing that erotic faith is "an emotional conviction, ultimately religious in nature, that meaning, value, hope, and even transcendence" can be found in "erotically focused love" (1), Polhemus begins his study with a critique of *Pride and Prejudice*, a work he calls "the archetypal romantic novel for countless readers and imitators" (28). In it, he says, the power of love allows Elizabeth to transcend the sordid convention-bound world, while it transforms Darcy into a better man. Their falling in love is a great event, equivalent to those one witnesses in the public sphere. As such, the novel "offers a challenge and an alternative to conventional notions of what constitutes 'great events'" (54).

Philosophical and Political Inquiries

In the early 1980s Austen's fiction continued to be of interest to philosophers as well as literary critics. The selections discussed in this section suggest the range of interest philosophers had in her work, and the continuing influence of philosophy on literary study. For example, in *After Virtue: A Study in Moral Theory* (1981) Alisdair MacIntyre describes Austen as a classic moralist, celebrating her for promoting virtue in her fiction. MacIntyre says Austen wrote comic novels because she was "a Christian" who "sees the *telos* of human life implicit in its everyday form" (226). Furthermore, she is "in a crucial way" the "last great representative of the classical tradition of the virtues" (226). George Anastaplo is more concerned with Austen's continuing relevance, asking in *The Artist as Thinker: From Shakespeare to Joyce* (1983) what Austen's work can teach late-twentieth-century readers. His sweeping survey of Austen's fiction, in which he examines her attitudes toward a variety of topics such as education, marriage, self-knowledge and self-control, leads him to conclude that her intent is to depict for readers of all times "what a virtuous human being" is (90).

In *The Thread of Connection* (1982), C. C. Barfoot explores Austen's use of the philosophical concept of fate. Interested in how notions of fate have developed since classical times, Barfoot argues that, despite the appearance that choice dominates Austen's interest — and making the right choices, especially of a life partner, is the most important activity for Austen's principal characters — the novels are filled with occurrences which suggest that fate, too, plays a role in the outcome of Austen's plots. Similarly, Richard Eldridge finds *Pride and Prejudice* a useful example of the philosophical principles he seeks to elucidate in *On Moral Personhood* (1989), a study of ways human beings come to know themselves and become more fully human through social relationships. Eldridge finds in the contradictory views put forth by critics of the novel an essential tension that exists within human society about the nature of, and motivations behind, personal relationships, especially the nature and function of marriage as a social institution and means of self-fulfillment.

Although not a philosopher, Marilyn Butler has been for nearly four decades one of the strongest advocates for a moral and politically conservative reading of Austen's fiction. In *Romantics, Rebels, and Reactionaries: English Literature and its Background, 1760–1830* (1981) she reiterates the argument she had made in *Jane Austen and the War of Ideas* (1975) that Austen was conservative in both her politics and her treatment of women. Although Austen gives her heroines "character and rationality," Butler says, her plots "rebuke individualistic female initiative" and "imply that the consummation of a woman's life lies in marriage to a commanding man" (98). Austen is "the gentry's greatest artist" (99), writing at a time when traditional roles for the various social classes, especially the gentry, were being challenged. Austen's novels all promote traditional values, Butler insists, although "she is as critical of the current practice of her class as she is admiring of the ethical theory that sustains it" (105). Because her satire of the gentry of her day is at times quite sharp, it is sometimes "tempting" to "see in her a critic of the old system, and perhaps in modern terminology a progressive." Butler cautions that "this would be to get her emphasis quite wrong" (108).

Like Butler, in *The Consoling Intelligence: Responses to Literary Modernism* (1982), David Kubal describes Austen as one of a handful of writers who stand in opposition to the trend toward modernism in literature and society as a whole. Linking her with such diverse figures as Matthew Arnold, Sigmund Freud, George Orwell, and John Fowles, Kubal shows how in her novels Austen advocates "reason and order" against the competing — and compelling — values of "imagination and flux" (33). In his extended discussion of *Emma* Kubal explains how Austen creates for her heroine a kind of dream-world in which order and repose are possible. But at the same time, he says, Austen recognized the persuasive power of forces that advocated for the importance of passion and self-fulfillment, making the final resolution of the novel more complex and tenuous than might be initially expected from a writer firmly committed to traditional ideals.

While Martin Price alleges in the first sentence of the introduction to *Forms of Life: Character and Moral Imagination in the Novel* (1983) that his book is "about ways in which character has been imagined and presented in some novels of the nineteenth and early twentieth centuries" (xi), his real aim is to extend the kind of critical commentary practiced by predecessors such as Lionel Trilling and Douglas Bush, whose constant search for the moral grounds of novelists' visions of society mark all of their work. Throughout his chapter on Austen, Price insists that Austen proves repeatedly that it is possible for a novelist to be at once comic and profound. She is, he says, a moralist who uses her considerable narrative skills to critique her society and the people who inhabit it. The lawyer and literary critic James Boyd White makes the same judgment in his comments on *Emma* in *When Words Lose Their Meaning* (1984). Austen is a moralist who creates from her inherited materials "a moral language of extraordinary range, discrimination and coherence" in order to teach readers how to make this language their own so they may use it in their own lives (163). *Emma* is a "deeply political" novel, he says, because it challenges discerning readers to think about how they should behave in community.

Grahame Smith is also concerned about Austen's portrayal of people in community, arguing in *The Novel and Society* (1984) that Austen's *Persuasion* is best understood when its social context is fully appreciated. His reading demonstrates "a heightened richness in the novel's social elements" (117) while acknowledging the intensely personal nature of the narrative. But Smith argues against strongly conservative interpretations of Austen. Instead, he claims that, far from being an unquestioning proponent of the dominant social and political values of her time, Austen continually questioned those values. Taking the opposing position in his essay on Austen in *Conservative Thinkers* (1988), R. A. D. Grant attempts to reclaim Austen for the conservative camp — and by conservative he means not simply aesthetic but political and moral as well. Operating from the premise expressed by the volume's editor Roger Scruton that the animating principle of conservatives is "a desire to record and respect the human condition" (8) and that conservatism "places duty before right" (9), Grant briefly traces Austen's debt to conservative thinkers, especially Samuel Johnson, before cataloging the virtues she upholds in her fiction. Her seemingly spontaneous support of conservative values emerges, Grant says, from her belief that "civilization and civilized behaviour" are "more truly 'natural' than any notionally primitive or 'unspoiled' humanity." Although Grant finds Austen's conservatism apparent and consistent, he believes it necessary to reassert her position in the tradition in light of recent critical trends, because "no work of literature can resist the *beau ideal* of modern critical theory, a really dedicated misreader" (173).

Austen's Relationship to the Romantics

The movement to determine Austen's relationship to the Romantics gathered steam during the early 1970s and was highlighted by the release of the special issue of *The Wordsworth Circle* (1976) devoted to her work. Of course, there had always been attempts made to determine Austen's proper place in literary history. Most take an approach similar to that employed by T. B. Tomlinson, who argues in *The English Middle-Class Novel* (1976) that Austen belongs at the head of the list of nineteenth-century novelists rather than as the final entrant in the catalog of eighteenth-century novelists. Tomlinson finds Austen to be intensely concerned with the same issues that would occupy her successors, sharing with them a sense of the increasingly complex social world that constantly impinges on the individual life.

It seems that most critics have found it easier to place Austen outside the Romantic tradition than to see how she might fit within it. In fact, when critics have considered Austen's relationship to her historical contemporaries, they have often found little in common. For example, In *The Romantic Novel in England* (1972) Robert Kiely offers a reading of *Northanger Abbey* that highlights Austen's attack on Romantic fiction, which often stressed the importance of strong feeling and imagination — emotions which words often could not describe. Kiely says Austen "thought the capabilities of language, correctly used, [were] considerable" (122). He claims *Northanger Abbey* is Austen's primer in the correct use of language as a means of apprehending reality. Through the use of irony, Austen points out the excesses of Romanticism, but also acknowledges that without proper education it is easy for one to succumb to such excess. So, too, in *Literature, the Individual, and Society* (1977), Raymond Southall suggests that Austen's view of the conflict between individual and society is a counterpoint to Wordsworth's response. Calling her the novelist most capable of "express[ing] society through character and dialogue" (123), Southall offers readings of *Pride and Prejudice*, *Mansfield Park*, and *Persuasion* as illustrations of the way Austen projects her social vision through her characters. And in "'Taste' and 'Tenderness' as Moral Values in the Novels of Jane Austen" (1976) Hermione Lee is equally adamant in placing Austen in the anti-Romantic camp. "Firmly accepting the fundamental idea of a relationship between taste and morality," Lee says, Austen was "thoroughly satirical of the excesses to which that idea could lead" (82). Lee devotes most of her essay to cataloging Austen's critiques of affectation.

Jay Clayton makes the case for Austen as an anti-Romantic even more forcefully in *Romantic Vision and the Novel* (1987), refuting claims that Austen was a Romantic by "examining the nature of her opposition to Romanticism," particularly as evidenced by her treatment of the Romantic visionary experience (61). Clayton focuses on *Mansfield Park* because he believes Austen's characterization of Fanny Price reveals her "deep concern with both the attractions and the dangers of a Romantic vision" (61). Just why Austen was not enamored with Romanticism is the subject of Anne Mellor's essay "Why Women Didn't Like Romanticism: The Views of Jane Austen and Mary Shelley" in Gene Ruoff's *The Romantics and Us: Essays on Literature and Culture* (1990). Mellor claims many women intellectuals, Austen among them, responded negatively to the tenets of Romanticism, especially the "celebration of the creative process and of passionate feeling" (278). Influenced by ideas found in Mary Wollstonecraft's *A Vindication of the Rights of Woman*, Austen was more prone to value women of sense rather than feeling. If Austen has any tendencies toward Romanticism, Mellor says, it is because she "celebrated the education of the rational woman, and an ethic of care" (285), not the more egocentric, sentimental romanticism promoted by male Romantics.

On the other hand, in her provocative study of the Gothic tradition *Ghosts of the Gothic: Austen, Eliot, Lawrence* (1980), Judith Wilt devotes considerable attention to exploring the persistence of Gothic elements in Austen's fiction, suggesting that the novelist was not totally divorced from the movement she seemed so happy to make fun of in *Northanger Abbey*. Wilt explains how Austen used and transformed Gothic machinery in works like *Emma*, where the everyday and commonplace are raised to the significance of the catastrophic in a fashion similar to their depictions in Gothic fiction. Wilt's study suggests that Austen had more in common with Gothic writers — and the Romantics — than she may have wanted to admit.

Another critic who attempts to integrate Austen into the primary literary movement of her time is Clifford Siskin. His *The Historicity of Romantic Discourse* (1988) is intended to reshape the idea of English Romanticism, making apparent its cultural and historical dimensions and revising ideas about the timelessness and inevitability of the ideology that informed it. Traditional definitions of Romanticism have made it difficult to see Austen as a Romantic, Siskin says. Furthermore, those who have stressed the timeless quality of Austen's writing, and her essential conservatism, or pushed for her consideration as a modernist, have added to this problem. Siskin sees tendencies of Romanticism in Austen's decision to move away from older models of fiction and reshape the novel for her own purposes. "Austen's rejection of epic and tragic models for the novel in favor of a turn to the probable confirms that the sense of the hierarchy of literary forms, like the social hierarchy, was undergoing significant change" (143). Austen is an innovator like Wordsworth, Siskin says, producing new forms for her chosen genre.

Strong arguments for and against Austen's inclusion among the Romantics may have influenced Gary Kelly's discussion of her in *English Fic-*

tion of the Romantic Period, 1789–1830 (1989). Kelly offers a kind of middle-ground assessment of Austen's novels, linking her to the Romantic movement in several ways while acknowledging that she was not a spiritual sister of the great Romantic poets. Kelly is concerned with what motivated Austen as a writer, as well as what use she made of the literary tradition she inherited and what she invented. He suggests that her place as a member of the minor gentry gave her ample opportunity to become familiar with "the mainstream of English culture and ideology," including the debate around the status of women (112). Kelly's real insight comes in his judgment of Austen fiction as a whole. Her works are "novels of epistemology," concerned with "the psychology of perception, the drama of consciousness played out in a comic universe with a romantic comedy plot" (119) — a judgment that seems closely aligned with the assessment of the Romantics being promoted at the time Kelly was writing.

Austen Outside Britain and America

While the present assessment of Austen criticism focuses overwhelmingly on works written in the United States, the United Kingdom, and Canada, there have always been critics abroad interested in Austen whose work has added to our understanding of the novelist and her fiction. Some have had direct influence on Anglo-American views about her, while others have had relatively little impact on her reputation outside the countries in which they were written. I have isolated them from my main discussion not because I believe these studies are unimportant, but rather to highlight the broad appeal Austen's fiction has had worldwide — a fact that might be lost were I to bury these critiques among the overwhelming number of British and American commentaries published at the same times.

One of the more intriguing European assessments of Austen is Pierre Goubert's *Jane Austen* (1975) — not so much for the conclusions he reaches, but for his methodology. Working in the heart of the country where postmodern theory had its origins, Goubert employs what can best be described as traditional approaches to reading Austen's fiction. Even his use of psychological theory looks back to early twentieth-century theorists rather than to figures like Lacan. German critic Renate Mann is similarly conventional in *Jane Austen: Die Rhetorik der Moral* (1975), discussing Austen as a transitional figure between the neoclassical eighteenth-century and the generation of novelists that followed her. Grete Ek's essay on *Pride and Prejudice* in *Fair Forms: Essays in English Literature from Spenser to Jane Austen* (1975), a collection that editor Maren-Sofie Røstvig says is intended to transform "theoretical interest in structure" into "practical criticism" (9), examines the structure of Austen's novel to produce a new reading of the text. Rather than being a novel of antithesis, *Pride and Prejudice* is a kind of "mystery story" whose substructure reveals to a

TRADITIONAL CRITICISM, 1976–1990 ♦ 165

careful reader that the hero and heroine are always alike in their attitudes toward individuals and social conventions (178–79).

Patricia Voss-Clesly's three-volume *Tendencies of Character Depiction in the Domestic Novels of Burney, Edgeworth, and Austen: A Consideration of Subjective and Objective World* (1979) is an exhaustive technical analysis of three women novelists who Voss-Clesly believes are responsible for advancing the novel as a genre in England. In a highly systematic way characteristic of Continental dissertation writers, Voss-Clesly examines a variety of devices including monologues, descriptions of characters' states of mind, point of view, and imagery. Voss-Clesly's study did not have great impact on Austen studies, perhaps because of the segmented nature of her critique and the rather stiff prose in which it is presented.

Austen has always been a popular novelist in India, where throughout the twentieth century critics frequently published articles on her work in Indian journals and guidebooks such as B. R. Mullik's *Jane Austen* (1957) in the Studies in Novelists for B.A. and M.A. Students of English Literature in Indian Universities series. During the 1980s a number of critical studies were published by Indian scholars. Leading the group was Atma Ram, who began publishing on Austen in the 1960s. Her first book, *Heroines in Jane Austen: A Study in Character* (1982) incorporates a number of her earlier articles in a study intended to explain why Austen appeals to Indian readers. Ram's 1989 study *Woman as Novelist: A Study of Jane Austen* collects a number of previously published essays in what could best be described as a complement to Park Honan's critical biography of the novelist.

In 1987 T. Vasudeva Reddy published two brief monographs on Austen. *Jane Austen: The Dialectics of Self Actualisation in Her Novels* links Austen with modern novelists because, Vasudeva Reddy says, her fiction "prob[es] human character and situations" without "attempting to establish any psychological truth or metaphysics of human behaviour"; instead, Austen allows her "fictional structures or representations to speak for themselves" (3–4). Vasudeva Reddy's examination of Austen's fiction traces "the growth in awareness experiences" by her heroines that leads them to achieve "self-actualization," which in turn leads to "self-fulfillment" (79). In *Jane Austen: The Matrix of Matrimony* (1987) Vasudeva Reddy explores the "ego dynamics" (i) of characters to explain how these reveal the moral values to which Austen subscribes. Vasudeva Reddy concludes that Austen was essentially a middle-class writer whose attitude toward love and marriage is conditioned by her own place in society. Her heroines live out the kind of love-and-marriage fantasy she believed most appropriate for everyone of her social class.

H. R. Dhatwalia's *Familial Relationships in Jane Austen's Novels* (1988) concentrates on parent-child relationships in the novels. Dhatwalia begins with a review of family relationships in eighteenth-century England, then describes Austen's own situation growing up in a large family. After what seem like obligatory comments on Austen's rather dismissive attitude toward small children, Dhatwalia looks more carefully at education for both sexes and the relationships that develop between mothers and daughters, fathers and daughters, and the less commonly discussed relationships — mother-son and father-son — in Austen's fiction. An examination of these relationships, Dhatwalia says, makes apparent one reason for Austen's universal appeal: she deals with a topic that transcends cultural differences, regardless of how cultures shape the specifics of these relationships.

Reeta Sahney's *Jane Austen's Heroes and Other Male Characters* (1990) attempts a systematic taxonomy of male characters created by Austen in her fiction. Seemingly more informed by contemporary critical theory, Sahney nevertheless continues the trend of Indian critics to view — and applaud — Austen as a conventionally conservative novelist whose work upholds traditional social and moral values in the face of impending changes to society. Finally, P. C. Chakrabarti's *Jane Austen: A Study of the Novels* (1992) is a systematic attempt "to trace in whatever detail possible the autobiographical elements which have been by and large woven into the texture of Jane Austen's novels" (preface). Chakrabarti mixes critical commentary with a good bit of speculation regarding the real-life models for many of Austen's characters and locales. While Chakrabarti admits that the "speculative linking of life and literature" is an "enterprise which has almost gone out of fashion" (135), it is likely that the dedicatees of Chakrabarti's volume — "Dear Janeites" — would have approved of the work.

Guidebooks, Case Studies, and Collections of Criticism

For decades the student market has proven to be a lucrative source of income for a number of publishers issuing guides to Austen's work or collections of critical essays about her fiction. Dozens of these volumes appeared between 1976 and 1990. While most are helpful principally to new scholars, some have proven to be important contributions to Austen studies. One such volume is *A Jane Austen Companion* (1986), issued in the United Kingdom as *The Jane Austen Dictionary* (1986). Neither title adequately describes this impressive volume. Edited by J. David Grey with the assistance of Walton Litz and Brian Southam, *A Jane Austen Companion* includes an alphabetical dictionary of real and fictional characters and sixty-four brief essays by a cadre of the most respected Austen scholars practicing at the time. A brief perusal suggests the range of current critical interest in Austen at the height of the revolution in literary studies. Contributors provide reliable background information on Austen's work, ranging from discussions of love and marriage to commentary on medicine, music, the military — the list can be (and is) extended substantially. It is not surprising that essays from this volume are frequently quoted in subsequent criticism of Austen's fiction. What seems missing from this compendium, however, is any real sense of the revolution in Austen studies going on as a result of new critical methodologies. Only feminism is treated in any detail (and even that only minimally). The contributors and the editor seem to ascribe to the observations made by Walton Litz in his review of critical studies published between 1939 and 1983: "Jane Austen's fiction has always been resistant to critical fashions and extremes of critical theory," remaining immune from "the work of doctrinaire Marxist, formalist, and archetypal critics" and sure to remain equally barren ground for the "more heavy-handed practitioners of structuralism and deconstruction." Good old-fashioned humanist commentary, historical study, and sound thematic interpretation seem to be just fine for Litz and many other contributors to this volume (although a perusal of contributors indicates that some, at least, might endorse readings by feminists and the yet-to-emerge postcolonial critics). Litz is convinced, though, that "the best criticism of Jane Austen has always been, and will remain, a reflection of her art — sensible, disciplined, and above all lucid" (117).

Less traditional in its discussion of Austen, June Dwyer's *Jane Austen* (1989) in the Continuum Publisher's "Literature and Life: British Writers" series provides the kind of introduction to the novelist and her works that made this series and its competitor, the Twayne British Authors series, staples of libraries and frequently cited sources in many undergraduate papers in the last half of the century. Dwyer offers what might be described as a moderate feminist approach to Austen, stressing the novelist's concern with women's issues. Although she notes with approval Austen's abilities as an ironist, Dwyer insists that Austen's "profoundly moral sensibility" gives all of the novels a common theme: "They are about behaving well and making the right choices" (40). Austen remains popular with students nearly two hundred years after she died, Dwyer says, because "most twentieth-century readers," beset by relativism and chaos around them, respond to her work with a "wistfulness to the moral order that reigns in Austen's novels" (41).

Casebooks on individual novels also grew in popularity during this period. Roger Gard's *Jane Austen: Emma and Persuasion* (1985) in the Penguin Masterstudies series highlights some of Austen's accomplishments. Gard is principally interested in explaining what he calls "the kind of creative control [Austen] exercises over her materials" (30), showing how she turns them into "high art in a comic drama of vital issues as opposed to sublimated gossip" (30). Gard's approach seems somewhat old school, especially in light of what was being published concurrently. Certainly it is free of contemporary critical jargon, a fact that Geoffrey Hoare, general editor of the Masterstudies series, considers "a refreshing change in the present literary arctic stream" (preface). There is one nod to contemporary trends, however — in the use of pronouns. Gard remarks early in his study that he has used "he" to identify the reader, but only "in the interests of economy rather than of sexual discrimination" (7). One suspects that quite a few of his fellow scholars would find that a rather unconvincing rationale. Also typical of student guides is Kenneth Moler's *Pride and Prejudice: A Student's Companion to the Novel* (1989) in the Twayne's Masterwork series. Far from being a simple "crib" on the novel's plot and major concerns, Moler's critique provides a systematic and well researched discussions of themes such as moral blindness and self-knowledge, the conflict of art and nature, the role of symbolism and conversation, and the importance of allusion.

In contrast to Gard's traditionalist approach, Isobel Armstrong's *Jane Austen: Mansfield Park* (1988), a brief but informative guide for students, incorporates a good bit of contemporary critical theory into descriptions of the social and political background of the novel as part of a reading that emphasizes the novelist's techniques. A concluding commentary on Austen's conservative nature contains some cogent observations on the dynamics of reader response. Historically, Armstrong observes, in times of national crisis "the harsher, satirical Jane Austen emerges in criticism" (98). Armstrong argues that, while not all views of Austen as either conservative or radical are equally valid, it is possible to entertain the idea that she can be read both ways — and that a "conservative reading" often "generates its radical opposition" (104).

But certainly no one has been more prolific in producing guidebooks to Austen than American scholar-turned-editor Harold Bloom. In 1986 Bloom issued the first of what would be more than a dozen books collecting criticism of Austen. *Jane Austen* (1986) contains thirteen essays reprinted from books and journals published during the 1970s and 1980s. While some of Bloom's selections were readily available at the time his *Jane Austen* was published, a number of essays in his collection had appeared only in scholarly publications not easily accessible to many undergraduates. Furthermore, at least one essay deals with each of Austen's major novels, and the book displays a happy blending of traditional and new theoretical approaches to her work. Bloom's subsequent volumes, notably essay collections published in 2000 and 2009, display some of the same perspicacity in selection. Although by necessity highly selective, the Bloom editions of Austen criticism offer a useful source for those wishing to get a sense of the critical tradition without having to wade through the hundreds of books and thousands of periodical articles produced since 1811.

However, let me end this section on a cautionary note. The availability of all these guidebooks and essay collections — both the ones discussed in this chapter and ones discussed earlier in this volume — has been a kind of double-edged sword. By making the work of earlier scholars easily accessible to students and non-specialists, editors have helped broaden knowledge of Austen's fiction — and of trends in critical analysis of the novels. At the same time, however, the presence of these texts suggests to those not fully versed in Austen criticism that what is collected is somehow privileged — that this material is, to borrow Matthew Arnold's term, "the best that has been thought and said" about her work. Anyone who has been commissioned to edit such a volume knows that often what is included is determined by the willingness of scholars and publishers to grant permissions for reprints (and to price that permission reasonably) as it is by the editor's wish to collect essays that he or she feels best represent the state of criticism at the present time. That has not been the case throughout the past century, and is likely not to be in the coming century as well.

Works Cited

Anastaplo, George. "Jane Austen (1775–1817)." *The Artist as Thinker: From Shakespeare to Joyce.* Chicago and Athens, OH: Swallow Press, 1983.

Armstrong, Isobel. *Jane Austen: Mansfield Park.* New York: Penguin, 1988.

Austen-Leigh, William, and Richard A. Austen-Leigh. *Jane Austen: Her Life and Letters: A Family Record.* London: Smith, Elder, 1913.

Barfoot, C. C. *The Thread of Connection: Aspects of Fate in the Novels of Jane Austen and Others.* Amsterdam: Rodolphi, 1982.

Bloom, Harold, ed. *Jane Austen.* Modern Critical Views. New York: Chelsea House, 1986.

———, ed. *Jane Austen.* New York: Chelsea House, 2000.

———, ed. *Jane Austen.* New York: Bloom's Literary Criticism, 2009.

Butler, Marilyn. "Novels for the Gentry." *Romantics, Rebels, and Reactionaries: English Literature and its Background, 1760–1830,* 94–112. New York: Oxford UP, 1981.

Cecil, David. *A Portrait of Jane Austen.* London: Constable, 1978. New York: Hill & Wang, 1979.

Chakrabarti, P. C. *Jane Austen: A Study of her Novels.* Calcutta: Sarat Book House, 1992.

Citron, Jo Ann. "Fantasy Life." Review of John Halperin, *The Life of Jane Austen* and John Hardy, *Jane Austen's Heroines: Intimacy in Human Relationships. Women's Review of Books* 2.1 (August 1985): 15–16.

Clayton, Jay. "*Mansfield Park.*" *Romantic Vision and the Novel,* 59–80. New York: Cambridge UP, 1987.

Cottom, Daniel. "Jane Austen." *The Civilized Imagination: A Study of Ann Radcliffe, Jane Austen, and Sir Walter Scott,* 69–123. New York: Cambridge UP, 1985.

De Rose, Peter L. *Jane Austen and Samuel Johnson.* Washington, DC: UP of America, 1980.

Dhatwalia, H. R. *Familial Relationships in Jane Austen's Novels.* New Delhi: National Book Organization, 1988.

Duckworth, Alistair M. "Jane Austen's Accommodations." In *The First English Novelists: Essays in Understanding,* edited by J. M. Armistead, 225–67. Knoxville: U of Tennessee P, 1985.

Dwyer, June. *Jane Austen.* New York: Continuum, 1989.

Ek, Grete. "Mistaken Conduct and Proper 'Feeling': A Study of Jane Austen's *Pride and Prejudice.*" In *Fair Forms: Essays in English Literature from Spenser to Jane Austen,* edited by Maren-Sofie Røstvig, 178–202. Cambridge: D. S. Brewer, 1975.

Eldridge, Richard. "Ideality, Materiality, and Value: *Pride and Prejudice* and Marriage." *On Moral Personhood: Philosophy, Literature, Criticism, and Self-Understanding,* 141–80. Chicago: U of Chicago P, 1989.

Fergus, Jan. *Jane Austen and the Didactic Novel.* Totowa, NJ: Barnes & Noble, 1983.

Furst, Lillian R. "Jane Austen: *Pride and Prejudice,* 1813." *Fictions of Romantic Irony,* 49–67. Cambridge, MA: Harvard UP, 1984.

Gard, Roger. *Jane Austen: Emma and Persuasion.* Penguin Masterstudies. New York: Penguin, 1985.

Goubert, Pierre. *Jane Austen: Étude Psychologique de la Romancière.* Paris: Presses Universitaires de France, 1975.

Grant, R. A. D. "Jane Austen as a Conservative Thinker." *Salisbury Review* 5 (January 1987): 43–47. Reprinted in *Conservative Thinkers: Essays from "The Salisbury Review,"* edited by Roger Scruton, 169–85. London: Claridge Press, 1988.

Grey, J. David, ed. *The Jane Austen Companion.* With the assistance of Walton Litz and Brian Southam. New York: Macmillan, 1986. Also published as *The Jane Austen Dictionary.* London: Athlone, 1986.

———, ed. *Jane Austen's Beginnings: The Juvenilia and* Lady Susan. Ann Arbor: UMI Research Press, 1989.

Halperin, John. *The Life of Jane Austen.* Baltimore: Johns Hopkins UP, 1984.

Hardy, John. *Jane Austen's Heroines: Intimacy in Human Relationships.* Boston: Routledge & Kegan Paul, 1984.

Harris, Jocelyn. *Jane Austen's Art of Memory.* New York: Cambridge UP, 1989.

Harrison, Bernard. "Muriel Spark and Jane Austen." In *The Modern English Novel: The Reader, The Writer, and The Work*, edited by Gabriel Josipovici. New York: Barnes and Noble, 1976.

Heilbrun, Carolyn. Review of John Halperin, *The Life of Jane Austen*. *Novel: A Forum in Fiction* 19.2 (Winter 1986): 183–85.

Honan, Park. *Jane Austen: Her Life*. London: Weidenfeld & Nicolson, 1987.

Kaplan, Deborah. Review of Park Honan, *Jane Austen: Her Life*. *Modern Language Studies* 19.2 (Spring 1989): 90–92.

Keener, Frederick W. "The Philosophical Tale, Jane Austen, and the Novel." *The Chain of Becoming: The Philosophical Tale, The Novel, and a Neglected Realism of the Enlightenment*, 241–307. New York: Columbia UP, 1983.

Kelly, Gary. "'Only a Novel': Jane Austen." *English Fiction of the Romantic Period, 1789–1830*, 111–38. New York: Longman, 1989.

Kiely, Robert. *The Romantic Novel in England*. Cambridge, MA: Harvard UP, 1972.

Koppel, Gene. *The Religious Dimension of Jane Austen's Novels*. Ann Arbor, MI: UMI Research Press, 1988.

Konigsberg, Ira. "*Pride and Prejudice*: The Paradigmatic Novel." *Narrative Technique in the English Novel: Defoe to Austen*, 213–56. Hamden, CT: Archon Books, 1985.

Kubal, David. "Jane Austen's 'Midsummer Night's Dream.'" *The Consoling Intelligence: Responses to Literary Modernism*, 33–51. Baton Rouge: Louisiana State UP, 1982.

Le Faye, Deirdre. *Jane Austen: A Family Record*. London: British Library; Boston: G. K. Hall, 1989.

———. Review of John Halperin, *The Life of Jane Austen*. *Review of English Studies* 37 (August 1986): 426–30.

Lee, Hermione. "'Taste' and 'Tenderness' as Moral Values in the Novels of Jane Austen." In *Literature of the Romantic Period, 1750–1850*, edited by R. T. Davies and B. G. Beatty, 82–95. Liverpool English Texts and Studies 14. Liverpool: Liverpool UP, 1976.

Lefkovitz, Lori Hope. "Shaping the Body to Fit the Eye: Austen's *Persuasion* as a Romantic Cinderella." *The Character of Beauty in the Victorian Novel*, 43–57. Ann Arbor, MI: UMI Research Press, 1987.

Levine, George. *The Realistic Imagination: English Fiction from Frankenstein to Lady Chatterley*. Chicago: U of Chicago P, 1981.

MacIntyre, Alisdair. *After Virtue: A Study in Moral Theory*. London: Duckworth; Notre Dame, IN: U of Notre Dame P, 1981.

Mann, Renate. *Jane Austen: Die Rhetorik der Moral*. Bern and Frankfurt am Main: Lang, 1975.

Mellor, Anne K. "Why Women Didn't Like Romanticism: The Views of Jane Austen and Mary Shelley." In *The Romantics and Us: Essays on Literature and Culture*, edited by Gene W. Ruoff, 274–87. New Brunswick, NJ: Rutgers UP, 1990.

Moler, Kenneth L. *Pride and Prejudice: A Study in Artistic Economy*. Twayne Masterworks Series. Boston: Twayne, 1989.

Mooneyham, Laura G. *Romance, Language, and Education in Jane Austen's Novels*. New York: St. Martin's, 1988.

Morgan, Susan. Review of Park Honan, *Jane Austen: Her Life*. *Modern Philology* 87.2 (November 1989): 191–94.

Morris, Ivor. *Mr. Collins Considered: Approaches to Jane Austen*. New York: Routledge & Kegan Paul, 1987. 2nd ed. issued as *Jane Austen and the Interplay of Character*. London and New Brunswick, NJ: Athlone, 1999.

Mullik, B. R. *Jane Austen*. Studies in Novelists for M.A. and B.A. Students of English Literature in Indian Universities 2. New Delhi: S. Chand & Co., 1957.

Nabokov, Vladimir. *Lectures on Literature*, edited by Fredson Bowers. New York: Harcourt Brace Jovanovich, 1980.

Polhemus, Robert M. "Austen's *Emma* (1816): The Comedy of Union." *Comic Faith: The Great Tradition from Austen to Joyce*, 24–59. Chicago: U of Chicago P, 1980.

———. *Erotic Faith: Being in Love from Jane Austen to D. H. Lawrence*. Chicago: U of Chicago P, 1990.

Price, Martin. "Austen: Manners and Morals." *Forms of Life: Character and Moral Imagination in the Novel*, 65–89. New Haven, CT: Yale UP, 1983.

Ram, Atma. *Heroines in Jane Austen: A Study in Character*. New Delhi: Kalyani, 1982.

———. *Woman as a Novelist: A Study of Jane Austen*. Delhi: Doaba House, 1989.

Roberts, Warren. *Jane Austen and the French Revolution*. New York: St. Martin's, 1979.

Sahney, Reeta. *Jane Austen's Heroes and Other Male Characters: A Sociological Study*. New Delhi: Abhiav, 1990.

Scott, P. G. M. *Jane Austen: A Reassessment*. London: Vision P; Totowa, NJ: Barnes & Noble, 1982.

Siskin, Clifford. *The Historicity of Romantic Discourse*. Oxford: Oxford UP, 1988.

Skilton, David. "Austen, Scott and the Victorians." *The English Novel: Defoe to the Victorians*, 80–98. Comparative Literature Series. Newton Abbott, England: David & Charles; New York: Barnes & Noble, 1977.

Smith, Grahame. *The Novel and Society: Defoe to George Eliot*. London: Batsford Academic & Educational, 1984.

Southall, Raymond. "The Social World of Jane Austen." *Literature, the Individual, and Society*, 105–39. London: Lawrence and Wishart, 1977.

Tanner, Tony. *Jane Austen*. Cambridge, MA: Harvard UP, 1986.

Tave, Stuart. Review of Park Honan, *Jane Austen: Her Life*. *Novel: A Forum on Fiction* 22.2 (Winter 1989): 231–33.

Tomlinson, Thomas B. *The English Middle-Class Novel*, 21–51. London: Macmillan, 1976.

Trowbridge, Hoyt. "Mind, Body, and Estate: Jane Austen's System of Values." *From Dryden to Jane Austen: Essays on English Critics and Writers, 1660–1818*, 275–92. Albuquerque: U of New Mexico P, 1977.

Vasudeva Reddy, T. *Jane Austen: The Dialectics of Self-Actualisation in Her Novels*. New York: Envoy Press, 1987.

———. *Jane Austen: The Matrix of Matrimony*. Jaipur: Bohra, 1987.

Vernon, John. "The Breaking up of the Estate: *Persuasion*." *Money and Fiction: Literary Realism in the Nineteenth and Early Twentieth Centuries*, 42–64. Ithaca, NY: Cornell UP, 1984.

Voss-Clesly, Patricia. *Tendencies of Character Depiction in the Domestic Novels of Burney, Edgeworth, and Austen: A Consideration of Subjective and Objective World*. Salzburg: Inst. f. Anglistik u. Amerikanistik, Univ. Salzburg, 1979.

White, James Boyd. "'Conversation, Rational and Playful': The Language of Friendship in Jane Austen's *Emma*." *When Words Lose Their Meaning: Constitutions and Reconstitutions of Language, Character and Community*, 163–69. Chicago: U of Chicago P, 1984.

Williams, Michael. *Jane Austen: Six Novels and Their Methods*. New York: St. Martin's, 1986.

Wilt, Judith. *Ghosts of the Gothic: Austen, Eliot, and Lawrence*. Princeton, NJ: Princeton UP, 1980.

Wordsworth Circle 7.4 (Autumn 1976). Special Issue on Jane Austen.

8: Theory-Based Criticism of Austen, 1991–2008

CRITICISM OF AUSTEN at the end of the twentieth century and for the first decade of the twenty-first continued to follow patterns established during the "revolutionary" 1970s and 1980s. Feminism continued as the dominant ideology informing Austen criticism during the 1990s and 2000s, but other critical methodologies gained in prominence and influence in shaping the novelist's reputation and aiding in understanding her fiction. While the preponderance of criticism written after 1990 reflects new theoretical methodologies, work by critics who practiced what had come to be called traditional methods of inquiry was also published routinely. In fact, however, a good bit of the criticism produced during this period can best be described as hybrid, combining techniques from two or more theoretical approaches to produce significant advances in the understanding and appreciation of Austen's accomplishments as a novelist.

A Snapshot of Feminist Criticism: 1991

To understand the trend in feminist studies, it might be useful to look briefly at work published in 1991, the beginning of a decade that one critic suggests ushered in a third wave of feminist studies which influenced perceptions of Austen's work. Critiques that faulted her for a tendency to succumb to the norms of the patriarchal society in which she lived were routinely balanced by those that found a strong revolutionary strain in her work. Meenakshi Mukherjee's *Jane Austen* (1991) carries on the feminist tradition of reading Austen's novels, explaining how Austen cleverly if somewhat obliquely rejected the norms of the society she ostensibly sought to uphold. In part, Mukherjee's study is aimed at correcting what she considers a sad situation among feminist critics. "The general belief that Jane Austen unquestioningly accepted patriarchal values alienated her from the majority of the serious feminist critics who came into prominence in the 1970s," she says (12). This has been unfortunate, since "a recurrent theme" of Austen's novels is "the heroine's resistance to the efforts of the patriarchal community to force her into a social role at the cost of her own identity" (27). Examining concepts such as Austen's attitudes toward marriage and women's education, as well as the influence and role of colonialism in shaping society and the importance of literary tradition and language, Mukherjee finds ample evidence to place Austen in the tradition that includes Mary Wollstonecraft and later writers such as George Eliot, the Brontës, and Virginia Woolf. Yet at the same time Mukherjee is forced to admit that it is possible to justify a reading of Austen's works that defends her as a conservative. She observes at another point that Austen was "not a consistent critic of" the "closeknit society with its chain of obligations, duties and shared values" (83). Instead, Austen's recurrent use of irony to describe the situations in which her heroines find themselves makes it impossible for critics — many of whom wish to arrive at a unitary interpretation of her works — to settle on any single view of the novelist's ideology. "Even while mocking some aspects of the dominant ideology of her time," Mukherjee says, Austen "did seem to subscribe to others" (138). That may be unfortunate for those wishing to provide ideological readings of her novels, but Mukherjee says it will have to do.

Deborah Ross's observations on Austen's work in *The Excellence of Falsehood: Romance, Realism, and Women's Contribution to the Novel* (1991), a feminist history that challenges traditional generic boundaries and the values assigned to them, suggests that women like Austen "used romance to assert the legitimacy of feminine 'truth'" (15). Austen is particularly noteworthy, Ross suggests, because she manages to describe women's daily struggles "in plentiful, believable detail," giving her works a cast of hard realism while still "envelop[ing] women's lives in romantic comedy" (167). Austen was important in the history of the form because she was successful in "moving the novel beyond narrow conduct-book didacticism" — a role assigned to it by men like Samuel Johnson — toward "a more subtle and searching, and thus more deeply moral, criticism of life" (207). Similarly, Patricia Ondek Laurence's brief comments on Austen in *The Reading of Silence: Virginia Woolf in the English Tradition* (1991) link her with Woolf and Charlotte Brontë as novelists who "realize more fully than male authors that there is power in the vantage point of an observer and value in silence" (66). These novelists value "the inner life," a condition originally prompted by their position in a patriarchal society but "transformed through the living of their lives" (66) into a quality that gives them authority as moral figures.

The ways feminism was revising traditional critical inquiry is evidenced by four studies, Marjorie McCormick's *Mothers in the English Novel: From Stereotype to Archetype* (1991), Gail David's *Female Heroism in the Pastoral* (1991), Katherine Green's *The Courtship Novel 1740–1820: A Feminized Genre* (1991), and Ruth Yeazell's *Fictions of Modesty: Women and Courtship in the English Novel* (1991). McCormick describes Austen as the first novelist "consistently to portray mothers as active, individually realized members of their fictional families and communities" who at the same time conform to "conventions of the maternal stereotype" (147).

However, it seems that at times McCormick engages in a bit of special pleading in order to recognize Austen's importance as an innovator while acknowledging the problems one encounters with the many conventional mothers in her texts. McCormick's solution is to suggest that Austen is able to create realistic characters that effectively disguise the fact that they are stereotypes. David examines the role and impact of the female heroine in pastoral novels, attempting to "isolate and trace a single, archetypal pattern, the movement of the hero-traveler between two symbolic landscapes, one rural and the other urban" (xiv). She is also intent on substituting her reading of the hero for the patriarchal descriptions found in the works of Erich Neumann and Joseph Campbell. Hence, she reads *Sense and Sensibility* as a novel illustrating "the difficulty confronted by the woman bent on bringing herself to completion" as an integrated self (113).

Green's analysis of Austen's handling of the courtship novel, informed by contemporary historicist and psychological theories, exposes the gradual shifts in attitudes about the importance of choice and compatibility in selecting partners that reshaped ideas about marriage during the latter half of the eighteenth century. Green reads Austen's novels as "the last grand flourish of the courtship novel" in which Austen "interrogate[s] the terms and practices of the marriage market" and "suggest[s] alternatives to the subject position society made available to women of her period" (153). Yeazell's commentary on *Mansfield Park* is placed in the context of a larger discussion of the development of notions of modesty. As represented in the English novel, Yeazell says, modesty is a desirable quality in women, and writers often find it a useful concept for exploring temptations that haunt both men and women. Focusing on *Mansfield Park* because Fanny Price is Austen's "most self-effacing heroine" (xi), Yeazell argues that the novel presents quite directly "the trials of modesty" (148), revealing how a self-effacing, modest young woman can be a source of great attraction to men. Austen uses Fanny's story as a means of distinguishing between real modesty and the empty conventions that had become attached to the term.

An interesting example of the way feminists made use of interdisciplinary study to alter the understanding of a novelist's canon is Paula Marantz Cohen's discussion of Austen in *The Daughter's Dilemma: Family Process and the Nineteenth-Century Domestic Novel* (1991). Combining elements of literary and social criticism and making extensive use of "family systems theory as a principal methodology" (4), Cohen examines *Mansfield Park* as novel in which "the life of the family takes precedence over the life of the individual" (59). She argues that in most nineteenth-century novels, what Tony Tanner describes as the conflict between law and sympathy tends to "tip the balance to the tragic or to the conventional happy ending." But in *Mansfield Park*, Cohen says, "a prefect balancing of these two forces produces a utopic ending that sets it apart from other novels of the century" (60). Additionally, Cohen says, the heroine receives emphasis in "much the same way that sick families place emphasis on the symptomatic individual — only Austen fashions admirable character traits" from what would ordinarily be seen as conditions that would produce symptoms of disease (84). This tendency accounts for part of the irony one senses in reading the novels, as "the notion of formed character takes on a different aspect when we see it as both the function of and the compensation for a disequilibrated family system" (85).

The influence of feminism in revising traditional scholarly analysis of Austen's work also can be seen in Barbara Horwitz's *Jane Austen and the Question of Women's Education* (1991). Like David Devlin did sixteen years earlier, Horwitz concentrates on ways Austen adopts or rejects prevailing notions about the proper form of education for women. Horwitz reviews the ideas of a number of educational theorists such as Locke, Jane West, the Edgeworths (father and daughter), and Wollstonecraft to give readers a sense of what ideas were in the air when Austen began writing. Horwitz believes Austen shared Locke's ideas that women "should be taught to know their duty, to act in the light of reason, to master their imaginations, to respect religion, to achieve fortitude" (72). Where Austen differs from prevailing ideas about education, however, is in her belief that its aim is not simply to produce good mothers but to provide women with self-knowledge, just as it does for men. In this respect, Horwitz says, Austen reveals radical tendencies that make her worthy of being considered a member of the feminist tradition.

However, in 1991 one of the most influential feminist critics of Austen, the British scholar Janet Todd, offered a cautionary note to feminists trying to claim Austen as a mother of the revolution. In "Jane Austen, Politics, and Sensibility" Todd suggests that too many feminist readings are "largely ahistorical and ungeneric," often "removing Austen from her contemporary context and from other women writers who preceded and surrounded her." These ahistorical interpretations, Todd says, "made her sisterhood across time but not within it" (71). Todd argues that "not all women of the past aspired to a modern feminist view," and to assume so is to "silence them as thoroughly as patriarchy silenced enlightened feminism" (71–72). She argues instead for a kind of *via media* in feminist studies of Austen, rejecting both the cult of sentimentality that characterizes conservative, patriarchal readings and those that are overly skeptical of the "pieties of home and hearth" (86). That more balanced view would be articulated by many of the feminists who published work on Austen during the next twenty years, although several would continue to claim her as a revolutionary or dismiss her as a conservative.

Books Influenced by Feminism and Gender Studies

By the 1990s, feminists were beginning to develop a more nuanced appreciation for Austen, as evidenced by Deborah Kaplan's intriguing analysis in *Jane Austen Among Women* (1992). Kaplan melds traditional feminist literary criticism with the theories of feminist cultural historians to answer the question, "what made it possible for Jane Austen to write?" (6). Recognizing the limitations imposed on women in the patriarchal, class-bound society in which Austen lived, Kaplan rejects as simplistic the theories of earlier Austen critics such as David Cecil and John Halperin that the novelist was a natural genius or that, as Cecil suggests, she was able to work simultaneously in two spheres, those of the solitary artist and the ordinary woman. There were two cultures in which Austen operated, Kaplan admits, but they were ones populated by large numbers of people: the gentry class, composed of men and women, which represented the large public sphere, and the community of women who formed a kind of private sphere that carried on women's work while encouraging each other to develop a sense of self. This community of women with whom Austen associated provided her the insights and the inner strength to carry out her role as a writer. Kaplan devotes less time to analyzing Austen's fiction than to explaining why it was possible for the novelist to write in a society that looked down on women who were too forward, too passionate, or too intellectual. At the same time, Kaplan admonishes feminists who would appropriate Austen to their cause as a subversive. "Austen's six novels express and obscure aspects of the women's culture," she says, but at the same time "they unequivocally endorse patriarchal ideology." The novels are filled with "inconsistencies of perspective," and feminists who wish to be fair to Austen "need to acknowledge these inconsistencies" and "relinquish some of our intimacy" with her work (204). Viewed as products of the culture in which they were written, Austen's novels are "sometimes hospitable and sometimes resistant, sometimes familiar and sometimes strange" (205).

Finding a way to appreciate Austen as a feminist while recognizing the resistant quality of her work toward feminist readings became something of a challenge. Glenda Hudson suggests in *Sibling Love and Incest in Jane Austen's Fiction* (1992) that readers can develop a new appreciation of Austen's novels by concentrating not on the love stories but on the relationships between siblings. Arguing that Austen "employs sibling relationships to negotiate within and to critique the complex ideology presented in her fiction" (2), Hudson examines the bonds between sisters, and between brothers and sisters, in a society where such relationships were often the most important ones young people forged. Calling Austen a herald of Victorian values in her portrait of the family circle "as an innovative social and moral power-base" (2), Hudson suggests that these relationships often border on the incestuous — but that in Austen's case, incest is not such a bad thing. "Fantasies of incestuous love" are intended by Austen to "provoke moral awareness rather than elicit immoral daydreams" (8). In the best cases, Hudson says, Austen suggests that healthy, loving sibling relations can lead to the creation of an ideal society.

Despite the growing interest in other relationships, however, the power struggle between the sexes continued to attract most attention in books about Austen. Witness, for example, the central argument of Moreland Perkins's *Reshaping the Sexes in "Sense and Sensibility"* (1998). Perkins claims that in Austen's first published novel, she "most aggressively undertakes to reconstruct dominant concepts of gender" (5), and that she would continue doing so, though more subtly, in later works. In all her fiction, Perkins argues, Austen struggled to critique patriarchy through characters whose gender identity (culturally speaking) is reversed. The same may be said of a number of essays in Devoney Looser's collection *Jane Austen and Discourses of Feminism* (1995). The assessment of Austen by contributors to the volume is mixed; some claim her as a champion of the feminist cause, while others see her as at best a reluctant warrior in the battle for women's rights. In a thoughtful introduction, Looser explains the ways in which Austen may be considered a feminist — and why her work elicits such mixed reaction from ardent practitioners of feminist criticism.

It is not surprising that, with the growing critical interest in "the body" as a topic or trope in literature, works on Austen's treatment of the physical should have appeared. One such work, Australian scholar John Wiltshire's *Jane Austen and the Body: "The Picture of Health"* (1992), is controversial on many fronts. First, Wiltshire openly challenges received opinion that Austen was simply not interested in matters pertaining to the body, that her novels lack references to matters involving corporeality — and as a consequence, lack a sense of passion. Second, Wiltshire expresses skepticism about readings of Austen produced by some feminists who he claims want to "theorize" the body, treating the idea of the body as a cultural construct and hence an ideologically charged concept that further demonstrates the insidious influence of patriarchy. Wiltshire constructs his study along lines suggested by the work of the psychiatrist and anthropologist Arthur Kleinman, whose explorations of the ways mental stress becomes expressed as physical ailment serves as the theoretical framework for Wiltshire's approach in reading Austen's fiction. Concentrating on four novels — curiously excluding *Pride and Prejudice* and *Northanger Abbey* — he explains how health and illness are important in furthering the plot of Austen's novels, and how these concepts also help reveal something about individual character and social relationships, especially gender relationships. In his estimate, illness becomes a means for women to exert power — either as patients or caregivers — in one of the few realms open to them in a society that severely restricted their activities. In this way, Wiltshire concludes, Austen demonstrates her subversive qualities and establishes her place in the sisterhood of feminist novelists.

Less polemic than Wiltshire's work but equally informative, Anita Gorman's *The Body in Illness and Health: Themes and Images in Jane Austen* (1993) examines Austen's depiction of both healthy and ill human beings. Gorman ranges outside literary study to determine just what Austen knew of medical practice in her own day and explains how that knowledge influenced her portrayal of characters. What interests Gorman principally is the way Austen "uses illness to define character, to design plot, and to refine her themes" (xiii–xiv). In another study focusing on issues of health in the novels, Gloria Gross celebrates Austen as a hard-nosed realist in "Flights into Illness: Some Characters in Jane Austen" (1993), applauding her "bold insights and audacious critiques" of society (188). Gross insists Austen's novels are radically subversive. Perhaps her "ultimate defiance" of conventional norms, Gross says, was her indictment of women "for unpalatable acts of manipulation and deception," a tendency that Austen brings "inescapably to light in her portrayal of characters who take flight into illness" (189). Finally, like similar studies of the role and function of the body in fiction, Mary Ann O'Farrell's commentary on Austen in *Telling Complexions: The Nineteenth-Century English Novel and the Blush* (1997) suggests that in both *Pride and Prejudice* and *Persuasion* Austen uses the physical phenomenon of the blush as a means of signaling character traits and revealing characters' inner thoughts without resorting either to dialogue or authorial intrusion.

The felicity with which feminist critics learned to blend different theoretical approaches is evident in several studies published during the mid-1990s. Maaja Stewart's *Domestic Realities and Imperial Fictions: Jane Austen's Novels in Eighteenth-Century Contexts* (1993) offers a revisioning of the Austen canon in which the conflict between older and younger brothers is highlighted in the narratives. Applying feminist and postcolonial theories to the novels, Stewart produces an interpretation that places women at the center of a domestic sphere where values are constantly shifting, as primacy once reserved for the landed aristocracy is shifting toward the merchant classes. In both worlds, of course, women are denied full rights as subjects. Published in the same year, Beth Tobin's *Superintending the Poor: Charitable Ladies and Paternal Landlords in British Fiction 1770–1800* (1993) focuses on "discursive strategies used by middle-class men and women to undermine the landed upper classes' control over the rural economy of early industrial Britain," largely through types of "self-regulation and surveillance" that discredit the landed gentry in favor of the talented middle class (1). Tobin suggests that Austen came down on both sides of this issue. *Emma* is a "defense of the landed classes" that simultaneously "idealiz[es] the landlord and criticiz[es] the monied status of the new gentry" (69). But in her other works Austen is almost always critical of the landed class for their "self-absorption and rampant consumerism." Tobin considers Austen's critique a "radical Tory condemnation of the gentry for failing to perform their duty and to fulfill their obligations to society" (96). Austen is not interested in radically changing society, Tobin says; she only wants to fix it. Gabriella Castellanos's *Laughter, War, and Feminism: Elements of Carnival in Three of Jane Austen's Novels* (1994) offers a feminist critique of the Austen canon that is at the same time heavily reliant on the theoretical work of Foucault and Bakhtin. Adopting Bakhtin's ideas about the nature of "carnival," viz., that there is a language and behavior of those outside official channels of authority that acts as a subversive force to undermine power relationships, Castellanos argues that Austen is writing in a feminist tradition in which her predecessors had already been exploring ways to subvert patriarchal ideas about women's appropriate roles in society. Castellanos is intent on disarming the notion of the conservative Austen, one supported by a general belief that Austen was "a conventional woman who would not have dared to challenge established social views." Such an assumption was easily accepted by readers "conditioned to see women as mostly conformists and followers, never as initiators" (13). But Castellanos also takes issue with feminists who believe Austen was alienated and angry. Above all, she insists, Austen was an ironist, but her "ironic laughter is animated by a peculiar type of opposition to traditional views of women's situation and abilities, an opposition whose feminism is best understood by recourse to the ambivalent stance typical of carnival" (20).

Perhaps the best example of recent criticism that blends feminist ideology with perceptive historicist reconstruction of Austen's work is Jillian Heydt-Stevenson's *Austen's Unbecoming Conjunctions: Subversive Laughter, Embodied History* (2005). In this volume Heydt-Stevenson expands ideas she developed in a series of essays published in the 1990s, offering a reading of the novels that stresses Austen's bawdy, sensual humor. Carefully explicating the contemporary meanings of many of Austen's phrases, Heydt-Stevenson explains how these comedic allusions serve to critique notions of female propriety that were taking root during the time Austen was writing. The use of "unbecoming conjunction[s]," a term used by Austen herself "to describe what happens when two ideas or images or people set side by side, reveal unforeseen similarities" (25) that defy reasonable interpretation and invite ridicule, allows the novelist to challenge preconceptions about important matters such as courtship and love. Heydt-Stevenson explains how "Austen's humor, her exploration of the body's expression of social constructions, and her presentation of women's histories through the everyday objects they handle all encourage a reassessment of cultural expectations" (27). In the course of her commentary, Heydt-Stevenson demonstrates that Austen's works consistently challenge patriarchal ideologies. As such, *Austen's Unbecoming Conjunctions* offers "a reevaluation of Austen's literary achievements and the place of the woman writer in the Romantic era" (28).

Another revisionist study, Barbara Wenner's *Prospect and Refuge in the Landscape of Jane Austen* (2006), also brings a feminist perspective to a topic that had heretofore received little attention among Austen scholars. "Readers of Jane Austen's novels might wonder how an entire book could be written about her landscapes," Wenner muses somewhat disingenuously at the beginning of her study (1). After all, she continues, received critical opinion has been that landscape and setting play only minor roles in Austen's fiction, at least until she wrote *Persuasion*. But Wenner describes with notable insight how Austen "interpreted the land around her aesthetically" and used it as a means of having her heroines "grow in their knowledge of society and themselves" (ix). Her study is informed by feminist theories of landscape and environment, particularly Gillian Rose's *Feminism and Geography: The Limits of Geographical Knowledge* (1993), and Jill Heydt-Stevenson's "Liberty, Connection, and Tyranny: The Novels of Jane Austen and the Aesthetic Movement of the Picturesque" (1998), which connects three important realms of study: nationhood, gender, and aesthetics. In Austen's fiction, Heydt-Stevenson claims, "arguments about the construction of a national identity converge with the arguments about the construction of womanhood and the construction of landscape" (261). Rose and Heydt-Stevenson's ideas help shape Wenner's notion that "Austen found a way of championing women through her use of picturesque landscape aesthetics" (8). Wenner acknowledges that she is in some ways responding to the commentary on Austen's use of landscape in Alistair Duckworth's *The Improvement of the Estate* (1971), differing from him in her belief that Austen wants her heroines to have opportunities to find freedom within the landscapes they inhabit, and never to become simply objects in landscapes designed and dominated by men.

And lest one think that British feminists remained aloof from the practice of highly theoretical critiques of Austen's fiction, Oxford scholar Ashley Tauchert disproves the notion convincingly in *Romancing Jane Austen: Narrative, Realism, and the Possibility of a Happy Ending* (2005). Tauchert offers a thoughtful analysis of Austen's use of the romance, a genre that Tauchert is quick to note has two meanings in contemporary criticism: the masculine medieval adventure tale, and its feminized version, the domestic fantasy. Interested in explaining what she sees as important relationships between past and present as exemplified by these two strands of the same creative impulse, Tauchert explores Austen's fiction to expose the "anachronistic implications of a resonance between the eighteenth-century feminist polemic of Mary Wollstonecraft and the twentieth-century 'feminine philosophy' of Luce Irigaray" (ix). In Tauchert's view, Austen is a pivotal figure in the transformation of the romance, refiguring its mythic dimensions into the feminine version that has survived in romance novels of the twentieth century. Austen at first appears contradictory. She adopts the form of romance, a genre that "structures femininity in a way that demands attention" (xii), but centers on what Tauchert calls "the basest of feminine fantasies" (xiii) — the rescue fantasy, in which the heroine, saved by a worthy hero, lives happily ever after. As Tauchert's close readings of Austen's novels demonstrate, however, the heroine does much to civilize her savior; these are real love stories, not simply escapist fantasies. Tauchert's analysis also reveals how Austen's novels offer complex examinations of the female subject struggling to attain (and maintain) personal identity and gain happiness. Austen believes love is a redemptive emotion, especially for women. Sadly, Tauchert reflects, in the postmodern world it is difficult to appreciate this fact, much less write about it sympathetically.

Finally, beginning in the 1990s interest in Austen's portrayal of men gained renewed interest. Two book-length studies capitalized on that trend. Unfortunately, Audrey Hawkridge's *Jane and Her Gentlemen* (2000), actually shows little evidence of having been influenced by recent discussions of gender identity or masculinity. Instead, Hawkridge offers some insight into what Austen thought of men by reviewing the details of her life, concentrating on her relationships with male family members and the young gentlemen who may have been potential husbands for her. From these personal encounters, Hawkridge says, Austen developed her notion of what the ideal man should be, and transposed many of the qualities she discovered in the men in her life into her fictional heroes. Although Austen may have been an incipient feminist with a passionate desire to see women given equal rights in society, in Hawkridge's opinion she remained all her life a romantic who desired male companionship, even marriage — but on her own terms.

Where Hawkridge's study is rather discursive and personalized, Michael Kramp's *Disciplining Love* (2007) reflects the work done since the mid-1990s when the Jane Austen Society of North America sponsored a conference focusing on Austen's treatment of men. Employing the theoretical work of Foucault and Gilles Deleuze, and integrating recent scholarship into his assessment, Kramp studies "the masculinity modeled by the men of Austen's novels" (x) not only to discover what Austen's fiction reveals about its own day but also why it has become particularly appealing to readers (and viewers of the many film and video adaptations) at the end of the twentieth century. Kramp demonstrates that the concept of masculinity was in serious question at the time Austen was writing. After reviewing historical and cultural background materials that reveal "England's ambitions for the modernizing nation and its men" (10), Kramp surveys Austen's fiction to explain how the novels reveal widespread anxiety about what it meant to be male. The fiction presents the struggle as dynamic and not necessarily linear. While *Pride and Prejudice* seems to celebrate new concepts of masculinity, *Mansfield Park* "dramatizes a society in denial of this transition" (12). In *Emma* Austen treats such resistance comically, representing Knightley as the New Man who "can preserve social/sexual identity, maintain a vital civic role, and keep the company of women by carefully regulating any amorous desire or sexual passion" (13). *Persuasion* is a kind of escapist fantasy wherein the lovers, by removing themselves from society, can pursue their passion only by becoming nomads. The lessons offered by Austen are important for contemporary society, Kramp says, in which men seem to struggle to find acceptable ways to express their sexual identity. Austen's men can serve "as useful early examples of our ongoing modern attempt to manage a disciplined masculinity that is sexually safe and socially useful" (149).

Feminist Biographies

Since the use of feminist theory to revisit traditional topics was a hallmark of scholarship during this period, it should not be surprising to find feminist biographies of Austen appearing during these decades. Two such works deserve special mention: Jan Fergus's *Jane Austen* (1991) and Emily Auerbach's *Searching for Jane Austen* (2004). Concentrating on Austen's professional life, Fergus explains how events in the novelist's home and family life served first as a kind of apprenticeship and then as a continuing spur to her creative efforts. Fergus provides an insightful survey of the publishing industry in the late eighteenth and early nineteenth centuries, demonstrating why Austen's decision — made early in her life — to become a published author was unconventional, even daring. Fergus believes Austen adopted many of the conventions of novel-writing as it was being practiced in her day to assure herself an audience for her novels. Her "political sympathies may be fundamentally conservative," Fergus admits, "but her mind is critical and her vision ironic" (67). Throughout her career, Austen offered in her fiction a "critique of conventional notions of women" (52) and society's expectations for them. Though not wedded to the radical ideologies of feminists or other theorists, Fergus nonetheless displays in her readings of the novels and Austen's letters a strong awareness of, and sympathy for, those who find in Austen's social comedies a strong critique of "the complex power relationships between women and a social world that reduces their options and makes them marginal" (146). While Austen often entertains her readers with "the highly comic mixture of sexual and economic motives that prompt courtship and marriage," she is equally concerned with "the much less comic operations of power — of dominance and submission — that occur within and around both institutions" (148). Fergus's assessment of Austen as a professional writer, and a brilliant, ironic commentator is at the same time a sober analysis of perennial gender issues that deny women equal status in society.

While solidly feminist in its approach to Austen's life and writing, Auerbach's *Searching for Jane Austen* (2004) makes use of both previously published scholarship and close analysis of Austen's fiction and her letters to reveal something about the essence of the woman who composed six of the most widely read novels in English. The principal task Auerbach sets for herself is to get beyond the myths created over nearly two centuries about Austen as a retiring, self-deprecating spinster who thought well of everyone and considered her novel-writing as little more than an interesting diversion. To fully appreciate Austen's accomplishments, Auerbach insists, "we must break free of dear Aunt Jane — and of two centuries of putdowns and touchups." When this is done, readers and critics will discover Austen's "sharp, uncompromising gaze" that allowed her to write some of the most penetrating commentaries on her own society and on the perennial struggles of women — and men — to find happiness and value in their lives (40). Throughout her critique of the fiction, Auerbach stresses Austen's sharp wit, her playfulness, and her delight in taking to task hypocrites and self-important people whose braggadocio and bluster get in the way of meaningful relationships.

Other Commentary Influenced by Feminism and Gender Studies

During the period covered in this chapter hundreds of articles and chapters in books provided analyses of Austen's fiction based on principles of feminist literary theory. Most demonstrate the growing trend to blend feminist analysis with other theories of narratology, aesthetics, or politics to produce more subtle readings of Austen's work. A representative example is Susan Sniader Lanser's essay on Austen in *Fictions of Authority: Women Writers and Narrative Voice* (1992), a book designed to help develop a feminist poetics of narrative voice by linking ideas regarding narratology with feminist concerns about women's point of view and experience. Relying on principles developed by Bakhtin, Lanser examines Austen's novels as "texts that engage questions of authority specifically through their production of narrative voice" (7). Austen, she says, concentrates on conflicts that arise when women presume to speak with authority — a lesson she learned early in her career, when *Northanger Abbey*, a novel with a radical narrative voice, was withheld from publication. Austen learned to make accommodations in her style to disguise her efforts to express resistance to the dominant patriarchal ideology. But as her career progressed, Lanser says, Austen moved gradually back towards an "overtly authorial form" (79) which can be detected in *Persuasion* and to an even greater degree in *Sanditon*. Similarly, Julia Giordano's "The World as Battleground in Jane Austen's *Persuasion*" in Carol Singley and Susan Sweeney's *Anxious Power: Reading, Writing, and Ambivalence in Narrative by*

Women (1993) examines Austen's use of indirect discourse as a means of simultaneously identifying with her romantic heroine while maintaining a certain ironic distance from her. The technique, Giordano says, makes the novel a subversive attack on the patriarchal society in which the heroine must negotiate her future.

Birgitta Berglund combines techniques of formalist criticism with a feminist's keen sensitivity to the nuances of the text in her examination of Austen's depiction of houses in *Woman's Whole Existence: The House as an Image in the Novels of Ann Radcliffe, Mary Wollstonecraft, and Jane Austen* (1993). Influenced by historical and sociological studies of women's changing roles in eighteenth-century society, Berglund argues that, like most women novelists of her time, Austen depicts the tension felt by middle-class and gentry women who were essentially confined to the domestic sphere. This tension is represented by the house, which is at once a symbol of the liberty they experience, being free from labor and titularly the figure of primary importance in their domicile, and the confinement they suffer within these walls where they are imprisoned by social convention.

Two studies of sisterhood in Austen's novels illustrate feminists' continuing interest in this important topic. In *The Suppressed Sister: A Relationship in Novels by Nineteenth- and Twentieth-Century British Women* (1992), Amy Levin finds Austen's novels "remarkable in the way they work and rework the elements of the traditional sister plot" (34). Not only are Austen's plots used to comment on the social status of women and establish character through contrasts, they often become "the locus of what is repressed or displaced from the marriage plot" (34). Noting that not all relationships between sisters are idyllic, Levin says these frequently "form part of that darker underside" of the novels, highlighting those qualities that must be "suppressed, distanced, or unfulfilled in a heroine for her to accept a traditional marriage and for the novelist to create a conventional ending" (52–53). In another study of sisterhood, "'Islands' of Peace: Female Friendships in Victorian Literature" (1993), Laurie Buchanan calls Austen the first novelist to attempt to create a new paradigm for living that would be parallel with, or even triumph over, the patriarchy, largely through her "portrayal of women's friendships" (79). Using *Sense and Sensibility* as her example, Buchanan explains how the sisters' friendship brings them together as they face the various crises in their lives, while simultaneously "allowing them to become independent individuals" and achieve a "new understanding of themselves" (86).

Feminists also continued to explore Austen's relationship to Romanticism — and in redefining the term to be more inclusive. Among those revisionists is Anne Mellor, who in *Romanticism and Gender* (1993) takes on the ambitious task of challenging the male-centered definitions of English Romanticism proposed by luminaries such as M. H. Abrams, Harold Bloom, Geoffrey Hartman, Paul de Man, Carl Woodring, and Je-

rome McGann. Mellor argues that by viewing the development of literature through the eyes of women (including Austen) writing during the
period traditionally designated as Romantic, a new vision of Romanticism
can be formulated. In a fashion similar to — but not identical with — the
bildungsroman, a popular genre for male Romantics, Austen concentrates
all her novels on "female education," in which "an intelligent but igno-
rant girl learns to perceive the world more accurately, to understand more
fully the ethical complexity of human nature and society, and to gain con-
fidence in the wisdom of her own judgment" (53). Austen recognized an
important truth for her time, Mellor says; for women to survive in society
they must "exercise good sense and self-control" (58). She also recognized that women endured a form of slavery within a society that limited
their freedoms in many ways. "Jane Austen wants us to see the myriad
ways in which patriarchal power — especially the possession of money —
can corrupt both men and women" (63). Mellor believes Austen's best
characters learn to use money for the betterment of society — presumably
not a typical patriarchal practice.

Occasionally, however, a dissenting voice emerged to challenge feminist appropriations of Austen. Mona Scheuermann argues forcefully in
Her Bread to Earn: Women, Money and Society from Defoe to Austen
(1993) that "the images of women in the eighteenth-century English
novel are more positive than much recent criticism of women in the novel
would suggest." Furthermore, the "recent central emphasis on images of
women in the works only of women novelists" tends to distort the reality
of the way women were perceived in the society at large, because this approach "overemphasizes the view of woman as victim" and as a "nonfunc-
tioning member of society." Besides, Scheuermann insists, "the majority
of the important novels of the eighteenth century were written by men"
(1). Unfortunately, Scheuermann does not provide the criteria by which
she judges certain novels "important," so it is difficult to challenge her assertion. Nevertheless, she insists that Austen's images of women are "less
critical than those of the radical novelists" who are her close contemporaries (199). Austen's women pursue marriage as a noble goal, and they
are "completely integrated into society" (199). Scheuermann believes that
Austen accepts the social constraints of her world as givens. Hence, the
novelist's focus on the importance of money is "not only reasonable but
unavoidable" (202). Ignoring the possibilities for irony, Scheuermann
provides a literal reading of Austen's texts that strongly supports claims
that the novelist endorsed the values of the world in which she lived.

Despite critiques such as Scheuermann's, many feminists were still very
willing to enlist Austen as a champion in their cause. The particularly subversive quality of Austen's humor is examined in Regina Barreca's *Untamed and Unabashed: Essays on Women and Humor in British Literature*
(1994), in which Barreca suggests that all women's comic writing "is

charracterized by its thinly disguised rage" (21). In comedies written by women — including Austen — "the straitjacket of conventional femininity is challenged, confronted, and, finally, thrown off" (32). Barreca questions the prevailing critical notion that Austen's heroines, despite their seeming independence, eventually succumb to the demands of the patriarchy. While they are subjected to "the authorized editions of their own lives," the values "shared by reader and author are not those of the didactic male teachers" in the novels, but "rather the values espoused by the uninitiated female protagonists" (44). Austen's novels, Barreca says, consistently point out the disparity between reality for women and the fictions about their nature and role created for them by men.

Audrey Bilger adopts the same stance toward Austen in *Laughing Feminism: Subversive Comedy in Fanny Burney, Maria Edgeworth, and Jane Austen* (1998), a study of the "intersection of feminism and comedy" in the eighteenth century (9). Interested in "gender politics in women's comic writing" (9), Bilger begins by noting how Austen's comedy was largely ignored by her earliest readers in favor of the "domestic aspects" of her fiction (29). Bilger finds Austen's humor "openly aggressive" (69) in her private correspondence, but muted somewhat in her published works. Still, Bilger insists, "a significant aspect" of Austen's humor connects her to feminists of her own day, as it derives from her belief in "an equality between men and women based upon rationality and a perception of the incongruity of women's lot" (70–71). Bilger finds that Austen's comic mask disguises her "anger both at the restrictions upon women's behavior and the lack of choices available to them" (71).

Eileen Gillooly paints a similar portrait of Austen in "Rehabilitating Mary Crawford: *Mansfield Park* and the Relief of 'Throwing Ridicule'" (1994), representing Austen as a member of the oppressed sisterhood who uses her work to strike back at the culture which restricts her freedoms because she is a woman. Focusing her comments on *Mansfield Park*, Gillooly demonstrates how, through the character of Mary Crawford, Austen is able to launch "her own subtle humorous assaults upon the patriarchal construction of nineteenth-century femininity" and obtain vicariously some "temporary relief from the contained aggression" she suffered in that culture (329).

Less strident than Bilger and Gillooly, Patrician Menon argues in *Austen, Eliot, Charlotte Brontë and the Mentor-Lover* (2003) that understanding the role of the "mentor-lover" can expose a "wide range of interconnected issues stemming from the relationship of love to morality, power, and judgment" (1). While Menon admits Austen is not obsessed with the mentor-lover relationship, she uses it in several of her works; hence, apprehending its significance can help readers see the moral intention of Austen's fiction. Austen's "treatment of the mentor-lover in her works," Menon says, "suggests that she is principally interested in the mentor-lover relationship as it contributes to, or works against, what she sees as an ideal end: a marriage founded on both moral equality and mutual sexual love, on both judgment and passion" (77).

During the 1970s and 1980s many feminist scholars were reluctant to use the theoretical work of Mikhail Bakhtin in critiquing literary works, primarily because there was a general sense that the Russian formalist's approach was incompatible with feminists' aims. However, in 1994 Karen Hohne and Helen Wussow edited *A Dialogue of Voices: Feminist Literary Theory and Bakhtin*, a collection of essays applying Bakhtin's theoretical principles to "problems raised by feminist analysis of cultural texts" (viii). Included in that volume is Julie Shaffer's "The Ideological Intervention of Ambiguities in the Marriage Plot: Who Fails Marianne in Austen's *Sense and Sensibility?*" Shaffer challenges the notion that the cultural viewpoint represented in the novel by Elinor Dashwood should be accepted as the norm by which all other characters — especially her sister Marianne — should be judged. "A better way of reading *Sense and Sensibility*," Shaffer says, would be to "avoid privileging one term over another" (130). This method would help make sense of readers' tendency to sympathize with Marianne. Shaffer suggests the novel's critique of society is "bidirectional" (131), revealing not only "the limitations of Marianne's approach to the world," but also the "limitations" of the "world with which Marianne is left after giving up her illusions" (131).

It is certainly not surprising to see Austen well represented in books dealing with the mother-daughter relationship. For example, Susan Greenfield's critique of *Emma* in *Mothering Daughters: Novels and the Politics of Family Romance: Fanny Burney to Jane Austen* (2002), a book tracing "the mother-daughter plot" (13) in eighteenth- and early nineteenth-century novels by women, melds feminist criticism with the tools of psychological criticism and new historicism in an insightful reading of Austen's novel. Claiming Austen and her contemporaries "helped construct" the concept of "modern maternity" (13), Greenfield gives Austen credit for her "artistic triumph" in *Emma* of modernizing "the absent mother plot" (145). What makes this novel modern is the success Austen enjoys in "conceal[ing] socioeconomic and political problems behind the illusion of 'private' experience" (147). These forces are at work on the characters and shape their universe, but Austen manages to obscure their presence as factors driving the story. But Greenfield insists *Emma* is modern in another way as well. It is "the first English novel in which the existence of the unconscious seems indubitable — the first in which the heroine's misunderstanding of her own mind is the subject of the story" (150).

There are also numerous examples to be found illustrating feminism's influence on traditional critical studies. Marea Mitchell and Diane Osland's essay on *Pride and Prejudice* in *Representing Women and Female Desire from Arcadia to Jane Eyre* (2005) provides a comparative analysis of Austen's novel and Sir Philip Sidney's *Arcadia* to expose "aspects of Austen's novel that are more thoroughly grounded in narrative conventions than its finely wrought social specificity might suggest" (159). Despite this, the authors admit, Austen takes seriously the gender and class issues that are simply ignored or covered over by the conventions of the tradition in which she is writing. Their careful reading of the novel illustrates how Elizabeth Bennet negotiates her own fate while remaining within the conventional boundaries of decorum.

Two final examples should suffice to illustrate the variety of approaches used by feminists to explore broad cultural themes. *Life After Death: Widows and the English Novel* (2005), Karen Gevirtz's study of widows in novels written during the decades when England was transitioning from an agrarian to an industrial society, tries to tease out a sense of Austen's position on an important social and gender issue. Gevirtz suggests that in portraying widows in her fiction, Austen takes a progressive position with respect to these women. While Gevirtz finds no consistent pattern for their treatment, she concludes that Austen's widows "offer different perspectives on the multitude of concerns facing women living in the middle stages of emerging mercantile capitalism and the industrial revolution" (167). Also on the family theme, Mary Jean Corbett argues in *Family Likenesses* (2008), a study of the representation of romantic relationships and marriages among family members, that Austen approved of such romances because the practice allowed young women the comfort of entering into long-term unions with people with whom they were already familiar and at the same time retain some of the close sisterly relationships they had developed prior to being married.

The "Masturbation" and "Lesbian" Controversy

One of the few controversies over Austen to spill outside academe erupted during the late 1990s. It began with the presentation of a paper at the Modern Language Association meeting in 1990 by the well known authority on queer studies, Eve Sokofsky Sedgwick. Provocatively titled "Jane Austen and the Masturbating Girl," Sedgwick's paper appeared a year later in *Critical Inquiry*, then in her 1993 collection *Tendencies*. Sedgwick intentionally interjects some controversy into her discussion by claiming that she wants not simply to expose some hidden tendencies in Jane Austen's fiction toward celebrating autoeroticism, but also — and maybe more importantly — to reveal what she sees as the tendency of twentieth-century critics to circumscribe readings of Austen so as to eliminate all possibility of recognizing homoerotic or autoerotic suggestions that arise from the novels. As Sedgwick sees it, "Austen criticism" as it has been practiced for over a century is distinguished "not just for its timidity and banality, but for its unresting exaction of the spectacle of a Girl Being Taught a

Lesson" (125). Not only must proper girls rid themselves of tendencies to feel fully female. Also implied in dominant critical practice is the notion that critics must deal with Austen's fiction in such a way as to insure that any tendency to see her as celebrating the full experience of womanhood is severely repressed.

What most other scholars interested in lesbian and queer studies would do as follow-up to Sedgwick's observations can be seen in Lisa Moore's discussion of *Emma* in *Dangerous Intimacies* (1997), an analysis of the representation of female friendship and lesbianism in eighteenth- and nineteenth-century literature. Moore concentrates on explaining how all other "social differences" in the novel are subordinated to "sexual questions about the heroine's relations with other women" (110). That kind of conclusion would hardly have surprised professionals engaged in Austen study, even if they did not agree with it.

It is likely, though, that the suggestions about Austen's novels somehow depicting autoerotic or lesbian tendencies might have remained confined to academic circles were it not for the publication of what was intended to be a well-written, thoughtful book review by Terry Castle of Deirdre Le Faye's 1995 edition of *Jane Austen's Letters* in the *London Review of Books*. The title of her review, "Sister, Sister," may not have raised any eyebrows either, had it not been for the publisher's decision to announce the review on the first page of the issue in which it appeared with the banner heading "Was Jane Austen Gay?" In the minds of devoted Janeites, this teaser served as confirmation of all that was wrong with academic criticism of their favorite author. Although Castle insisted in a statement published by the press office at Stanford University where she held a faculty appointment that she did not intend to suggest Austen was a lesbian, her scholarly application of recent theories of the importance of erotic bonds between sisters in the eighteenth and nineteenth centuries caused something of a tempest in a teapot for those accustomed to thinking of Austen as a proper lady. What Castle makes clear in her review is the importance of the close association between the two Austen girls — a relationship that lasted a lifetime and probably influenced the shape of Jane Austen's fiction more than has been acknowledged by earlier critics.

This flurry of activity in scholarly and popular journals had its amusing moments, as Austen's conservative defenders railed against the radical left, which in turn seemed perfectly comfortable in defending the notion that Austen had more than a passing interest in other women. Claudia Johnson manages to put the controversy in historical context in "The Divine Miss Jane: Jane Austen, Janeites, and the Discipline of Novel Studies" (2001), an essay that reprises her 1997 article from the *Cambridge Companion to Jane Austen* (1997) and adds a commentary on the controversy stirred up by Sedgwick's article and Castle's review. Johnson thinks the supposed controversy is neither new nor particularly warranted. Despite efforts by Janeites to preserve Austen's reputation as a retiring spinster who was proper in everything — including her views on sex — Johnson notes that there have always been dissenting voices pointing out the subversive qualities of her work or taking decidedly different positions on her value as an artist.

Readings Influenced by
Poststructuralism and Narratology

Deconstruction, narratology and other poststructuralist theories have never gained prominence as methods for examining Austen's work. Nevertheless, a number of studies employing these methodologies have provided important insights into the novels. A review of selected writings illustrates how attitudes regarding Austen's craftsmanship and the ideology behind her fiction have been altered by critics using these approaches to her work. For example, Michael Boardman's *Narrative Innovation and Incoherence: Ideology in Defoe, Goldsmith, Austen, Eliot, and Hemingway* (1992) offers a reading of *Persuasion* that attempts to explain the many anomalies other critics cite as reasons for finding the novel problematic. Boardman suggests that critiques that dismiss the novel as being somewhat flawed are based on misreadings that insist it belongs to the same genre as Austen's earlier work. Boardman says the novel represents an innovation — not in structure alone but in ideology. In it Austen rejects the notion expressed in all her earlier fiction that merit will bring reward to the heroine if she perseveres against social sham and economic deprivation. Instead, in her last work Austen focuses on the pain that unrequited love has caused her powerless heroine. There are some instances of incoherence, Boardman admits, but these are caused by the novelist's struggling to adapt her work to the new outlook she has discovered regarding the society in which she lives. Similarly, Susan Payne's essay on *Northanger Abbey* in *The Strange within the Real: The Function of Fantasy in Austen, Brontë, and Eliot* (1992) explores the ways Austen uses fantasy and the Gothic to critique the realist tradition. Using the tools of contemporary narratology, Payne demonstrates that the novel has an underlying substratum of irony that can easily evade readers who accept too willingly the notion that Austen is poking fun at the fantastic by setting it off against a more realist vision of the world.

Grounded in the work of Hayden White, Paul de Man and others, Eugene Hollahan's *Crisis-Consciousness and the Novel* (1992), a study of the importance of "crisis" as a defining term for the development of the novel, focuses on Austen's use of what Hollahan calls a "*crisis*-trope" (62) in structuring *Emma*. In what Hollahan considers an advance over *Pride and Prejudice*, Austen presents her heroine moving from the use of crisis as a manipulative device to an acceptance of crisis as "an existential principle of self-discovery and self-acceptance" (63). At the other end of the spectrum, the concept of playfulness is the subject of Kulip Kuwahara's *Jane Austen at Play: Self-Consciousness, Beginnings, Endings* (1993), in which Kuwahara applies aesthetic principles developed by Austen's contemporary Friedrich von Schiller to an examination of her fiction. Not claiming that Schiller influenced Austen directly, Kuwahara nevertheless finds a key to appreciating Austen's fiction in the German philosopher's argument that play is as important as reason and sentiment to human nature. Describing Austen as "a self-conscious artist at play absorbed in a discovery of the truth" (13), Kuwahara explains how she plays with conventions of fiction-writing, initially setting up readers' expectations through "verbal patterns" and the interplay of denotation and connotation, and then skillfully resolving dilemmas she has raised as she brings closure to her novels." In her fiction, Kuwahara says, Austen creates an "ideal world" that is "clearly rooted in the finite world" (14).

As its title suggests, Cates Baldridge's *The Dialogics of Dissent in the English Novel* (1994) is a Bakhtinian critique of fiction (supplemented by ideas gleaned from Foucault, Terry Eagleton, and Raymond Williams) in which Baldridge argues that "any balanced perspective on the politics of the novel must take into account not only the ways in which it records and promotes the hegemonic discourses of bourgeois culture but of those means by which it occasionally obstructs, exposes, decenters, and subverts them" (xii). In his analysis of *Mansfield Park*, Baldridge relies on D. A. Miller's insights into Austen's problems with trying to be a novelist and a narrativist simultaneously in order to explain how she "champions the middle-class desideratum of tranquility so relentlessly as to bring herself in conflict with the structural necessities of her chosen medium" (40). Bakhtin's theory of dialogism is also at the center of Barbara Seeber's rather brief but exceptionally insightful monograph *General Consent in Jane Austen: A Study in Dialogism* (2000). Seeber attempts to reconcile the two competing and antithetical views of Austen. "Austen is subversive," Seeber argues, but not simply in the sublimated subtext of her novels. "It is in the interplay between main text and subtext that the subversive effect lies" (8). Seeber encourages a reading of the fiction that "expand[s] the space that Jane Austen inhabits in traditional criticism by presenting readings that fully acknowledge the dialogism of Austen's texts and its implications" (137). In yet another study informed by theories of narratology, *Jane Austen and Narrative Authority* (1995), Tara Ghoshal Wallace argues that each of Austen's major works "interrogates the claims of authoritative narrators" and "challenge[s] and enable[s] readers to move beyond a deconstructive dismantling of her texts toward an effective theory of narrative interpretation" (1). Austen's novels represent, either explicitly or in veiled terms, "a treatment of the intersection of gender, language, and authority" (2–3) and "thematize the problems of narrative authority" (15), creating in the course of her career a canon that urges readers to "practice what modern critical discourse calls the hermeneutics of suspicion" (16).

Strong arguments such as those put forward by Seeber and Wallace did not go unchallenged, however. Defending traditional critical constructs and philosophical concepts regarding realism against what he sees as threats posed by these new narratological approaches to literary study, in *Narrating Reality: Austen, Scott, Eliot* (1999) Harry Shaw begins his discussion of Austen from the premise that "realist plots are, for readers, primarily a matter of developing affect, not of objective structural patterning" (126). Using Austen's novels as test cases for exploring "the place of the plot in the realist novel" (127), and relying on theories of mimesis developed half a century earlier by the German critic Eric Auerbach, Shaw looks at how Austen constructs her plots. However, Shaw is equally interested in revealing how many critical assessments of her novels "betray a suspicion of plots in general" (128) and of realism in general. Shaw argues for reading *with* the grain — opposing contemporary efforts by critics such as Terry Eagleton to promote resistant readings. The real problem with writing about Austen, he says, is "the problem of finding a way to remain engaged with, but unmastered by, her mode of processing reality" (144).

Another area in which theorists have been helpful in expanding notions of Austen's artistry has been in assessing her handling of tropes and literary techniques. Austen's fiction is placed in the service of a greater theoretical project in Deidre Lynch's *The Economy of Character* (1998), a study that challenges traditionalist readings of characterization and character-formation. Lynch examines ways writers and readers in the long eighteenth century came to "make the character the center of their stories," linking this phenomenon with "new protocols" that developed at the time "for organizing class relations and for dividing a feminine world from a masculine one" (5). In studying Austen's development of Elinor Dashwood and Anne Elliot, Lynch extends her discussion beyond ways Austen individuates characters to examine her use of crowd scenes as a means of contrasting the individual and the larger social whole. By these means, Lynch says, Austen "supplements the opportunities her readers have for practice in sympathetic feeling by inviting them to partake in lighthearted games of stereotype-recognition and cliché-busting" (212).

Relying on the theoretical work of Mark Johnson and George Lakoff, Margaret Wye offers a reading in *Jane Austen's Emma: Embodied Metaphor as a Cognitive Constraint* (1998) that rebuts the notion that Austen was not given to the use of metaphor. Instead, Wye says, applying techniques of analysis that rely on the recognition of cognitive metaphors reveals the pervasiveness of metaphoric language in this novel, and by extension, in all of Austen's fiction. Anne Gaylin's *Eavesdropping in the*

Novel from Austen to Proust (2002) investigates ways Austen and other novelists portray human curiosity through the technique of eavesdropping. Gaylin suggests that the propensity for eavesdropping reveals something about human beings' desire to know, because knowledge can bring closure (for characters and readers). Austen's novels, she says, offer abundant examples of "how eavesdropping provokes or resolves narrative situations" (18); Gaylin sets these scenes against those involving conversation, which she calls "a counter-narrative paradigm weighted toward discovery of information and narrative closure" (19).

Revisionist criticism has also reshaped the way we view Austen as a rhetorician. In *Jane Austen's Discourse With New Rhetoric* (1999) Lynn Rigberg examines Austen's fiction in light of theories of rhetoric prevalent during her day. Informed by late twentieth-century theories regarding the ideological assumptions of rhetorical study and strategies for its use, Rigberg explains how Austen relies on the work of eighteenth-century rhetoricians Hugh Blair and George Campbell to stress the need for female education in rhetoric as a means of improving and sustaining the moral order. Patricia Michaelson's *Speaking Volumes: Women, Reading, and Speech in the Age of Austen* (2002), an interdisciplinary examination intended to "recapture" the "linguistic practices of individual women" (1), helps dispel the myth that there is a unified female voice. Positing that by Austen's time novels had replaced "conversation manuals in educating speakers" (20), Michaelson looks specifically at *Pride and Prejudice* as a novel that places "emphasis on speech" and "the rules governing conversation" (181), concentrating on what Austen's "attention to dialogue meant for the *reader*" (182). In this novel "Austen is optimistic about the possibilities of constructing a self through speech" (212). As Austen's career progressed, however, she became less sanguine about such possibilities; by the time she wrote *Persuasion*, she was becoming intrigued with the "value of silence" (213).

Several other narratological critiques published just after the turn of the twenty-first century are worth noting as well. In *Jane Austen, Or the Secret of Style* (2003) D. A. Miller continues the exploration of Austen's fiction begun nearly two decades earlier in *Narrative and its Discontents*, combining personal experience with his usual perceptive insights and sound command of critical theory to offer an analysis of the quality of Austen's writing that has most intrigued scholars and critics for nearly two centuries. As an artist, Miller says, Austen makes a conscious effort to keep "style" and "personality" separate, and in the process produces stories that contain the most impersonal narrators in English fiction. Miller also discovers that style is an important element within the stories, and that Austen frequently sets style and "substance" in opposition; only when characters are willing to get beyond their style — that is, their conscious way of presenting themselves to the world — can they engage in meaningful relationships with others.

Like Miller's work on Austen's style, Madeline Wing-chi Ki's *Jane Austen and the Dialectic of Misrecognition* (2005) presents a provocative and controversial view of the novelist's attitude toward self and society. Grounding her analysis in the work of Hegel and Lacan, Wing-chi Ki argues that both conservative and liberal proponents of Austen — those in the "containment" and "subversive" groups — have not provided an adequate explanation for the novelist's vision. What is needed, she says, is an appreciation of Austen's more complex notion of "enlightenment," which is frequently represented in the novels as a "dialectic between progress and non-improvement." Wing-Chi Ki demonstrates how Austen's fiction is "dominated by a love of enlightened recognition" (323) in which Austen's protagonists go through a process of education that leads them to recognize both the importance of the Self *and* the essentiality of the Other. Many of Austen's characters recognize the shortcomings of the conservative society in which they live, but they engage in a process of "misrecognition" that allows them to operate as if they accept those values. Austen's "dialectics of misrecognition" support neither "docile conformism" nor "subversive changes," but instead highlight the "struggle between on-going analytical recognition in the midst of persisting misrecognition" (325).

Marxist, New Historical, and Political Criticism

Trying to separate new historicism from older forms of historical study is not always easy. Traditional historical analysis is often still practiced, but it is frequently informed by the work of New Historicists whose work began to gain widespread attention during the 1980s. The blending of "old" and "new" is evident in Tom Winnifrith's examination of the "fallen woman" in Austen's fiction in *Fallen Women in the Nineteenth-Century Novel* (1994). Seeing Austen as the first in a line a writers who did not treat such women kindly, Winnifrith warns that it is unwise to judge the novelist by contemporary standards. Rather, we should see her in historical context to gain some appreciation of her ideas about illicit sex and understand how her views reflect the society that produced them. Another example of this kind of blended historical analysis is Roger Sales's well-researched and deftly presented assessment, *Jane Austen and Representations of Regency England* (1994). Although ostensibly written for students wishing to understand something of the context of Austen's novels, Sales's book is actually a carefully crafted argument stressing the importance of understanding the historical context to appreciate fully Austen's achievement. His interest in Austen's handling of various political, social, cultural, and medical issues contextualizes the novelist within her own age rather than making her out to be someone uninterested in events happening around her as she wrote.

More typical of New Historical criticism is Nicola Watson's *Revolution and the Form of the British Novel 1790–1825* (1994). Watson stresses the cultural and political reasons that motivated Austen to transform some of her early epistolary work into narratives before they were published. By the time she was ready to publish, Watson says, the letter as a form of communication had become suspect among the general public because of the ways private correspondence had been used subversively during the French Revolution. Austen and her contemporaries were engaged in "projects of recuperation, conversion, and purgation" from that "great cataclysm" (20), and Austen saw the necessity of recasting her work to avoid the appearance of its being revolutionary.

Employing both eighteenth-century and contemporary theories of political economics to an examination of the development of the genre of romance, Miranda Burgess deftly explains in *British Fiction and the Production of Social Order, 1740–1830* (2000) how "the conjunction of Toryism, parody, and history" helps to shape "a crucial place for Austen's fiction among the early-nineteenth-century ideologies of British social and economic cohesion" (151). To read Austen's novels "as national romances that engage and ironically resolve problems of national history," Burgess says, "is to map Austen's position on a chart of contemporary contradiction and crisis" (157). Similarly, Edward Copeland combines feminist and Marxist techniques of analysis to Austen's fiction in *Women Writing about Money: Women's Fiction in England* (1995), revealing how intensely Austen was interested in matters of economy, specifically consumption. Concerned about attempts by his own contemporaries to transpose their values onto Austen's work, Copeland cautions that Austen and her contemporaries "approach consumption through the much narrower gates of rank and custom" than do modern-day consumers — and critics (89).

In *The Politics of Jane Austen* (1999) Edward Neill seeks to "'liberate' the reading of Jane Austen" from traditional conservative views which he believes Austen would have abhorred (ix). But he does not consider her a radical; rather, he says, she is more a skeptic. Neill sets out to explode previous theories of her fiction, especially conservative ones, such as Marilyn Butler's argument in *Jane Austen and the War of Ideas*, or what Neill calls naïve ones, such as Roger Gard's in *Jane Austen's Novels: The Art of Clarity* (discussed in the next chapter). He is also bothered by readings that attempt to explain Austen simply as the product of her times, because these invariably fail to "show *why she emerged from that context* as a massive textual and cultural force" (12). What interests him most is why Austen's novels "have acted as continuously circulating cultural energies" that are taken to represent the concept of Englishness while "rais[ing] gender and general political issues in a compelling and continuously interesting way" (12). Similarly, Melora Giardetti argues rather ingeniously in *Personal and Political Transformations in the Texts of Jane Austen* (2003) that Austen "defies categorical definitions of conservative and radical" in order to present a "transcendent message" (1) that supports conservative ends, but does so subversively.

Like Neill, in *Jane Austen and the Enlightenment* (2004) Peter Knox-Shaw mounts an attack on Marilyn Butler's *Jane Austen and the War of Ideas*, employing the tools of historicist scholarship to debunk many of her arguments. Using family documents as well as the work of various Enlightenment writers, he demonstrates that Austen was keenly aware of the Enlightenment's view of humankind and sympathetic to many of the tenets of the movement's most notable philosophers, particularly Adam Smith, making her views "typical of the skeptical Enlightenment" (11). Austen's skepticism was bred at home, Knox-Shaw says, and her satire "belongs to a tradition that is liberal in character" (55). While she may not have been a supporter of the French Revolution, she does not deserve to be labeled an anti-Jacobin in the sense in which that term is normally applied. What is more, Knox-Shaw concludes, Austen was not — as Butler asserts — averse to matters of sensibility. Instead, she was "a mistress of 'the sensuous, the irrational, and the involuntary'" — qualities Butler says are missing from Austen's writings. On the contrary, Knox-Shaw says, "she represents them in her novels with unprecedented insight and skill" (253).

Perhaps the most strident turn-of-the-century Marxist analysis of Austen's fiction is Moyra Haslett's in *Marxist Literary and Cultural Theories* (2000). Although Haslett concentrates on film adaptations of Austen's novels produced during the 1980s and 1990s, she makes it clear that her complaints are with the novels as well. The re-visionings of Austen's texts on screen, Haslett says, are less objectionable for their anachronisms — a topic of endless annoyance to devotees of Austen among the general public — than for the producers' and directors' consistent efforts to sanitize living conditions and ignore the plight of the poor and working classes on which the gentry depended for their elegant lifestyles. The movies and television series almost always play to conservative preconceptions of Austen and Regency England — notions that, in Haslett's view, are far from the truth. Ironically, one film that does receive some praise is *Clueless*, a modern re-telling of *Emma*. By avoiding the trappings of "period piece" costuming and setting, the film is able to expose "some of the purely monetary and capitalist aspects" of Austen's novel (219). Like Haslett, William Galperin in *The Historical Austen* (2003) is interested in discerning the history behind the fiction by concentrating on what Frances Ferguson, in a review of his study, calls the "history of the declining and the vanquished" (133). However, in contrast to Haslett and most other Marxists, Galperin challenges the notion that Austen was a supporter of the existing social order who advocated for regulating behavior as a moral imperative. The subversive qualities of Austen's fiction, he says, are most evident in her narrative techniques, where her use of indirection helps mask the revolutionary character of her fiction.

Even the field of textual studies was influenced by new historicist approaches to literary analysis. In *Jane Austen's Textual Lives: From Aeschylus to Bollywood* (2005) Kathryn Sutherland examines the novels' initial appearances, nineteenth- and early twentieth-century editions of the novels, the establishment of the Austen canon through the editorial work of R. W. Chapman, and the contrasting modes of interpretation offered by scholarly analysis and screen adaptations. In the same year, Janet Todd and a panel of distinguished scholars assisting her began publication of The Cambridge Edition of the Works of Jane Austen, a nine-volume set intended to supplant Chapman's work as the standard edition of the novelist's fiction. The careful planning that went into this project is evidenced in part by the fact that all nine volumes were in print within five years, and by the meticulous attention to detail Todd and her co-editors give to textual and historical matters great and small. Todd's 2005 *Jane Austen in Context*, intended as a general introduction to the edition, contains forty essays by a veritable "who's who" among Austen scholars, although it should be noted that the contributions are largely intended to provide background information to help readers understand the fiction. There are, however, several fine essays outlining Austen's critical reputation in which some of the major approaches to the novels are suggested.

Finally, in *Jane Austen and the Popular Novel: The Determined Author* (2007) Anthony Mandal builds his argument around the double meaning of "determined" to describe ways the contemporary atmosphere in which Austen created her novels affected their production. While Austen may have been "determined" — that is, resolute — to become a published novelist, she was also "determined" in the Darwinian sense, in that her environment provided the conditions favorable for her to get published. Challenging notions about the late-Georgian period as one of literary stasis, Mandal centers Austen's fiction in the cultural milieu of the 1810s, when women's work was serving as proof that the novel as a form was still evolving. Read in this light, Austen is a revolutionary — because she helped to revolutionize the production of fiction rather than challenge social norms.

Postcolonial Studies

In 1989 Edward Said, the Palestinian-born Columbia University professor whose 1978 volume *Orientalism* helped launch interest in cultural studies, provided the impetus for postcolonial investigations of Austen's fiction in an essay for a festschrift honoring the British cultural critic

Raymond Williams. In his oft-reprinted essay "Jane Austen and Empire" (1989) Said argues that the "imperial map of the world in English literature" (152) began to take shape before the great colonial expansion of the late nineteenth century made it a political reality. Austen "is more implicated in the rationale for imperialist expansion" than has been generally recognized (154). His reading of *Mansfield Park* suggests that considering ideas of imperialism and the hegemony of British values can "provide a fascinatingly expanded dimension" to one's understanding of the novel (153). Said lays stress on the importance of the Antigua estate from which the Bertrams earn the money they need to live in style at Mansfield Park; as part of her education Fanny must learn her place in the social hierarchy supported by colonial (slave) labor. Said's reading on the margins reveals the political subtext of the novel, identifying *Mansfield Park* as "part of the structure of an expanding imperialist venture" (163) and *not* an ahistorical moral masterpiece. Following Said's lead, in *Reaches of Empire: The English Novel from Edgeworth to Dickens* (1991) his disciple Suvendrini Perera explains how the ideology of empire, with its concurrent creation of the notion of Englishness, is a subtext in Austen's fiction. Though Austen's novels seldom seem to touch openly on matters of colonial expansion, the "presence of empire" exists "at the edges of Austen's texts," in which the "spatial interrelation between country village and colonies is enacted in the text through the working out of new sets of social relationships" (43).

Works such as Said's and Perera's seemed to open the floodgates, allowing a steady flow of postcolonial commentary to rush into print, much of it focused on *Mansfield Park*. Moira Ferguson's reading of that novel in *Colonialism and Gender from Mary Wollstonecraft to Jamaica Kincaid* (1993) stresses the importance of Thomas Bertram's ties to the West Indian plantations that supply his revenues and supplement the livelihood of his English country estate. Ferguson offers an interpretation of the novel in which Sir Thomas is seen as a slave owner and Fanny as his slave, who has been taken from her natural home and taught new values designed to raise her above the society from which she has been removed. Sir Thomas's treatment of her is what would have been expected from any male head of household in providing for the proper education — and subjugation — of young women in his care. Hence, Ferguson believes there are parallels to be drawn between the condition of slaves in British colonies and women at home. Austen's novel is "a post-abolition narrative" that simultaneously "intertwines with a critique, conscious or unconscious, of gender relations" (88). Less focused on Austen than Ferguson's study, Katie Trumpener's *Bardic Nationalism: The Romantic Novel and the British Empire* (1997), an examination of literature of the late eighteenth and early nineteenth centuries, concentrates on Austen's reaction to the problems of slavery within the Empire, arguing that while many might consider *Mansfield Park* a "conservative retrenchment from the political issues that slavery raised," it can also be read as "an abolitionist novel in its own right" (172). And while it may be primarily a tale of female education, it is simultaneously "a more wide-ranging meditation on the reproduction and transformation of power relations" (175).

Carl Plasa's commentary on Austen in *Textual Politics from Slavery to Postmodernism* (2000) supplements and at times refutes the work of earlier postcolonial critics, arguing that "questions of colonialism and slavery in Austen's post-abolitionist novel [*Mansfield Park*] are fully interwoven with what might be called its textual strategies" (5). Focusing on what he calls the "repressed history" (5) of the novel, Plasa faults Austen for not fully acknowledging the true horrors of slavery. Her attempts to equate the conditions of slavery with the plight of the Englishwoman is simply a false comparison, Plasa says, and further evidence of her reticence to confront this abomination head-on. By contrast, Gabrielle D. V. White makes Austen's views on slavery and abolition the principal subject of *Jane Austen in the Context of Abolition* (2006), a bold (if somewhat disjointedly organized and repetitive) work that challenges Said's claim about Austen's lack of sympathy for slaves. Concentrating on the novels written while Austen was living at Chawton Cottage, White shows that not only *Mansfield Park*, but *Persuasion* and especially *Emma*, reveal Austen's great support for abolition and her hopes that chattel slavery would be totally abolished throughout the Empire.[1]

One of the most intriguing studies of Austen's fiction to emerge as a result of new historicist and postcolonial inquiries is Franco Moretti's *Atlas of the European Novel, 1800–1900* (1998). Attempting to explain how plotting the locales of novels can help readers understand something about their characters' values and the social order in which their action takes place, Moretti suggests that Austen is one of the first novelists to take advantage of geography to create a comfortable "home" environment for her gentry — one that conveniently ignores the lower classes and centers itself on the country homes and spas outside the great metropolis of London. These comfortable environs provide a kind of safety net for Austen's heroines while introducing an element of the unknown, as they pursue marriage and its attendant requirement to situate in new homes. Like so many others who find Austen swept up in stereotypes about Britain's colonial possessions, Moretti notes that Austen makes use of this unknown territory symbolically in *Mansfield Park* to provide a source of wealth for the upper classes that allows them to enjoy the benefits of money without having to confront directly the gruesome conditions under which it is produced.

Writing about colonialism closer to Austen's home, in *The Grammar of Empire in Eighteenth-Century British Writing* (2000), a study of the rather complex, often stormy relationship between England and Scotland as evidenced in language and literature, Janet Sorensen examines Austen's language to determine if received opinion concerning her firm commitment to English culture and customs is borne out in her fiction. Sorensen notes that many critics have suggested that, given the realist nature of her fiction, Austen's words could stand for the reality of England itself. Sorensen suggests, however, that Austen's works actually confirm "the impossibility of word-world correspondence and of the common language that might collectively articulate such correspondence" (208).

How Jane Austen influenced readers and writers throughout the British Empire — both before and after most colonial nations gained independence — is the subject of You-me Park and Rajeswari Sunder Rajan's collection, *Austen in the World: Postcolonial Mappings* (2000). Essays in this volume, many by scholars from countries that were once colonies of Britain, provide interesting and often provocative reassessments of Austen's fiction, proposing that a careful reading of her novels at the margins reveals her complicity with the colonial enterprise that was for her contemporaries one of the great contributions Britain was making to world civilization — whether the natives wanted it or not.

Psychological Studies

Without meaning to create prejudice against some truly fine works of critical analysis, I believe it is fair to say that the volume and quality of psychological studies of Austen lags significantly behind work done from other perspectives. The first wave of interest in psychological criticism, largely Freudian or Jungian, hardly affected critical opinion of her work. Studies employing new psychological approaches, influenced by Lacan and the neo-Freudians, are equally scarce, and some are of questionable value. However, there is merit in Diana Postlethwaite's rather traditionalist psychological study of *Persuasion*, "Sometimes I Feel Like a Motherless Child: Austen's Anne Elliot and Freud's Anna O." (1992). Postlethwaite approaches the novel "from a Freudian view of causality" in which "the recovery of the missing mother provides the secret of transformation and rebirth" (42). Another good example of late-century psychological criticism of Austen's work is Anita Sokolsky's "The Melancholy Persuasion" in *Psychoanalytical Literary Criticism* (1994). Applying theories of melancholy developed by Freud and adapted by Melanie Klein, Sokolsky explains not only why in Austen's final novel Anne Elliot's inability to break the grasp of melancholy delays her gratification (and the happy ending), but also why many readers are particularly frustrated by Anne's apparent unwillingness to dispel the feeling of melancholy that forces her into mute passivity.

On the other hand, Julian Wynne's reading of Austen's novels under the auspices of Freudian psychology in *Jane Austen and Sigmund Freud*

(1998) seems less effective, perhaps because Wynne make great claims for his work as being the first to break free from the clutches of "Janeism" to present a reading of the novels that truly illuminates Austen's insights into human behavior. It may be hard for other critics to accept Wynne's assertion that Austen's work "has been *fundamentally* misunderstood" since it was first published (xiii), and to see that he introduces dozens of his predecessors only to demolish their arguments. One might wonder, too, about the premise on which Canadian speech pathologist Phyllis Ferguson Bottomer bases *So Odd a Mixture: Along the Autistic Spectrum in Pride and Prejudice* (2007). Bottomer applies clinical methodology used to detect and describe autism, specifically Asperger's syndrome, to characters in *Pride and Prejudice* in an attempt to offer some explanation for their behavior. Finding evidence that at least eight characters show some signs of this condition, Bottomer explains how Austen may have become familiar with this syndrome (even though it was not a diagnosable disease at the time), and how recognizing the impact of autism on Austen's characters helps readers understand why they behave as they do. Some critics, however, may not be convinced that such a reading of the novel carries the kind of weight Bottomer attaches to it.

Notes

[1] White is only one of several Austen scholars to challenge Said's reading of *Mansfield Park*; among the better critiques is Susan Fraiman, "Jane Austen and Edward Said: Gender, Culture and Imperialism" (1995).

Works Cited

Auerbach, Emily. *Searching for Jane Austen*. Madison: U of Wisconsin P, 2004.

Baldridge, Cates. "The Anti-Romantic Polemics of *Mansfield Park*." *The Dialogics of Dissent in the English Novel*, 40–62. Hanover, NH: UP of New England, 1994.

Barreca, Regina. "Dearly Loving a Good Laugh: Humor in Charlotte Lennox and Jane Austen." *Untamed and Unabashed: Essays on Women and Humor in British Literature*, 34–60. Detroit: Wayne State UP, 1994.

Berglund, Birgitta. *Woman's Whole Existence: The House as an Image in the Novels of Ann Radcliffe, Mary Wollstonecraft, and Jane Austen*. Lund, Sweden: Lund UP; Bromley, Kent: Chartwell-Bratt, 1993.

Bilger, Audrey. *Laughing Feminism: Subversive Comedy in Frances Burney, Maria Edgeworth, and Jane Austen*. Detroit: Wayne State UP, 1998.

Boardman, Michael M. "Comic Fiction and Ideological Instability: Gold-smith and Austen." *Narrative Innovation and Incoherence: Ideology in Defoe, Goldsmith, Austen, Eliot, and Hemingway*, 59–103. Durham, NC: Duke UP, 1992.

Bottomer, Phyllis Ferguson. *So Odd a Mixture: Along the Autistic Spectrum in Pride and Prejudice*. London and Philadelphia: Jessica Kingsley, 2007.

Buchanan, Laurie. "'Islands' of Peace: Female Friendships in Victorian Literature." In *Communication and Women's Friendships*, edited by Janet Doubler Ward and JoAnna Stephens Mink, 77–96. Bowling Green, OH: Bowling Green State UP, 1993.

Burgess, Miranda. *British Fiction and the Production of Social Order, 1740–1830*. New York: Cambridge UP, 2000.

Castellanos, Gabriela. *Laughter, War, and Feminism: Elements of Carnival in Three of Jane Austen's Novels*. New York: Lang, 1994.

Castle, Terry. "Sister-Sister." Review of Deirdre Le Faye, *Jane Austen's Letters. London Review of Books*, 2 August 1995. Reprinted in *London Review of Books: An Anthology*, edited by Jane Hindle, 138–48. London: Verso, 1996.

Cohen, Paula Marantz. *The Daughter's Dilemma: Family Process and the Nineteenth-Century Domestic Novel*. Ann Arbor: U of Michigan P, 1991.

Copeland, Edward. "Shopping for Signs: Jane Austen and the Pseudo-Gentry." *Women Writing about Money: Women's Fiction in England, 1790–1820*, 89–117. Cambridge: Cambridge UP, 1995.

Copeland, Edward, and Juliet McMaster, eds. *The Cambridge Companion to Jane Austen*. Cambridge; New York: Cambridge UP, 1997.

Corbett, Mary Jean. *Family Likenesses: Sex, Marriage, and Incest from Jane Austen to Virginia Woolf*. Ithaca, NY: Cornell UP, 2008.

David, Gail. "Shared Heroics." *Female Heroism in the Pastoral*, 113–69. New York: Garland, 1991.

Duckworth, Alistair. *The Improvement of the Estate: A Study of Jane Austen's Novels*. Baltimore and London: Johns Hopkins UP, 1971.

Fergus, Jane. *Jane Austen: A Literary Life*. New York: St. Martin's, 1991.

Ferguson, Frances. Review of William Galperin, *The Historical Austen. Albion* 36.1 (Spring 2004): 133–34.

Ferguson, Moira. "*Mansfield Park*: Slavery, Colonialism, and Gender." *Oxford Literary Review* 13 (1991): 118–39. Reprinted in *Colonialism and Gender Relations from Mary Wollstonecraft to Jamaica Kincaid: East Caribbean Connections*, 65–89. New York: Columbia UP, 1993.

Fraiman, Susan. "Jane Austen and Edward Said: Gender, Culture, and Imperialism. *Critical Inquiry* 21.4 (Summer 1995): 805–21.

Galperin, William. *The Historical Austen*. Philadelphia: U of Pennsylvania P, 2003.

Gaylin, Ann Elizabeth. *Eavesdropping in the Novel from Austen to Proust.* Cambridge and New York: Cambridge UP, 2002.

Gevirtz, Karen Bloom. "A State of Alteration, Perhaps of Improvement: Jane Austen's Widows." *Life after Death: Widows and the English Novel, Defoe to Austen*, 137–68. Cranbury, NJ: Associated UP, 2005.

Gillooly, Eileen. "Rehabilitating Mary Crawford: *Mansfield Park* and the Relief of 'Throwing Ridicule.'" In *Feminist Nightmares; Women at Odds — Feminism and the Problem of Sisterhood*, edited by Susan Ostrov Weisser and Jennifer Fleischner, 328–42. New York: New York UP, 1994.

Giardetti, Melora. *Personal and Political Transformation in the Texts of Jane Austen*. Lewiston, NY: Edwin Mellen Press, 2003.

Giordano, Julia. "The Word as Battleground in Jane Austen's *Persuasion*." In *Anxious Power: Reading, Writing, and Ambivalence in Narrative by Women*, edited by Carol J. Singley and Susan E. Sweeney, 107–23. Albany: State U of New York P, 1993.

Gorman, Anita G. *The Body in Illness and Health: Themes and Images in Jane Austen*. New York: Lang, 1993.

Green, Katherine Sobba. "Jane Austen: The Blazon Overturned." *The Courtship Novel 1740–1820: A Feminized Genre*, 153–59. Lexington: UP of Kentucky, 1991.

Greenfield, Susan C. *Mothering Daughters: Novels and the Politics of Family Romance: Fanny Burney to Jane Austen*, 145–68. Detroit: Wayne State UP, 2002.

Gross, Gloria S. "Flights into Illness: Some Characters in Jane Austen." In *Literature & Medicine During the Eighteenth Century*, edited by Marie Mulvey Roberts and Roy Porter, 188–99. New York: Routledge, 1993.

Haslett, Moyra. *Marxist Literary and Cultural Theories*. New York: St. Martin's, 2000.

Hawkridge, Audrey. *Jane and her Gentlemen: Jane Austen and the Men in her Life and Novels*. London: Peter Owen; Chester Springs, PA: Dufour Editions, 2000.

Heydt-Stevenson, Jillian. *Austen's Unbecoming Conjunctions: Subversive Laughter, Embodied History*. New York: Palgrave Macmillan, 2005.

———. "Liberty, Connection, and Tyranny: The Novels of Jane Austen and the Aesthetic Movement of the Picturesque." In *Lessons of Romanticism: A Critical Companion*, edited by Thomas Pfau and Robert F. Gleckner, 261–79. Durham, NC and London: Duke UP, 1998.

Hohne, Karen, and Helen Wussow, eds. *A Dialogue of Voices: Feminist Literary Theory and Bakhtin*. Minneapolis: U of Minnesota P, 1994.

Hollahan, Eugene. "Ideology and Crisis-Consciousness: Jane Austen, Emily Brontë, and George Eliot." *Crisis-Consciousness and the Novel*, 56–95. Cranbury, NJ: Associated UP, 1992.

Horwitz, Barbara J. *Jane Austen and the Question of Women's Education.* New York: Lang, 1991.

Hudson, Glenda A. *Sibling Love and Incest in Jane Austen's Fiction.* New York: St. Martin's, 1992.

Johnson, Claudia L. "Austen Cults and Cultures." In *The Cambridge Companion to Jane Austen*, edited by Edward Copeland and Juliet McMaster, 211–26. Cambridge; New York: Cambridge UP, 1997.

———. "The Divine Miss Jane: Jane Austen, Janeites, and the Discipline of Novel Studies." In *Reception Studies: From Literary Theory to Cultural Criticism*, edited by James L. Machor and Philip Goldstein, 118–32. New York and London: Routledge, 2001.

Kaplan, Deborah. *Jane Austen Among Women.* Baltimore: Johns Hopkins UP, 1992.

Knox-Shaw, Peter. *Jane Austen and the Enlightenment.* Cambridge and New York: Cambridge UP, 2004.

Kramp, Michael. *Disciplining Love: Austen and the Modern Man.* Columbus: Ohio State UP, 2007.

Kuwahara, K. K. *Jane Austen at Play: Self-Consciousness, Beginnings, Endings.* New York: Lang, 1993.

Lanser, Susan Sniader. "Sense and Reticence: Jane Austen's 'Indirections.'" *Fictions of Authority: Women Writers and Narrative Voice*, 61–80. Ithaca, NY: Cornell UP, 1992.

Laurence, Patricia Ondek. "Keeping and Breaking the Silence." *The Reading of Silence: Virginia Woolf in the English Tradition*, 56–88. Stanford, CA: Stanford UP, 1991.

Levin, Amy K. "Jane Austen: The Sister Plots." *The Suppressed Sister: A Relationship in Novels by Nineteenth- and Twentieth-Century British Women*, 33–53. Cranbury, NJ: Associated UP, 1992.

Looser, Devoney, ed. *Jane Austen and Discourses of Feminism.* New York: St. Martin's, 1995.

Lynch, Deidre. *The Economy of Character: Novels, Market Culture, and the Business of Meaning.* Chicago: U of Chicago P, 1998.

Mandal, Anthony. *Jane Austen and the Popular Novel: The Determined Author.* New York: Palgrave Macmillan, 2007.

McCormick, Marjorie. "'Occasionally Nervous and Invariably Silly': Mothers in Jane Austen." *Mothers in the English Novel: From Stereotype to Archetype*, 47–75. New York: Garland, 1991.

Mellor, Anne K. *Romanticism and Gender*. London: Routledge, 1993.

Menon, Patricia. *Austen, Eliot, Charlotte Brontë and the Mentor-Lover*. Houndsmill, Basingstoke, Hampshire; New York: Palgrave Macmillan, 2003.

Michaelson, Patricia Howell. *Speaking Volumes: Women, Reading, and Speech in the Age of Austen*. Stanford, CA: Stanford UP, 2002.

Miller, D. A. *Jane Austen, or, The Secret of Style*. Princeton, NJ: Princeton UP, 2003.

Mitchell, Marea, and Diane Osland. "'It Was Happy She Took a Good Course': Saving Elizabeth Bennet in *Pride and Prejudice*." *Representing Women and Female Desire from Arcadia to Jane Eyre*, 158–74. Houndsmill, Basingstoke, Hampshire; New York: Palgrave Macmillan, 2005.

Moore, Lisa. *Dangerous Intimacies: Toward a Sapphic History of the British Novel*. Durham, NC: Duke UP, 1997.

Moretti, Franco. *Atlas of the European Novel, 1800–1900*. London: Verso, 1998.

Mukherjee, Meenakshi. *Jane Austen*. New York: St. Martin's, 1991.

Neill, Edward. *The Politics of Jane Austen*. New York: St. Martin's, 1999.

O'Farrell, Mary Ann. *Telling Complexions: The Nineteenth-Century English Novel and the Blush*. Durham, NC: Duke UP, 1997.

Park, You-me, and Rajeswari Sunder Rajan, eds. *Austen in the World: Postcolonial Mappings*. London and New York: Routledge, 2000.

Payne, Susan. "The Author and the Text: Parodic Strategy and Metafiction in Jane Austen's *Northanger Abbey*." *The Strange Within the Real: The Function of Fantasy in Austen, Brontë, and Eliot*, 17–60. Rome: Bulzone, 1992.

Perera, Suvendrini. "Proper Places: Spatial Economics in Austen and Gaskell." *Reaches of Empire: The English Novel from Edgeworth to Dickens*, 35–57. New York: Columbia UP, 1991.

Perkins, Moreland. *Reshaping the Sexes in "Sense and Sensibility."* Charlottesville: UP of Virginia, 1998.

Plasa, Carl. "'What Was Done There is Not to be Told': *Mansfield Park*'s Colonial Unconscious." *Textual Politics from Slavery to Postmodernism*, 32–59. London: Palgrave, 2001.

Postlethwaite, Diana. "Sometimes I Feel Like a Motherless Child: Austen's Anne Elliot and Freud's Anna O." In *The Anna Book: Searching for Anna in Literary History*, edited by Mickey Pearlmann, 37–48. Westport, CT: Greenwood, 1992.

Rigberg, Lynn R. *Jane Austen's Discourse With New Rhetoric*. New York: Peter Lang, 1999.

Rose, Gillian. *Feminism and Geography: The Limits of Geographical Knowledge*. Minneapolis: U of Minnesota P, 1993.

Ross, Deborah. "Jane Austen's Novels: The Romantic Denouement." *The Excellence of Falsehood: Romance, Realism, and Women's Contribution to the Novel*, 166–207. Lexington: UP of Kentucky, 1991.

Said, Edward W. "Jane Austen and Empire." In *Raymond Williams: Critical Perspectives*, edited by Terry Eagleton, 150–64. Cambridge and Oxford: Polity Press, 1989. Reprinted in: *Contemporary Marxist Literary Criticism*, edited by Francis Mulhern, 97–113. New York: Longmans, 1992; Edward Said, *Culture and Imperialism*, 80–97. New York: Knopf, 1993.

———. *Orientalism*. New York: Vintage Books, 1978.

Sales, Roger. *Jane Austen and Representations of Regency England*. New York: Routledge, 1994.

Scheuermann, Mona. "Jane Austen: *Pride and Prejudice* and *Emma*." *Her Bread to Earn: Women, Money, and Society from Defoe to Austen*, 199–238. Lexington: UP of Kentucky, 1993.

Sedgwick, Eve Kosofsky. "Jane Austen and the Masturbating Girl." *Critical Inquiry* 17 (1991): 818–37. Reprinted in *Tendencies*, 109–29. Durham, NC: Duke UP, 1993. Reprinted in *Close Reading: The Reader*, edited by Frank Lentricchia and Andrew DuBois, 301–20. Durham, NC: Duke UP, 2001.

Seeber, Barbara Karolina. *General Consent in Jane Austen: A Study of Dialogism*. Montreal and Ithaca, NY: McGill-Queen's UP, 2000.

Shaffer, Julie A. "The Ideological Intervention of Ambiguities in the Marriage Plot: Who Fails Marianne in Austen's *Sense and Sensibility*?" In *A Dialogue of Voices: Feminist Literary Theory and Bakhtin*, edited by Karen Hohne and Helen Wussow, 128–51. Minneapolis: U of Minnesota P, 1994.

Shaw, Harry E. *Narrating Reality: Austen, Scott, Eliot*. Ithaca, NY: Cornell UP, 1999.

Sokolsky, Anita. "The Melancholy Persuasion." In *Psychoanalytic Literary Criticism*, edited by Maud Ellman, 128–42. New York: Longman, 1994.

Sorensen, Janet. "Epilogue: Jane Austen's Language and the Strangeness at Home in the Center." *The Grammar of Empire in Eighteenth-Century British Writing*, 197–223. Cambridge: Cambridge UP, 2000.

Stewart, Maaja A. *Domestic Realities and Imperial Fictions: Jane Austen's Novels in Eighteenth-Century Contexts*. Athens: U of Georgia P, 1993.

Sutherland, Kathryn. *Jane Austen's Textual Lives: From Aeschylus to Bollywood*. Oxford and New York: Oxford UP, 2005.

Tauchert, Ashley. *Romancing Jane Austen: Narrative, Realism, and the Possibility of a Happy Ending*. Houndsmill, Basingstoke, Hampshire; New York: Palgrave Macmillan, 2005.

Tobin, Beth Fowkes. *Superintending the Poor: Charitable Ladies and Paternal Landlords in British Fiction, 1770–1860*, 50–73. New Haven, CT: Yale UP, 1993.

Todd, Janet. "Jane Austen, Politics, and Sensibility." In *Feminist Criticism: Theory and Practice*, edited by Susan Sellers, 71–87. New York: Harvester Wheatsheaf, 1991. Reprinted in Janet Todd, *Gender, Art, and Death*, 136–54. New York: Continuum, 1993.

———, ed. *The Cambridge Edition of the Works of Jane Austen*. 9 volumes. Cambridge: Cambridge UP, 2005–9.

———, ed. *Jane Austen in Context*. Cambridge: Cambridge UP, 2005.

Trumpener, Katie. *Bardic Nationalism: The Romantic Novel and the British Empire*. Princeton, NJ: Princeton UP, 1997.

Wallace, Tara Ghoshal. *Jane Austen and Narrative Authority*. New York: St. Martin's, 1995.

Watson, Nicola J. *Revolution and the Form of the British Novel 1790–1825*, 87–108. Oxford: Oxford UP, 1994.

Wenner, Barbara Britton. *Prospect and Refuge in the Landscape of Jane Austen*. Aldershot, England; Burlington, VT: Ashgate, 2006.

White, Gabrielle D. V. *Jane Austen in the Context of Abolition: "A Fling at the Slave Trade."* Houndsmill, Basingstoke, Hampshire; New York: Palgrave Macmillan, 2006.

Wiltshire, John. *Jane Austen and the Body: "The Picture of Health."* New York: Cambridge UP, 1992.

Wing-chi Ki, Madeline. *Jane Austen and the Dialectic of Misrecognition*. New York: Lang, 2005.

Winnifrith, Tom. "Austen." *Fallen Women in the Nineteenth-Century Novel*, 13–29. New York: St. Martin's, 1994.

Wye, Margaret Enright. *Jane Austen's Emma: Embodied Metaphor as a Cognitive Construct*. Lewiston, NY: Edwin Mellen Press, 1998.

Wynne, Julian Wilmot. *Jane Austen and Sigmund Freud: An Interpretation*. London: Plume Publications, 1998.

Yeazell, Ruth Bernard. "Fanny Price's Modest Loathings." *Fictions of Modesty: Women and Courtship in the English Novel*, 143–68. Chicago: U of Chicago P, 1991.

9: Traditional Approaches to Austen, 1991–2008

I T MAY BE BEST TO BEGIN THIS CHAPTER with a cautionary note. It is almost impossible to find any criticism of Austen written after the 1970s that does not somehow take into account the work of theorists, especially feminist critics and those who have made great advances in placing Austen's fiction in its historical and cultural context. Nevertheless, there continue to be studies published that, in the main, use methodologies developed in the nineteenth century and the first half of the twentieth — critical biographies, influence studies, and comparative analyses, to name a few. The books and essays discussed below are representative of these approaches. As the sheer number of these studies suggests, despite the emphasis in academic circles on new theoretical approaches to critical analysis, there has been no dearth of traditional studies of Austen published between 1990 and the present.

Biographies

What the novelist and essayist John Updike described as the problem of producing competent biographies of great writers like Austen, whom he calls an "exalted literary performer about whom we seem to know so little" (*Due Consideration*, 7), seems not to have stopped scholars from writing new studies of her life, and during the past twenty years a handful have appeared. As one might expect, each biographer attempts to take a new slant on Austen's life in order to say something that has not been said, or at least not said so well as he or she can say it. For example, the central premise of Keith Odom's *Jane Austen: Rebel of Time and Place* (1991) is that, far from being an inheritor of and spokesperson for conservative values, Austen was from her earliest years "a social rebel" (42) who poked fun at and challenged conventions — especially those that relegated women to a subordinate place in society. She was also a rebel in a literary sense as well, rejecting the forms and subjects of eighteenth-century models in favor of new ones that herald the novels of the nineteenth century. Although Odom seems aware of the history of Austen criticism — he often devotes considerable space to summarizing views of his own predecessors — there is little evidence in this formalist, humanist assessment that he has been influenced by any new critical theory with the possible exception of feminism. George Holbert Tucker, historian and author of an earlier volume on the Austen family, *A Goodly Heritage: Jane Austen's Family* (1983), says that in writing *Jane Austen the Woman* (1994) he consciously avoids literary commentary so he might present the novelist "as she actually was" (xiii). He insists his portrait of Austen demonstrates that she was radically different from the retiring spinster most people have made her out to be. Instead, he argues that she was a vibrant, somewhat saucy commentator on people and morals. Tucker tries to stick close to his sources, but his premise seems dated; the work of Harding, Mudrick, and the feminists had already destroyed the idea that Austen was the saint her descendants tried to make her out to be in the 1870 *Memoir* and other family compilations of her life.

By what can only be described as a happy coincidence, in 1997 three new studies of Austen's life were published. By far the longest and most detailed is David Nokes's *Jane Austen: A Life* (1997). Nokes ranges far beyond his principal subject to describe the people whose lives touched Austen's (sometimes only tangentially) and the events to which she was a witness (however indirectly). Long passages on figures like British politician Warren Hastings and Austen's cousin Eliza De Feuillide, and ones on her brothers, especially Frank and Charles, interrupt the principal tale. Accounts of the Napoleonic wars provide some insight into the troubled times in which Austen lived, and serve as a dramatic contrast to her rather simple life as a poor relation in her extended family. Although Nokes is more interested in describing Austen's life than analyzing her novels, he does provide sufficient commentary to explain how they came to be written, what Austen drew from life and what was purely invention, and how her wit and occasional *hauteur* are invested in her characters. Nokes's Austen is certainly not the "dear Aunt Jane" of the 1870 *Memoir*, a selfless and self-effacing soul who cared about everyone but herself.

In fact, that Austen was *not* such a woman is the major point Nokes makes in his study. And he does it in a rather curious, if sometimes irritating, way. Determined to return to primary sources for his information about Austen, Nokes virtually ignores the work of Honan and Jenkins in favor of letters and other documents that Austen and her contemporaries left behind. Of course, as Nokes points out early, for more than a century scholars had understood that the surviving letters were but a fraction of what Austen had written. Her sister Cassandra had made sure that any embarrassing missives were not saved for posterity — and if any slipped by her, there was a good chance that nineteenth-century descendants would have suppressed any evidence that might challenge the family myth about "dear Aunt Jane." Wanting to be certain that the family portrait is thoroughly discredited, Nokes takes every opportunity to paint Cassandra Austen as a kind of villain with a deep-seated need to control Jane's image. By relying on innuendo gleaned from correspondence that did not end up in the fire, and by imaginatively extrapolating evidence from the portraits of the women in Austen's fiction, Nokes creates what he asserts is a more balanced portrait of the novelist. While *his* Jane Austen is sometimes arch, catty, and even vindictive, she is also passionate, keenly interested in the world around her, sensible and even businesslike about her writing, and above all genuinely concerned about her family's happiness. *This* Jane Austen is a godmother not only of Henry James but of Ernest Hemingway: she knows much more than she writes, but her wide understanding of human nature comes through in understated tones throughout her fiction.

Like Nokes's study, Valerie Grosvenor Myer's portrait of the novelist in *Jane Austen: Obstinate Heart* (1997) is of a woman who is "tougher, more irritable and more sardonic" (4) than her family admitted. Shorter than Nokes's study and clearly aimed at a more general audience, *Jane Austen: Obstinate Heart* is reminiscent of Myer's earlier (and shorter) *Jane Austen* (1980), in which Austen's work is seen as reflecting the social, cultural, and ethical mores of its time. Myer suggests that Austen's life was one of constant disappointment. Bitter at never having married, she made up for not having children by attaching herself to her novels. Myer considers Austen a quiet rebel who chose to take out her anger toward the society in which she was little more than a helpless dependent by painting unflattering portraits of social customs and people who seemed to get ahead by dint of luck or position rather than native intelligence. However, there is little of what might be called literary criticism in Myer's narrative. Instead, she concentrates on the novelist's personal relationships to point out how people in Austen's life appear (transformed, of course) in her fiction. However, two figures come off better in Myer's account than in Nokes's book: Jane's brother Henry is not dismissed as an inept literary agent, nor is Cassandra vilified for her handling of Jane's personal papers after her death. Still, despite its chatty style and attempts to offer a rounded portrait, *Jane Austen: Obstinate Heart* seems destined to rankle Janeites who wished to cling to the vision of the novelist created during the first century after her death.

The third biography, Claire Tomalin's *Jane Austen: A Life* (1997), stands midway between Nokes and Myer in length but above both in style and insight. By the time she began her biography of Austen, the former literary editor for the *New Statesman* and the London *Sunday Times* had already produced notable (and award-winning) biographies of Mary Wollstonecraft, Katherine Mansfield, Dickens's mistress Ellen Ternan, and Dora Jordan, actress and longtime mistress to King George IV. Tomalin's ability to weave an intriguing story from Austen's letters (a scant collection, she laments) and other documents is her particular strength. She, too, is interested in debunking the notion that Austen was a demure wallflower. However, where Nokes sees Cassandra as a villain, Tomalin fixes that label on Austen's parents. Their actions to "banish" their daughter — to a nurse in the village when she was an infant, to schools when she was a girl, and away from Steventon parsonage where she had lived her whole life until her father's retirement in 1801 (although in this case Jane did not leave her family) — left a kind of psychic scar on Austen's personality that determined her desire to be a writer and influenced the themes she pursued. Throughout her life Austen felt deeply the inequities of her station as a poor relation, and almost every one of her heroines struggles to find happiness in a world where the deck is stacked against her.

While Tomalin covers much of the same ground as Nokes and Myer, she does so more efficiently than the former and more effectively than the latter. Deftly weaving in commentary on the novels with her account of Austen's life, she manages to give a sense of what Austen was forced to put up with as she pursued her vocation. Tomalin accounts for the great decade of silence by suggesting that Austen needed the stability of a home and routine in order for her creative juices to flow. Because there was no stable environment for her between 1801 and 1808, she simply could not bring herself to work on her fiction. In commenting on the novels, Tomalin takes care to point out how real-life people and places affected Austen's imagination. She also finds something worthwhile to say about some characters typically dismissed or disdained, including Willoughby in *Sense and Sensibility*, and both Mrs. Bennet and Mr. Collins in *Pride and Prejudice*. And she insists that anyone who believes *Persuasion* is Austen's quiet farewell to fiction and to life needs to take a good look at the unfinished *Sanditon*, which shows the novelist tackling a new subject in a fresh way.

The Austen community of scholars was divided in its opinion regarding the relative merits of these three volumes, although each had at least one champion. In an essay in *Atlantic Monthly* (1998) Lee Siegel finds Nokes perceptive but guilty of claiming too much originality for his approach. Additionally, "his details tend to pile up into a blearing mélange" (95). Tomalin is a better writer than Nokes, Siegel continues, but her account is at times more fanciful. Tomalin won praise from Nancy Mairs in a 1998 *Women's Review of Books* article, while Myer was applauded by Christopher Lehmann-Haupt in the *New York Times* for being "sensible and intriguing" (C17). Most notably, Lehmann-Haupt says, her work is an improvement on John Halperin's disdainful portrait in his 1984 biography.

A year later M. C. Hammond combined biography and critical analysis in *Relating to Jane* (1998) in an effort to rescue the novelist from both the Janeites and academic critics alike. Hammond feels compelled to explain why Austen is neither the sweet maiden aunt imagined by the former nor the cynical satirist who seems (in Hammond's view) to have captured the fancy of high-brow critics. Although more than half of *Re-*

lating to Jane is given over to a biography of one of Austen's nieces and brief sketches of other family members, Hammond's review of Austen's career concentrates on rescuing her from charges that she was too narrow in her focus and unkind to children, while defending her as a highly capable stylist and portrayer of character. The result of Hammond's rather eclectic assessment is that Austen comes off as being *all* of the things people have said of her, continuing to interest readers through novels that retain their vibrancy and interest over generations.

Those wishing to read a more condensed version of Austen's life could turn to several brief biographies published near the turn of the century. Helen Lefroy's *Jane Austen* (1997) offers a succinct introduction to Austen's life that concentrates on her relationships with family and friends. Lefroy also examines Austen's various romantic attachments (including her first, with Lefroy's distant ancestor Tom Lefroy). Nigel Nicolson's *The World of Jane Austen* (1991), Maggie Lane's *Jane Austen's World* (1996), and Deirdre Le Faye's *Jane Austen* (1998) are coffee-table books, profusely illustrated with reproductions of artwork, manuscripts, and photographs. But Le Faye provides an accurate and often insightful account of Austen's life. The same can be said of her *Jane Austen: The World of Her Novels* (2002), a lavishly produced book filled with color photographs surrounding a text describing Austen's life and times — a volume sure to appeal to a general readership but also useful for serious students (as long as one recognizes Le Faye's conservative bias in interpreting Austen's life and values). Marilyn Butler's "bite-size" *Jane Austen* (2007) (the publisher's phrase) offers a good entree to Austen for anyone seeking to learn the basic facts of her life and get a brief but sound introduction to the major fiction from a writer who values Austen's conservatism.

In keeping with its practice of choosing noted writers as biographers for their Viking Lives series, the editors at Viking Press commissioned Canadian novelist Carol Shields to write Austen's life story. Noting that her own work has sometimes been compared to Austen's, Shields takes up the task with a little bit of reverence and a good bit of critical discipline. Consequently, although she breaks no new ground, her *Jane Austen* (2001) offers general readers a good introduction to the novelist and her work. Shields is a strong believer that Austen was a chronicler of her times — not always directly, but with what she calls a "glance" (2), saying much by mere allusion or hint. In the same way, Shields suggests, "by indirection, by assumption, by reading what is implicit" it is possible to discover in Austen's novels "a steady, intelligent witness to a world that was rapidly reinventing itself" (4). Shields's study, as much critical commentary and psychological analysis as it is biography, paints a portrait of a woman constantly searching for "home" — by which Shields means that place of security and stability where she could be independent. Not finding it in life, Austen created it in her fiction. While the novels are not strictly autobiographical, Shields says, they are revelatory. Additionally, Austen's ability to use what she had at hand becomes important not only for chronicling her own life but for using it as a means of reporting on "sociological change" (97). With a woman's eye toward the experiences of another woman, Shields manages to depict the growth of a young author who finds in fiction a means of realizing her full potential as a woman. In her final summation, Shields asserts that the novels are not *really* autobiography but more akin to drama. "Jane Austen is a dramatic rather than a descriptive writer, concerned with morality and using speech as her medium" (179). But the bulk of Shields's book is given over to suggesting that Austen's fiction is principally a psychodrama of the author's attempt to create a self amid a turbulent and changing society.

It might be hard to imagine that a biography of Austen published in 2003 could provide any truly new insights into her character or throw new light on her fiction. But Jon Spence's *Becoming Jane Austen* seems to have accomplished both of those feats. Building on letters, family documents, and a good bit of materials he uncovered in more than a decade of research, Spence weaves a tale of Austen's life, concentrating on the early years in which the girl who would become one of England's great novelists was educated in a most fruitful setting: her own family. Spence's central thesis is that Austen's life served as the basis for all her fiction, and her novels are all inspired by the people and events she knew as she grew up in the parsonage at Steventon. The young Jane was attached to her siblings, especially Cassandra and Henry, so what happened to them became important to her. She was fascinated by her elder cousin Eliza de Feuillide, whose story she weaves into many of her juvenile tales (most of which Spence explicates in detail). And most of all, Spence says, she was shaped by the one true love affair of her life, her fleeting but intense relationship with Tom Lefroy. Making much from the scant evidence available, Spence creates an intriguing account of the brief period in which Lefroy visited his relatives near the Austen's home, parsing phrases and even individual words from the few extant letters that allude to this formative liaison. There would be other loves — or at least, Spence suggests, other men whose love Austen could have returned — but the feelings she had for Lefroy stayed with her throughout her life and shaped all her mature fiction.

While it is certainly true that others had pointed out the potential influence of Austen's relationship with Lefroy in helping her gain first-hand experience of the emotions about which she writes in her fiction, no one had made the case in such detail as Spence does that Lefroy was the muse who inspired her work. The argument might be dismissed out of hand were it not for Spence's ability to marshal his evidence with precision and present it in a narrative that reads much like a novel. Perhaps that is why so many in the community of Austen scholars gave the book high marks.

In his review for the newsletter of the Jane Austen Society of North America, Joseph Wiesenfarth went so far as to anoint it as "one of the best half-dozen books published on Austen in the last quarter century" (23). Reviewing the book for the Jane Austen Society of Australia, Penny Gay echoes Wiesenfarth's admiration, but wonders if Spence might be stretching things to claim that Austen "encoded her feeling for Tom Lefroy into virtually every novel." Additionally, in a development particularly fortuitous for Spence, his book became the basis for the 2007 hit movie *Becoming Jane,* with current box-office favorite Anne Hathaway in the title role. One can only imagine what Spence felt like while serving as "historical advisor" for the film.

Hermione Lee, whose 1976 essay on Austen placed the novelist firmly among the anti-Romantics of her generation, turned once again to a consideration of the novelist in *Virginia Woolf's Nose: Essays on Biography* (2005). Applying a methodology made popular in academic circles a half-century earlier by Richard Altick in *The Scholar Adventurers* (1950), Lee explains how biographers have taken bits and pieces from various sources to construct a coherent portrait of the novelist. Lee focuses on the famous incident in which Austen is reputed to have fainted at the news of her family's imminent departure from Steventon Rectory, the only home she had ever known. By examining various recent biographies in close detail, Lee points out how Austen's story can be — and has been — interpreted very differently depending on the approach individual biographers have taken toward their subjects. Hence, Lee suggests, whether one finds Austen weak in spirit or resolute often depends not so much on what happened in her life but on the "spin" biographers have placed on key incidents.

Studies Focused Principally on Austen

In the midst of the wave of studies based on new theoretical approaches to literature and culture, historian Oliver MacDonagh provides a more traditional assessment of Austen's life and times in *Jane Austen: Real and Imagined Worlds* (1991). By design the book is light on literary criticism, as MacDonagh aims instead to demonstrate how historical events shaped Austen's fiction and how her novels can be read as an accurate record of the times. A similar study useful in understanding the historical context of Austen's novels is Myra Stokes's *The Language of Jane Austen: A Study of Some Aspects of her Vocabulary* (1991). Much more than a catalog of unusual words or a compendium of extended definitions, Stokes's book explains much about the culture and conventions of Austen's age and helps readers distanced from her novels by as much as two centuries understand what Austen meant when discussing matters of character, intellect, or feeling.

Traditional critical studies written during these decades tend to hark back to those that stressed Austen's conservative views regarding literature, society, and morality. One important example is Roger Gard's *Jane Austen's Novels: The Art of Clarity* (1992). Gard makes the argument that Austen is, above all, an exceptionally precise and clear writer — and that her critics, especially recent ones, would do well to heed her example. She is, he insists, "obviously one of the most challenging moralists in European fiction and one of its most brilliantly accomplished creative practitioners" (2). Gard's critique of the novels is reminiscent of those by proponents of the "Austen as a great moralist" school, although he takes exception with what he considers some of the more outlandish claims for the seriousness of Austen's world view. But Gard's harshest criticism is leveled at practitioners of the "new" critical tradition — by which he means those influenced by literary theories emerging after the Second World War. Gard has little use for people who find hidden subtexts and undiscovered ambiguities lurking beneath Austen's straightforward narratives. Given Gard's critical predilections, one might assume he would disdain attempts at playful readings or approaches to Austen's fiction; surprisingly, however, two of his chapters are dialogues between fictional readers whose comments on Austen's novels are intended to reflect the joyful surprise one gets when encountering her for the first time.

It also seems somewhat surprising that the Twayne English Authors volume on Austen did not appear until three decades after the series began. From the appearance of the first Twayne books in the 1960s, these studies had been a mainstay for undergraduate research. So while John Lauber's *Jane Austen* (1993) makes no significant original contribution to Austen scholarship, his commentary is worth noting since it undoubtedly has helped shape opinion among college-educated readers of the past two decades who have not gone on to further study of the novelist. Most simply stated, Lauber's principal interest lies in explicating Austen's novels to reveal their technical merit and explain the morality behind them. While such an approach would have been published without comment before 1970, Lauber realizes that changes in critical practice demand that he make clear his own biases. On occasion Lauber makes oblique references to the various "-isms" that have grown up in the latter half of the century, but it would be hard to discern the influence of feminism, narratology, or new cultural studies on his attitudes toward Austen and her work. In his brief survey of the critical history of Austen's novels, he admits that "ideology is inescapable" (130). Nevertheless, Lauber insists, literary and aesthetic qualities are very real as well, and they — not ideology — determine the staying power of an artist. "Readers turn to novels not so much to confirm their own beliefs or prejudices as for essentially literary reasons — above all, for the pleasure of entering and experiencing a favorite writer's imagined world" (130–31). Austen's fairy-tale comedies continue to appeal to readers because her characters, especially her hero-ines, exist and thrive in a world where freedom can be experienced within an ordered society that does make some legitimate demands on people. Her novels "are on the side of freedom and of feeling," Lauber concludes, "although with inevitable limits, determined first by morality, secondarily by social convention and status" (144). Consequently, they "can never be acceptable to extreme romantics or to political and social radicals" (144). So much, he seems to say, for those feminists, Marxists, and cultural crit-ics who have found Austen inadequate for their ideological needs.

Although biographers had on occasion offered some comments about Austen's views on religion — after all, she was a clergyman's daughter — relatively little attention had been paid to that aspect of her life and work since the Victorians glibly asserted that she was devout and respectfully high-church. Hence, Irene Collins's *Jane Austen and the Clergy* (1993) seems to serve a useful function, bridging the fields of historical and liter-ary scholarship to find in Austen's letters and novels some idea of what the life of the clergy was like in the novelist's lifetime and explain how Austen felt about the clergy and, more generally, about matters of reli-gion. Five years later in a companion piece, *Jane Austen, the Parson's Daughter* (1998), Collins turns her gaze more explicitly on Austen her-self, explaining how growing up and living in the household of a clergy-man influenced her writing. A similar study written by William Jarvis, an Anglican clergyman with a lifelong interest in Austen's relationship to matters of religion and spirituality, appeared after his death under the title *Jane Austen and Religion* (1996).

However, the most detailed and critically satisfying study of the reli-gious dimensions of Austen's life and work, extending and expanding Gene Koppel's 1988 study, is Michael Giffin's *Jane Austen and Religion* (2002). Arguing that mainstream academic criticism for the past century has wrongly stressed Austen's role as a realist and naturalist, Giffin offers a powerful, sometimes even contentious, counterargument to critiques that celebrate Austen as a revolutionary and proto-feminist. Placing her firmly in the midst of her Georgian contemporaries and insisting that she was thoroughly imbued with and supportive of the Anglican theology she learned at home, Giffin argues that she was "an anti-revolutionary au-thor" whose novels "describe the codes that govern the social contract" (21). Her novels, all "metafictional works" intended "to convey a mes-sage about life outside the text" (4), depict heroines striving to achieve balance between reason and emotion. Austen comes down on the side of neoclassical balance, not romantic excess. She "does not see women as victims," Giffin says (31), but instead as partners with men in making good marriages, which are essential to preserving social order and helping individuals achieve salvation. Giffin's discussion of Austen's major fiction describes in detail how the novelist sorts through the many impediments to good marriages and traces the heroine's education and preparedness to enter into matrimony. If that rather conservative interpretation were not enough to cause a host of feminists and New Historicists to grit their teeth, Giffin goes out of his way to point out his dissent from what he believes has been the main current in academic thought for at least a century.

Giffin's is one of several studies in the "Jane Austen and . . ." category, most of which explore a single theme in her novels. A few deserve mention here, however. Maggie Lane's *Jane Austen and Food* (1995) is notable for the intriguing way Lane approaches serious issues in Austen's fiction by focusing on "all the different things which Jane Austen finds to do, artistically, with the humdrum commodity of food" (xi). Lane, a life-long devotee of Austen and prolific writer about the novelist and her times, had already demonstrated her ability to combine historical skills with close reading of Austen's works in her 1986 book *Jane Austen's England*, a compendium of background information about people, places, and events of Austen's time. Far from being another table-top book, *Jane Austen and Food* uses food as the entrée to exploring themes of love and friendship in the fiction. Austen was spare in her descriptions of setting, Lane notes, so it is safe to assume that when she does take time to describe events such as meals, she has special reason for doing so. Lane argues that in many instances, references to food reveal something about the characters who partake of it. This is especially true in *Emma*, she says, where Austen's references to food become symbolic of larger cultural matters; in this novel food is "the voluntary currency of love and caring" (168).

Three other books in the "Austen and . . ." variety also reveal ways a competent scholar can employ traditional methodology to enhance readers' understanding of Austen's fiction. David Selwyn's *Jane Austen and Leisure* (1999) provides an exceptionally detailed and nuanced look at how leisure activities are represented in Austen's novels. Selwyn makes a strong case that understanding what society thought of leisure, what public and domestic pursuits were appropriate, and the role of reading, theatricals, and games in Austen's day are indispensable for properly understanding the fiction. Brian Southam's *Jane Austen and the Navy* (2000) is more than a detailed history of the Austen family's dealings with naval officers, including Jane's two brothers; it also provides insightful commentary on ways those interactions affected the novelist's understanding of, and appreciation for, the naval service and its influence in shaping her fiction, especially *Mansfield Park* and *Persuasion*. Susannah Fullerton's *Jane Austen and Crime* (2004), another historical background study, seems at first glance to be one in which the author might have to stretch to find relevant materials to fill out a book. However, Fullerton has a deep understanding of Austen's fiction and an equally good grasp of the historical period in which Austen lived. She examines the nature and consequences of various crimes in which Austen showed enough interest to include in her novels (and a few that she did not), helping readers rein-terpret some key scenes that have in the past been dismissed as comic in-terludes. Most interestingly, Fullerton writes about the symbolic nature of imprisonment, a feature quite prominent in *Mansfield Park*, suggesting a way of reading the novel much as one might expect from a scholar con-versant with the social theories of Foucault. Curiously, Fullerton does not refer explicitly to Foucault in her work, but *Jane Austen and Crime* does not seem to suffer from this omission.

Traditional critics following the "Austen and . . ." format often con-centrated on questions regarding Austen's relationship to the literary tra-dition. For example, in *Jane Austen and Eighteenth-Century Courtesy Books* (1997) Penelope Joan Fritzer demonstrates how closely Austen fol-lows the advice provided in courtesy books that express eighteenth-century attitudes about women's moral and social development. Fritzer's carefully developed argument challenges feminist critiques that stress Aus-ten's rebellious nature. Mary Waldron's *Jane Austen and the Fiction of her Time* (1999) stands out for its careful attention to details that demon-strate how much Austen depended on the fictional conventions of her day — and how much she deviated from them to create what was essentially a new form of fiction, the modern psychological novel.

Austen's craftsmanship also remained a subject of keen interest for traditional critics, notable among them the Canadian scholar Juliet McMaster. Her *Austen the Novelist* (1996) collects a number of essays she published during the previous three decades, including those that had ap-peared in a small monograph, *Jane Austen on Love* (1978). Some range widely to discuss topics such as hospitality or human relationships; others provided detailed critical assessments of individual works. What is particu-larly noteworthy about the collection is that McMaster did little to revise essays for the new volume. Hence, by reading through it one can see how her thinking about Austen changed over time as she was influenced by new developments in literary theory, especially feminist criticism. In 1996 McMaster and Bruce Stovel brought together essays originally delivered as papers at the 1993 Jane Austen Society of North America conference in *Jane Austen's Business: Her World and Her Profession,* a volume that cele-brates the novelist's abilities as a realistic writer whose fiction speaks si-multaneously for its own age and for all time. However, contributors demonstrate keen awareness of new approaches to Austen. Essays by Gary Kelly, Elaine Showalter, Jane Millgate, Jane Fergus and others provide a useful starting point for discerning the state of Austen criticism at the end of the twentieth century.

By that time, the idea that Austen stood apart from the literary and intellectual tradition had effectively been discredited, and a number of critics devoted considerable attention to the books and ideas that shaped her fiction, and to ways Austen affected those who came after her. Three studies are illustrative of this critical trend. First, Jo Alyson Parker's *The Author's Inheritance: Henry Fielding, Jane Austen, and the Establishment of the Novel* (1998) provides an extended study of these two figures, concentrating on issues of authority (both moral and literary) and the legitimacy of the novel as an art form. Parker explains how both sought to legitimize this new form of writing and how they agree on many points about the power of the novel as an instrument for displaying, and perhaps correcting, the faults of society. However, they differ, Parker says, on matters of gender: Fielding accepts without question the idea that experience is masculinized, while Austen works diligently to present female experience as essentially different from, although sometimes complementary to, that of men. A second study of influence, Gloria Sybil Gross's *In A Fast Coach with a Pretty Woman: Jane Austen and Samuel Johnson* (2002) offers a detailed analysis of how Johnson's ideas and rhetorical strategies affected the young novelist. Gross suggests that Austen revered Johnson as a larger-than-life cultural hero who revolutionized the study of literature and aesthetics. From Johnson, Gross says, Austen learned to have great "irreverence" for stale conventions and discovered in him a principal theme for all her fiction: the battle of "unbounded freedom versus control" (6). Part of Gross's task is to rehabilitate Austen from charges that she is limited in her perception of human nature, too distanced and intellectual to capture "the fire of human experience" (7) — including women's sexuality. In fact, Gross insists, Austen views women as "intelligent, sexual being[s]" (192). A third study, Peter Graham's *Jane Austen & Charles Darwin: Naturalists and Novelists* (2008) offers an intriguing, often thought-provoking analysis that juxtaposes the two writers to illustrate how both were great empiricists whose way of representing the world offers keen insight into nature, both human and otherwise.

Austen's fascination with drama and the dramatic qualities of her writing have long been critical commonplaces, but several recent studies have provided additional insight into this aspect of her work. In *Jane Austen and the Theatre* (2002) Penny Gay attempts to "tease out both the theatrical context of Austen's writing" and demonstrate how "she deals in each of the major novels with a society that she perceives to be inescapably theatrical" (ix). Gay notes how dozens of plays find their way into Austen's fiction, often deeply disguised but nevertheless influencing her portraits of people (especially her heroines) and her construction of scene and dialogue. Paula Byrne's book, also titled *Jane Austen and the Theatre* (2002), sets her work in the dramatic traditions of the great eighteenth-century dramatists and in the line of succession from Shakespeare and his contemporaries. Nora Nachumi's discussion of Austen in *Acting Like A Lady: British Women Novelists and the Eighteenth-Century Theater* (2008) argues that Austen's use of *Lover's Vows* in a key scene in *Mansfield Park* displays "her engagement in contemporary debates about the effect of the drama on the emotions of theatergoers" and "signals her interest in the question of how one ought to respond to all kinds of fiction" (148).

Richard Jenkyns's *A Fine Brush on Ivory: An Appreciation for Jane Austen* (2004) is clear proof that it is still possible to get an academic publisher to underwrite works that offer close readings not overwhelmed with the language of theory. Although Jenkyns claims to have read most contemporary criticism, his discussion of Austen's novels is really a personal reading that explains how they work (technique) and what they say (theme). Like Jenkyns's study, Peter Leithart's *Miniatures and Morals: The Christian Novels of Jane Austen*, published in the same year, also provides a close reading of Austen's texts. A theologian by training, Leithart relies considerably less on the few sources he lists in his bibliography than on his own sensitivity to the moral dimensions of Austen's fiction.

Finally, Austen's juvenilia continued to draw critical attention as worthy of study in its own right. Margaret Anne Doody offers a cogent assessment in "Jane Austen, That Disconcerting Child" (2005), noting that the clichéd judgments about early works being harbingers of a novelist's mature output do not fully describe the quality of the fiction Austen wrote during her apprentice years. The works she produced while a teenager "seem not readily classifiable," Doody says, "and not 'juvenile.' The stories are very polished, disconcertingly sophisticated" (103). But they do not always suggest the direction Austen would take in her mature fiction. They do exhibit Austen's free spirit and keen sense of the world around her, showcasing something of the *joie de vivre* that is lost in the later work. Austen "had to give up a good deal of her own ruthless and exuberant style of comic vision in order to be published," Doody concludes. Hence, "the six novels are very fine, but the works of the 'child' have their own validity" (119).

Studies of Values, Virtues, and Ethics

A new emphasis on ethical criticism in the 1990s led to a number of discussions of Austen's work during the next two decades. One of the first is Tobin Siebers's "Jane Austen and Comic Virtue" in his *Morals and Stories* (1992), a book built on Siebers's assertion that "the nature of literature cannot be separated from ethics" (8). He finds Austen's novels good subjects for philosophical examination because Austen envisions "a human community in which individuals exist in close association with each other," giving her fiction "a political and ethical dimension that surpasses others" (137). Curiously, though, Siebers insists she is not the last of the classical novelists; instead, her works "describe a truly romantic view of morality," and her "ideas about ethics are all geared toward obtaining successful relationships between men and women" (137–38). Austen is actually a counterpoint to Aristotle and Kant, Siebers says; and because she has this romantic vision of society, her novels are comedies rather than tragedies.

The conservative philosopher and classicist Allan Bloom disagrees with Siebers. In a discussion of *Pride and Prejudice* in *Love and Friendship* (1993), a monumental study of love in Western literature and life, Bloom suggests Austen serves as a kind of counterweight to the followers of Rousseau, who introduced to Western culture "the frantic sexual search for genuine human contact and reciprocity in the isolation of bourgeois life" (39). Austen, he says, was a "steadfast defender of *bon sens* against self-expression and commitment" (191). Taking what many of his contemporaries would call both a conservative and patriarchal position on Austen's work, Bloom says that "nothing much really happens" in her novels (192), yet "when one actually reads Austen, the intensity and excitement are as great as or greater than what one discovers in other writers" (192). In all her novels, "the adjustment of the sexual passion to the love of virtue" is the "central question" (192). His close reading of *Pride and Prejudice* leads him to conclude that Austen promotes "classical friendship as the core of romantic love" (208). In a similar critique, James Boyd White, the lawyer and literary critic known best for his promotion of literary study by lawyers, includes a discussion of *Mansfield Park* in *Acts of Hope* (1994), a book that examines "the way authority is thought about and constituted in a series of texts" (xi). White claims the central problem of the novel revolves around Fanny's ability to find her way through the confusion of multiple points of authority "to any sort of clarity of vision and solidity of judgment" (209). *Mansfield Park*, he says, is "the story of the development of [Fanny's] character as a principled one," able to trust her own judgments; in short, it is the development of her "identity" (214).

Both Bloom and White offer traditional humanist readings that stand in opposition to those of most postmodern critics. An even more daring challenge to postmodern assessments of Austen is Anne Crippen Ruderman's *The Pleasures of Virtue: Political Thought in the Novels of Jane Austen* (1995). Ruderman begins by asserting that attempts to claim Austen as either conservative or subversive are both inadequate because they miss the essential quality of her fiction: its classical bent. Austen is principally concerned with displaying the relationship between virtue and happiness — and by virtue Ruderman means something akin to the idea Aristotle promotes in his philosophy. Austen's heroines achieve happiness by learning to think and act virtuously, by putting the needs of others ahead of their own when situations demand it. They are not engaged in some sort of power struggle, as feminists claim, to assert their independence in a society that wishes to keep them imprisoned and subjected to male dominance. In fact, Ruderman argues, the idea of marriage was for Austen a good which, when it brought together a virtuous woman and a virtuous man, led to genuine happiness. Ruderman traces Austen's attitudes toward, and general approval of, the classical virtues: prudence, sensibility, justice, and modesty. The last "is generally portrayed as a *positive* quality in Austen's novels," not a "duty imposed by an unfeeling society" (164). Above all, Austen celebrates the virtue of moderation, a kind of classical alternative to the excesses of romanticism which she felt got in the way of developing a mature, sensible, and truly sensitive relationship that heterosexual love could bring.

Less polemic in its assertions about Austen's conservatism than Ruderman's study, Jeffrey Moxham's *Interfering Values in the Nineteenth-Century British Novel: Austen, Dickens, Eliot, Hardy and the Ethics of Criticism* (2002) includes a discussion of *Mansfield Park* that claims it "anticipates and responds to the focus of relativism" that seemed to be undermining older, more stable systems of belief and behavior (2). Moxham says *Mansfield Park* poses "absorbing questions about how to affirm or revise moral guidelines in a society becoming increasing unsure about absolutes and about the justice of applying generalized codes of conduct to individually lived experience" (2). Revising readings of the novel by Lionel Trilling, Tony Tanner, and Marilyn Butler, Moxham tries to resolve the vexing question of whether Fanny Price is unlovable or simply unloved.

Another study concerned with ethical criticism — and much else besides — is Bharat Tandon's *Jane Austen and the Morality of Conversation* (2003). Tandon claims that Austen's fiction "goes beyond simply portraying or reflecting" the mores of her time to engage readers "in experiences of perception, judgment and puzzlement" which are measured against the manners displayed by her characters (xiii). He presents Austen as a conservative willing to challenge and experiment with accepted social and moral conventions, an inheritor of an ethical tradition that was under siege when she was writing. Although Tandon claims his chief interest is in exploring "the central role played in Jane Austen's art by her creative ear for familiar and familial conversation" (3), his book ranges widely into discussions of eighteenth-century polity, culture, and ethics, and examines critical readings of Austen from the nineteenth and twentieth century. In fact, Austen becomes a touchstone for launching discussions of several larger philosophical issues, especially the ethics of reading. Less sweeping in scope but equally compelling in its argumentation, Sarah Emsley's *Jane Austen's Philosophy of the Virtues* (2005) is a direct challenge to those who see Austen as radical or subversive. Interested in what she calls Austen's "approach to philosophy" (2) and following the arguments advanced by Alisdair MacIntyre in *After Virtue* (1981), Emsley documents the process by which Austen's heroines "come to learn about the ethical life" (11). Emsley believes Austen follows a kind of virtue ethic that combines classical and Christian values; while she scrutinizes carefully — and often criticizes — the practices and principles of her society, ultimately she is interested in promoting betterment, not revolution.

Jenny Davidson's *Hypocrisy and the Politics of Politeness: Manners and Morals from Locke to Austen* (2004) is a particularly intriguing assessment of a behavioral trait that she says was viewed quite differently in the eighteenth century than it is in the twenty-first. In the decades before Austen wrote, Davidson says, hypocrisy came to be accepted as useful in promoting polite, civilized society — but it also fostered a climate of dominance/dependence. Combining the techniques of cultural and rhetorical criticism, Davidson engages in close readings of a number of texts in which hypocrisy, masked often as politeness or civility, plays an important role. In this context she offers an analysis of *Mansfield Park* that suggests Austen was at least partially complicit in supporting the role of hypocrisy in society. In fact, Davidson says, "hypocrisy is central" to the aims Austen sets for herself in writing the novel (146). Fanny Price's surface modesty is a strategy she employs to achieve her own goals. By extension, Davidson suggests, such hypocrisy is one of the means by which women dependent in society negotiate their futures.

Valerie Wainwright's *Ethics and the English Novel from Austen to Forster* (2007) suggests that one can discern in an increasing number of novels through the nineteenth and into the twentieth century "an influential line of thought which privileges personal flourishing" (2). While Wainwright agrees that "Austen's fiction constitutes an important moment in the story of modern literature" because it "envisions a more active and expansive concept of well-being" (60), her analysis of *Mansfield Park* demonstrates that this novel does not fit that pattern very easily. Fanny certainly faces almost insurmountable difficulties, but the ethical uprightness of her actions, Wainwright says, is questionable at times. More expansive in its assessment of Austen is Gregory Tague's *Ethics and Behavior: The English Novel from Jane Austen to Henry James* (2008). Described in the Introduction by Daniel Meyer-Dinkgräfe as a "dense argument" about the "relevance of fiction for real life" (x) and heavily reliant on previously published scholarship, Tague's book focuses on responsibility as it is portrayed in fictional characters. Tague operates from the premise that "the question of scholarship" is "ultimately the question of what it means to be human and how to find meaning in life" (xv). In that light he examines five Austen novels (excluding *Northanger Abbey*, perhaps because it is not as realistic as the others) to reveal what he describes as her ethic of life — how it should be lived and what qualities are necessary for one to be fully human.

Austen's Relationship to the Romantics

One way traditional boundaries outside of and especially within the discipline of literary studies have influenced our reading of Austen has been to force us to classify her as a throwback to the Augustan age of satire or as a precursor of the Victorian realist novel — because we have not been able to situate her within the primary literary movement of her day, Romanticism. Until the 1970s, only an occasional essay on her work can be found tracing similarities between her work and that of her Romantic contemporaries. In the past thirty years, however, a serious, sustained effort been mounted to see her as shaped by, and helping to shape, the idea of Romanticism. The effort has been made possible, of course, by new critical theories that either intentionally break down the formalist and historical boundaries set up earlier in the twentieth century within the academic community, or ignore them altogether.

During the 1990s critics continued work begun two decades earlier in trying to establish Austen's relationship with her contemporaries who embraced the tenets of Romanticism. Three studies illustrate the advances made in this line of critical inquiry. In *The Western Canon: The Books and School of the Ages* (1994), Harold Bloom describes Austen as a transitional figure between what he calls the Aristocratic Age (a period beginning with the Renaissance) and the Democratic Age (ushered in by the Romantic movement). Bloom says Austen expresses a sense of self akin to the Romantics, especially the early Wordsworth. She "shares with Wordsworth an art dependent upon a split between a waning Protestant will and a newly active sympathetic imagination, with memory assigned the labor of healing the divide" (263). The many ways in which Austen shares kinship with, or differs from, the Romantics who were her contemporaries is also the subject of Laura Dabundo's essay on Austen in *Jane Austen and Mary Shelley and Their Sisters* (2000). Dabundo says Austen is linked with women of the period through her use of language and in her recognition of the "aesthetic boundaries to what language can convey" (55). In *British Romanticism and the Science of the Mind* (2001), a study tracing the relationship between the new science of the brain being developed at the time and the production of creative work, Alan Richardson claims that "Austen anticipates Victorian novelists in looking to biological and innate concepts of mind and character." Her "innovative style for conveying the heroine's impressions" in the novel "speaks as much to a new psychological appreciation" of her character's mental life as it does to "a new esthetic model for representing the flux of conscious experience" (94).

Clara Tuite also employs new theories to link Austen with the Romantics in *Romantic Austen: Sexual Politics and the Literary Canon* (2002). Tuite sets out to consider "ways in which Austen's fictions participate in the production of a specifically Romantic form of British national culture to anticipate the terms of their own canonization" (2). Deftly moving between cultural studies and feminist analysis of literary production, Tuite demonstrates how closely Austen's work reflects the social, political, and larger cultural dimensions of her age, and how its statement about British nationality and culture reflects a Romantic caste as much as it does an Augustan view of both public and domestic relationships. By contrast, Colin Winborn's *The Literary Economy of Jane Austen and George Crabbe* (2004) explores the relationship between the novelist and her favorite poet, linking them not only in their apparent anti-Romantic tendencies but in their concern for what Winborn calls "spatial economy," the "turning of available resources to the best possible account" (1). Situating the novelist in historical context, Winborn demonstrates how Austen's deep concern for historical events helped shape her fiction, and how an understanding of the work of some of her contemporaries — Malthus, William Spence, William Cobbett, Arthur Young, and Humphry Repton — can offer readers a richer appreciation of her novels. The same argument is made by Inger Sigrun Brodey in *Ruined by Design: Shaping Novels and Gardens in the Culture of Sensibility* (2008), a study of the late eighteenth-century cult of sensibility that influenced Austen and shaped her first published novel.

In another attempt to read Austen in historical context, William Deresiewicz argues in *Jane Austen and the Romantic Poets* (2004) that the novels of Austen's maturity were influenced by the Romantic poets — specifically Wordsworth, Coleridge, Scott, and Byron, all of whom were popular during the time she was composing *Mansfield Park, Emma*, and *Persuasion*. Deresiewicz demonstrates how her early compositions, all of which involve "essentially straightforward marriage plots" (1), differ from the later ones, and how her reading of the Romantic poets specifically shaped the last three novels she completed. "Austen's encounter with the Romantics deepened her art," Deresiewicz says, "darkened it, made it more intuitive, ambiguous, and unsettled, but also more bold and mature" (3). That influence is not always in the form of direct borrowing, he continues; it is "not a shackling of consciousness into imitative postures," but instead is "a startling of the imagination into the pursuit of new possibilities" (4). Whether Deresiewicz is right to claim that he is the first to trace so minutely the influence of the Romantics on Austen's fiction, it is clear that anyone writing about Austen after him must consider his well-documented argument for this important influence on her fiction.

Guidebooks and Collections of Criticism

Students at the end of the century found no shortage of new books aimed at assisting them in learning to read and understand Austen. Of course, the quality of these handbooks varies widely. For example, British novelist and essayist Violet Powell's *A Jane Austen Compendium: The Six Major Novels* (1993) offers little critical commentary, but rather is simply a series of extended plot summaries into which Powell inserts observations on auto-biographical or historical allusions in the novels. By contrast, Nicholas Marsh's *Jane Austen: The Novels* (1998) applies the practice of close textual reading and explores the social context in which Austen's novels were produced. Marsh's guide focuses on Austen's style, quoting extensively from the novels to illustrate her ability to create comedy through the skilful use of irony and highlighting the serious moral purpose of her fiction.

One of the best new guidebooks appeared in 1997. *The Cambridge Companion to Jane Austen*, edited by Edward Copeland and Juliet McMaster, contains work by some of the most distinguished Austen scholars of the late century. To satisfy the editors' aim of creating a collection that would "recover and illuminate elements of [Austen's] culture" (xii), the volume includes a chronology of Austen's life, commentary on her work as a professional writer, two essays treating the major novels and one each on her short fiction and letters, as well as background essays on the class structure, money, religion and politics, Austen's style, and her place in and use of the literary tradition. Clarice Swisher's *Readings on Jane Austen* (1997) is more akin to the Prentice Hall series of earlier days; in her volume Swisher collects essays from the 1940s through the 1990s to provide students a representative sampling of critical opinion on the novels. Laura and Robert Lambdin's *A Companion to Jane Austen Studies* (2000) is also of value to students because essays in this volume treat each of the novels in some detail. Generally, works are examined using techniques of reader-response theory, and lengthy discussions of the critical history of each work supplement each essayist's own critique.

Josephine Ross's *Jane Austen: A Companion* (2002) offers useful definitions of words, phrases, or customs in Austen's fiction that might seem foreign to twenty-first century readers. Ross comments on daily living in Austen's day, fashions of the time, literature that influenced Austen and her contemporaries, eighteenth-century ideas about love and marriage, the landscapes of country and city, rank and social status, and politics. Two other, similar books are worth noting because of the approach they take to categorizing Austen's work and for the style in which critical commentary is presented. Robert Miles's *Jane Austen* (2003) concentrates on the generic and technical aspects of her work. Miles explains how Austen creates what he calls "personality" in her fiction, then examines her use of comic structures, handling of point-of-view, and treatment of issues of class, gender, and nationalism. Darryl Jones's *Jane Austen* (2004) in the Critical Issues Series contains readings of each of the major novels and of many of the juvenilia and unfinished works. Jones displays keen awareness of the critical controversies in Austen scholarship during the past several decades, and his grounding of Austen's texts in their historical moment provides insights into their revolutionary character and their engagement with issues of topical importance.

Robert Irvine's *Jane Austen* (2005) in the Routledge Guides to Literature series provides background on the novelist's life and times and critiques of individual novels, a very informative summary of the literary tradition which influenced Austen's work, and an equally helpful discussion of the history of Austen criticism from the early nineteenth century to the present. Irvine also deals with the issue of Austen's conservatism and her relationship with the feminist movement, both in her own day and in the twentieth century. Similarly, Janet Todd's *The Cambridge Introduction to Jane Austen* (2006), a brief but reliable guide to the novelist and her age, provides critical readings of Austen's six published novels, stressing Austen's originality and her willingness to experiment. Although Todd is well grounded in contemporary theory, this work is virtually devoid of the jargon that has come to be associated with so much scholarly writing. At the same time, Todd acknowledges the various angles of vision from which Austen's work may be viewed, and she encourages thoughtful multifaceted approaches that might open up new vistas on the novelist.

Finally, two additional guidebooks deserve some mention, largely because of the audience they attempt to reach and the tone in which critical commentary is presented. Richard Gill and Susan Gregory's *Mastering the Novels of Jane Austen* (2003) is aimed at readers outside academe who simply want to gain a more sophisticated appreciation of Austen, a writer Gill and Gregory compare with Shakespeare, Wordsworth, and Dickens. Joan Klingel Ray's *Jane Austen for Dummies* (2006) provides similar survey information and offers some cogent analysis of individual works. Unfortunately, while both volumes are critically sound and reflect current scholarship, they may be ignored by many who associate the "Mastering" and "for Dummies" series with crib sheets and jaunty how-to guides designed for neophytes in areas as widely spread as sailing, sewing, gardening, poker playing, French cooking, and financial management.

A sampling of essay collections indicates that interest in assembling previously published work on Austen for students (and professors short on time for research) remained high. For example, continuing the Prentice Hall collections of the 1960s and 1970s, G. K. Hall's Critical Essays on British Literature issued Laura Mooneyham White's *Critical Essays on Jane Austen* in 1998. White excerpts commentary from influential scholars such as Nancy Armstrong, Mary Poovey, John Halperin, and D. A. Miller, providing readers a sense of trends in Austen criticism during the last two decades of the twentieth century. White's brief introductory essay traces the history of Austen studies back to its origins. In 2003 John Wiltshire collected a number of his own previously published essays in *Jane Austen: Introductions and Interventions,* which he says are intended to "accompany the reader through the experience of first acquaintance with

Austen's work, followed up by a more informed and sophisticated understanding" (ix). Essays on individual novels offer informative commentary,
while Wiltshire's concluding discussion of the world depicted in Austen's
fiction explains how Austen uses elements of the real world to create a fictional universe where human relationships are paramount. In *Reading the
Nineteenth Century Novel: Austen to Eliot* (2008), Alison Case and Harry
Shaw offer readings of *Pride and Prejudice* and *Persuasion* to make these
novels more accessible to twenty-first century readers, filling in gaps and
highlighting differences in the cultural milieus of Austen's age and the
present.

Austen on Screen

Beginning in the last half of the twentieth century, critical interest in
adaptations of Austen's novels for movies and television grew notably.
While it is not my intention to provide an extensive analysis of this bur-
geoning sub-set of Austen criticism, some commentary seems in order to
suggest the level of interest these adaptations are attracting. Linda Troost
and Sayre Greenfield's *Jane Austen in Hollywood* (1998) collects work by
a number of respected Austen scholars whose commentary reflects the seriousness with which the literary establishment has begun to deal with the
transformation of texts into other media. Anke Werker's *By a Lady: Jane
Austen's Female Archetypes in Fiction and Film* (1998) argues that Austen
relied heavily on certain archetypes for many of her women, but managed
to individualize them so that they become something more than stock
characters. She goes on to examine several film adaptations to demonstrate how easily Austen's literary figures can be transposed to the screen.
Deborah Cartmell and Imelda Whelehan's *Adaptations: From Text to
Screen, Screen to Text* (1999) contains two essays on films adapted from
Austen's texts, one a discussion of how Austen's radical critique of the
treatment of women in *Sense and Sensibility* is transformed into a conservative commentary in the 1995 film version, and another using *Clueless*,
the 1995 retelling of *Emma*, as a jumping-off point for a lengthy commentary on the theories behind film interpretation.

   Scholarly efforts to examine the implications of the transformation of
Austen's work from print to visual media abound, and quite a few are excellent. Among those that can offer a glimpse of this fascinating branch of
Austen studies is Erica Sheen's "'Where the Garment Gapes': Faithfulness
and Promiscuity in the 1995 BBC *Pride and Prejudice*" (2000), in which
Sheen applies contemporary sociological theory (especially that of Fou-
cault) in examining the highly popular BBC production of *Pride and
Prejudice* to explain what "adaptation" and "faithfulness" mean when discussing transformations between media. In *Recreating Jane Austen* (2001)
John Wiltshire discusses a number of recent film adaptations of Jane Aus-

ten's work to expose some of the key relationships between the text and the film. Wiltshire's larger aim is to develop a general theory of adaptation, explaining the psychology behind filmmakers' attempts to recreate Austen in their medium.

Sue Parrill offers extensive critical commentary on all the major adaptations in *Jane Austen on Film and Television* (2002), a book that provides much in the way of sensible critiques of the process of adaptation and a helpful list of casts of characters from the various cinematic versions of the novels. In *Jane Austen on Screen* (2003) editors Gina and Andrew MacDonald bring together essays examining various film adaptations of Austen's novels, highlighting the debate between purists who bemoan the loss of complexity and richness of the text when adapted for the movies or television and those who see the explosion of adaptations of Austen's work as a sign of their continuing vitality. The essays collected in Suzanne Pucci and James Thompson's *Jane Austen and Co.: Remaking the Past in Contemporary Culture* (2003) examine ways Austen's novels (and some by other writers as well) have been refashioned for the screen or adapted in other media to suit contemporary tastes, sometimes at the expense of the original historical context. Martina Anzinger makes a similar argument in *Gainsborough Pictures Reframed* (2003), in which she examines in detail the transformation of *Sense and Sensibility* and *Persuasion* into films in 1995. Anzinger argues that, far from being literal adaptations of Austen's conservative texts, the movies present a liberal, even feminist, portrait of their heroines. Marc DiPaolo's *Emma Adapted* (2007) offers a historical perspective on efforts to adapt Austen's novel for the screen, at the same time providing some insights into problems of adaptation in general and commenting on ways important topics like gender relationships are affected by the transformation between media.

Articles on film adaptations of Austen stand side-by-side with those that directly address the novels, and appear in reputable scholarly journals, suggesting that this form of critical inquiry has achieved legitimacy in Austen circles. In fact, two issues of *Persuasions On-Line* have been devoted to critiques of film adaptations: the Fall 1999 "Occasional Papers" on screen versions of *Emma*, and the Summer 2007 issue focused on Joe Wright's *Pride and Prejudice*.

The three authors of *The Cinematic Jane Austen* (2009) take a much wider and more theoretical approach to the issue of film adaptations of Austen's work. The eight essays in this collection, all written by David Monaghan, Ariane Hudelet, and John Wiltshire, "explore the various ways in which Jane Austen can be described as a cinematic novelist" (5). However, the focus is not on proving that Austen had an eye for a medium that had not yet been invented when she wrote. Rather, the authors explain how her fiction is transposed to the screen, challenging semiotic approaches to the novels and explaining how adaptations can at once be faithful to

Austen's fiction and be works of art in and of themselves. Of special interest is Wiltshire's concluding essay which addresses directly the issue of fidelity, critiquing the position of those whose blind insistence on literal redaction of novels into film has hindered the study of film adaptations.

Works Cited

Altick, Richard D. *The Scholar Adventurers.* New York: Macmillan, 1950.

Anzinger, Martina. *Gainsborough Pictures Reframed, or, Raising Jane Austen for 1990s Film.* Frankfurt am Main and New York: Peter Lang, 2003.

Bloom, Allan. "Austen, *Pride and Prejudice.*" *Love and Friendship*, 191–208. New York: Simon & Schuster, 1993.

Bloom, Harold. "Canonical Memory in Early Wordsworth and Jane Austen's *Persuasion.*" *The Western Canon: The Books and School of the Ages*, 239–63. New York: Harcourt, 1994.

Brodey, Inger Sigrun. *Ruined by Design: Shaping Novels and Gardens in the Culture of Sensibility.* New York: Routledge, 2008.

Butler, Marilyn. *Jane Austen.* Oxford and New York: Oxford UP, 2007.

Byrne, Paula. *Jane Austen and the Theatre.* London: Hambledon, 2002.

Cartmell, Deborah, and Imelda Whelehan, eds. *Adaptations: From Text to Screen, Screen to Text.* London: Routledge, 1999.

Case, Alison, and Harry E. Shaw. *Reading the Nineteenth Century Novel: Austen to Eliot.* Maldon, MA; Oxford: Blackwell, 2008.

The Cinematic Jane Austen. See Monaghan, David.

Collins, Irene. *Jane Austen and the Clergy.* London and Rio Grande OH: Hambledon Press, 1993.

———. *Jane Austen, the Parson's Daughter.* London and Rio Grande, Ohio: Hambledon Press, 1998.

Copeland, Edward, and Juliet McMaster, eds. *The Cambridge Companion to Jane Austen.* Cambridge and New York: Cambridge UP, 1997.

Dabundo, Laura, ed. *Jane Austen and Mary Shelley, and Their Sisters.* Lanham, MD: UP of America, 2000.

Davidson, Jenny. "Hypocrisy and the Novel: A Modest Question about *Mansfield Park.*" *Hypocrisy and the Politics of Politeness: Manners and Morals from Locke to Austen.* New York: Cambridge UP, 2004.

Deresiewicz, William. *Jane Austen and the Romantic Poets.* New York: Columbia UP, 2004.

Di Paolo, Marc. *Emma Adapted: Jane Austen's Heroine from Book to Film.* New York: Peter Lang, 2007.

Doody, Margaret Anne. "Jane Austen, That Disconcerting 'Child.'" In *The Child Writer from Austen to Woolf*, edited by Christine Alexander and Juliet McMaster, 101–21. Cambridge: Cambridge UP, 2005.

———, ed. *Jane Austen: Catherine, and Other Writings*. Oxford: Oxford UP, 1993.

Emsley, Sarah Baxter. *Jane Austen's Philosophy of the Virtues*. New York: Palgrave Macmillan, 2005.

Fritzer, Penelope Joan. *Jane Austen and Eighteenth-Century Courtesy Books*. Westport, CT: Greenwood Press, 1997.

Fullerton, Susannah. *Jane Austen and Crime*. Sydney: Jane Austen Society of Australia, 2004. Madison: Jones Books, 2008.

Gard, Roger. *Jane Austen's Novels: The Art of Clarity*. New Haven, CT: Yale UP, 1992.

Gay, Penny. *Jane Austen and the Theatre*. Cambridge: Cambridge UP, 2002.

———. Review of Jon Spence, *Becoming Jane Austen. Sensibilities: The Jane Austen Society of Australia* 26 (June 2003): 43–46.

Giffin, Michael. *Jane Austen and Religion: Salvation and Society in Georgian England*. Houndsmill, Basingstoke, Hampshire; New York: Palgrave Macmillan, 2002.

Gill, Richard, and Susan Gregory. *Mastering the Novels of Jane Austen*. New York: Palgrave Macmillan, 2003.

Graham, Peter W. *Jane Austen & Charles Darwin: Naturalists and Novelists*. Aldershot, England; Burlington, VT: Ashgate, 2008.

Gross, Gloria Sybil. *In a Fast Coach with a Pretty Woman: Jane Austen and Samuel Johnson*. New York: AMS Press, 2002.

Halperin, John. *The Life of Jane Austen*. Baltimore: Johns Hopkins UP, 1984.

Hammond, M. C. *Relating to Jane: Studies on the Life and Novels of Jane Austen with a Life of Her Niece Elizabeth Austen*. London and Atlanta: Minerva Press, 1998.

Irvine, Robert P. *Jane Austen*. Routledge Guides to Literature Series. London and New York: Routledge, 2005.

Jarvis, William. *Jane Austen and Religion*. Whitney, Oxfordshire: Stonefield Press, 1996.

Jenkyns, Richard. *A Fine Brush on Ivory: An Appreciation of Jane Austen*. Oxford and New York: Oxford UP, 2004.

Jones, Darryl. *Jane Austen*. Critical Issues Series. Houndsmill, Basingstoke, Hampshire; New York: Palgrave Macmillan, 2004.

Lambdin, Laura Coomer, and Robert Thomas Lambdin. *A Companion to Jane Austen Studies*. Westport, CT: Greenwood Press, 2000.

Lane, Maggie. *Jane Austen and Food*. London and Rio Grande, OH: Hambledon Press, 1995.

———. *Jane Austen's England*. New York: St. Martin's, 1986.

———. *Jane Austen's World: The Life and Times of England's Most Popular Author*. London: Carlton, 1996.

Lauber, John. *Jane Austen*. Twayne's English Authors Series. New York: Twayne, 1993.

Le Faye, Deirdre. *Jane Austen*. London: British Library, 1998.

———. *Jane Austen: The World of Her Novels*. London: Frances Lincoln; New York: Harry Abrams, 2002.

Lee, Hermione. "Jane Austen Faints." *Virginia Woolf's Nose: Essays on Biography*, 63–94. Princeton, NJ: Princeton UP, 2005.

Lefroy, Helen. *Jane Austen*. Thrupp, Gloucestershire: Sutton, 1997.

Lehmann-Haupt, Christopher. *New York Times* 16 April 1997, C17.

Leithart, Peter J. *Miniatures and Morals: The Christian Novels of Jane Austen*. Moscow, ID: Canon Press, 2004.

MacDonagh, Oliver. *Jane Austen: Real and Imagined Worlds*. New Haven, CT: Yale UP, 1991.

MacDonald, Gina, and Andrew MacDonald. *Jane Austen on Screen*. Cambridge and New York: Cambridge UP, 2003.

MacIntyre, Alisdair. *After Virtue: A Study in Moral Theory*. London: Duckworth; Notre Dame, IN: U of Notre Dame P, 1981.

Mairs, Nancy. "Single Blessedness." *Women's Review of Books* 15.8 (May 1998): 13.

Marsh, Nicholas. *Jane Austen: The Novels*. New York: St. Martin's, 1998.

McMaster, Juliet. *Austen the Novelist: Essays Past and Present*. Basingstoke, Hampshire: Macmillan; New York: St. Martin's, 1996.

———. *Jane Austen on Love*. English Literary Studies Monographs, 13. Victoria, BC: U of Victoria P, 1978.

McMaster, Juliet, and Bruce Stovel, eds. *Jane Austen's Business: Her World and her Profession*. Houndsmill, Basingstoke, Hampshire: Macmillan; New York: St. Martin's, 1996.

Miles, Robert. *Jane Austen*. Writers and Their Work Series. Plymouth, UK: Northcote House, 2003.

Monaghan, David, Ariane Hudelet, and John Wiltshire. *Cinematic Jane Austen: Essays on the Filmic Sensibility of the Novels*. Jefferson, NC: McFarland, 2009.

Moxham, Jeffrey. *Interfering Values in the Nineteenth-Century British Novel: Austen, Dickens, Eliot, Hardy, and the Ethics of Criticism*. Westport, CT: Greenwood Press, 2002.

Myer, Valerie Grosvenor. *Jane Austen, Obstinate Heart: A Biography.* New York: Arcade, 1997.

Nachumi, Nora. *Acting Like a Lady: British Women Novelists and the Eighteenth-Century Theater.* New York: AMS Press, 2008.

Nicolson, Nigel. *The World of Jane Austen.* London: Weidenfeld & Nicolson, 1991.

Nokes, David. *Jane Austen: A Life.* New York: Farrar, Straus, and Giroux, 1997.

Odom, Keith C. *Jane Austen: Rebel of Time & Place.* Arlington, TX: Liberal Arts Press, 1991.

Parker, Jo Alyson. *The Author's Inheritance: Henry Fielding, Jane Austen, and the Establishment of the Novel.* DeKalb: Northern Illinois UP, 1998.

Parrill, Sue. *Jane Austen on Film and Television: A Critical Study of the Adaptations.* Jefferson, NC: McFarland, 2002.

Persuasions On-Line Occasional Papers 3 (Fall 1999). Special Issue on Film Versions of *Emma*.

Persuasions On-Line 27.2 (Summer 2007). Special Issue on Joe Wright's *Pride and Prejudice*.

Powell, Violet. *A Jane Austen Compendium: The Six Major Novels.* London: Heinemann, 1993.

Pucci, Suzanne R., and James Thompson, eds. *Jane Austen and Co.: Remaking the Past in Contemporary Culture.* Albany: State U of New York P, 2003.

Ray, Joan Klingel. *Jane Austen for Dummies.* Hoboken, NJ: Wiley, 2006.

Richardson, Alan. "Of Heartache and Head Injury: Minds, Brains, and the Subject of *Persuasion*." *British Romanticism and the Science of Mind.* Cambridge: Cambridge UP, 2001.

Ross, Josephine. *Jane Austen: A Companion.* London: John Murray, 2002. New Brunswick, NJ: Rutgers UP, 2003.

Ruderman, Anne Crippen. *The Pleasures of Virtue: Political Thought in the Novels of Jane Austen.* Lanham, MD: Rowman & Littlefield, 1995.

Selwyn, David. *Jane Austen and Leisure.* London: Hambledon Press, 1999.

Sheen, Erica. "'Where the Garment Gapes': Faithfulness and Promiscuity in the 1995 BBC *Pride and Prejudice*." In *The Classic Novel from Page to Screen*, edited by Robert Giddings and Erica Sheen, 14–30. Manchester, Eng. and New York: Manchester UP, 2000.

Shields, Carol. *Jane Austen.* New York: Viking, 2001.

Siebers, Tobin. "Jane Austen and Comic Virtue." *Morals & Stories*, 135–58. New York: Columbia UP, 1992.

Siegel, Lee. "A Writer Who is Good for You." *Atlantic Monthly* 281.1 (January 1998): 95.

Southam, B. C. *Jane Austen and the Navy*. London: Hambledon and London, 2000.

Spence, Jon. *Becoming Jane Austen: A Life*. London and New York: Hambledon & London, 2003.

Stokes, Myra. *The Language of Jane Austen: A Study of Some Aspects of Her Vocabulary*. New York: St. Martin's, 1991.

Swisher, Clarice, ed. *Readings on Jane Austen*. San Diego, CA: Greenhaven Press, 1997.

Tague, Gregory F. *Ethics and Behavior: The English Novel from Jane Austen to Henry James*. Introduction by Daniel Meyer-Dinkgräfe. Bethesda, MD: Academica Press, 2008.

Tandon, Bharat. *Jane Austen and the Morality of Conversation*. London: Anthem, 2003.

Todd, Janet M. *The Cambridge Introduction to Jane Austen*. Cambridge and New York: Cambridge UP, 2006.

Tomalin, Claire. *Jane Austen: A Life*. New York: Knopf, 1997.

Troost, Linda, and Sayre Greenfield, eds. *Jane Austen in Hollywood*. Lexington: UP of Kentucky, 1998.

Tucker, George Holbert. *A Goodly Heritage: Jane Austen's Family*. Thrupp, Gloucester, England: Sutton, 1983.

———. *Jane Austen the Woman: Some Biographical Insights*. New York: St. Martin's, 1994.

Tuite, Clara. *Romantic Austen: Sexual Politics and the Literary Canon*. Cambridge; New York: Cambridge UP, 2002.

Updike, John. "On Literary Biography." *Due Considerations*, 3–13. New York: Knopf, 2007.

Wainwright, Valerie. *Ethics and the English Novel from Austen to Forster*. Aldershot, England: Ashgate, 2007.

Waldron, Mary. *Jane Austen and the Fiction of her Time*. Cambridge; New York: Cambridge UP, 1999.

Werker, Anke. *By a Lady: Jane Austen's Female Archetypes in Fiction and Film*. Tilburg, The Netherlands: Tilburg UP, 1998.

White, James Boyd. "Austen's *Mansfield Park*: Making the Self Out of — and Against — the Culture." *Acts of Hope: Creating Authority in Literature, Law, and Politics*. Chicago: U of Chicago P, 1994.

White, Laura Mooneyham. *Critical Essays on Jane Austen*. New York: G. K. Hall; London: Prentice Hall International, 1998.

Wiesenfarth, Joseph. Review of Jon Spence, *Becoming Jane Austen*. *JASNA News* 19.3 (Winter 2003): 28.

Wiltshire, John. *Jane Austen: Introductions and Interventions*. New Delhi: Macmillan, 2003.

———. *Recreating Jane Austen*. Cambridge and New York: Cambridge UP, 2001.

Winborn, Colin. *The Literary Economy of Jane Austen and George Crabbe*. Burlington, VT: Ashgate, 2004.

10:   Speculations on the Future

A S WE ENTER THE SECOND DECADE of the twenty-first century and
approach the bicentennial of the publication of Austen's first novel,
there seems to be no letup in the outpouring of commentary on Austen
and her fiction. Articles on Austen are as likely to be found today in *Critical Inquiry* or *Studies in English Literature* as they are in *Eighteenth-
Century Studies* or *Victorians Institute Journal*. Perhaps the best evidence
of the continuing interest can be seen by looking at the activities of the
Jane Austen Society of North America. In 1981 JASNA, which boasts a
healthy mix of American and Canadian scholars, launched the scholarly
journal *Persuasions*. In 1999 the society began a second publication, *Persuasions On-Line*, that now rivals its printed sister in length and quality.
One can gain some idea of the breadth of scholarly inquiry that Austen's
work inspires by inspecting the "Table of Contents" of the 2008 issue of
Persuasions. Among the nine articles grouped on the theme of Austen's
legacy are Claudia Johnson's "A Name to Conjure With," Jocelyn Harris's "Jane Austen, Samuel Johnson, and the Academy," Janine Barchas's
"Mrs. Gaskell's *North and South*: Austen's Early Legacy," and Sarah Parry's "The Pemberley Effect: Austen's Legacy to the Historic House Industry." Turning to the thirteen essays in the "Miscellany" section, one
can read Thomas Rand's "*Emma* and *Twelfth Night*," Rana Tekcan's
"Notes on a Turkish Edition of *Pride and Prejudice*," and Freydis Jane
Welland's "The History of Jane Austen's Writing Desk" — and more. As
Dryden said of Chaucer, "here is God's plenty." And it's only one journal
in one year.

Whether there is something new *and* worthwhile to say about Austen
may be a matter of debate, though. Audrey Hawkridge laments in the introduction to *Jane and Her Gentlemen* (2000) that "trying to write something fresh about Jane Austen is like tiptoeing through a ploughed field in
the hope of finding virgin soil" (7). And yet, despite the sizeable amount
of Austen criticism already on library shelves (and on the Internet), apparently there is still opportunity to produce original scholarship. Witness
Massimiliano Morini's *Jane Austen's Narrative Techniques* (2009), a
Bakhtinian assessment in which Austen's novels are seen as "dialogic
machines" (7) with no fixed meanings; Morini says he was driven to write
by his discovery that many of the "new critical ideas" and "modern Austen commonplaces" do not "pass the test of close linguistic scrutiny" (1).
Or consider E. M. Daldez's *Mirrors of One Another: Emotion and Value*

in Jane Austen and David Hume (2009), which demonstrates that familiarity with Hume's writings can illuminate our understanding of Austen's fiction — and vice versa. Mona Scheuermann reprises her staunchly conservative critique of Austen's fiction in *Reading Jane Austen* (2009), a study that operates from the premise that "Austen writes from the core beliefs in her period, and her perspective carries the whole authority of her society" (2). In 2010, the Ohio State University Press brought out two new studies that range widely among academic disciplines to provide fresh perspectives on Austen's fiction: Kay Young's *Imagining Mind: The Neuro-Aesthetics of Austen, Eliot and Hardy*, and Leona Toker's *Toward the Ethics of Form in Fiction.*

In light of the mountain of scholarship already in print about Austen's views on courtship and matrimony, the appearance of another book on the subject may seem surprising, but Hazel Jones seems to have been undaunted by the challenge to find something new to say. Her *Jane Austen and Marriage* (2009) foregoes recent critical commentary in favor of eighteenth-century sources and a few twentieth-century histories of that period from which she derives a fresh reading of the novels as documents about the marriage business. Jones believes Austen appreciated all the benefits of married life, and at times wished she had been fortunate enough to experience them, but in the end she found being an "old maid" quite satisfying, because it offered her the "best chance of self-fulfillment" (208). Austen's status as an "old maid" is also the subject of Devoney Looser's perceptive chapter on the novelist in *Women Writers and Old Age in Great Britain, 1750–1850* (2008). Although, as Looser knows, Austen did not live into old age, her works are worthy of study beside those of other women who did, because she has come to be labeled an "old maid" by succeeding generations. Looser explores ways this idea has affected our study of Austen and examines Austen's treatment of older women in her fiction. Perhaps with a note of sadness, Looser concludes that, while Austen's "young heroines may rightly be labeled feminist," the novelist "appears not to have chosen to overturn dominant representations of old maids," instead displaying "a willingness to conform to, rather than to overturn, prevalent stereotypes" (76–77). Looser's more nuanced understanding of Austen's feminist sensibilities suggests that critics might still find something to glean from the seemingly inexhaustible suggestivity of Austen's fiction. Eric Walker also manages to write fresh, nuanced account of Austen's views on marriage in *Marriage, Writing, and Romanticism: Wordsworth and Austen After War* (2009).

Might there be new biographies as well? It seems hard to imagine that anyone will discover a cache of letters or family documents that will materially add to the ones already available — the well-rehearsed story of "Aunt Cassandra" burning those of Jane's letters she thought too personal for public viewing has by now taken on the mantle of fact — but no doubt people will try to offer a fresh take on the well-known tale. The subtitle of Andrew Norman's *Jane Austen: An Unrequited Love* (2009) suggests how that might be accomplished. Although Norman includes brief summaries and commentary on Austen's fiction, his real interest is in explaining why Austen never married. While most of his biography reflects the work of earlier biographers (and not all of them, as his rather brief bibliography indicates), Norman offers some rather intriguing observations on what he sees as Cassandra Austen's attempts to undermine her sister's budding romances.

Just how far "Austen" has become a touchstone or catchphrase for attracting readers to projects that often have only tangential relationship to her fiction can be seen in the entertaining collection *Jane Austen Sings the Blues* (2009), edited by Nora Foster Stovel. Poems, critical essays, and even a compact disc of twelve songs, which Stovel insists were inspired by Austen, make up this unusual collection. Not to be left out, fiction writers continue to crank out sequels or produce serious (or sometimes just clever) fiction based on Austen's work. Karen Joy Fowler's *The Jane Austen Book Club* (2004), a modern-day novel in which the six main characters' stories are linked to Austen's fiction, was a national best-seller, and was adapted for the big screen. In 2010 more than a dozen sequels, take-offs, or "inspired by Austen" books appeared on bookshelves in America and Britain. Among the oddest adaptations, Seth Grahame-Smith's *Pride and Prejudice and Zombies* (2009) — published, most appropriately, by Quirk Books — has generated a large following and actually renewed interest in Austen among many who thought she was too stuffy until they read this version of Elizabeth Bennet's two-fold struggle to win Mr. Darcy *and* ward off a hoard of flesh-eating undeads that threaten all of England. Ben Winters's *"Sense and Sensibility" and Sea Monsters* and Wayne Josephson's *Emma and the Vampires* (2010), two of at least a half-dozen such titles, suggest that the trend in this sort of fiction is likely to continue. One can only wonder if there will be movies about these books, too.

Two recently published essay collections indicate that publishers continue to have interest in capitalizing on the academic community's perpetual fascination with Austen. *Issues of Class in Jane Austen's Pride and Prejudice* (2009) edited by Claudia Durst Johnson (of the University of Alabama) in the Gale Group's "Social Issues in Literature" series collects brief essays from a number of prominent Austen scholars who provide background on topics such as the rural gentry in Austen's time, rank and social class, gender relationships, and morality — along with a handful of what are described as "Contemporary Perspectives on Class Issues" designed to help students in relating the novel to their own lives. Claudia L. Johnson (of Princeton) and Clara Tuite's *A Companion to Jane Austen* (2009) collects forty-two essays by leading Austen scholars that survey Austen's life, examine the production of her texts, offer reader-response and genre critiques, provide cultural and political context, and explore the novelist's shifting reputation over time. Neither disdainful not condescending to the group they call "ordinary readers" (xviii), the editors and their contributors acknowledge the important role lovers of Austen outside academic circles have had in preserving her popularity and holding scholars accountable for claims made about her novels. Many contributors suggest directions for new work in understanding Austen, her fiction, and her age — and the interactions among the three. How future studies such as these might be shaped was the general topic of "New Directions in Austen Studies," a conference held at Chawton House Library in 2009. Some of the papers from the conference appear in a special issue of *Persuasions On-Line* (2010).

There will certainly be books like the present study. As I was preparing *Jane Austen: Two Centuries of Criticism* there appeared Claire Harman's *Jane's Fame: How Jane Austen Conquered the World* (2009), a study attempting to explain why Austen has remained of interest to so many people for so long. Joanne Wilkes's *Women Reviewing Women in Nineteenth-Century Britain* (2010) shows that we have not yet mined the historical record for what it can tell us about Austen's appeal in prior generations. Even if these books prove sufficient for the moment, in a decade or two there will be need for a new "history of criticism" because that history will have been expanded exponentially. For example, the new "Critical Insights" series initiated in 2009 by Salem Press, collections of new and previously published criticism includes a volume on Austen among the first ten issued on authors of what the Press calls the most studied literature in the world. A volume on *Pride and Prejudice* in the same series is forthcoming in 2011.

There are also strong indications that Austen's fiction will continue to make its way to the screen. "Hollywood Can't Get Enough of Jane Austen" screams a headline in the August 10, 2007 issue of the *Pittsburgh Post Gazette*. Whether faithfully transferred to the screen or freely adapted, Austen's novels continue to bring millions into the theater and millions more to television screens — and produce millions in revenue for the producers. Remakes or one novel or another seem to pop up every ten years or so, and the 2009 BBC production of *Emma* (a fairly loose rendition of the text of the novel) played to large national audiences on both sides of the Atlantic. Given this trend, one can expect additional critical commentary on screen adaptations.

And if all the critical attention went away, it is likely that Austen would continue to have a large following among readers who are proud to be labeled "Janeites." They meet in book clubs or over coffee to discuss Austen's works, paying meticulous attention to details and becoming self-styled experts on the food, fashion, customs, and domestic politics of Austen's age. They have entered cyberspace, too. Among the most popular sites featuring Austen and her work is "The Republic of Pemberley" (www.pemberley.com), which bills itself as the largest, most comprehensive site about all things Austen and has hundreds of thousands of "hits" each year. On the site one can find links to the texts of Austen's novels, information about sequels, lists of recommended reading, chat rooms and message boards where fans can exchange ideas and opinions about the fiction (or about many other subjects as well), and a rather robust gift store where one can order mugs, tote bags, clothing (styled after that which Austen wore), and magnets with pithy quotations from the novels. Before one assumes that Austen fans are all cut from the same cloth, however, it might be good to review the accolades for her fiction offered by the thirty-three writers whose comments are collected in Susannah Carson's *A Truth Universally Acknowledged: 33 Great Writers on Why We Read Jane Austen* (2009). Figures as diverse in their literary outlook as Somerset Maugham and A. S. Byatt suggest with equal fervor that reading Austen is both aesthetically and intellectually satisfying.

Why is it that Austen has generated such critical interest and retained such wide appeal? Brian Southam proposed an answer to that question nearly four decades ago in his brief volume, *Jane Austen*, for the Longmans series (1975): Austen, he says, is one of the few writers who appeals equally to "interpretive critics," "literary historians," and "an audience quite unconcerned with Jane Austen's critical reputation and status, who turn to the novels simply for enjoyment" (3). She continues to attract readers, he says, because of her "readability" and her "capacity to engage us imaginatively, emotionally, and intellectually" (4). Twenty-five years later Harold Bloom found additional reasons for her enduring appeal. "In the Dark Ages ahead of us," he writes in somewhat apocalyptic tones in the introduction to his 2000 Chelsea House volume of critical essays on Austen, "when the visual media will reduce everything to virtual reality, Jane Austen will survive, together with Shakespeare and Dickens. These seem the three great writers in the language who require least mediation" (ix).

I think Bloom is right, and not only because Austen is accessible to modern readers. Austen seems to be one of those few authors who, though clearly attuned to and influenced by the conventions and culture of her time, truly understood the "truths" that, while not always "universally acknowledged," lie at the heart of human nature. As a consequence, the works she has left us are likely to compel our attention for decades to come.

Works Cited

Barchas, Janine. "Mrs. Gaskell's *North and South*: Austen's Early Legacy." *Persuasions* 30 (2008): 53–66.

Bloom, Harold, ed. *Jane Austen*. New York: Chelsea House, 2000.

Carson, Susannah. *A Truth Universally Acknowledged: 33 Great Writers on Why We Read Jane Austen*. New York: Random House, 2009.

Daldez, E. M. *Mirrors of One Another: Emotion and Value in Jane Austen and David Hume*. West Sussex, UK: Wiley-Blackwell, 2009.

Fowler, Karen Joy. *The Jane Austen Book Club*. New York: Putnam, 2004.

Grahame-Smith, Seth. *Pride and Prejudice and Zombies*. Philadelphia: Quirk Books, 2009.

Harman, Claire. *Jane's Fame: How Jane Austen Conquered the World*. Edinburgh: Canongate, 2009; New York: Henry Holt, 2010.

Harris, Jocelyn. "Jane Austen, Samuel Johnson, and the Academy." *Persuasions* 30 (2008): 27–37.

Hawkridge, Audrey. *Jane and her Gentlemen: Jane Austen and the Men in her Life and Novels*. London: Peter Owen; Chester Springs, PA: Dufour Editions, 2000.

"Hollywood Can't Get Enough of Jane Austen." *Pittsburgh Post Gazette*, 10 August 2007.

Johnson, Claudia Durst, ed. *Issues of Class in Jane Austen's Pride and Prejudice*. Social Issues in Literature Series. Detroit: Gale, 2009.

Johnson, Claudia L. "A Name to Conjure With." *Persuasions* 30 (2008): 15–26.

Johnson, Claudia L., and Clara Tuite, eds. *A Companion to Jane Austen*. Malden, MA: Blackwell, 2009.

Jones, Hazel. *Jane Austen and Marriage*. New York: Continuum, 2009.

Josephson, Wayne. *Emma and the Vampires*. Naperville, IL: Sourcebooks Landmark, 2010.

Lynch, Jack, ed. *Jane Austen*. Critical Insights Series. Englewood Cliffs, NJ: Salem Press, 2009.

Looser, Devoney. "What is Old in Jane Austen?" *Women Writers and Old Age in Great Britain, 1750–1850*. Baltimore: Johns Hopkins UP, 2008.

Morini, Massimiliano. *Jane Austen's Narrative Techniques*. Burlington, VT: Ashgate, 2009.

Norman, Andrew. *Jane Austen: An Unrequited Love*. Stroud, Gloucestershire: The History Press, 2009.

Parry, Sarah. "The Pemberley Effect: Austen's Legacy to the Historic House Industry." *Persuasions* 30 (2008): 113–22.

Persuasions On-Line 30.2 (Spring 2010). Special Issue: "New Directions in Austen Studies."

Rand, Thomas. "*Emma* and *Twelfth Night*." *Persuasions* 30 (2008): 181–86.

"The Republic of Pemberley." http://www.pemberley.com (2004–2010).

Scheuermann, Mona. *Reading Jane Austen*. New York: Palgrave Macmillan, 2009.

Southam, B. C. *Jane Austen*. Writers and Their Work Series. London: Longman, 1975.

Stovel, Nora Foster, ed. *Jane Austen Sings the Blues*. Edmonton: U of Alberta P, 2009.

Tekcan, Rana. "Notes on a Turkish Edition of *Pride and Prejudice*." *Persuasions* 30 (2008): 241–54.

Toker, Leona. *Toward the Ethics of Form in Fiction*. Columbus: Ohio State UP, 2010.

Walker, Eric. *Marriage, Writing, and Romanticism: Wordsworth and Austen After War*. Stanford, CA: Stanford UP, 2009.

Welland, Freydis Jane. "The History of Jane Austen's Writing Desk." *Persuasions* 30 (2008): 125–28.

Wilkes, Joanne. *Women Reviewing Women in Nineteenth-Century Britain*. Aldershot, England: Ashgate, 2010.

Winters, Ben H. "*Sense and Sensibility*" and Sea Monsters*. Philadelphia: Quirk Books, 2009.

Young, Kay. *Imagining Mind: The Neuro-Aesthetics of Austen, Eliot, and Hardy*. Columbus: Ohio State UP, 2010.

Works by Jane Austen

Juvenilia. Three volumes, written circa 1786–92. Volume 2 first published as *Love and Friendship and Other Early Works*, edited by G. K. Chesterton. London: Chatto & Windus, 1922. Vol. 1 first published as *Volume The First*, edited by R. W. Chapman. Oxford: Clarendon Press, 1933. Vol. 3 first published as *Volume The Third*, edited by R. W. Chapman. Oxford: Clarendon Press, 1954.

Sense and Sensibility. London: Thomas Egerton, 1811.

Pride and Prejudice. London: Thomas Egerton, 1813.

Mansfield Park. London: Thomas Egerton, 1814.

Emma. London: John Murray, 1815.

Persuasion. In *Northanger Abbey and Persuasion*, with an introduction by Henry Austen. London: John Murray, 1817.

Northanger Abbey. Written ca. 1798–99. First published in *Northanger Abbey and Persuasion*, with an introduction by Henry Austen. London: John Murray, 1817.

Lady Susan. A fragment, written ca. 1794. First published in *Jane Austen: A Memoir*, edited by James Edward Austen-Leigh. 2nd edition. London: Richard Bentley, 1871.

The Watsons. A fragment, begun ca. 1804. First published in *Jane Austen: A Memoir*, edited by James Edward Austen-Leigh. 2nd edition. London: Richard Bentley, 1871.

Sanditon. A fragment, written ca. 1817. First published in *Jane Austen: A Memoir*, edited by James Edward Austen-Leigh. 2nd edition. London: Richard Bentley, 1871.

Chronological List of Works Cited

1810s

Notice of *Sense and Sensibility*. *British Critic* 39 (May 1812): 527.

Notice of *Sense and Sensibility*. *Critical Review* n.s. 4.1 (February 1812): 149–57.

Notice of *Pride and Prejudice*. *British Critic* 41 (February 1813): 189–90.

Review of *Pride and Prejudice*. *Critical Review* 4th ser., no. 3 (March 1813): 318–24.

Scott, Walter. Unsigned review of *Emma*. *Quarterly Review* 14 (March 1816): 188–201.

Notice of *Emma*. *Gentleman's Magazine* 86 (September 1816): 248–49.

Austen, Henry. "Biographical Notice of the Author." *Northanger Abbey and Persuasion*. London: John Murray, 1817. Reprinted in *Persuasion*, edited by Janet Todd and Antje Blank. Cambridge: Cambridge UP, 2006.

Notice of *Northanger Abbey* and *Persuasion*. *Blackwood's Edinburgh Magazine* n.s. 2 (May 1818): 453–55.

Review of *Northanger Abbey* and *Persuasion*. *British Critic* n.s. 9 (March 1818): 293–301.

1820s

Whately, Richard. Review of *Northanger Abbey* and *Persuasion*. *Quarterly Review* 24 (January 1821): 352–76.

1830s

Lister, Thomas Henry. Review of Catherine Gore, *Women as They Are*. *Edinburgh Review* 53 (July 1830): 448–51.

Cunningham, Alan. "Biographical and Critical History of the Literature of the Last Fifty Years: British Novels and Romances." *Athenaeum* 316 (16 November 1833): 773–77.

Lockhart, John Gibson. *Memoirs of the Life of Sir Walter Scott*. 7 vols. Edinburgh: R. Cadell, 1837–38. Single-volume abridgment, *The Life of Sir Walter Scott*, edited by R. H. Hutton. Philadelphia: J. D. Morris & Co., 1897.

1840s

Chambers, Robert, ed. *Cyclopaedia of English Literature*, 2:571–72. Edinburgh: William & Robert Chambers, 1843–44.

Elwood, Anne Katherine. *Memoirs of the Literary Ladies of England, From the Commencement of the Last Century*, 2:174–86. London: Henry Colburn, 1843.

Macaulay, Thomas Babington. "The Diary and Letters of Mme D'Arblay." *Edinburgh Review* 76 (January 1843): 561–62.

Lewes, G. H. "Recent Novels: French and English." *Fraser's Magazine* 36 (December 1847): 687.

Shaw, T. B. *Outlines of English Literature*, 479–80. Philadelphia: Blanchard & Lee, 1849.

1850s

Jacox, Francis. "Female Novelists, No. I: Miss Austen." *New Monthly Magazine* 95 (May 1852): 17–23.

Lewes, George Henry. "The Lady Novelists." *Westminster Review* n.s. 2 (1852): 129–41.

"The Progress of Fiction as an Art." *Westminster Review* n.s. 4 (1853): 342–74.

Jeaffreson, John Cordy. *Novels and Novelists, From Elizabeth to Victoria*, 2:84–87. London: Hurst and Blackett, 1858.

Lewes, George Henry. "The Novels of Jane Austen." *Blackwood's Edinburgh Magazine* 86 (1859): 99–113. Reprinted in *Littell's Living Age* 62 (1859): 424–36.

Masson, David. *British Novelists and Their Styles*, 188–89. London: Macmillan; Boston: Gould and Lincoln, 1859.

1860s

Kavanagh, Julia. "Miss Austen's Six Novels." *English Women of Letters: Biographical Sketches*, 188–236. Leipzig: Tauchnitz, 1862; London: Hurst & Blackett, 1863.

Dallas, E. S. Review of George Eliot, *Felix Holt, the Radical. The Times*, 26 June 1866, p. 6.

"Miss Austen." *Englishwoman's Domestic Magazine* 3rd ser. 2 (1866): 237–40, 278–82.

1870s

Austen-Leigh, James Edward. *A Memoir of Jane Austen*. London: Richard Bentley, 1870. 2nd ed., expanded, 1871. Reprinted with introduction and notes by R. W. Chapman. Oxford: Clarendon Press, 1926.

Oliphant, Margaret. "Miss Austen and Miss Mitford." *Blackwood's Edinburgh Magazine* 107 (March 1870): 294–305.

Pollock, Juliet. "Jane Austen." *St. Paul's Magazine* 5 (March 1870): 631–43.

Simpson, Richard. Review of James Edward Austen-Leigh, *A Memoir of Jane Austen*. *North British Review* 52 (April 1870): 129–52.

Forsyth, William. *The Novels and Novelists of the Eighteenth Century*. London: John Murray; New York: D. Appleton, 1871.

Murch, Jerome. *Mrs. Barbauld and her Contemporaries*. London: Longmans, Green, 1877.

Lefroy, Fanny Caroline. "Hunting for Snarkes at Lyme Regis." *Temple Bar* 57 (1879): 391–97.

1880s

Tytler, Sarah [Henrietta Keddie]. *Jane Austen and Her Works*. London: Cassell, Petter, Galpin, 1880.

Oliphant, Margaret. *The Literary History of England*, 3:203–50. London: Macmillan, 1882.

Lefroy, Fanny Caroline. "A Bundle of Letters." *Temple Bar* 67 (1883): 258–88.

———. "Is It Just?" *Temple Bar* 67 (1883): 270–84.

Pellew, George. *Jane Austen's Novels*. Boston: Cupples, Upham & Co., 1883.

Braeburn, Edward Lord (Edward Knatchbull), ed. *Letters of Jane Austen*. 2 vols. London: Bentley, 1884.

Stephen, Leslie. *Dictionary of National Biography*, 1:731–32. London: Smith, Elder, 1885.

Fawcett, Millicent. *Some Eminent Women of Our Times: Short Biographical Sketches*, 136–44. London: Macmillan, 1889.

Malden, S. F. *Jane Austen*. Famous Women Series. London: W. H. Allen & Co., 1889. Boston: Roberts Bros., 1889.

1890s

Hutton, R. H. "The Charm of Miss Austen." Review of Goldwyn Smith's *Life of Jane Austen*. *Spectator* 64 (1890): 403–4. Reprinted in *Brief Literary Criticisms*, 168–74. London: Macmillan, 1906.

Smith, Goldwyn. *Life of Jane Austen*. Great Writers Series. London: Walter Scott, 1890.

Adams, Oscar Fay. *The Story of Jane Austen's Life*. Chicago: A. C. McClurg, 1891.

Howells, William Dean. *Criticism and Fiction*, 73–77. New York: Harper; London: Osgood, McIlvane & Co., 1891.

Hamilton, Catherine J. *Women Writers: Their Works and Ways*, 191–206. London: Ward, Lock, Bowden, 1892.

Walford, Lucy Bethia. *Twelve English Authoresses*, 65–81. London: Longmans, Green, 1892.

Meynell, Alice. "The Classic Novelist." *Pall Mall Gazette* 58 (16 February 1894): 4. Reprinted in *The Second Person Singular and Other Essays*, 62–67. London: Oxford UP, 1921.

Raleigh, Walter. *The English Novel*, 253–75. London: John Murray. New York: Scribner, 1894.

Saintsbury, George. *A History of Nineteenth Century Literature (1780–1895)*. London: Macmillan, 1896.

Jack, Adolphus A. *Essays on the Novel as Illustrated by Scott and Miss Austen*. London and New York: Macmillan, 1897.

Twain, Mark [Samuel Langhorne Clemens]. *Following the Equator*. 3 vols. New York: Doubleday & McClure, 1897.

Gosse, Edmund. *A Short History of Modern English Literature*. London: Heinemann, 1898.

Cross, Wilbur L. "Jane Austen: The Critic of Romance and Manners." *The Development of the English Novel*, 114–24. New York and London: Macmillan, 1899.

Gwynn, Stephen. "The Decay of Sensibility." *Cornhill* n.s. 7 (1899): 18–30. Reprinted in *The Decay of Sensibility and Other Essays and Sketches*, 1–33. London and New York: John Lane, The Bodley Head, 1900.

Oliphant, James. *Victorian Novelists*, 14–30. London: Blackie & Son, 1899.

Pollock, Walter H. *Jane Austen: Her Contemporaries and Herself: An Essay in Criticism*. London: Longmans, Green, 1899.

Walkley, Arthur B. *Frames of Mind*, 107–12. London: Grant Richards, 1899.

1900s

Stoddard, Francis H. *The Evolution of the English Novel.* New York and London: Macmillan, 1900.

Hill, Constance. *Jane Austen: Her Homes and Her Friends.* London and New York: John Lane, 1901.

Howells, William Dean. *Heroines of Fiction,* 1:37–78. London and New York: Harper & Bros., 1901.

Bonnell, Henry H. *Charlotte Brontë, George Eliot, Jane Austen: Studies in their Works,* 323–475. New York: Longmans, Green, 1902.

Fitzgerald, Percy. "Jane Austen's Novels." *Gentleman's Magazine* 295 (1903): 399–413.

Garnett, Richard, and Edmund Gosse. *English Literature: An Illustrated Record in Four Volumes,* 4:91–97. London: William Heinemann; New York: Macmillan, 1903.

Dawson, William J. *The Makers of English Fiction,* 38–52. New York: Revell, 1905.

James, Henry. *The Question of Our Speech: The Lesson of Balzac: Two Lectures.* Boston: Houghton Mifflin, 1905.

Mitton, Geraldine E. *Jane Austen and Her Times.* London: Methuen, 1905.

Wilmot-Buxton, Ethel Mary. *A Book of Noble Women,* 207–17. London: Methuen, 1907.

Jackson, Holbrook. *Great English Novelists.* London: R. Richards, 1908.

Burton, Richard. "Realism: Jane Austen." *Masters of the English Novel,* 102–22. New York: Henry Holt, 1909.

Helm, William H. *Jane Austen and Her Country-House Comedy.* London: Eveleigh Nash, 1909.

Magnus, Laurie. *English Literature in the Nineteenth Century,* 49–52. London: Andrew Melrose; New York: Putnam, 1909.

1910s

Whitmore, Clara H. *Women's Work in English Fiction from the Restoration to the Mid-Victorian Period,* 157–78. New York and London: G. P. Putnam's Sons, 1910.

Williams, Harold H. "Jane Austen (1775–1817)." *Two Centuries of the English Novel,* 132–48. London: Smith, Elder, 1911.

Elton, Oliver. *A Survey of English Literature, 1780–1830,* 191–201. London: Edward Arnold, 1912.

Fitzgerald, Percy. *Jane Austen: A Criticism and Appreciation*. London: Jarrold & Sons, 1912.

Lang, Andrew. *History of English Literature from "Beowulf" to Swinburne*, 536–40. London: Longmans Green, 1912.

Austen-Leigh, William, and Richard A. Austen-Leigh. *Jane Austen: Her Life and Letters: A Family Record*. London: Smith, Elder, 1913.

Saintsbury, George. "Scott and Miss Austen." *The English Novel*, 189–210. London: J. M. Dent, 1913.

Warre Cornish, Francis W. *Jane Austen*. English Men of Letters series. London: Macmillan, 1913.

Phelps, William Lyon. "Jane Austen." *Essays on Books*, 129–77. New York: Macmillan, 1914.

Rague, Kate, and Paul Rague. *Jane Austen*. Paris: Bloud & Gay, 1914.

Child, Harold H. "Jane Austen." *Cambridge History of English Literature*, 12:257–71. Cambridge: Cambridge UP, 1915.

Villard, Léonie. *Jane Austen: Sa Vie et Son Oeuvre, 1775–1817*. Saint-Étienne: Société Anonyme de l'Imprimerie Mulcey, 1915. English ed., *Jane Austen: A French Appreciation*, translated by Veronica Lucas. London: Routledge & Sons, 1924.

Phelps, William Lyon. *The Advance of the English Novel*. New York: Dodd, 1916.

Descours, Paul. "The Centenary of Jane Austen." *Positivist Review* 25 (1917): 180–84.

Farrer, Reginald. "Jane Austen, *ob*. July 18 1817." *Quarterly Review* 228 (1917): 1–30.

Leo, Brother [Francis J. G. Meehan]. "Jane Austen and the Comic Spirit." *Catholic World* 106 (1917–18): 752–63.

Mais, Stuart P. B. "The Centenary of Jane Austen." *Fortnightly Review* 108 (1917): 257–66.

Shelley, Henry C. "Centenary of Jane Austen's Death." *Book News Monthly* 35 (1917): 397–99.

Woodbridge, H. E. "Jane Austen." *Texas Review* 3 (1917–18): 195–207.

Johnson, R. Brimley. *The Women Novelists*, 66–130. London: W. Collins & Sons, 1918.

Summers, Montague. "Jane Austen: An Appreciation." *Transactions of the Royal Society of Literature of the United Kingdom* 2nd ser. 36 (1918): 1–33.

Walters, J. Cuming. "Jane Austen: A Centenary Tribute." *Manchester Quarterly* 148 (October 1918): 295–311.

1920s

Austen-Leigh, Mary Augusta. *Personal Aspects of Jane Austen.* London: John Murray, 1920.

Firkins, Oscar W. *Jane Austen.* New York: Henry Holt, 1920.

Bald, Marjory A. *Women Writers of the Nineteenth Century,* 1–27. Cambridge: Cambridge UP, 1923.

Chapman, R. W., ed. *The Novels of Jane Austen: The Text Based on Collations of the Early Editions.* 5 vols. Oxford: Clarendon Press, 1923.

Walkley, Arthur B. "Jane's Prejudice." *More Prejudice,* 26–30. London: Heinemann, 1923.

Woolf, Virginia. "How It Strikes a Contemporary." *Times Literary Supplement,* 25 April 1923. Reprinted in *The Common Reader,* 231–41. 1st series. New York: Harcourt, Brace, Jovanovich, 1925.

Cazamian, Louis, and Émile Legouis. *Histoire de la Litterature Anglaise.* 2 vols. Paris: Hachette, 1924. English ed., *A History of English Literature,* translated by Helen D. Irvine and W. D. MacInnes, 1:944–97. London: J. M. Dent, 1926–27; New York: Macmillan, 1929.

Forster, E. M. Review of *The Novels of Jane Austen. Nation* 34 (5 January 1924): 512. Reprinted in *Abinger Harvest.* London: Edward Arnold, 1936.

Kipling, Rudyard. "The Janeites." *Story-Teller* (May 1924): 139–50. Reprinted in *Debits and Credits,* 147–74. London: Macmillan, 1926.

Woolf, Virginia. "Jane Austen." *The Common Reader,* 134–45. 1st series. New York: Harcourt, Brace, Jovanovich, 1925. Reprint New York: Harvest Books, 1984.

Forster, E. M. "Notes on the English Character." *Atlantic Monthly* 137 (1926): 30–37. Reprinted in *Abinger Harvest,* 3–14. London: Edward Arnold, 1936.

Williams, Orlo. *Some Great English Novels: Studies in the Art of Fiction,* 149–78. London: Macmillan, 1926.

Forster, E. M. *Aspects of the Novel.* London: Edward Arnold, 1927.

Johnson, R. Brimley. *Jane Austen.* London: Sheed & Ward, 1927. Reprinted as *Jane Austen: Her Life, Her Work, Her Family, and Her Critics.* London and Toronto: J. M. Dent & Sons; New York: E. P. Dutton, 1930.

Ralli, Augustus. "The Home-Land of Jane Austen." *Critiques,* 67–92. London: Longmans, Green, 1927.

Garrod, H. W. "Jane Austen: A Depreciation." In *Essays by Divers Hands, being the Transactions of the Royal Society of Literature of the United Kingdom* n.s. 8 (1928): 21–40.

Muir, Edwin. *The Structure of the English Novel*, 42–45. London: Hogarth, 1928.

Keynes, Geoffrey. *Jane Austen: A Bibliography*. London: Nonesuch Press, 1929.

Priestley, J. B. *English Humour*, 116–25. London: Longmans, Green, 1929.

Thomson, Clara Linklater. *Jane Austen: A Survey*. London: Horace Marshall & Son, 1929.

1930s

Ford, Ford Madox. *The English Novel: From the Earliest Days to the Death of Conrad*. London: Constable, 1930.

Lawrence, D. H. *Apropos of Lady Chatterley's Lover*. London: Mandrake Press, 1930.

Bailey, John Cann. *Introductions to Jane Austen*. London: Oxford UP, 1931.

Chapman, R. W. "Jane Austen: A Reply to Mr. Garrod." In *Essays by Divers Hands, being the Transactions of the Royal Society of Literature of the United Kingdom* n.s. 10 (1931): 17–34.

Knight, Grant C. *The Novel in English*, 150–59. New York: Richard C. Smith, 1931.

Collins, Norman. "Jane Austen's Unheavenly World." *The Facts of Fiction*, 104–15. London: Gollancz, 1932.

Lovett, Robert M. and Helen S. Hughes. *The History of the Novel in England*, 165–71. Boston: Houghton Mifflin, 1932.

Rhydderch, David. *Jane Austen: Her Life and Art*. London: Jonathan Cape, 1932.

Edgar, Pelham. *The Art of the Novel from 1700 to the Present Time*, 93–116. New York: Macmillan, 1933.

O'Malley, Ida B. *Women in Subjection: A Study of the Lives of Englishwomen before 1832*. London: Duckworth, 1933.

Moore, Virginia. *Distinguished Women Writers*, 97–107. New York: E. P. Dutton, 1934.

Rawlence, Guy. *Jane Austen*. Great Lives series. London: Duckworth, 1934.

Baker, Ernest A. *The History of the English Novel*. Vol. 6, *Edgeworth, Austen, Scott*, 57–121. London: H. F. & G. Witherby, 1935.

Cecil, David. *Jane Austen*. Cambridge: Cambridge UP, 1935.

Clarke, Isabel C. *Six Portraits*, 93–134. London: Hutchinson, 1935.

Squire, John Collins. "Jane Austen." *Reflections and Memories*, 254–73. London: Heinemann, 1935.

Lawrence, Margaret. *The School of Femininity*, 32–59. New York: Frederick Stokes, 1936.

Rinaker, Clarissa. "A Psychoanalytical Note on Jane Austen." *Psychoanalytical Quarterly* 5 (1936): 108–15.

Seymour, Beatrice Kean. *Jane Austen: Study for a Portrait*. London: Michael Joseph, 1937.

Jenkins, Elizabeth. *Jane Austen: A Biography*. London: Gollancz, 1938.

Wilson, Mona. "Jane Austen 1775–1817." *Jane Austen and Some Contemporaries*, 1–42. London: Cresset, 1938.

Gorer, Geoffrey. "The Myth in Jane Austen." *Life and Letters Today* 21 (May 1939): 38–44. Reprinted in *American Imago* 2.3 (1941): 197–204. Reprinted in *Five Approaches to Literary Criticism*, edited by Wilbur S. Scott, 91–98. New York and London: Macmillan, 1962.

Harding, Denys Wyatt. "Regulated Hatred: An Aspect of the Work of Jane Austen." *Scrutiny* 8 (1939–40): 346–62. Reprinted in *Regulated Hatred and Other Essays on Jane Austen*, edited by Monica Lawlor, 1–26. London: Atlantic Highlands, NJ: Athlone Press, 1998.

Lascelles, Mary. *Jane Austen and Her Art*. Oxford: Clarendon Press, 1939.

1940s

Chapman, R. W. "Jane Austen (1775–1817)." *The Cambridge Bibliography of English Literature*, edited by F. W. Bateson, 3:381–84. Cambridge: Cambridge UP, 1940.

Leavis, Q. D. "A Critical Theory of Jane Austen's Writings." *Scrutiny* 10 (1941–42): 61–87, 114–42, 272–94; *Scrutiny* 12 (1944–45): 104–19. Reprinted in *The Englishness of the English Novel*. Vol. 1 of *Collected Essays*, edited by G. Singh, 61–146. New York: Cambridge UP, 1983.

Gerould, Gordon. *The Patterns of English and American Fiction: A History*. Boston: Little, Brown, 1942.

Wagenknecht, Edward. *Cavalcade of the English Novel*, 142–51. New York: Holt, Rinehart & Winston, 1943.

Wilson, Edmund. "A Long Talk about Jane Austen." *New Yorker* 20 (24 June 1944): 70, 72–74, 77–78. Reprinted in *Edmund Wilson: Literary Essays and Reviews of the 1930s–40s*, 620–35. New York: Library of America, 2007.

Kliger, Samuel. "Jane Austen's *Pride and Prejudice* in the Eighteenth Century Mode." *University of Toronto Quarterly* 16 (1946–47): 357–70.

MacCarthy, Bridget G. *The Later Women Novelists, 1744–1818: The Female Pen*, 235–81. Cork, Ireland: Cork UP; Oxford: Blackwell, 1947.

Aldington, Richard. *Jane Austen*. Pasadena, CA: Ampersand Press, 1948.

Chapman, R. W. *Jane Austen: Facts and Problems.* Oxford: Clarendon Press, 1948.

Chew, Samuel C. *A Literary History of England*, edited by Albert C. Baugh, et al., 4:1200–1206. New York: Appleton Century Crofts, 1948.

Leavis, F. R. *The Great Tradition: George Eliot, Henry James, Joseph Conrad.* London: Chatto & Windus, 1948.

Schorer, Mark. "Fiction and the 'Matrix of Analogy.'" *Kenyon Review* 11 (1949): 539–60.

1950s

Altick, Richard D. *The Scholar Adventurers.* New York: Macmillan, 1950.

Kennedy, Margaret. *Jane Austen.* London: Arthur Baker, 1950.

Kettle, Arnold. *An Introduction to the English Novel*, 1:90–104. London: Hutchinson's University Library, 1951.

Neill, S. Diana. *A Short History of the English Novel.* London: Jarrolds, 1951; New York: Macmillan, 1952. Rev. ed., New York: Collier; London: Collier-Macmillan, 1964.

Warner, Sylvia Townsend. *Jane Austen.* Writers and Their Work Series. London: Longmans, 1951. Rev. ed., London: Longmans, 1957.

Mudrick, Marvin. *Jane Austen: Irony as Defense and Discovery.* Princeton, NJ: Princeton UP, 1952.

Chapman, R. W. *Jane Austen: A Critical Bibliography.* Oxford: Clarendon Press, 1953.

King, Noel J. "Jane Austen in France." *Nineteenth-Century Fiction* 8 (1953–54): 1–26.

Rubinstein, Annette T. "Jane Austen." *The Great Tradition in English Literature from Shakespeare to Shaw*, 1:328–74. New York: Citadel Press, 1953.

Van Ghent, Dorothy. *The English Novel: Form and Function*, 99–112, 346–59. New York: Holt, Rinehart & Winston, 1953.

Wright, Andrew H. *Jane Austen's Novels: A Study in Structure.* London: Chatto & Windus, 1953.

Allen, Walter. *The English Novel: A Short Critical History*, 113–26. New York: E. P. Dutton, 1954.

O'Connor, Frank [Michael Donovan]."Jane Austen and the Flight from Fancy." *Yale Review* 45 (1955–56): 31–47. Reprinted in *The Mirror in the Roadway*, 17–41. New York: Knopf, 1956.

Bush, Douglas. "Mrs. Bennet and the Dark Gods: The Truth about Jane Austen." *Sewanee Review* 64 (1956): 591–96. Reprinted in *Engaged and Disengaged*, 20–26. Cambridge, MA: Harvard UP, 1966.

Freeman, Kathleen. *T'Other Miss Austen*. London: Macdonald, 1956.

Schorer, Mark. "Pride Unprejudiced." *Kenyon Review* 19 (1956): 72–91.

Harding, Denys Wyatt. "Jane Austen and Moral Judgment." In *From Blake To Byron*, edited by Boris Ford, 51–59. Harmondsworth: Penguin, 1957.

Mullik, B. R. *Jane Austen*. Studies in Novelists for M.A. and B.A. Students of English Literature in Indian Universities, 2. New Delhi: S. Chand & Co., 1957.

Trilling, Lionel. "*Emma*." *Encounter* 8.6 (June 1957): 49–59. Reprinted in *Beyond Culture: Essays on Literature and Learning*. New York: Viking, 1965.

———. "*Emma* and the Legend of Jane Austen." Introduction to *Emma*. Boston: Houghton Mifflin, 1957.

Babb, Howard S. "Dialogue with Feeling: A Note on *Pride and Prejudice*." *Kenyon Review* 20 (1958): 203–16.

Leavis, Q. D. "Introduction to *Mansfield Park*." London: Macdonald, 1958. Reprinted in *The Englishness of the English Novel*. Vol. 1 of *Collected Essays*, edited by G. Singh, 161–94. New York: Cambridge UP, 1983.

McKillop, Alan D. "Critical Realism in *Northanger Abbey*." In *From Jane Austen to Joseph Conrad*, edited by Robert Rathburn and Martin Steinman, 35–45. Minneapolis: U of Minnesota P, 1958.

Murrah, Charles. "The Background of *Mansfield Park*." In *From Jane Austen to Joseph Conrad*, edited by Robert Rathburn and Martin Steinman, 23–34. Minneapolis: U of Minnesota P, 1958.

Rathburn, Robert, and Martin Steinman, eds. *From Jane Austen to Joseph Conrad*. Minneapolis: U of Minnesota P, 1958.

Schorer, Mark. "The Humiliation of Emma Woodhouse." *Literary Review* 2 (1959): 547–63. Reprinted in *The World We Imagine: Selected Essays*. New York: Farrar, Straus, & Giroux, 1969.

1960s

Cook, Albert. "Modes of Irony: Jane Austen and Stendhal." *The Meaning of Fiction*, 38–63. Detroit: Wayne State UP, 1960.

Daiches, David. *A Critical History of English Literature*, 3:743–65. London: Secker & Warburg, 1960.

Kirschbaum, Leo. "The World of *Pride and Prejudice*." In *Twelve Original Essays on Great English Novels*, edited by Charles Shapiro, 69–85. Detroit: Wayne State UP, 1960.

Krieger, Murray. *The Tragic Vision: Variations on a Theme in Literary Interpretation*. New York: Holt, Rinehart, Winston, 1960.

Mullik, B. R. *Jane Austen's "Emma."* Critical Studies for M.A. & B.A. Students of English Literature in Indian Universities, 14. New Delhi: S. Chand & Co., 1960.

Stevenson, Lionel. *The English Novel: A Panorama*, 185–93. Boston: Houghton Mifflin; London: Constable, 1960.

Booth, Wayne. "Point of View and Control of Distance in *Emma*." *The Rhetoric of Fiction*, 243–66. Chicago: U of Chicago P, 1961.

Heath, William, ed. *Discussions of Jane Austen*. Boston: D. C. Heath, 1961.

Babb, Howard S. *Jane Austen's Novels: The Fabric of Dialogue*. Columbus: Ohio State UP, 1962.

Craig, G. Armour. "Jane Austen's *Emma*: The Truths and Disguises of Human Discourse." In *In Defense of Reading: A Reader's Approach to Literary Criticism*, edited by R. A. Brower and Richard Poirier, 235–55. New York: E. P. Dutton, 1962.

Dalglish, Jack. *"Pride and Prejudice": Jane Austen*. Notes on English Literature. Oxford: Basil Blackwell, 1962.

Farrar, Sidney. *Jane Austen: "Northanger Abbey."* Guides to English Literature. London: Hulton Educational Publications, 1962.

Lobb, Kenneth M. *Jane Austen: "Pride and Prejudice."* Guides to English Literature. London: Hulton Educational Publications, 1962.

Marshall, Percy. *Masters of the English Novel*. London: Dennis Dobson, 1962.

Poirier, Richard. "Mark Twain, Jane Austen, and the Imagination of Society." In *In Defense of Reading: A Reader's Approach to Literary Criticism*, edited by R. A. Brower and Richard Poirier, 282–309. New York: E. P. Dutton, 1962.

Southam, B. C. "Mrs. Leavis and Miss Austen: The 'Critical Theory' Reconsidered." *Nineteenth-Century Fiction* 17 (1962–63): 21–32.

Drew, Elizabeth. *The Novel: A Modern Guide to Fifteen English Masterpieces*, 95–110. New York: Dell, 1963.

Liddell, Robert. *The Novels of Jane Austen*. London: Longmans, Green, 1963.

Renwick, William L. *English Literature, 1789–1815*. Vol. 9 of *The Oxford History of English Literature*, edited by F. P. Wilson and Bonamy Dobrée, 89–100. Oxford: Clarendon Press, 1963.

Watt, Ian, ed. *Jane Austen: A Collection of Critical Essays*. Twentieth Century Views. Englewood Cliffs, NJ: Prentice-Hall, 1963.

Karl, Frederick R. *An Age of Fiction: The Nineteenth Century British Novel*. New York: Noonday Press, 1964. Reprinted as *A Reader's Guide to the Nineteenth-Century British Novel*. New York: Octagon, 1972.

Southam, B. C. *Jane Austen's Literary Manuscripts: A Study of the Novelist's Development Through the Surviving Papers.* London: Oxford UP, 1964. Rev. ed., London: Athlone, 2004.

Ten Harmsel, Henrietta. *Jane Austen: A Study in Fictional Conventions.* The Hague: Mouton, 1964.

Craik, Wendy Ann. *Jane Austen: The Six Novels.* London: Methuen; New York: Barnes & Noble, 1965.

Demarest, David P., Jr. "*Reductio ad Absurdum*: Jane Austen's Art of Satiric Qualification." *Six Satirists.* Carnegie Series in English, No. 9, 51–68. Pittsburgh: Carnegie Institute of Technology, 1965.

Gillie, Christopher. "The Heroine Victim." *Character in English Literature,* 117–24. London: Chatto & Windus, 1965.

Litz, A. Walton. *Jane Austen: A Study of Her Artistic Development.* London: Chatto & Windus; New York: Oxford UP, 1965.

Steeves, Harrison Ross. *Before Jane Austen: The Shaping of the English Novel in the Eighteenth Century.* New York: Holt, Rinehart, & Winston, 1965; London: Allen & Unwin, 1965.

Bradbrook, Frank W. *Jane Austen and Her Predecessors.* Cambridge: Cambridge UP, 1966.

Donovan, Robert A. "*Mansfield Park* and Jane Austen's Moral Universe." *The Shaping Vision: Imagination in the English Novel from Defoe to Dickens,* 140–72. Ithaca, NY: Cornell UP, 1966.

Lodge, David. *Language of Fiction: Essays in Criticism and Verbal Analysis of the English Novel,* 94–113. London: Routledge & Kegan Paul; New York: Columbia UP, 1966.

Ryle, Gilbert. "Jane Austen and the Moralists." *Oxford Review* 1 (1966): 5–18. Reprinted in *English Literature and British Philosophy: A Collection of Essays,* edited by S. P. Rosenbaum, 168–84. Chicago: U of Chicago P, 1971.

Sherry, Norman. *Jane Austen.* With preface by Kenneth Gross. Literature in Perspective Series. London: Evans Brothers, 1966.

Walcutt, Charles C. "Jane Austen's Minuet: *Pride and Prejudice*." *Man's Changing Mask: Modes and Methods of Characterization in Fiction,* 71–90. Minneapolis: U of Minnesota P, 1966.

Collected Reports of the Jane Austen Society, 1949–1965. London: Dawson, 1967.

Crane, Ronald S. "Jane Austen: *Persuasion*." *The Idea of the Humanities and Other Essays Critical and Historical,* 2:283–302. Chicago and London: U of Chicago P, 1967.

Fleishman, Avrom. *A Reading of "Mansfield Park": An Essay in Critical Synthesis.* Minneapolis: U of Minnesota P, 1967.

Lerner, Laurence. *The Truthtellers: Jane Austen, George Eliot, D. H. Lawrence.* London: Chatto & Windus; New York: Schocken Books, 1967.

Marshall, William H. *The World of the Victorian Novel,* 37–72. New York: A. S. Barnes; London: Thomas Yoseloff, 1967.

Paulson, Ronald. *Satire and the Novel in Eighteenth-Century England,* 291–306. New Haven and London: Yale UP, 1967.

Waldron, Philip. "Style in *Emma.*" *Approaches to the Novel,* edited by John Colmer, 59–70. Edinburgh: Oliver & Boyd, 1967.

Wiesenfarth, Joseph. *The Errand of Form: An Assay of Jane Austen's Art.* New York: Fordham UP, 1967.

Harding, D. W. "Character and Caricature in Jane Austen." In *Critical Essays on Jane Austen,* edited by B. C. Southam, 83–106. London: Routledge & Kegan Paul, 1968; New York: Barnes & Noble, 1969.

Inglis, Fred. *An Essential Discipline: An Introduction to Literary Criticism,* 212–24. London: Methuen Educational, 1968.

Lodge, David, ed. *Jane Austen: 'Emma' — A Casebook.* London: Macmillan, 1968. Rev. ed., London: Macmillan Education, 1991.

Moler, Kenneth L. *Jane Austen's Art of Allusion.* Lincoln: U of Nebraska P, 1968.

Southam, B. C., ed. *Critical Essays on Jane Austen.* London: Routledge & Kegan Paul, 1968; New York: Barnes & Noble, 1969.

————, ed. *Jane Austen: The Critical Heritage.* London: Routledge & Kegan Paul; New York: Barnes & Noble, 1968.

Corsa, Helen S. "A Fair but Frozen Maid: A Study of Jane Austen's *Emma.*" *Literature and Psychology* 19 (1969): 101–24.

Craik, Wendy Ann. *Jane Austen in Her Time.* London: Thomas Nelson & Sons; New York: New York UP, 1969.

Mews, Hazel. *Frail Vessels: Woman's Role in Women's Novels from Fanny Burney to George Eliot.* London: Athlone Press, 1969.

Myers, Sylvia H. "Womanhood in Jane Austen's Novels." *Novel* 3 (1969–70): 225–32.

Rubenstein, Elliot L., ed. *Twentieth Century Interpretations of "Pride and Prejudice": A Collection of Critical Essays.* Englewood Cliffs, NJ: Prentice-Hall, 1969.

1970s

Gooneratne, Yasmine. *Jane Austen.* Cambridge: Cambridge UP, 1970.

Harding, Denys W. "Two Aspects of Jane Austen's Development." *Theoria* 35 (1970): 1–16.

Millett, Kate. *Sexual Politics.* Garden City, NY: Doubleday, 1970.

O'Neill, Judith, ed. *Critics on Jane Austen.* London: Allen & Unwin; Coral Gables, FL: U of Miami P, 1970.

Phillips, Kenneth C. *Jane Austen's English.* London: Deutsch, 1970.

Pritchett, V. S. *George Meredith and English Comedy.* London: Chatto & Windus; New York: Random House, 1970.

Williams, Raymond. *The English Novel from Dickens to Lawrence.* London: Chatto & Windus; New York: Oxford UP, 1970.

Duckworth, Alistair. *The Improvement of the Estate: A Study of Jane Austen's Novels.* Baltimore and London: Johns Hopkins UP, 1971.

Krieger, Murray. *The Classic Vision: The Retreat from Extremity in Modern Literature,* 221–43. Baltimore and London: Johns Hopkins UP, 1971.

Kroeber, Karl. *Styles in Fictional Structure: The Art of Jane Austen, Charlotte Brontë and George Eliot.* Princeton, NJ: Princeton UP, 1971.

Pilgrim, Constance. *Dear Jane: A Biographical Study of Jane Austen.* London: William Kimber, 1971.

Burgan, Mary Alice. "Feeling and Control: A Study of the Proposal Scenes in Jane Austen's Major Novels." In *The English Novel in the Nineteenth Century,* edited by George Goodin, 25–51. Urbana: U of Illinois P, 1972.

Hodge, Jane Aiken. *The Double Life of Jane Austen.* London: Hodder & Stoughton, 1972. Issued as *Only a Novel: The Double Life of Jane Austen.* New York: Coward, McCann & Geoghegan, 1972.

Kiely, Robert. *The Romantic Novel in England.* Cambridge, MA: Harvard UP, 1972.

Page, Norman. *The Language of Jane Austen.* Oxford: Basil Blackwell, 1972.

Trilling, Lionel. *Sincerity and Authenticity,* 72–83. London: Oxford UP; Cambridge, MA: Harvard UP, 1972.

Bradbury, Malcolm. "Persuasions: Moral Comedy in *Emma* and *Persuasion.*" *Possibilities: Essays on the State of the Novel,* 55–78. London: Oxford UP, 1973.

Brown, Lloyd W. *Bits of Ivory: Narrative Techniques in Jane Austen's Fiction.* Baton Rouge: Louisiana State UP, 1973.

Halperin, John. *The Language of Meditation: Four Studies in Nineteenth-Century Fiction,* 19–50. Ilfracombe, England: Stockwell, 1973.

Hardwick, Michael. *A Guide to Jane Austen.* Reading, England: Osprey; New York: Scribner's, 1973.

Mansell, Darrel. *The Novels of Jane Austen: An Interpretation.* London: Macmillan, 1973.

Nardin, Jane. *Those Elegant Decorums: The Concept of Propriety in Jane Austen's Novels.* Albany: State U of New York P, 1973.

Pinion, F. B. *A Jane Austen Companion: A Critical Survey and Reference Book.* London: Macmillan, 1973.

Roth, Barry, and Joel C. Weinsheimer, comps. *An Annotated Bibliography of Jane Austen Studies, 1952–1972.* Charlottesville: UP of Virginia, 1973.

Tave, Stuart M. *Some Words of Jane Austen.* Chicago and London: U of Chicago P, 1973.

Beer, Patricia. *Reader, I Married Him,* 45–83. London: Macmillan; New York: Barnes & Noble, 1974.

Gillie, Christopher. *A Preface to Jane Austen.* London: Longman, 1974.

Halperin, John. *Egoism and Self-Discovery in the Victorian Novel: Studies in the Ordeal of Knowledge,* 1–30. New York: Burt Franklin, 1974.

Kestner, Joseph. *Jane Austen: Spatial Structure of Thematic Variations.* Salzburg: Institut für Englische Sprache und Literatur, 1974.

Leeming, Glenda. *Who's Who in Jane Austen and the Brontës.* London: Elm Tree Books, 1974.

Whitten, Benjamin. *Jane Austen's Comedy of Feeling: A Critical Analysis of 'Persuasion.'* Ankara: Hacettepe UP, 1974.

Williams, Ioan. "The Novels of Jane Austen: Conservatism and Innovation." *The Realist Novel in England: A Study in Development,* 12–24. London: Macmillan, 1974.

Bush, Douglas. *Jane Austen.* Masters of World Literature Series. New York: Macmillan, 1975.

Butler, Marilyn. *Jane Austen and the War of Ideas.* Oxford: Clarendon Press, 1975.

Devlin, David D. *Jane Austen and Education.* London: Macmillan, 1975.

Ek, Grete. "Mistaken Conduct and Proper 'Feeling': A Study of Jane Austen's *Pride and Prejudice.*" In *Fair Forms: Essays in English Literature from Spenser to Jane Austen,* edited by Maren-Sofie Røstvig, 178–202. Cambridge: D. S. Brewer, 1975.

Goubert, Pierre. *Jane Austen: Étude Psychologique de la Romancière.* Paris: Presses Universitaires de France, 1975.

Halperin, John, ed. *Jane Austen: Bicentenary Essays.* Cambridge: Cambridge UP, 1975.

Hardy, Barbara. *A Reading of Jane Austen.* London: Peter Owen, 1975.

Mann, Renate. *Jane Austen: Die Rhetorik der Moral.* Bern and Frankfurt am Main: Lang, 1975.

Nineteenth-Century Fiction 30.3 (December 1975). Special Issue on Jane Austen.

Rodway, Allan. *English Comedy: Its Role and Nature from Chaucer to the Present Day*, 182–201. London: Chatto & Windus, 1975.

Southam, B. C. *Jane Austen*. Writers and Their Work Series. London: Longman, 1975.

Spacks, Patricia Meyer. *The Female Imagination: A Literary and Psychological Investigation of Women's Writing*. New York: Knopf, 1975. London: Allen & Unwin, 1976.

Studies in the Novel 7.1 (Spring 1975). Special Issue on Jane Austen.

Weinsheimer, Joel C., ed. *Jane Austen Today*. Athens: U of Georgia P, 1975.

Harrison, Bernard. "Muriel Spark and Jane Austen." In *The Modern English Novel: The Reader, The Writer, and The Work*, edited by Gabriel Josipovici. New York: Barnes and Noble, 1976.

Lee, Hermione. "'Taste' and 'Tenderness' as Moral Values in the Novels of Jane Austen." In *Literature of the Romantic Period, 1750–1850*, edited by R. T. Davies and B. G. Beatty, 82–95. Liverpool English Texts and Studies, 14. Liverpool: Liverpool UP, 1976.

McMaster, Juliet, ed. *Jane Austen's Achievement*. London: Macmillan, 1976.

Moers, Ellen. *Literary Women: The Great Writers*. New York: Doubleday, 1976. London: W. H. Allen, 1977. Reprinted New York: Oxford UP, 1985.

Rees, Joan. *Jane Austen: Woman and Writer*. London: Robert Hale; New York: St. Martin's, 1976.

Tomlinson, Thomas B. *The English Middle-Class Novel*, 21–51. London: Macmillan, 1976.

Trilling, Lionel. "Why We Read Jane Austen." *TLS* 5 (March 1976): 250–52. Reprinted in *The Last Decade: Essays and Reviews 1965–1975*, edited by Diana Trilling, 204–25. New York: Harcourt Brace Jovanovich, 1979.

Wordsworth Circle 7.4 (Autumn 1976). Special Issue on Jane Austen.

Cockshut, A. O. J. *Man and Woman: A Study of Love and the Novel, 1740–1940*, 54–72. London: Collins, 1977.

Collected Reports of the Jane Austen Society, 1966–1975. Folkestone: Dawson, 1977.

Lovell, Terry. "Jane Austen and Gentry Society." In *Literature, Society, and the Sociology of Literature*, ed. Francis Barker et al., 118–32. Colchester: U of Essex P, 1977.

Skilton, David. "Austen, Scott and the Victorians." *The English Novel: Defoe to the Victorians*, 80–98. Comparative Literature Series. Newton Abbott, England: David & Charles; New York: Barnes & Noble, 1977.

Southall, Raymond. "The Social World of Jane Austen." *Literature, the Individual, and Society*, 105–39. London: Lawrence and Wishart, 1977.

Todd, Janet. "Female Friendship in Jane Austen's Novels." *Journal of the Rutgers University Libraries* 39 (1977): 29–43.

Trowbridge, Hoyt. "Mind, Body, and Estate: Jane Austen's System of Values." *From Dryden to Jane Austen: Essays on English Critics and Writers, 1660–1818*, 275–92. Albuquerque: U of New Mexico P, 1977.

Zeman, Anthea. *Presumptuous Girls: Women and Their World in the Serious Woman's Novel*. London: Weidenfeld & Nicolson, 1977.

Auerbach, Nina. *Communities of Women: An Idea in Fiction*. Cambridge, MA: Harvard UP, 1978.

Cecil, David. *A Portrait of Jane Austen*. London: Constable, 1978. New York: Hill & Wang, 1979.

Grylls, David. *Guardians and Angels: Parents and Children in Nineteenth-Century Literature*, 111–32. London: Faber & Faber, 1978.

Kennard, Jean E. "Jane Austen: The Establishment." *Victims of Convention*, 21–45. Hamden, CT: Archon Books, 1978.

McMaster, Juliet. *Jane Austen on Love*. English Literary Studies Monographs, 13. Victoria, BC: U of Victoria P, 1978.

Paris, Bernard J. *Character and Conflict in Jane Austen's Novels: A Psychological Approach*. Detroit: Wayne State UP, 1978.

Robinson, Lillian S. "Why Marry Mr. Collins?" *Sex, Class, and Culture*, 178–99. Bloomington: Indiana UP, 1978.

Said, Edward W. *Orientalism*. New York: Vintage Books, 1978.

Siefert, Susan. *The Dilemma of the Talented Heroine: A Study in Nineteenth-Century Fiction*. St. Albans, VT: Eden Press, 1978.

Sternberg, Meir. "The Rhetoric of Anticipatory Caution: First Impressions in 'First Impressions' and the Poetics of Jane Austen." *Expositional Modes and Temporal Ordering in Fiction*, 129–58. Baltimore: Johns Hopkins UP, 1978.

Brown, Julia Prewitt. *Jane Austen's Novels: Social Change and Literary Form*. Cambridge, MA: Harvard UP, 1979.

Gilbert, Sandra M. and Susan Gubar. *The Madwoman in the Attic: The Woman Writer and the Nineteenth-Century Literary Imagination*, 107–83. New Haven, CT: Yale UP, 1979.

Monaghan, David. "Jane Austen and the Feminist Critics." *Room of One's Own: A Feminist Journal of Literature and Criticism* 4.3 (1979): 34–39.

Roberts, Warren. *Jane Austen and the French Revolution*. New York: St. Martin's, 1979.

Voss-Clesly, Patricia. *Tendencies of Character Depiction in the Domestic Novels of Burney, Edgeworth, and Austen: A Consideration of Subjective and Objective World*. Salzburg: Inst. f. Anglistik u. Amerikanistik, Univ. Salzburg, 1979.

1980s

Brewer, Derek. "Mainly on Jane Austen." *Symbolic Stories: Traditional Narratives of the Family Drama in English Literature*, 148–67. Totowa, NJ: Rowman & Littlefield, 1980.

De Rose, Peter L. *Jane Austen and Samuel Johnson*. Washington, DC: UP of America, 1980.

MacDonald, Susan Peck. "Jane Austen and the Tradition of the Absent Mother." In *The Lost Tradition: Mothers and Daughters in Literature*, edited by Cathy Davidson and E. M. Broner, 58–69. New York: Ungar, 1980.

Monaghan, David. *Jane Austen: Structure and Social Vision*. Totowa, NJ: Barnes & Noble, 1980.

Morgan, Susan. *In the Meantime: Character and Perception in Jane Austen's Fiction*. Chicago: U of Chicago P, 1980.

Nabokov, Vladimir. *Lectures on Literature*, edited by Fredson Bowers. New York: Harcourt Brace Jovanovich, 1980.

Polhemus, Robert M. "Austen's *Emma* (1816): The Comedy of Union." *Comic Faith: The Great Tradition from Austen to Joyce*, 24–59. Chicago: U of Chicago P, 1980.

Todd, Janet. *Women's Friendship in Literature*. New York: Columbia UP, 1980.

Wilt, Judith. *Ghosts of the Gothic: Austen, Eliot, and Lawrence*. Princeton, NJ: Princeton UP, 1980.

Aers, David. "Community and Morality: Towards Reading Jane Austen." In *Romanticism and Ideology: Studies in English Writing, 1765–1830*, edited by David Aers, Jonathan Cook, and David Punter, 118–36. Boston: Routledge & Kegan Paul, 1981.

Butler, Marilyn. "Novels for the Gentry." *Romantics, Rebels, and Reactionaries: English Literature and its Background, 1760–1830*, 94–112. New York: Oxford UP, 1981.

Harris, Laurie, ed. *Nineteenth-Century Literature Criticism*. Detroit: Gale, 1981.

Levine, George. *The Realistic Imagination: English Fiction from Frankenstein to Lady Chatterley*. Chicago: U of Chicago P, 1981.

MacIntyre, Alisdair. *After Virtue: A Study in Moral Theory*. London: Duckworth; Notre Dame, IN: U of Notre Dame P, 1981.

McMaster, Juliet, and Rowland McMaster. *The Novel from Sterne to James: Essays on the Relation of Literature to Life.* Totowa, NJ: Barnes & Noble, 1981.

Miller, D. A. "The Danger of Narrative in Jane Austen." *Narrative and Its Discontents: Problems of Closure in the Traditional Novel,* 3–106. Princeton, NJ: Princeton UP, 1981.

Monaghan, David, ed. *Jane Austen in a Social Context.* Totowa, NJ: Barnes & Noble, 1981.

Newton, Judith L. *Women, Power, and Subversion: Social Strategies in British Fiction, 1778–1860.* Athens: U of Georgia P, 1981.

Odmark, John. *An Understanding of Jane Austen's Novels: Character, Value, and Ironic Perspective.* Oxford: Basil Blackwell, 1981; Totowa, NJ: Barnes & Noble, 1981.

Phelan, James. "Determinate and Indeterminate Value in the Linguistic System: J. Hillis Miller and the Language of *Persuasion.*" *Worlds from Words: A Theory of Language in Fiction,* 117–52. Chicago: U of Chicago P, 1981.

Webb, Igor. *From Custom to Capital: The English Novel and the Industrial Revolution.* Ithaca, NY: Cornell UP, 1981.

Wilt, Judith. "Jane Austen's Men: Inside/Outside 'The Mystery.'" In *Men by Women,* edited by Janet Todd, 59–76. New York: Holmes & Meier, 1981.

Barfoot, C. C. *The Thread of Connection: Aspects of Fate in the Novels of Jane Austen and Others.* Amsterdam: Rodolphi, 1982.

Brownstein, Rachel W. "Getting Married: Jane Austen." *Becoming a Heroine: Reading About Women in Novels,* 79–136. New York: Viking, 1982.

Figes, Eva. "The Supremacy of Sense." *Sex and Subterfuge: Women Novelists to 1850,* 76–112. London: Macmillan, 1982.

Gilson, David. *A Bibliography of Jane Austen.* Oxford: Clarendon Press, 1982. Updated ed., Winchester, UK: St. Paul's Bibliographies; New Castle, DE: Oak Knoll Press, 1997.

Kubal, David. "Jane Austen's 'Midsummer Night's Dream.'" *The Consoling Intelligence: Responses to Literary Modernism,* 33–51. Baton Rouge: Louisiana State UP, 1982.

Ram, Atma. *Heroines in Jane Austen: A Study in Character.* New Delhi: Kalyani, 1982.

Scott, P. G. M. *Jane Austen: A Reassessment.* London: Vision P; Totowa, NJ: Barnes & Noble, 1982.

Anastaplo, George. "Jane Austen (1775–1817)." *The Artist as Thinker: From Shakespeare to Joyce.* Chicago and Athens, OH: Swallow Press, 1983.

Ermarth, Elizabeth. "Jane Austen's Critique of Distance." *Realism and Consensus in the English Novel,* 144–77. Princeton, NJ: Princeton UP, 1983.

Fergus, Jan. *Jane Austen and the Didactic Novel*. Totowa, NJ: Barnes & Noble, 1983.

James, Selma. *The Ladies and the Mammies: Jane Austen and Jean Rhys*. Old Market, Bristol, England: Falling Wall Press, 1983.

Keener, Frederick W. "The Philosophical Tale, Jane Austen, and the Novel." *The Chain of Becoming: The Philosophical Tale, The Novel, and a Neglected Realism of the Enlightenment*, 241–307. New York: Columbia UP, 1983.

Kirkham, Margaret. *Jane Austen: Feminism and Fiction*. Totowa, NJ: Barnes & Noble, 1983.

Price, Martin. "Austen: Manners and Morals." *Forms of Life: Character and Moral Imagination in the Novel*, 65–89. New Haven, CT: Yale UP, 1983.

Smith, LeRoy. *Jane Austen and the Drama of Woman*. New York: St. Martin's, 1983.

Todd, Janet, ed. *Jane Austen: New Perspectives*. New York: Holmes & Meier, 1983.

Tucker, George Holbert. *A Goodly Heritage: Jane Austen's Family*. Thrupp, Gloucester, England: Sutton, 1983.

Caywood, Cynthia. "*Pride and Prejudice* and the Belief in Choice: Jane Austen's Fantastical Vision." In *Portraits of Marriage in Literature*, edited by Anne C. Hargrove and Maurine Magliocco, 31–37. Macomb: Western Illinois UP, 1984.

Edwards, Lee R. "Heroes into Heroines: The Limits of Comedy in *Emma*, *Jane Eyre*, and *Middlemarch*." *Psyche as Hero: Female Heroism and Fictional Form*, 62–103. Middletown, CT: Wesleyan UP, 1984.

Furst, Lillian R. "Jane Austen: *Pride and Prejudice*, 1813." *Fictions of Romantic Irony*, 49–67. Cambridge, MA: Harvard UP, 1984.

Halperin, John. *The Life of Jane Austen*. Baltimore: Johns Hopkins UP, 1984.

Hardy, John. *Jane Austen's Heroines: Intimacy in Human Relationships*. Boston: Routledge & Kegan Paul, 1984.

Higbie, Robert. *Character and Structure in the English Novel*. Gainesville: U of Florida P, 1984.

Langland, Elizabeth. "Social Contexts for Judgment of Austen." *Society in the Novel*, 25–44. Chapel Hill: U of North Carolina P, 1984.

Poovey, Mary. *The Proper Lady and the Woman Writer: Ideology as Style in the Works of Mary Wollstonecraft, Mary Shelley, and Jane Austen*. Chicago: U of Chicago P, 1984.

Smith, Grahame. *The Novel and Society: Defoe to George Eliot*. London: Batsford Academic & Educational, 1984.

Vernon, John. "The Breaking up of the Estate: *Persuasion*." *Money and Fiction: Literary Realism in the Nineteenth and Early Twentieth Centuries*, 42–64. Ithaca, NJ: Cornell UP, 1984.

White, James Boyd. "'Conversation, Rational and Playful': The Language of Friendship in Jane Austen's *Emma*." *When Words Lose Their Meaning: Constitutions and Reconstitutions of Language, Character and Community*, 163–69. Chicago: U of Chicago P, 1984.

Williams, Merryn. "Jane Austen." *Women in the English Novel, 1800–1900*, 44–52. New York: St. Martin's, 1984.

Citron, Jo Ann. "Fantasy Life." Review of John Halperin, *The Life of Jane Austen* and John Hardy, *Jane Austen's Heroines: Intimacy in Human Relationships*. *Women's Review of Books* 2.1 (August 1985): 15–16.

Cottom, Daniel. "Jane Austen." *The Civilized Imagination: A Study of Ann Radcliffe, Jane Austen, and Sir Walter Scott*, 69–123. New York: Cambridge UP, 1985.

Duckworth, Alistair M. "Jane Austen's Accommodations." In *The First English Novelists: Essays in Understanding*, edited by J. M. Armistead, 225–67. Knoxville: U of Tennessee P, 1985.

Gard, Roger. *Jane Austen: Emma and Persuasion*. Penguin Masterstudies. New York: Penguin, 1985.

Konigsberg, Ira. "*Pride and Prejudice*: The Paradigmatic Novel." *Narrative Technique in the English Novel: Defoe to Austen*, 213–56. Hamden, CT: Archon Books, 1985.

Lanser, Susan Sniader. "No Connections Subsequent: Jane Austen's World of Sisterhood." In *The Sister Bond: A Feminist View of a Timeless Connection*, edited by Toni A. H. McNaron, 51–67. New York: Pergamon Press, 1985.

Neale, R. S. "Zapp Zapped: Property and Alienation in *Mansfield Park*." *Writing Marxist History: British Society, Economy, and Culture since 1700*, 87–108. New York: Basil Blackwell, 1985.

Roth, Barry, comp. *An Annotated Bibliography of Jane Austen Studies, 1973–83*. Charlottesville: UP of Virginia, 1985.

Bloom, Clive. "Sexuality in Jane Austen's Fanny, and *Mansfield Park*." *The "Occult" Experience and the New Criticism: Daemonism, Sexuality, and the Hidden in Literature*, 12–26. Brighton, Sussex: Harvester P; Totowa, NJ: Barnes & Noble, 1986.

Bloom, Harold, ed. *Jane Austen*. Modern Critical Views. New York: Chelsea House, 1986.

Dalsimer, Katherine. "Late Adolescence: *Persuasion*." *Female Adolescence: Psychoanalytic Reflections on Works of Literature*, 113–38. New Haven, CT: Yale UP, 1986.

Grey, J. David, ed. *The Jane Austen Companion*. With the assistance of Walton Litz and Brian Southam. New York: Macmillan, 1986. Also published as *The Jane Austen Dictionary*. London: Athlone, 1986.

Heilbrun, Carolyn. Review of John Halperin, *The Life of Jane Austen*. *Novel: A Forum in Fiction* 19.2 (Winter 1986): 183–85.

Lane, Maggie. *Jane Austen's England*. New York: St. Martin's, 1986.

Le Faye, Deirdre. Review of John Halperin, *The Life of Jane Austen*. *Review of English Studies* 37 (August 1986): 426–30.

Miller, Jane. *Women Writing About Men*. New York: Pantheon, 1986.

Schofield, Mary Anne, and Cecilia Macheski, eds. *Fetter'd or Free? British Women Novelists, 1670–1815*. Athens: Ohio UP, 1986.

Shaffer, Julie. "Not Subordinate: Empowering Women in the Marriage Plot in the Novels of Fanny Burney, Maria Edgeworth, and Jane Austen." In *Reading with a Difference: Gender, Race, and Cultural Identity*, edited by Arthur F. Marotti, et al., 21–44. Detroit: Wayne State UP, 1986.

Spencer, Jane. "Reformed Heroines: The Didactic Tradition." *The Rise of the Woman Novelist: From Aphra Behn to Jane Austen*, 140–80. New York: Basil Blackwell, 1986.

Sulloway, Alison G. "Jane Austen's Mediative Voice." In *Nineteenth-Century Women Writers of the English-Speaking World*, edited by Rhoda B. Nathan, 193–99. New York and Westport, CT: Greenwood Press, 1986.

Tanner, Tony. *Jane Austen*. Cambridge, MA: Harvard UP, 1986.

Williams, Michael. *Jane Austen: Six Novels and Their Methods*. New York: St. Martin's, 1986.

Armstrong, Nancy. *Desire and Domestic Fiction: A Political History of the Novel*. New York: Oxford UP, 1987.

Boone, Joseph A. "Narrative Structure in the Marriage Tradition: Paradigmatic Plots of Courtship, Seduction, and Wedlock." *Tradition Counter Tradition: Love and the Form of Fiction*, 65–137. Chicago: U of Chicago P, 1987.

Brodsky, Claudia J. "Austen: The Persuasions of Sensibility and Sense." *The Imposition of Form: Studies in Narrative Representation and Knowledge*, 141–87. Princeton, NJ: Princeton UP, 1987.

Burrows, J. F. *Computation into Criticism: A Study of Jane Austen's Novels and an Experiment in Method*. Oxford: Clarendon Press, 1987.

Clayton, Jay. "*Mansfield Park*." *Romantic Vision and the Novel*, 59–80. New York: Cambridge UP, 1987.

Evans, Mary. *Jane Austen and the State*. New York: Tavistock, 1987.

Fulbrook, Kate. "Jane Austen and the Comic Negative." In *Women Reading Women's Writing*, edited by Sue Row, 37–57. New York: St. Martin's, 1987.

Holbrook, David. "The Novel and Moral Concern: *Mansfield Park*." *The Novel and Authenticity*, 21–59. Totowa, NJ: Barnes & Noble, 1987.

Honan, Park. *Jane Austen: Her Life*. London: Weidenfeld & Nicolson, 1987.

Lefkovitz, Lori Hope. "Shaping the Body to Fit the Eye: Austen's *Persuasion* as a Romantic Cinderella." *The Character of Beauty in the Victorian Novel*, 43–57. Ann Arbor, MI: UMI Research Press, 1987.

Morris, Ivor. *Mr. Collins Considered: Approaches to Jane Austen*. New York: Routledge & Kegan Paul, 1987. 2nd ed. issued as *Jane Austen and the Interplay of Character*. London and New Brunswick, NJ: Athlone, 1999.

Musselwhite, David E. "Return to *Mansfield Park*." *Partings Welded Together: Politics and Desire in the Nineteenth-Century English Novel*, 16–42. London and New York: Methuen, 1987.

Sabiston, Elizabeth Jean. "'Emma's Daughters': A Study in Isolation and Creativity." *The Prison of Womanhood: Four Provincial Heroines in Nineteenth-Century Fiction*, 18–41. New York: St. Martin's, 1987.

Southam, B. C., ed. *Jane Austen: The Critical Heritage, 1870–1940*. New York: Routledge & Kegan Paul, 1987.

Vasudeva Reddy, T. *Jane Austen: The Dialectics of Self-Actualisation in Her Novels*. New York: Envoy Press, 1987.

———. *Jane Austen: The Matrix of Matrimony*. Jaipur: Bohra, 1987.

Weissman, Judith. "Jane Austen: Loving and Leaving." *Half Savage and Hardy and Free: Women and Rural Radicalism in the Nineteenth-Century Novel*, 47–75. Middletown, CT: Wesleyan UP, 1987.

Wright, Andrew. "The Emergent Woman." *Fictional Discourse and Historical Space*, 44–73. New York: St. Martin's, 1987.

Armstrong, Isobel. *Jane Austen: Mansfield Park*. New York: Penguin, 1988.

Booth, Wayne C. "Doctrinal Questions in Jane Austen, D. H. Lawrence, and Mark Twain." *The Company We Keep: An Ethics of Fiction*, 421–82. Berkeley: U of California P, 1988.

Dhatwalia, H. R. *Familial Relationships in Jane Austen's Novels*. New Delhi: National Book Organization, 1988.

Dussinger, John A. "'The Language of Real Feeling': Internal Speech in the Jane Austen Novel." In *The Idea of the Novel in the Eighteenth Century*, edited by Robert Uphaus, 97–115. East Lansing, MI: Colleagues Press, 1988.

Grant, R. A. D. "Jane Austen as a Conservative Thinker." *Salisbury Review* 5 (January 1987): 43–47. Reprinted in *Conservative Thinkers: Essays from "The Salisbury Review*," edited by Roger Scruton, 169–85. London: Claridge Press, 1988.

Hunt, Linda C. "A Woman's Portion: Jane Austen and the Female Character." *A Woman's Portion: Ideology, Culture, and the British Female Novel Tradition*, 17–48. New York: Garland, 1988.

Johnson, Claudia L. *Jane Austen: Women, Politics, and the Novel*. Chicago: U of Chicago P, 1988.

Koppel, Gene. *The Religious Dimension of Jane Austen's Novels*. Ann Arbor, MI: UMI Research Press, 1988.

Levine, George. "*Mansfield Park*: Observation Rewarded." *Darwin and the Novelists*, 56–83. Cambridge, MA: Harvard UP, 1988.

Mayne, Judith. "Two Narratives of Private and Public Life." *Private Novels, Public Films*, 40–67. Athens: U of Georgia P, 1988.

Mooneyham, Laura G. *Romance, Language, and Education in Jane Austen's Novels*. New York: St. Martin's, 1988.

Siskin, Clifford. *The Historicity of Romantic Discourse*. Oxford: Oxford UP, 1988.

Thompson, James. *Between Self and World: The Novels of Jane Austen*. University Park, PA: Penn State UP, 1988.

Tracy, Laura. "Jane Austen: Letting Go." *"Catching the Drift": Authority, Gender, and Narrative Strategy in Fiction*, 133–87. New Brunswick, NJ: Rutgers UP, 1988.

Ahearn, Edward J. "Radical Jane and the Other Emma." *Marx and Modern Fiction*, 31–75. New Haven, CT: Yale UP, 1989.

Chase, Karen. ""Bad" Was My Commentary': Propriety, Madness, Independence in Feminist Literary History." In *Victorian Connections*, edited by Jerome J. McGann, 11–30. Charlottesville: UP of Virginia, 1989.

Collected Reports of the Jane Austen Society, 1976–1985. Overton, Hampshire: Jane Austen Society, 1989.

Drabble, Margaret. "Introduction." *Emma*, by Jane Austen, v–xix. London: Virago Press, 1989.

———. "Introduction." *Mansfield Park*, by Jane Austen, v–xvii. London: Virago Press, 1989.

———. "Introduction." *Northanger Abbey*, by Jane Austen, v–xvii. London: Virago Press, 1989.

———. "Introduction." *Persuasion*, by Jane Austen, v–xvi. London: Virago Press, 1989.

———. "Introduction." *Pride and Prejudice*, by Jane Austen, v–xvi. London: Virago Press, 1989.

———. "Introduction." *Sense and Sensibility*, by Jane Austen, v–xviii. London: Virago Press, 1989.

Dwyer, June. *Jane Austen*. New York: Continuum, 1989.

Eldridge, Richard. "Ideality, Materiality, and Value: *Pride and Prejudice* and Marriage." *On Moral Personhood: Philosophy, Literature, Criticism, and Self-Understanding*, 141–80. Chicago: U of Chicago P, 1989.

Fraiman, Susan. "The Humiliation of Elizabeth Bennet." In *Refiguring the Father: New Feminist Readings of Patriarchy*, edited by Patricia Yeager and Beth Kowaleski-Wallace, 168–87. Carbondale and Edwardsville: Southern Illinois UP, 1989. Reprinted in *Unbecoming Women: British Women Writers and the Novel of Development*, 59–87. New York: Columbia UP, 1993.

Grey, J. David, ed. *Jane Austen's Beginnings: The Juvenilia and* Lady Susan. Ann Arbor: UMI Research Press, 1989.

Harris, Jocelyn. *Jane Austen's Art of Memory*. New York: Cambridge UP, 1989.

Holly, Grant I. "*Emma*grammatology." *Studies in Eighteenth-Century Culture* 19, edited by Leslie Ellen Brown and Patricia Craddock, 39–51. East Lansing, MI: Colleagues Press, 1989.

Kaplan, Deborah. Review of Park Honan, *Jane Austen: Her Life. Modern Language Studies* 19.2 (Spring 1989): 90–92.

Kelly, Gary. "'Only a Novel': Jane Austen." *English Fiction of the Romantic Period, 1789–1830*, 111–38. New York: Longman, 1989.

Le Faye, Deirdre. *Jane Austen: A Family Record*. London: British Library; Boston: G. K. Hall, 1989.

Moler, Kenneth L. *Pride and Prejudice: A Study in Artistic Economy*. Twayne Masterworks Series. Boston: Twayne, 1989.

Morgan, Susan. Review of Park Honan, *Jane Austen: Her Life. Modern Philology* 87.2 (November 1989): 191–94.

———. "Why There's No Sex in Jane Austen's Fiction." *Sisters in Time: Imagining Gender in Nineteenth-Century British Fiction*, 23–55. Oxford: Oxford UP, 1989.

Phelan, James. *Reading People, Reading Plots: Character, Progression, and the Interpretation of Narrative*. Chicago: U of Chicago P, 1989.

Ralph, Phyllis C. "Jane Austen: Precursor of the Victorians." *Victorian Transformations: Fairy Tale, Adolescence, and the Novel of Female Development*, 59–85. New York: Lang, 1989.

Ram, Atma. *Woman as a Novelist: A Study of Jane Austen*. Delhi: Doaba House, 1989.

Said, Edward W. "Jane Austen and Empire." In *Raymond Williams: Critical Perspectives*, edited by Terry Eagleton, 150–64. Cambridge and Oxford: Polity Press, 1989. Reprinted in: *Contemporary Marxist Literary Criticism*, edited by Francis Mulhern, 97–113. New York: Longmans, 1992; Edward Said, *Culture and Imperialism*, 80–97. New York: Knopf, 1993.

Steig, Michael. "Making *Mansfield Park* Feel Right." *Stories of Reading: Subjectivity and Literary Understanding*, 157–79. Baltimore: Johns Hopkins UP, 1989.

Sulloway, Alison G. *Jane Austen and the Province of Womanhood*. Philadelphia: U of Pennsylvania P, 1989.

Tave, Stuart. Review of Park Honan, *Jane Austen: Her Life*. *Novel: A Forum on Fiction* 22.2 (Winter 1989): 231–33.

1990s

Brown, Julia Prewitt. "The Feminist Depreciation of Austen: A Polemical Reading." *Novel* 23 (1990): 303–13.

Dussinger, John A. *In the Pride of the Moment: Encounters in Jane Austen's World*. Columbus: Ohio State UP, 1990.

Gibson, Walter. "Contrarieties of Emotion; Or, Five Days with *Pride and Prejudice*." In *Conversations: Contemporary Critical Theory and the Teaching of Literature*, edited by Charles Moran and Elizabeth F. Penfield, 114–19. Urbana, IL: National Council of Teachers of English, 1990.

Goodwin, Sarah Webster. "Knowing Better: Feminism and Utopian Discourse in *Pride and Prejudice*, *Villette*, and *Babette's Feast*." In *Feminism, Utopia, and Narrative*, edited by Libby Falk Jones and Sarah Webster Goodwin, 1–20. Knoxville: U of Tennessee P, 1990.

Handler, Richard, and Daniel Segal. *Jane Austen and the Fiction of Culture: An Essay on the Narration of Social Realities*. Tucson: U of Arizona P, 1990.

Mellor, Anne K. "Why Women Didn't Like Romanticism: The Views of Jane Austen and Mary Shelley." In *The Romantics and Us: Essays on Literature and Culture*, edited by Gene W. Ruoff, 274–87. New Brunswick, NJ: Rutgers UP, 1990.

Polhemus, Robert M. *Erotic Faith: Being in Love from Jane Austen to D. H. Lawrence*. Chicago: U of Chicago P, 1990.

Sahney, Reeta. *Jane Austen's Heroes and Other Male Characters: A Sociological Study*. New Delhi: Abhiav, 1990.

Spacks, Patricia Meyer. "'The Novel's Wisdom': Austen and Scott." *Desire and Truth: Functions of Plot in Eighteenth-Century English Novels*, 203–34. Chicago: U of Chicago P, 1990.

Stevenson, John Allen. "*Emma*: The New Courtship." *The British Novel, Defoe to Austen: A Critical History*, 110–28. Boston: Twayne, 1990.

Stout, Janis P. "What They Don't Say: Conversational and Narrative Withholdings in Austen's Novels." *Strategies of Reticence: Silence and Meaning in the Works of Jane Austen, Willa Cather, Katherine Anne Porter, and Joan Didion*, 24–65. Charlottesville: UP of Virginia, 1990.

Carr, Jean Ferguson. "The Polemics of Incomprehension: Mother and Daughter in *Pride and Prejudice*." In *Tradition and the Talents of Women*, edited by Florence Howe, 68–86. Urbana and Chicago: U of Illinois P, 1991.

Cohen, Paula Marantz. *The Daughter's Dilemma: Family Process and the Nineteenth-Century Domestic Novel.* Ann Arbor: U of Michigan P, 1991.

David, Gail. "Shared Heroics." *Female Heroism in the Pastoral*, 113–69. New York: Garland, 1991.

Fergus, Jane. *Jane Austen: A Literary Life.* New York: St. Martin's, 1991.

Ferguson, Moira. "*Mansfield Park*: Slavery, Colonialism, and Gender." *Oxford Literary Review* 13 (1991): 118–39. Reprinted in *Colonialism and Gender Relations from Mary Wollstonecraft to Jamaica Kincaid: East Caribbean Connections*, 65–89. New York: Columbia UP, 1993.

Goldstein, Philip. "Criticism and Institutions: The Conflicted Reception of Jane Austen's Fiction." *Studies in the Humanities* 18 (1991): 35–55.

Green, Katherine Sobba. "Jane Austen: The Blazon Overturned." *The Courtship Novel 1740–1820: A Feminized Genre*, 153–59. Lexington: UP of Kentucky, 1991.

Horwitz, Barbara J. *Jane Austen and the Question of Women's Education.* New York: Lang, 1991.

Laurence, Patricia Ondek. "Keeping and Breaking the Silence." *The Reading of Silence: Virginia Woolf in the English Tradition*, 56–88. Stanford, CA: Stanford UP, 1991.

McCormick, Marjorie. "'Occasionally Nervous and Invariably Silly': Mothers in Jane Austen." *Mothers in the English Novel: From Stereotype to Archetype*, 47–75. New York: Garland, 1991.

MacDonagh, Oliver. *Jane Austen: Real and Imagined Worlds.* New Haven, CT: Yale UP, 1991.

Mukherjee, Meenakshi. *Jane Austen.* New York: St. Martin's, 1991.

Nicolson, Nigel. *The World of Jane Austen.* London: Weidenfeld & Nicolson, 1991.

Odom, Keith C. *Jane Austen: Rebel of Time & Place.* Arlington, TX: Liberal Arts Press, 1991.

Perera, Suvendrini. "Proper Places: Spatial Economics in Austen and Gaskell." *Reaches of Empire: The English Novel from Edgeworth to Dickens*, 35–57. New York: Columbia UP, 1991.

Ross, Deborah. "Jane Austen's Novels: The Romantic Denouement." *The Excellence of Falsehood: Romance, Realism, and Women's Contribution to the Novel*, 166–207. Lexington: UP of Kentucky, 1991.

Sedgwick, Eve Kosofsky. "Jane Austen and the Masturbating Girl." *Critical Inquiry* 17 (1991): 818–37. Reprinted in *Tendencies*, 109–29. Durham, NC: Duke UP, 1993. Reprinted in *Close Reading: The Reader*, edited by Frank Lentricchia and Andrew DuBois, 301–20. Durham, NC: Duke UP, 2001.

Stokes, Myra. *The Language of Jane Austen: A Study of Some Aspects of Her Vocabulary.* New York: St. Martin's, 1991.

Todd, Janet. "Jane Austen, Politics, and Sensibility." In *Feminist Criticism: Theory and Practice*, edited by Susan Sellers, 71–87. New York: Harvester Wheatsheaf, 1991. Reprinted in Janet Todd, *Gender, Art, and Death*, 136–54. New York: Continuum, 1993.

Wiesenfarth, Joseph. Review of John Dussinger, *In The Pride of the Moment.* *Nineteenth Century Literature* 46.3 (December 1991): 408–11.

Yeazell, Ruth Bernard. "Fanny Price's Modest Loathings." *Fictions of Modesty: Women and Courtship in the English Novel*, 143–68. Chicago: U of Chicago P, 1991.

Boardman, Michael M. "Comic Fiction and Ideological Instability: Goldsmith and Austen." *Narrative Innovation and Incoherence: Ideology in Defoe, Goldsmith, Austen, Eliot, and Hemingway*, 59–103. Durham, NC: Duke UP, 1992.

Chakrabarti, P. C. *Jane Austen: A Study of her Novels.* Calcutta: Sarat Book House, 1992.

Gard, Roger. *Jane Austen's Novels: The Art of Clarity.* New Haven, CT: Yale UP, 1992.

Handley, Graham. *Criticism in Focus: Jane Austen.* New York: St. Martin's, 1992.

Hollahan, Eugene. "Ideology and Crisis-Consciousness: Jane Austen, Emily Brontë, and George Eliot." *Crisis-Consciousness and the Novel*, 56–95. Cranbury, NJ: Associated UP, 1992.

Hudson, Glenda A. *Sibling Love and Incest in Jane Austen's Fiction.* New York: St. Martin's, 1992.

Kaplan, Deborah. *Jane Austen Among Women.* Baltimore: Johns Hopkins UP, 1992.

Lanser, Susan Sniader. "Sense and Reticence: Jane Austen's 'Indirections.'" *Fictions of Authority: Women Writers and Narrative Voice*, 61–80. Ithaca, NY: Cornell UP, 1992.

Levin, Amy K. "Jane Austen: The Sister Plots." *The Suppressed Sister: A Relationship in Novels by Nineteenth- and Twentieth-Century British Women*, 33–53. Cranbury, NJ: Associated UP, 1992.

Marshall, Christine. "'Dull Elves' and Feminists: A Summary of Feminist Criticism of Jane Austen." *Persuasions* 14 (1992): 39–45.

Monaghan, David, ed. *Emma: Jane Austen.* New Casebooks. New York: St. Martin's, 1992.

Payne, Susan. "The Author and the Text: Parodic Strategy and Metafiction in Jane Austen's *Northanger Abbey.*" *The Strange Within the Real: The Function of Fantasy in Austen, Brontë, and Eliot,* 17–60. Rome: Bulzone, 1992.

Postlethwaite, Diana. "Sometimes I Feel Like a Motherless Child: Austen's Anne Elliot and Freud's Anna O." In *The Anna Book: Searching for Anna in Literary History,* edited by Mickey Pearlmann, 37–48. Westport, CT: Greenwood, 1992.

Siebers, Tobin. "Jane Austen and Comic Virtue." *Morals & Stories,* 135–58. New York: Columbia UP, 1992.

Wiltshire, John. *Jane Austen and the Body: "The Picture of Health."* New York: Cambridge UP, 1992.

Berglund, Birgitta. *Woman's Whole Existence: The House as an Image in the Novels of Ann Radcliffe, Mary Wollstonecraft, and Jane Austen.* Lund, Sweden: Lund UP; Bromley, Kent: Chartwell-Bratt, 1993.

Bloom, Allan. "Austen, *Pride and Prejudice.*" *Love and Friendship,* 191–208. New York: Simon & Schuster, 1993.

Buchanan, Laurie. "'Islands' of Peace: Female Friendships in Victorian Literature." In *Communication and Women's Friendships,* edited by Janet Doubler Ward and JoAnna Stephens Mink, 77–96. Bowling Green, OH: Bowling Green State UP, 1993.

Collins, Irene. *Jane Austen and the Clergy.* London and Rio Grande OH: Hambledon Press, 1993.

Doody, Margaret Anne, ed. *Jane Austen: Catherine, and Other Writings.* Oxford: Oxford UP, 1993.

Giordano, Julia. "The Word as Battleground in Jane Austen's *Persuasion.*" In *Anxious Power: Reading, Writing, and Ambivalence in Narrative by Women,* edited by Carol J. Singley and Susan E. Sweeney, 107–23. Albany: State U of New York P, 1993.

Gorman, Anita G. *The Body in Illness and Health: Themes and Images in Jane Austen.* New York: Lang, 1993.

Gross, Gloria S. "Flights into Illness: Some Characters in Jane Austen." In *Literature & Medicine During the Eighteenth Century,* edited by Marie Mulvey Roberts and Roy Porter, 188–99. New York: Routledge, 1993.

Harris, Jocelyn. Review of Alison Sulloway, *Jane Austen and the Province of Womanhood. Eighteenth-Century Studies* 27.1 (Autumn, 1993): 186–93.

Kuwahara, K. K. *Jane Austen at Play: Self-Consciousness, Beginnings, Endings.* New York: Lang, 1993.

Lauber, John. *Jane Austen.* Twayne's English Authors Series. New York: Twayne, 1993.

Le Faye, Deirdre. Review of Alison Sulloway, *Jane Austen and the Province of Womanhood*. *Review of English Studies* 44 (February 1993): 115–16.

Mellor, Anne K. *Romanticism and Gender*. London: Routledge, 1993.

Powell, Violet. *A Jane Austen Compendium: The Six Major Novels*. London: Heinemann, 1993.

Rose, Gillian. *Feminism and Geography: The Limits of Geographical Knowledge*. Minneapolis: U of Minnesota P, 1993.

Scheuermann, Mona. "Jane Austen: *Pride and Prejudice* and *Emma*." Her *Bread to Earn: Women, Money, and Society from Defoe to Austen*, 199–238. Lexington: UP of Kentucky, 1993.

Stewart, Maaja A. *Domestic Realities and Imperial Fictions: Jane Austen's Novels in Eighteenth-Century Contexts*. Athens: U of Georgia P, 1993.

Tobin, Beth Fowkes. *Superintending the Poor: Charitable Ladies and Paternal Landlords in British Fiction, 1770–1860*, 50–73. New Haven, CT: Yale UP, 1993.

Baldridge, Cates. "The Anti-Romantic Polemics of *Mansfield Park*." *The Dialogics of Dissent in the English Novel*, 40–62. Hanover, NH: UP of New England, 1994.

Barreca, Regina. "Dearly Loving a Good Laugh: Humor in Charlotte Lennox and Jane Austen." *Untamed and Unabashed: Essays on Women and Humor in British Literature*, 34–60. Detroit: Wayne State UP, 1994.

Bloom, Harold. "Canonical Memory in Early Wordsworth and Jane Austen's *Persuasion*." *The Western Canon: The Books and School of the Ages*, 239–63. New York: Harcourt, 1994.

Castellanos, Gabriela. *Laughter, War, and Feminism: Elements of Carnival in Three of Jane Austen's Novels*. New York: Lang, 1994.

Gillooly, Eileen. "Rehabilitating Mary Crawford: *Mansfield Park* and the Relief of 'Throwing Ridicule.'" In *Feminist Nightmares; Women at Odds — Feminism and the Problem of Sisterhood*, edited by Susan Ostrov Weisser and Jennifer Fleischner, 328–42. New York: New York UP, 1994.

Hohne, Karen, and Helen Wussow, eds. *A Dialogue of Voices: Feminist Literary Theory and Bakhtin*. Minneapolis: U of Minnesota P, 1994.

Laurence, Patricia. "Women's Silence as a Ritual of Truth." In *Listening to Silences: New Essays in Feminist Criticism*, edited by Shelley Fisher Fishkin, 156–67. New York: Oxford UP, 1994.

Park, Catherine. Review of John Dussinger, *In The Pride of the Moment*. *English Language Notes* 31.3 (March 1994): 79–81.

Sales, Roger. *Jane Austen and Representations of Regency England*. New York: Routledge, 1994.

Shaffer, Julie A. "The Ideological Intervention of Ambiguities in the Marriage Plot: Who Fails Marianne in Austen's *Sense and Sensibility*." In *A Dialogue of Voices: Feminist Literary Theory and Bakhtin*, edited by Karen Hohne and Helen Wussow, 128–51. Minneapolis: U of Minnesota P, 1994.

Sokolsky, Anita. "The Melancholy Persuasion." In *Psychoanalytic Literary Criticism*, edited by Maud Ellman, 128–42. New York: Longman, 1994.

Tucker, George Holbert. *Jane Austen the Woman: Some Biographical Insights*. New York: St. Martin's, 1994.

Watson, Nicola J. *Revolution and the Form of the British Novel 1790–1825*, 87–108. Oxford: Oxford UP, 1994.

Weisser, Susan Ostrov and Jennifer Fleischner, eds. *Feminist Nightmares: Women at Odds — Feminism and the Problem of Sisterhood*. New York: New York UP, 1994.

White, James Boyd. "Austen's *Mansfield Park*: Making the Self Out of — and Against — the Culture." *Acts of Hope: Creating Authority in Literature, Law, and Politics*. Chicago: U of Chicago P, 1994.

Winnifrith, Tom. "Austen." *Fallen Women in the Nineteenth-Century Novel*, 13–29. New York: St. Martin's, 1994.

Castle, Terry. "Sister-Sister." Review of Deirdre Le Faye, *Jane Austen's Letters*. *London Review of Books*, 2 August 1995. Reprinted in *London Review of Books: An Anthology*, edited by Jane Hindle, 138–48. London: Verso, 1996.

Copeland, Edward. "Shopping for Signs: Jane Austen and the Pseudo-Gentry." *Women Writing about Money: Women's Fiction in England, 1790–1820*, 89–117. Cambridge: Cambridge UP, 1995.

Fraiman, Susan. "Jane Austen and Edward Said: Gender, Culture, and Imperialism. *Critical Inquiry* 21.4 (Summer 1995): 805–21.

Jehmlich, Reimer. *Jane Austen*. Darmstadt: Wissenschaftliche Buchgesellschaft, 1995.

Johnson, Claudia L. "'Not At All What a Man Should Be': Remaking English Manhood in *Emma*." *Equivocal Beings: Politics, Gender, and Sentimentality in the 1790s: Wollstonecraft, Radcliffe, Burney, Austen*, 191–204. Chicago: U of Chicago P, 1995.

Lane, Maggie. *Jane Austen and Food*. London and Rio Grande, OH: Hambledon Press, 1995.

Looser, Devoney, ed. *Jane Austen and Discourses of Feminism*. New York: St. Martin's, 1995.

Ruderman, Anne Crippen. *The Pleasures of Virtue: Political Thought in the Novels of Jane Austen*. Lanham, MD: Rowman & Littlefield, 1995.

Wallace, Tara Ghoshal. *Jane Austen and Narrative Authority*. New York: St. Martin's, 1995.

Jarvis, William. *Jane Austen and Religion*. Whitney, Oxfordshire: Stonefield Press, 1996.

Lane, Maggie. *Jane Austen's World: The Life and Times of England's Most Popular Author*. London: Carlton, 1996.

Lynch, Deidre. "At Home with Jane Austen." In *Cultural Institutions of the Novel*, edited by Deidre Lynch and William B. Warner, 159–92. Durham, NC: Duke UP, 1996.

McMaster, Juliet. *Austen the Novelist: Essays Past and Present*. Basingstoke, Hampshire: Macmillan; New York: St. Martin's, 1996.

McMaster, Juliet, and Bruce Stovel, eds. *Jane Austen's Business: Her World and her Profession*. Houndsmill, Basingstoke, Hampshire: Macmillan; New York: St. Martin's, 1996.

Roth, Barry, comp. *An Annotated Bibliography of Jane Austen Studies, 1984–94*. Athens: Ohio UP, 1996.

Copeland, Edward, and Juliet McMaster, eds. *The Cambridge Companion to Jane Austen*. Cambridge and New York: Cambridge UP, 1997.

Fritzer, Penelope Joan. *Jane Austen and Eighteenth-Century Courtesy Books*. Westport, CT: Greenwood Press, 1997.

Johnson, Claudia L. "Austen Cults and Cultures." In *The Cambridge Companion to Jane Austen*, edited by Edward Copeland and Juliet McMaster, 211–26. Cambridge and New York: Cambridge UP, 1997.

Lefroy, Helen. *Jane Austen*. Thrupp, Gloucestershire: Sutton, 1997.

Lehmann-Haupt, Christopher. *New York Times* 16 April 1997, C17.

Moore, Lisa. *Dangerous Intimacies: Toward a Sapphic History of the British Novel*. Durham, NC: Duke UP, 1997.

Myer, Valerie Grosvenor. *Jane Austen, Obstinate Heart: A Biography*. New York: Arcade, 1997.

Nokes, David. *Jane Austen: A Life*. New York: Farrar, Straus, and Giroux, 1997.

O'Farrell, Mary Ann. *Telling Complexions: The Nineteenth-Century English Novel and the Blush*. Durham, NC: Duke UP, 1997.

Swisher, Clarice, ed. *Readings on Jane Austen*. San Diego, CA: Greenhaven Press, 1997.

Tomalin, Claire. *Jane Austen: A Life*. New York: Knopf, 1997.

Trumpener, Katie. *Bardic Nationalism: The Romantic Novel and the British Empire*. Princeton, NJ: Princeton UP, 1997.

Bilger, Audrey. *Laughing Feminism: Subversive Comedy in Frances Burney, Maria Edgeworth, and Jane Austen*. Detroit: Wayne State UP, 1998.

Collins, Irene. *Jane Austen, the Parson's Daughter.* London and Rio Grande, Ohio: Hambledon Press, 1998.

Gilson, David. *Jane Austen: Collected Articles and Introductions.* [England]: D. Gilson, 1998.

Hammond, M. C. *Relating to Jane: Studies on the Life and Novels of Jane Austen with a Life of Her Niece Elizabeth Austen.* London and Atlanta: Minerva Press, 1998.

Harding, Denys Wyatt. *Regulated Hatred and Other Essays on Jane Austen,* edited by Monica Lawlor. London and Atlantic Highlands, NJ: Athlone, 1998.

Heydt-Stevenson, Jillian. "Liberty, Connection, and Tyranny: The Novels of Jane Austen and the Aesthetic Movement of the Picturesque." In *Lessons of Romanticism: A Critical Companion,* edited by Thomas Pfau and Robert F. Gleckner, 261–79. Durham, NC and London: Duke UP, 1998.

Le Faye, Deirdre. *Jane Austen.* London: British Library, 1998.

Littlewood, Ian, ed. *Jane Austen: Critical Assessments.* 4 vols. Mountfield, East Sussex: Helm Information, 1998.

Lynch, Deidre. *The Economy of Character: Novels, Market Culture, and the Business of Meaning.* Chicago: U of Chicago P, 1998.

Mairs, Nancy. "Single Blessedness." *Women's Review of Books* 15.8 (May 1998): 13.

Marsh, Nicholas. *Jane Austen: The Novels.* New York: St. Martin's, 1998.

Moretti, Franco. *Atlas of the European Novel, 1800–1900.* London: Verso, 1998.

Parker, Jo Alyson. *The Author's Inheritance: Henry Fielding, Jane Austen, and the Establishment of the Novel.* DeKalb: Northern Illinois UP, 1998.

Perkins, Moreland. *Reshaping the Sexes in "Sense and Sensibility."* Charlottesville: UP of Virginia, 1998.

Poplawski, Paul. *A Jane Austen Encyclopedia.* Westport, CT: Greenwood Press, 1998.

Siegel, Lee. "A Writer Who is Good for You." *Atlantic Monthly* 281.1 (January 1998): 95.

Troost, Linda, and Sayre Greenfield, eds. *Jane Austen in Hollywood.* Lexington: UP of Kentucky, 1998.

Werker, Anke. *By a Lady: Jane Austen's Female Archetypes in Fiction and Film.* Tilburg, The Netherlands: Tilburg UP, 1998.

White, Laura Mooneyham. *Critical Essays on Jane Austen.* New York: G. K. Hall; London: Prentice Hall International, 1998.

Wye, Margaret Enright. *Jane Austen's Emma: Embodied Metaphor as a Cognitive Construct.* Lewiston, NY: Edwin Mellen Press, 1998.

Wynne, Julian Wilmot. *Jane Austen and Sigmund Freud: An Interpretation*. London: Plume Publications, 1998.

Auerbach, Emily. "'A Barkeeper Entering the Kingdom of Heaven': Did Mark Twain Really Hate Jane Austen?" *Virginia Quarterly Review* 75.1 (Winter 1999): 109–20. Reprinted in *Searching for Jane Austen*. Madison: U of Wisconsin P, 2004.

Brooke, Christopher. *Jane Austen: Illusion and Reality*. Woodbridge, Suffolk; Rochester, NY: D. S. Brewer, 1999.

Cartmell, Deborah, and Imelda Whelehan, eds. *Adaptations: From Text to Screen, Screen to Text*. London: Routledge, 1999.

Neill, Edward. *The Politics of Jane Austen*. New York: St. Martin's, 1999.

Persuasions On-Line Occasional Papers 3 (Fall 1999). Special Issue on Film Versions of *Emma*.

Rigberg, Lynn R. *Jane Austen's Discourse With New Rhetoric*. New York: Peter Lang, 1999.

Selwyn, David. *Jane Austen and Leisure*. London: Hambledon Press, 1999.

Shaw, Harry E. *Narrating Reality: Austen, Scott, Eliot*. Ithaca, NY: Cornell UP, 1999.

Waldron, Mary. *Jane Austen and the Fiction of her Time*. Cambridge and New York: Cambridge UP, 1999.

2000s

Bloom, Harold, ed. *Jane Austen*. New York: Chelsea House, 2000.

Burgess, Miranda. *British Fiction and the Production of Social Order, 1740–1830*. New York: Cambridge UP, 2000.

Dabundo, Laura, ed. *Jane Austen and Mary Shelley, and Their Sisters*. Lanham, MD: UP of America, 2000.

Haslett, Moyra. *Marxist Literary and Cultural Theories*. New York: St. Martin's, 2000.

Hawkridge, Audrey. *Jane and her Gentlemen: Jane Austen and the Men in her Life and Novels*. London: Peter Owen; Chester Springs, PA: Dufour Editions, 2000.

Lambdin, Laura Coomer, and Robert Thomas Lambdin. *A Companion to Jane Austen Studies*. Westport, CT: Greenwood Press, 2000.

Lynch, Deidre, ed. *Janeites: Austen's Disciples and Devotees*. Princeton, NJ: Princeton UP, 2000.

Park, You-me, and Rajeswari Sunder Rajan, eds. *Austen in the World: Postcolonial Mappings*. London and New York: Routledge, 2000.

Seeber, Barbara Karolina. *General Consent in Jane Austen: A Study of Dialogism*. Montreal and Ithaca, NY: McGill-Queen's UP, 2000.

Sheen, Erica. "'Where the Garment Gapes': Faithfulness and Promiscuity in the 1995 BBC *Pride and Prejudice.*" In *The Classic Novel from Page to Screen*, edited by Robert Giddings and Erica Sheen, 14–30. Manchester, Eng., and New York: Manchester UP, 2000.

Sorensen, Janet. "Epilogue: Jane Austen's Language and the Strangeness at Home in the Center." *The Grammar of Empire in Eighteenth-Century British Writing*, 197–223. Cambridge: Cambridge UP, 2000.

Southam, B. C. *Jane Austen and the Navy*. London: Hambledon and London, 2000.

Burt, Daniel. *The Literary 100: A Ranking of the Most Influential Novelists, Playwrights, and Poets of All Time*. New York: Facts on File, 2001.

Johnson, Claudia L. "The Divine Miss Jane: Jane Austen, Janeites, and the Discipline of Novel Studies." In *Reception Studies: From Literary Theory to Cultural Criticism*, edited by James L. Machor and Philip Goldstein, 118–32. New York and London: Routledge, 2001.

Plasa, Carl. "'What Was Done There is Not to be Told': *Mansfield Park*'s Colonial Unconscious." *Textual Politics from Slavery to Postmodernism*, 32–59. London: Palgrave, 2001.

Richardson, Alan. "Of Heartache and Head Injury: Minds, Brains, and the Subject of *Persuasion.*" *British Romanticism and the Science of Mind*. Cambridge: Cambridge UP, 2001.

Shields, Carol. *Jane Austen*. New York: Viking, 2001.

Southam, B. C. *Jane Austen's Literary Manuscripts: A Study of the Novelist's Development Through The Surviving Papers*. London and New York: Athlone Press, 2001.

Wiltshire, John. *Recreating Jane Austen*. Cambridge and New York: Cambridge UP, 2001.

Byrne, Paula. *Jane Austen and the Theatre*. London: Hambledon, 2002.

Gay, Penny. *Jane Austen and the Theatre*. Cambridge: Cambridge UP, 2002.

Gaylin, Ann Elizabeth. *Eavesdropping in the Novel from Austen to Proust*. Cambridge and New York: Cambridge UP, 2002.

Giffin, Michael. *Jane Austen and Religion: Salvation and Society in Georgian England*. Houndsmill, Basingstoke, Hampshire; New York: Palgrave Macmillan, 2002.

Greenfield, Susan C. *Mothering Daughters: Novels and the Politics of Family Romance: Fanny Burney to Jane Austen*, 145–68. Detroit: Wayne State UP, 2002.

Gross, Gloria Sybil. *In a Fast Coach with a Pretty Woman: Jane Austen and Samuel Johnson.* New York: AMS Press, 2002.

Le Faye, Deirdre. *Jane Austen: The World of Her Novels.* London: Frances Lincoln; New York: Harry Abrams, 2002.

Michaelson, Patricia Howell. *Speaking Volumes: Women, Reading, and Speech in the Age of Austen.* Stanford, CA: Stanford UP, 2002.

Moxham, Jeffrey. *Interfering Values in the Nineteenth-Century British Novel: Austen, Dickens, Eliot, Hardy, and the Ethics of Criticism.* Westport, CT: Greenwood Press, 2002.

Parrill, Sue. *Jane Austen on Film and Television: A Critical Study of the Adaptations.* Jefferson, NC: McFarland, 2002.

Ross, Josephine. *Jane Austen: A Companion.* London: John Murray, 2002. New Brunswick, NJ: Rutgers UP, 2003.

Tuite, Clara. *Romantic Austen: Sexual Politics and the Literary Canon.* Cambridge and New York: Cambridge UP, 2002.

Anzinger, Martina. *Gainsborough Pictures Reframed, or, Raising Jane Austen for 1990s Film.* Frankfurt am Main; New York: Peter Lang, 2003.

Galperin, William. *The Historical Austen.* Philadelphia: U of Pennsylvania P, 2003.

Gay, Penny. Review of Jon Spence, *Becoming Jane Austen. Sensibilities: The Jane Austen Society of Australia* 26 (June 2003): 43–46.

Giardetti, Melora. *Personal and Political Transformation in the Texts of Jane Austen.* Lewiston, NY: Edwin Mellen Press, 2003.

Gill, Richard, and Susan Gregory. *Mastering the Novels of Jane Austen.* New York: Palgrave Macmillan, 2003.

MacDonald, Gina, and Andrew MacDonald. *Jane Austen on Screen.* Cambridge and New York: Cambridge UP, 2003.

Menon, Patricia. *Austen, Eliot, Charlotte Brontë and the Mentor-Lover.* Houndsmill, Basingstoke, Hampshire; New York: Palgrave Macmillan, 2003.

Miles, Robert. *Jane Austen.* Writers and Their Work Series. Plymouth, UK: Northcote House, 2003.

Miller, D. A. *Jane Austen, or, The Secret of Style.* Princeton, NJ: Princeton UP, 2003.

Pucci, Suzanne R. and James Thompson, eds. *Jane Austen and Co.: Remaking the Past in Contemporary Culture.* Albany: State U of New York P, 2003.

Spence, Jon. *Becoming Jane Austen: A Life.* London and New York: Hambledon & London, 2003.

Tandon, Bharat. *Jane Austen and the Morality of Conversation.* London: Anthem, 2003.

Wiesenfarth, Joseph. Review of Jon Spence, *Becoming Jane Austen*. *JASNA News* 19.3 (Winter 2003): 28.

Wiltshire, John. *Jane Austen: Introductions and Interventions*. New Delhi: Macmillan, 2003.

Auerbach, Emily. *Searching for Jane Austen*. Madison: U of Wisconsin P, 2004.

Byrne, Paula, ed. *Jane Austen's Emma: A Sourcebook*. New York and London: Routledge, 2004.

Davidson, Jenny. "Hypocrisy and the Novel: A Modest Question about *Mansfield Park*." *Hypocrisy and the Politics of Politeness: Manners and Morals from Locke to Austen*. New York: Cambridge UP, 2004.

Deresiewicz, William. *Jane Austen and the Romantic Poets*. New York: Columbia UP, 2004.

Duckworth, Alistair, ed. *Emma*. London: Palgrave, 2004.

Ferguson, Frances. Review of William Galperin, *The Historical Austen*. *Albion* 36.1 (Spring 2004): 133–34.

Folsom, Marcia McClintock, ed. *Approaches to Teaching Austen's* Emma. New York: Modern Language Association of America, 2004.

Fowler, Karen Joy. *The Jane Austen Book Club*. New York: Putnam, 2004.

Fullerton, Susannah. *Jane Austen and Crime*. Sydney: Jane Austen Society of Australia, 2004. Madison, WI: Jones Books, 2008.

Jenkyns, Richard. *A Fine Brush on Ivory: An Appreciation of Jane Austen*. Oxford and New York: Oxford UP, 2004.

Jones, Darryl. *Jane Austen*. Critical Issues Series. Houndsmill, Basingstoke, Hampshire; New York: Palgrave Macmillan, 2004.

Knox-Shaw, Peter. *Jane Austen and the Enlightenment*. Cambridge and New York: Cambridge UP, 2004.

Leithart, Peter J. *Miniatures and Morals: The Christian Novels of Jane Austen*. Moscow, ID: Canon Press, 2004.

"The Republic of Pemberley." http://www.pemberley.com (2004–2010).

Winborn, Colin. *The Literary Economy of Jane Austen and George Crabbe*. Burlington, VT: Ashgate, 2004.

Doody, Margaret Anne. "Jane Austen, That Disconcerting 'Child.'" In *The Child Writer from Austen to Woolf*, edited by Christine Alexander and Juliet McMaster, 101–21. Cambridge: Cambridge UP, 2005.

Emsley, Sarah Baxter. *Jane Austen's Philosophy of the Virtues*. New York: Palgrave Macmillan, 2005.

Gevirtz, Karen Bloom. "A State of Alteration, Perhaps of Improvement: Jane Austen's Widows." *Life after Death: Widows and the English Novel, Defoe to Austen*, 137–68. Cranbury, NJ: Associated UP, 2005.

Heydt-Stevenson, Jillian. *Austen's Unbecoming Conjunctions: Subversive Laughter, Embodied History.* New York: Palgrave Macmillan, 2005.

Irvine, Robert P. *Jane Austen.* Routledge Guides to Literature Series. London; New York: Routledge, 2005.

Lee, Hermione. "Jane Austen Faints." *Virginia Woolf's Nose: Essays on Biography,* 63–94. Princeton, NJ: Princeton UP, 2005.

Mitchell, Marea, and Diane Osland. "'It Was Happy She Took a Good Course': Saving Elizabeth Bennet in *Pride and Prejudice.*" *Representing Women and Female Desire from* Arcadia *to* Jane Eyre, 158–74. Houndsmill, Basingstoke, Hampshire; New York: Palgrave Macmillan, 2005.

Sutherland, Kathryn. *Jane Austen's Textual Lives: From Aeschylus to Bollywood.* Oxford and New York: Oxford UP, 2005.

Tauchert, Ashley. *Romancing Jane Austen: Narrative, Realism, and the Possibility of a Happy Ending.* Houndsmill, Basingstoke, Hampshire; New York: Palgrave Macmillan, 2005.

Todd, Janet, ed. *The Cambridge Edition of the Works of Jane Austen.* 9 volumes. Cambridge: Cambridge UP, 2005–9.

———, ed. *Jane Austen in Context.* Cambridge: Cambridge UP, 2005.

Wing-chi Ki, Madeline. *Jane Austen and the Dialectic of Misrecognition.* New York: Lang, 2005.

Le Faye, Deirdre. *A Chronology of Jane Austen and her Family.* Cambridge and New York: Cambridge UP, 2006.

Ray, Joan Klingel. *Jane Austen for Dummies.* Hoboken, NJ: Wiley, 2006.

Todd, Janet M. *The Cambridge Introduction to Jane Austen.* Cambridge and New York: Cambridge UP, 2006.

Wenner, Barbara Britton. *Prospect and Refuge in the Landscape of Jane Austen.* Aldershot, England; Burlington, VT: Ashgate, 2006.

White, Gabrielle D. V. *Jane Austen in the Context of Abolition: "A Fling at the Slave Trade."* Houndsmill, Basingstoke, Hampshire; New York: Palgrave Macmillan, 2006.

Bautz, Annika. *The Reception of Jane Austen and Walter Scott: A Comparative Longitudinal Study.* London and New York: Continuum, 2007.

Bottomer, Phyllis Ferguson. *So Odd a Mixture: Along the Autistic Spectrum in* Pride and Prejudice. London and Philadelphia: Jessica Kingsley, 2007.

Butler, Marilyn. *Jane Austen.* Oxford and New York: Oxford UP, 2007.

Di Paolo, Marc. *Emma Adapted: Jane Austen's Heroine from Book to Film.* New York: Peter Lang, 2007.

Harris, Jocelyn. *A Revolution Almost Beyond Expression: Jane Austen's* Persuasion. Newark: U of Delaware P, 2007.

"Hollywood Can't Get Enough of Jane Austen." *Pittsburgh Post Gazette*, 10 August 2007.

Kramp, Michael. *Disciplining Love: Austen and the Modern Man*. Columbus: Ohio State UP, 2007.

Mandal, Anthony. *Jane Austen and the Popular Novel: The Determined Author*. New York: Palgrave Macmillan, 2007.

Mandal, Anthony, and B. C. Southam. *The Reception of Jane Austen in Europe*. New York: Continuum International, 2007.

Persuasions On-Line 27.2 (Summer 2007). Special Issue on Joe Wright's *Pride and Prejudice*.

Stafford, Fiona, ed. *Jane Austen's* Emma: *A Casebook*. Oxford: Oxford UP, 2007.

Wainwright, Valerie. *Ethics and the English Novel from Austen to Forster*. Aldershot, England: Ashgate, 2007.

Updike, John. "On Literary Biography." *Due Considerations*, 3–13. New York: Knopf, 2007.

Baker, William. *Critical Companion to Jane Austen: A Literary Reference to Her Life and Work*. New York: Facts on File, 2008.

Barchas, Janine. "Mrs. Gaskell's *North and South*: Austen's Early Legacy." *Persuasions* 30 (2008): 53–66.

Brodey, Inger Sigrun. *Ruined by Design: Shaping Novels and Gardens in the Culture of Sensibility*. New York: Routledge, 2008.

Case, Alison, and Harry E. Shaw. *Reading the Nineteenth Century Novel: Austen to Eliot*. Maldon, MA; Oxford: Blackwell, 2008.

Corbett, Mary Jean. *Family Likenesses: Sex, Marriage, and Incest from Jane Austen to Virginia Woolf*. Ithaca, NY: Cornell UP, 2008.

Graham, Peter W. *Jane Austen & Charles Darwin: Naturalists and Novelists*. Aldershot, England; Burlington, VT: Ashgate, 2008.

Harris, Jocelyn. "Jane Austen, Samuel Johnson, and the Academy." *Persuasions* 30 (2008): 27–37.

Johnson, Claudia L. "A Name to Conjure With." *Persuasions* 30 (2008): 15–26.

Looser, Devoney. "What is Old in Jane Austen?" *Women Writers and Old Age in Great Britain, 1750–1850*. Baltimore: Johns Hopkins UP, 2008.

Nachumi, Nora. *Acting Like a Lady: British Women Novelists and the Eighteenth-Century Theater*. New York: AMS Press, 2008.

Parry, Sarah. "The Pemberley Effect: Austen's Legacy to the Historic House Industry." *Persuasions* 30 (2008): 113–22.

Rand, Thomas. "*Emma* and *Twelfth Night*." *Persuasions* 30 (2008): 181–86.

Tague, Gregory F. *Ethics and Behavior: The English Novel from Jane Austen to Henry James.* Introduction by Daniel Meyer-Dinkgräfe. Bethesda, MD: Academica Press, 2008.

Tekcan, Rana. "Notes on a Turkish Edition of *Pride and Prejudice.*" *Persuasions* 30 (2008): 241–54.

Welland, Freydis Jane. "The History of Jane Austen's Writing Desk." *Persuasions* 30 (2008): 125–28.

Bloom, Harold, ed. *Jane Austen.* New York: Bloom's Literary Criticism, 2009.

Carson, Susannah. *A Truth Universally Acknowledged: 33 Great Writers on Why We Read Jane Austen.* New York: Random House, 2009.

Daldez, E. M. *Mirrors of One Another: Emotion and Value in Jane Austen and David Hume.* West Sussex, UK: Wiley-Blackwell, 2009.

Grahame-Smith, Seth. *Pride and Prejudice and Zombies.* Philadelphia: Quirk Books, 2009.

Johnson, Claudia Durst, ed. *Issues of Class in Jane Austen's Pride and Prejudice.* Social Issues in Literature Series. Detroit: Gale, 2009.

Johnson, Claudia L. and Clara Tuite, eds. *A Companion to Jane Austen.* Malden, MA: Blackwell, 2009.

Jones, Hazel. *Jane Austen and Marriage.* New York: Continuum, 2009.

Leithart, Peter J. *Jane Austen: Writer of Fancy.* Nashville, TN: Cumberland House, 2009.

Lynch, Jack, ed. *Jane Austen.* Critical Insights Series. Englewood Cliffs, NJ: Salem Press, 2009.

Monaghan, David, Ariane Hudelet, and John Wiltshire. *Cinematic Jane Austen: Essays on the Filmic Sensibility of the Novels.* Jefferson, NC: McFarland, 2009.

Morini, Massimiliano. *Jane Austen's Narrative Techniques.* Burlington, VT: Ashgate, 2009.

Norman, Andrew. *Jane Austen: An Unrequited Love.* Stroud, Gloucestershire: The History Press, 2009.

Scheuermann, Mona. *Reading Jane Austen.* New York: Palgrave Macmillan, 2009.

Stovel, Nora Foster, ed. *Jane Austen Sings the Blues.* Edmonton: U of Alberta P, 2009.

Walker, Eric. *Marriage, Writing, and Romanticism: Wordsworth and Austen After War.* Stanford, CA: Stanford UP, 2009.

Winters, Ben H. *"Sense and Sensibility" and Sea Monsters.* Philadelphia: Quirk Books, 2009.

Harman, Claire. *Jane's Fame: How Jane Austen Conquered the World.* Edinburgh: Canongate, 2009; New York: Henry Holt, 2010.

Josephson, Wayne. *Emma and the Vampires.* Naperville, IL: Sourcebooks Landmark, 2010.

Persuasions On-Line 30.2 (Spring 2010). Special Issue: "New Directions in Austen Studies."

Toker, Leona. *Toward the Ethics of Form in Fiction.* Columbus: Ohio State UP, 2010.

Villaseñor, Alice Marie. "Fanny Caroline Lefroy: A Feminist Critic in the Austen Family." *Persuasions On-Line* 30.2 (Spring 2010).

Wilkes, Joanne. *Women Reviewing Women in Nineteenth-Century Britain.* Aldershot, England: Ashgate, 2010.

Young, Kay. *Imagining Mind: The Neuro-Aesthetics of Austen, Eliot, and Hardy.* Columbus: Ohio State UP, 2010.

Index

Mudrick, Marvin, 1, 10, 59, 70–71, 72, 77, 88, 93, 96, 105, 143, 147, 149, 150, 211, 256
Mukherjee, Meenakshi, 174–75, 207, 274
Mullik, B. R., 87, 96, 165, 172, 257, 258
Murch, Jerome, 22, 40, 259
Murrah, Charles, 81, 96, 257
Musselwhite, David E., 139, 145, 270
Myer, Valerie Grosvenor, 212, 213, 235, 279
Myers, Sylvia, 90, 96, 260
myth criticism, 81, 141–42, 182–83

Nabokov, Vladimir, 155, 172, 265
Nachumi, Nora, 221–22, 235, 286
Napoleonic wars, 83, 89, 150, 152, 211
Nardin, Jane, 77, 78, 96, 132, 143, 262
narratology, 8, 91, 124, 126, 131–35 *passim*, 157, 185, 192–96 *passim*, 217
Neale, R. S., 138, 145, 268
Neill, Edward, 105, 106, 197–98, 207, 281
Neill, S. Diana, 68, 96, 256
Neumann, Erich, 176
New Criticism, 8, 12, 43–52 *passim*, 66–75 *passim*, 78, 80–83, 86–87, 88, 99, 126, 152, 157
New Historicism, 8, 89, 131, 137–39, 152, 189, 196–99 *passim*, 201, 219
Newton, Judith L., 115, 129, 266
Nicolson, Nigel, 214, 235, 274
Nokes, David, 211–12, 213, 235, 279
Norman, Andrew, 240, 243, 287
novel of manners, 21, 23, 28, 49, 68, 83, 89, 109, 110

O'Connor, Frank [Michael Donovan], 80–81, 96, 256
Odmark, John, 132–33, 145, 266
Odom, Keith C., 210, 235, 274
Oliphant, James, 26, 40, 250

Oliphant, Margaret, 19–20, 22, 40, 249
O'Malley, Ida B., 49, 64, 254
O'Neill, Judith, 6, 10, 261
Orwell, George, 160
Osland, Diane, 189–90, 207, 285
Oxford Edition (of Austen's novels), 46–47
Oxford University, 46

Page, Norman, 76, 96, 261
Paris, Bernard J., 140–41, 145, 264
Park, Catherine, 135, 145, 277
Park, You-me, 202, 207, 281
Parker, Jo Alyson, 221, 235, 280
Parrill, Sue, 231, 235, 283
Parry, Sarah, 238, 244, 286
Paulson, Ronald, 83, 96, 260
Payne, Susan, 192, 207, 276
Pellew, George, 22–23, 40, 249
Perera, Suvendrini, 200, 207, 274
Perkins, Moreland, 179, 207, 280
Persuasions (journal), 6, 238
Persuasions Online (journal), 6, 22, 231, 238, 241
Phelan, James, 133–34, 145, 266, 272
Phelps, William Lyon, 34, 40, 252
Phillips, Kenneth C., 76, 96, 261
philosophical criticism, 84, 85, 141, 158, 159–60, 222–25
Pilgrim, Constance, 79, 96, 261
Pinion, F. B., 89, 96, 262
Plasa, Carl, 201, 207, 282
Poirier, Richard, 83, 96, 258
Polhemus, Robert, 156–57, 159, 172, 265, 273
Pollock, Juliet, 19, 40, 249
Pollock, Walter H., 26, 41, 250
Poovey, Mary, 121–22, 129, 229, 267
Poplawski, Paul, 4, 10, 280
postcolonial studies (postcolonial criticism), 8, 167, 180, 199–202
Postlethwaite, Diana, 202, 207, 276
poststructuralist criticism, 4, 131, 192–96 *passim*
Poulet, Georges, 91